New Worlds to Seek

New Worlds to Seek

Pioneer Heinrich Lienhard in Switzerland and America, 1824–1846

Translated and Annotated by
Raymond J. Spahn

Edited by
John C. Abbott

With a Foreword by
John H. Lienhard IV

Southern Illinois University Press

Carbondale and Edwardsville

Printed in the United States of America

03 02 01 00 4 3 2 1

Publication partially funded by a subvention grant from the Friends of Lovejoy Library.

Frontispiece: Earliest known photo of Heinrich Lienhard, taken in 1855 or 1856.
Courtesy John H. Lienhard IV.

Endpapers: Facsimile of a manuscript page from Johann Heinrich Lienhard, Memoirs
of a Trip to California, Life at Sutter's Fort, and Return to Switzerland, 1846–1850
(BANC MSS C-D 5024), the Bancroft Library, University of California, Berkeley.
Reproduced by permission of John H. Lienhard IV and the Bancroft Library.

Library of Congress Cataloging-in-Publication Data
Lienhard, Heinrich, 1822–1903.
New worlds to seek : pioneer Heinrich Lienhard in Switzerland and America,
1824–1846 / translated and annotated by Raymond J. Spahn ; edited by
John C. Abbott ; with a foreword by John H. Lienhard, IV.
p.   cm.
Translation of folio one through folio 51, page one, line 22 of Lienhard's
manuscript autobiography, which is located at the Bancroft Library,
University of California at Berkeley.
Includes bibliographical references and index.
1. Lienhard, Heinrich, 1822–1903. 2. Pioneers—West (U.S.) Biography. 3. Frontier
and pioneer life—West (U.S.) 4. West (U.S.)—Description and travel. 5. Illinois—
Description and travel. 6. Iowa—Description and travel. 7. Swiss Americans—West
(U.S.) Biography. 8. Highland (Ill.) Biography. 9. Glarus (Switzerland : Canton)
Biography. I. Spahn, Raymond Jürgen. II. Abbott, John Cushman, 1921– . III. Title.
F592.L54 1999
978'.02'092
[B]—DC21   99-21412
ISBN 0-8093-2233-1 (alk. paper)   CIP

To Jennie Latzer Kaeser
of Swiss background,
for her innumerable contributions
to her beloved Highland,
and to much else

Also to the Lienhard-Schiess family,
who descend from Heinrich's younger brother, Caspar,
and still carry on with grace
at the old family homestead in Canton Glarus

Contents

Contents

2

By Land, Sea and Upriver to St. Louis

55

3

Becoming More or Less American

89

Contents

Contents

Illustrations

Foreword

IT IS WITH considerable anticipation that I await this first complete English edition of the portion of my great-grandfather's manuscript autobiography dealing with the years from his birth in Switzerland in 1822 to the time of his departure for Sutter's Fort in 1846. Much of my knowledge of Johann Heinrich Lienhard comes from reading the two earlier English language editions. In those accounts he tells about his trek across the Great Plains and Rockies in 1846 and about what life was like in Sutter's Fort before and during the Gold Rush. That may seem like a great deal; yet he has much more to tell us.

Since I do not read the old German script of the manuscript, I have not had access to the rest of this tale of immigration and adventure. Now, at last, Dr. Spahn makes it possible for all of us to experience the entire sweep of Heinrich Lienhard's story. You and I will finally be able to see this complex man, and those exciting times, with a far better perspective.

Great-grandpa has always been a mind-catching, if somewhat shadowy, figure for me. I grew up seeing him through the eyes of my father—through the eyes of his young grandson. In 1856 he settled into the German-Swiss community of Nauvoo, Illinois, formerly the domain of the Latter-day Saints and the Icarians. With his Gold Rush wealth he bought the fine mansion that had belonged to Heber C. Kimball, a member, while in Nauvoo, of the Mormon Quorum of Twelve Apostles and later First Counselor to Brigham Young.

Nauvoo grew into a sober, conservative, largely German-speaking community—strong in the same settled values that Heinrich had left behind in Switzerland. The character of the community grew away from the restless, unconstrained nature that had brought him to America in the first place. His son (my grandfather) Johann Heinrich Lienhard II lived almost his entire, orderly life in Nauvoo. He was a successful Midwestern businessman.

The first Johann Heinrich appears to have lived out the balance of his life dancing to his own drum—pursuing his love of horticulture and agriculture, raising a large family, serving a term as mayor of Nauvoo, and writing his memoirs. He gathered in the prize of his early exploits. That prize was a life of great personal freedom in a green and fertile land.

Certain family writings and comments suggest that my grandfather had trouble understanding Heinrich's "who-cares" attitude toward the consumption of his fortune. The irony is clear. Heinrich's fortune was the result of his pursuit of *freedom,* not of *fortune.* His son enjoyed the settled life that Heinrich's gains had provided. My grandfather could far better understand "good business" than the forces driving Heinrich.

Restlessness, discontent, and the craving for freedom were the great engines of mid-nineteenth-century America. That restlessness takes another important form in Heinrich Lienhard's writings. It appears as an almost Faustian hunger for understanding. With clinical fascination, Heinrich studies the ways of the Indians, the flora and fauna of the West, Sutter's excesses, and the patterns of generosity and greed around him. He hands us, at last, a portrait of the West as swirling human comedy.

The history of our westward expansion was the history of adventurism in the mind as well as in the harsh outer world. The historian Lynn White Jr. has pointed out that the technologies of the West mirrored those of the eleventh, twelfth, and thirteenth centuries.[1] He explains this by noting that both periods were ones of great intellectual freedom and technological expansion in a world where there was room for growth.

Even as Heinrich Lienhard wrote, the technology of his world was expanding like a blast front. When he first crossed the plains, the very path was unclear. For example, he survived while most of the Donner party, which left Wyoming about the same time, perished. It was only because he and his friends took a chance and picked their way down the Weber River into the Great Salt Lake Basin. The Donners took the more obvious route through Emigrant Canyon. They were delayed just long enough by a treacherous willow thicket to be caught in the first Sierra Nevada snows that winter.

Yet, when he returned to Switzerland to get Sutter's family, a few years later, Heinrich simply booked passage on a steam-driven packet boat. The trip still included a land crossing over the Isthmus of Panama. But in four years' time, transportation had leapt from the Stone Age to nineteenth-century high-tech. A scant fifteen years after his crossing, he could have telegraphed ahead to California. Twenty-three years later he could have made the same trip by rail.

I had the opportunity to lecture at Utah State University, in Ogden, in the spring of 1990. Two miles south of the campus, we passed the mouth of Weber Canyon. I saw exactly where Great-grandpa had come out of the wild, imposing hills. It was a daunting sight. So I went back to read his account of that day. Here's what I found:

> We reached the shallow shores of the magnificent Salt Lake, with its waters crystal clear but as salty as the strongest brine. It is a broad expanse of water

and offers toward the northeast a view of nothing but sky and water. . . . The land slopes gradually from the mountains to the lake in a beautiful oblique plane, traversed only by . . . streams of the freshest water. . . . All day long I felt like singing and whistling.[2]

Of course, Great-grandpa was singing a song of *freedom*. He was twenty-four years old and he was free. He was in real danger, but freedom is dangerous and he knew that.

Technology and exploration were both being swept on by the same remarkable breed of risk-taking adventurers. For me, Heinrich Lienhard is prototypical of the creative, dream-driven, slightly arrogant, insatiably curious person who was, after all, the only sort who would have or could have stepped off into the brooding vastness that waited just beyond the Mississippi River in 1846.

John H. Lienhard I V

Notes

1. Lynn White Jr., *Medieval Religion and Technology* (Berkeley: University of California Press, 1978).

2. Heinrich Lienhard, *From St. Louis to Sutter's Fort, 1846,* trans. and ed. Erwin G. Gudde and Elisabeth K. Gudde (Norman: University of Oklahoma Press, 1961), 103.

Preface

REGARDING EDITORIAL MATTERS, the following should be noted. On the first page of each folded folio sheet, Lienhard wrote on the left-hand margin a summary of most of the contents of the neighboring text. These notations were reproduced, with general minor differences, in a separate table at the end of the manuscript. It is the former that are reproduced here as section headings, translated from copy supplied by Christa Landert. However, the editor is responsible for dividing the translation into four chapters and for devising titles for each.

Citations of Lienhard's manuscript first give the folio number, second the page number within the folio, and then the line or line numbers, for example 12/1/18–19.

The German language vowel modifications, *ä, ö,* and *ü,* are rendered throughout as *ae, oe,* and *ue* respectively.

Lienhard's spelling of English language personal and place names is often that of a German-speaking person's phonetic rendering. Where sufficient documentation clearly establishes a different spelling, that spelling is used in its modern form; a note at the point of first use indicates Lienhard's spelling. However, the names of churches, taverns, and inns, when given in German are translated into English, the departure from Lienhard's text again being noted at the point of first use.

Lienhard's travels took him into territories not yet organized as states, Iowa not being admitted as such until December 1846, Wisconsin in 1848, and Minnesota in 1858; for convenience, place names are indicated as though they were already in those states.

Heinrich Lienhard's manuscript autobiography is located at the Bancroft Library, University of California at Berkeley. It consists of two hundred thirty-eight once-folded folio sheets, adding up to nine hundred fifty-two pages. This book is a translation of folio one through folio fifty-one, page one, line twenty-two.

The following are translations of subsequent portions from the original text:

From St. Louis to Sutter's Fort, 1846, trans. and ed. Erwin G. Gudde and Elisabeth K. Gudde (Norman: University of Oklahoma Press, 1961). This book begins in folio fifty-one, where the present book ends, and goes to folio eighty-three.

"The Lienhard Journal," trans. Dale L. Morgan. Published in *West from Fort Bridger: The Pioneering of Immigrant Trails Across Utah,* which title comprises the whole of volume nineteen (1951) of the *Utah Historical Quarterly.* In 1994 *West from Fort Bridger* (Logan: Utah State University Press) was printed in a revised edition. In the former edition, "The Lienhard Journal" appears on pages 117–76; in the latter, on pages 127–84. Except for minor note changes, Lienhard's text is the same in both editions.

A Pioneer at Sutter's Fort, 1846–1850, The Adventures of Heinrich Lienhard, trans., ed., and annot. Marguerite Eyer Wilbur (Los Angeles: Calafía Society, 1941). Wilbur's text commences in folio eighty-three, where the Guddes' text ends. It is an abridged translation that concentrates largely on Lienhard's time with Captain Sutter.

Lienhard's life and manuscript are most authoritatively described and analyzed in two works by Christa Landert:

Das Amerika-Bericht des Johann Heinrich Lienhard (1822–1903) (Lizentiatsarbeit, University of Zurich, 1986).

"Johann Heinrich Lienhard (1822–1903) and His Manuscript: A Biographical Sketch," *Yearbook of German-American Studies,* 25 (1990): 131–49.

John C. Abbott

Acknowledgments

THIS IS THE FIFTH BOOK relating to the history of Highland, Illinois, founded as New Switzerland by Swiss settlers in 1831, to be published with support from the Friends of Lovejoy Library of Southern Illinois University Edwardsville. In all probability none of these works would have been undertaken had it not been for the initiative of a daughter of Swiss background, Mrs. Jennie Latzer Kaeser. One fall day, Mrs. Kaeser, then in her ninetieth year, brought to the library her translation of the virtually unknown 1859 *Die Geschichte der Ansiedlung von Highland*, written by one of Highland's founders, Salomon Koepfli. In due course it was published as *The Story of the Settling of Highland*. A few years later she provided further impetus to the Friends' emerging program of publishing Highland histories with her translation of Dr. Kaspar Koepfli's also rare *Spiegel von Amerika*, published in Lucerne in 1849; as "Mirror of America" it became book one of *New Switzerland in Illinois*, published by the Friends in 1977.

One person, Dr. Raymond Jurgen Spahn, Professor Emeritus of German at Southern Illinois University Edwardsville, often with his wife, Betty Alderton Spahn, has been indispensable to all five books relating to Highland's history published in association with the library's Friends. As editor and annotator of *The Story of the Settling of Highland*, he made it possible to publish that work in a seemingly impossible short period of time. Next he and Mrs. Spahn edited and annotated *New Switzerland in Illinois*. In addition to the already mentioned book one (Dr. Kaspar Koepfli's "Mirror of America"), it included as book two Jacob Eggen's "Chronicles of Early Highland" (for Its Fiftieth Anniversary Celebration) (*Aufzeichnungen aus Highlands Gruendungszeit zum fuenfzigjaehrigen Jubilaeum*). Already the most important source for early Highland history, it was substantially augmented — twenty-two of the sixty-eight pages of the translation — by material Eggen had considered too controversial to include in the original edition. Then came *The Swiss on Looking Glass Prairie; A Century and a Half, 1831–1981*, written and documented by Professor Spahn. The fourth book was his translation of the *Reisebericht*, which was published in 1986 under the title *Journey to New Switzerland: Travel Account of the Koepfli and Suppiger Family to*

xix

St. Louis on the Mississippi and the Founding of New Switzerland in the State of Illinois. And lastly, he is the translator and annotator of the book the reader is holding.

All five books have relied heavily upon a card file of about twelve thousand entries for persons whose names seemed to indicate Swiss or German origins and who lived in the four-township area surrounding New Switzerland. It was compiled over a period of several years by Professor and Mrs. Spahn from gravestones, cemetery and church records, newspaper obituaries, and histories that deal with Highland and its environs. This file has made it possible to solve a multitude of problems of identification, spelling, relationships, etc. Also of special value were the many indexes to census, marriage, naturalization, and cemetery and other records compiled by members of the Madison County Genealogical Society.

No person can begin to match Christa Landert's exhaustive knowledge of Heinrich Lienhard and of his entire manuscript. Her article, "Johann Heinrich Lienhard (1822–1903) and His Manuscript: A Biographical Sketch," *Yearbook of German-American Studies* 25 (1990), stands alone as an admirably accurate and analytical account of Lienhard's life and his manuscript, and it has been relied upon heavily by the editor. For permission to reproduce parts of her article, I thank the journal editors. Over a period of several years, as will be evident throughout this work, the translator and the editor have profited greatly from Ms. Landert's assistance, without which this book would be far less complete and accurate. In addition, a copy of her transcript of the original text has been most helpful. She cannot, of course, be held responsible for any errors and deficiencies that may remain.

The editor spent several very profitable weeks in Zurich with Ms. Landert reviewing difficult passages and discussing editorial questions. Together we went by train to the Lienhard-Schiess homestead at the Ussbuehl, Bilten, Canton Glarus, where Heinrich spent his first twenty-one years and where his brother Caspar and descendants have lived ever since. For the editor there followed two unforgettable days spent with Rosmarie and Caspar Lienhard-Schiess and their offspring, taking in the topography and scenes that Heinrich wrote of. Frequently Ms. Landert would phone on our behalf to Rosmarie or Caspar for the meaning of a word, phrase, or custom peculiar to Canton Glarus. If an answer could be found, a correct or useful response invariably followed.

We are most grateful to the Bancroft Library at the University of California, Berkeley, for permission to publish part of the manuscript and especially to John Hugo Lienhard and John Heinrich Lienhard IV for granting permission to use this portion of their forebear's manuscript. Further, the latter, in his foreword to this book, has provided the special perspective of one who sees Heinrich through passed-down memories and study of his published work. Dr. Bonnie Hardwick of the Bancroft Library, University of California, Berkeley, provided an enlarged photocopy of the first section of Lienhard's increasingly fragile manuscript. We are grateful to the Missouri Historical Society for permission to quote in our notes a passage by Charles Van Ravenswaay that appears in *Saint Louis: An Informal History of the City and Its People, 1764–1865,* edited by Candace O'Connor (St. Louis: Missouri Historical Society Press, 1991). Thanks are also due to Diane Clements, who has granted us permission to publish the maps she has prepared.

The following have been most helpful in responding to requests for information: Virginia Bryan, New Glarus (Wisconsin) Public Library; Hans Faeh, Landesbibliothek des Kantons Glarus; Michael D. Gibson, Archivist, Center for Dubuque (Iowa) History; Lezann V. Pilgrim, University of Utah Library; Alissa Rosenberg, Minnesota Historical Society Library; and H. Scott Wolfe, Galena Public Library. In addition, the Illinois State Archives provided copies of census documents; the Illinois State Historical Library responded to requests for copies of obituaries appearing in newspapers; and the Illinois Regional Archives Depository in Carbondale supplied copies of probate records.

In addition to Lovejoy Library, Southern Illinois University Edwardsville, the following have provided indispensable access to their collections: Louis Latzer Public Library, Highland, Illinois; Missouri Historical Society Library, St. Louis; Newberry Library, Chicago; Northwestern University Library, Evanston, Illinois; St. Louis Public Library; University of Arizona Library, Tucson; and the Zentralbibliothek, Zurich.

For editorial and textual assistance we are greatly indebted to Gisela Behrendt Estes, Mark Kanak, Betty A. Spahn, and most especially to Christa Oxford. Special thanks also go to Laura R. Abbott and Jeanine Pendersen for their proofreading and to John R. Abbott for his contributions to the introduction. Maxine Bell patiently typed a small mountain of texts and graciously put up with the editor's notoriously bad handwriting. Finally, the entire project could not have come to fruition without the support and assistance of the Friends of Lovejoy Library, Southern Illinois University Edwardsville, and of its Director of Development for Lovejoy Library, Donna Bardon.

Introduction

THIS TRANSLATION represents the first appearance, in either English or in the original German, of the initial portion of [Johann] Heinrich Lienhard's[1] enormous manuscript autobiography. An account of the first twenty-four years of his life, it consists of four segments: (1) early years and young manhood in the Swiss canton of Glarus, 1822–1843; (2) journey to America, August to November 1843; (3) his two-and-a-half years in Highland, Illinois, and (4) in the upper Mississippi Valley, up to April 21, 1846, when he commenced the arduous and often dangerous journey from St. Louis to Captain John Sutter's Fort at New Helvetia, California.

This portion of his memoir, though it makes up but 21 percent of the total text of well over a half million words, provides vitally important insights into Lienhard's character and presents themes that are resumed in subsequent text. Given the overall work's sheer magnitude, it is understandable that most who have dealt with his autobiography in a substantial way have treated it piecemeal, as an historical document. In so doing, and lacking sufficient knowledge of his earlier life, they have sometimes misconstrued his motivations and demonstrated an inadequate understanding of his character.

Heinrich Lienhard was born January 19, 1822, at a place called the Ussbuehl, a small collection of farms two miles west of the village of Bilten, that fell under its jurisdiction.[2] There, in the far northwestern corner of the alpine canton of Glarus, he was raised on the small farm of his parents, Caspar and Dorothea Lienhard. Here Heinrich would work along with his two older siblings, Peter and Barbara, and his younger brother, Caspar, until age twenty-one, when he departed, in August 1843, on the journey to America.

The Swiss Background

The Lienhards, like their fellow Glarners, were Alemanni, members of Germanic tribes who, in the fifth century A.D., became dominant in what is now north central and eastern Switzerland. Those who settled in the topographically constricted mountain valleys—Glarus among them—found it necessary to define the inhabitants' rights to the *Alleweide,* common lands consisting of meadows,

xxiii

pasture, forest, etc. Those rights were established by councils that in time came to be known as *Landesgemeinde,* annual assemblies of male citizens in which cantonal legislative authority was vested. This system of democratic governance also prevailed immediately to the west of Glarus in the Forest Cantons, which controlled access to the Gotthard Pass, the shortest trade route from the north to Italy. Foreseeing that the Hapsburgs would attempt to take over this strategic and profitable territory, the cantons of Uri, Schwyz, and Nidwalden in 1291 entered into a defensive alliance, which the Swiss celebrate as the founding date of their Confederation. Subsequently, at the Battle of Mortgarten in 1315, the Hapsburgs suffered a crushing defeat, losing three-quarters of their two thousand mounted troops to a much smaller force of Confederate foot soldiers armed with halberds.[3]

Though not one of the original member cantons, the people of Canton Glarus were also threatened by Hapsburg efforts to incorporate them into the family domains. Thus, when in 1352 the original cantons annexed Glarus by a show of force, the invaders were welcomed as liberators, and Glarus thereby became one of the early Swiss Confederation members, all of them speaking various Alemannic dialects derived from Old or Middle High German. However, full membership did not come until 1388, when on the morning of April 9, at the Battle of Naefels, fought just a few miles southwest of Bilten, an Austrian army of from five to six thousand, on horse and on foot, were overwhelmed by a force of about six hundred Glarus foot soldiers, with an estimated loss on the Austrian side of seventeen hundred, compared to fifty-four men of Glarus.[4] Ever since, Naefels Day has been observed in Glarus as an annual patriotic festival. A year before the Battle of Naefels, Canton Glarus held its first *Landesgemeinde.*[5]

Another defining event in the history of Glarus was the Reformation led by Ulrich Zwingli, whose first service to the church began in 1506 in Glarus, where he served until 1516 as parish priest. While the Counter Reformation succeeded in restoring Catholicism to the Forest Cantons, it met with much opposition in Glarus, where the Protestant Reformed Church gained the upper hand; by 1837 over 86 percent were Protestant, with most of the Catholic community confined to Naefels. In contrast, the Forest Cantons remained 100 percent Catholic.[6]

Designed by nature as a geographic entity, Canton Glarus is topographically defined by the Linth River, which flows about twenty-five miles, from south to north, through a valley enclosed by high, virtually impassable mountains, which, from one side of the river to the other, are at times barely a gunshot apart. Only toward the north, around Naefels, does the valley broaden out into a flood-prone plain, through which the Linth empties into a large lake, the Walensee. It flows westward from there and empties into Lake Zurich.

Due to a shortage of tillable land in the narrow valley, combined with short hours of sunshine, agriculture alone could not meet the needs of the population.

Thus, as elsewhere in Switzerland, for several centuries a principal export had been young males to serve in foreign armies. Upon their return, the veteran warriors not only brought back much needed pension incomes but also a knowledge of the outside world, which helped to enrich the local culture and industry. Such products as were exported passed toward Zurich by way of the Linth.

In 1798 came the Napoleonic invasion and conquest of Switzerland; in its wake a strong centralized government, new to the Swiss, ran roughshod over time-honored local rights and privileges. Fierce armed resistance in Glarus and other cantons was ruthlessly suppressed. The defeated cantons were for a time reorganized and administered after Napoleonic design, while a sullen Glarus population was subjected to large-scale pillage, farmers being forced to give up their draft animals and to bear on their backs the spoils of war confiscated by the enemy.[7] Widespread misery and starvation also resulted when Napoleon's continental blockade devastated the vitally important textile industry's ability to import raw materials.

Governmental centralization introduced by Napoleon did bring one lasting benefit to Glarus, especially to the lower Linth, where the Lienhards lived. By the eighteenth century, over-cutting of the forested mountainsides had resulted in the lower course of the Linth becoming so silted that the area had turned into one vast malarial marshland. In response, the Napoleon-instigated Swiss Diet devised a scheme whereby, during the first two decades of the nineteenth century, the Linth was diverted by way of the Escher Canal into the Walensee, then westward through the Linth Canal into Lake Zurich. Once again the river was open to shipping and the people of the area were no longer afflicted by the "marsh fever."

Bilten had been one of the first in the canton to open a free school, going back to the 1760s.[8] By about 1828, when Heinrich commenced his schooling, the curriculum had greatly expanded from its initial offerings of reading and writing, singing, and religious instruction. Heinrich's father was fond of reading newspapers, a habit in which earlier generations almost certainly could not have indulged. The first newspaper was published in Canton Glarus during the French occupation and continued under various titles until 1804. Thereafter, shorter-lived newspapers were published. It was not until 1833, with the founding of the *Glarus Zeitung,* that Glarus had a newspaper with a continuous existence; it was almost certainly the paper read at the Lienhard household.[9]

The changes indicated by the introduction of public schools, the expansion of their curricula, and the publication of newspapers had been preceded and then paralleled by industrial developments that reached even into remote villages in the upper lateral valleys. Relatively unimpeded by guild restrictions and feudal institutions, local handicrafts, such as those made of slate and especially of wood, had found ready foreign markets as early as the 1600s. For a time Glarus prospered from export of woven woolens and hemp textiles, which were later superseded by handspun cotton. The resulting prosperity led, in the seventeen hundreds, to a doubling of the canton's population. However, the arrival of the new century signaled not only an end to this era of prosperity, but also to decades of economically, socially, and demographically chaotic conditions. Growing competition from English cotton textiles, the restrictions on trade imposed by Napoleon's Continental System, Napoleon's impressment of Swiss into his armies, and several crop failures (from 1805 to 1818) were largely responsible for a drastic reduction in the canton's population, and only in 1824 did the population recover to about its former level. Meanwhile, disruptive changes in textile production were underway. From 1818 on, handspinning of cotton was almost entirely superseded by handweaving, which in turn gave way to factory production using waterpowered mechanical looms, leaving many unemployed, at least in the short term.

Though remote from the great urban centers, the residents of the canton were predominantly engaged in nonagricultural pursuits. Of the 11,853 males indicated as being gainfully employed in 1837, the vast majority were factory workers, producers of textiles, artisans, or were engaged in miscellaneous other occupations. Only 1,092 were engaged, as were the Lienhards, in farming, many of them doubtless on the flood plain and mountainsides from Naefels north;[10] simple peasants they were not.

Lienhard's Early Life

Lienhard's parents were hardworking, God-fearing, upright, literate, farm folk whose children learned early the meaning of strict discipline. The father was given to frequent fits of temper, which he would later regret. The mother's approach was temperate and reasonable, and her discipline sensible and more effective. Lienhard's father was obsessed by a determination that his three sons should farm, as he had. His motto was: "Stay on the land and make an honest living; you will have food and live as I have if you remain here." In order to acquire sufficient land for all, the father went into debt to buy the additional parcels of land on the mountainside that lay behind the family homestead and on the flood plain of the Linth River that stretched in front of their home. To pay off the debts incurred, family members had to work especially hard. The source of the required funds was mainly, if not wholly, derived from the sale of cattle that grazed on the mountain during the seasons when weather permitted.

As early as his sixth year, Heinrich was put to work tending the homestead cow. A couple of years later he began to herd ten to fifteen head of cattle. The herd grew, and by his ninth year he was tending cattle well up the often dangerous mountainside. There, narrow brushes with death—and undeserved punishment from his father—only served to increase his dislike of his duties on the precipitous terrain. By his late teens, Heinrich had begun to yearn to emigrate to America, which, when later expressed openly, resulted in considerable discord between father and son.

At the end of his fifth year, Heinrich began attending the Bilten School. By all accounts the school was exceptional, offering an advanced and extensive curriculum, without peer among the twenty-eight district schools in Canton Glarus. This distinction owed mainly to its enlightened direction under Pastor Rudolf Schuler, who, in addition to preaching on Sundays and other pastoral duties, supervised the entire school and taught the upper classes for students aged thirteen to sixteen. While Schuler enjoyed a fearsome reputation as a strict disciplinarian, his students came to know that honest effort would be appreciated and evidence of creativity encouraged. The pastor certainly won Heinrich's trust and affection from his first day.

During the winter, school was in session mornings and afternoons, Monday through Friday, and for three hours on Saturday mornings, during which time the pastor would review the students' compositions, and then expect the students to have made indicated corrections by ten A.M.[11] In the summer, school was held on two days, from six to eight A.M. Exact records of school attendance were kept and, when justified, parents and students admonished for truancy. Every month judgments regarding attendance, zeal, and good behavior were communicated to the local school board. To encourage parents and students, yearly exams were held in the church, where,

> as in the school, there was reading, mathematics, speaking, story telling, questions put to the students, essays read aloud, actual school being held. . . . In the upper classes there was language instruction, religion, mathematics, history of the "fatherland," biblical history and geography.

The latter subject apparently including natural history, at least in Schuler's classes. The pastor's requiring essays of ten to twenty pages, forcing some students to work late into the night, met with so much parental opposition that it was forbidden by local ordinances passed in 1837, and again in 1839 and 1853.[12]

Lienhard tells us that he "enjoyed geography . . . and compositions, and if for a change we studied natural history I was absorbed body and soul." He later regretted not having applied himself more diligently to learning "orthographically correct spelling," which required conversion of the Alemannic Swiss dialect text into High German.[13]

Indications of Lienhard's capacity for picturesque and accurate recollection were evident from an early age. Describing some of his earliest memories he writes, "I still remember exactly how I used . . . to draw, with a slate pencil, all sorts of pictures on the big slate table, which I often covered completely."[14] Early in his school years at Bilten, Pastor Schuler happened to pass Heinrich's seat and notice a drawing of a partridge done on his slate. The pastor first commented that drawing classes were not allowed there, but then said, "The bird is very accurate even though done with only a few strokes." He believed he had found a special talent, and praised the bird even more. Discovering more skillfully done sketches, the pastor gave him a variety of drawing assignments to be completed at home. "Naturally this increased my passion even more," and Heinrich went on to increasingly difficult assignments. He would have liked to have used rainy days for the purpose, in reaction to which his father would say, "Out with the lazy fellow. . . . Your drawing craze doesn't bring any bread into the house, and is completely useless for farming people." The pastor attempted, without success, to persuade the parents to allow Heinrich to "become a painter, designer, or a sculptor, arguing that it would be a sin not to develop such a fine talent by which [he] could expect to make a good living."[15] Even so he did not completely give up on his artistic ambitions until about age fifteen, when his brother Peter married and bought a nearby farm. This required that the already hard-working family work all the harder, leaving Heinrich with "rarely a moment in which I could have practiced my drawing."[16] While he never mentions the matter again, his talent for accurate, graphic recollection had already become a permanent trait. It is likely also that his phenomenal ability to recall conversations and events was in large part due to his not infrequent need to explain misdeeds of which he was likely to be accused by his father and his brother Peter.

Having completed his schooling at age sixteen and being confirmed in the Bilten church as a Swiss Reformed Protestant on Palm Sunday 1838, Lienhard would have liked to have continued his schooling, but for him there was no choice but to become, according to his father's wishes, a full-time farmer. Heinrich's father had a typically conservative attitude toward farming methods, being insistent upon sticking to traditional practices. The son was of a contrary disposition. He bought a book that dealt "with almost every branch of agriculture," quite rare in those days, and set out to learn from it. Much to his surprise, his father allowed him to follow its advice for planting some fruit trees. Though he planted his in the poorest soil, he got appreciably better results than his brother Caspar, who planted his in moderately good soil, and Peter, who planted his in the best. Nevertheless, his father absolutely forbade his trying anything further that he had read there, declaring that such books might be useful for those wealthy enough to experiment, "but would be of little value for our kind of folk."[17] Thereafter, always looking for new and better ways of doing things, Heinrich's creative energies found outlets in more acceptable enterprises, such as fashioning various home and farm articles from wood.

Though frustrated over his father's insistence that he become a full-fledged farmer, Heinrich knew that he

had to put up with it, much as my thoughts might soar out into the big, wide world—and how often they did, especially when I was working on the mountain! The beautiful view of the broad valley in which our home stood; the mountains, valleys, rivers, and lakes of the four bordering cantons, and the magnificent view of Lake Zurich with its many splendid towns! Down there, over there, I always knew I would have to go some day. But for the time being these were only idle, wishful dreams, and there seemed little likelihood that those dreams would ever be realized.[18]

Heinrich, who was inclined to speak out when he saw an injustice being done, one day got up his courage to remonstrate with his father over his hurtful arguments with his mother, whose delicate health suffered as a result. To the son's astonishment, the father took the rebuke to heart and sought afterwards to follow his son's advice. This he would admit to Heinrich later, after the mother's death, an event that left both men disconsolate; for a time Heinrich feared for his father's health. By then he had come to understand that his father's intemperate behavior derived from having lost his own mother when he was ten or eleven and having been, along with his siblings, raised in poverty by an irresponsible father.[19]

Throughout this period, Heinrich's ambition to emigrate to America only grew stronger. Yet, he was reluctant to do so without his father's consent. He therefore decided to try to learn a trade, apprenticing himself first to a furniture maker and then to a gunsmith. In both instances the masters failed to live up to their agreements. Paternal consent finally came in the summer of 1843, when Lienhard's father was momentarily caught off guard by arguments of his brother, Peter Lienhard, whose son and nephew[20] had both gone to America. When Heinrich at last did depart for America, he and his father quietly sat down and, over glasses of wine, forgave each other whatever wrongs might have been committed. Thus on August 24 Heinrich, with a congenial distant relative, Jacob Aebli, finally left, traveling with a group of Swiss emigrants to the French port of Le Havre. From there they traveled by ship to New Orleans, from where they journeyed by boat to St. Louis, Missouri, some thirty miles west of their final destination, Highland, Illinois.

By the time of Lienhard's departure, Swiss emigration to America was growing more common, partly in response to the worsening economic situation of the 1840s. An earlier core of Swiss settlers had already struck roots in the New World, thereby expediting the settlement of additional family and friends. Highland itself had been founded, in 1831, by one such group of Swiss emigrants, led by the physician and free-thinker Dr. Kaspar Koepfli. The Swiss settlers of this fledgling New Switzerland were soon joined by others, prominently General James Semple, whose political connections and enterprise quickly established him as a leading force in local development. It was Semple's idea to name the town Highland; he felt a more American-sounding name (he was of Scotch descent himself) would better attract investment than Helvetia, the name preferred by the Swiss. This change notwithstanding, Swiss settlement in the area continued to grow; by the mid-1850s it was probably the largest rural Swiss community in the country.[21]

This was the Highland area in which Lienhard arrived in November 1843. Back in Canton Glarus, meanwhile, mounting interest in New World settlement soon led to the founding of an Emigration Society, with the express aim of finding an American site that would offer Glarners a similar climate, soil, and general character. A group of over one hundred soon departed for what would become New Glarus, Wisconsin; en route the party had an amusing encounter with Lienhard in Galena, Illinois, in August 1845. Two years later, the New Glarus party was joined by twelve Bilten families, who established nearby a New Bilten, or Bilten Settlement, which, in a few years, merged with New Glarus.[22]

For Lienhard the impetus for emigrating was not economic, but an intense intellectual curiosity that could only be satisfied by taking in whatever was novel: identifying and describing the vast variety of flora and fauna, soil types, landscapes, or vividly characterizing the multitude of new acquaintances, casual or otherwise. During the voyage to New Orleans, when approaching some new landmark, he would be the last one to go to sleep and the first one up in the morning. Nearing New Orleans, he learns of tropical lands to the south and immediately feels a longing to visit those regions. Not yet arrived at his planned destination, Highland, Illinois, he hears of groups making the arduous trek across the plains and mountains to California and Oregon and is immediately seized with a desire to do the same—as he indeed did two-and-a-half years later. Leaving the love of his life in Highland, Lienhard journeyed to the lead mines of Galena in order to replenish his diminishing stock of funds and "see more of the world."

Only toward the end of his journeys, when he returned in 1850 to Switzerland, worn out, and on several occasions seriously ill, did Lienhard's seemingly unquenchable thirst for adventure and travel become satiated. He was now more than ready to take medical advice and settle down as a married man.[23] On July 3, 1851 he was married by Pastor Schuler to Elsbeth Blumer of Bilten, who, being an orphan, had no parents to oppose his return to America, should he wish to do so. Using the small fortune in gold he had gained in California, the couple settled down on a substantial homestead at Kilchberg, near Zurich, where their first two sons were born. In 1854 Lienhard returned to America, bringing his family with him. They first lived in Madison, Wisconsin. Then in 1856 they established their permanent residence at Nauvoo, Illinois, a beautiful Mississippi River town, which he had passed several times during his trips to the upper regions of the valley. Here they bought the finest mansion in the community, that of Heber C. Kimball, the Mormon apostle. By 1856 Nauvoo's tumultuous years were over, including those under the Mormons (1839–1846), during which time it became by far the most populous community in the state, and then (1849–1856) under the Icarians, a group of French utopian communists. Though the Lienhards probably did not fully realize it in 1856, Nauvoo was to become one of the larger German-speaking towns in Illinois. By 1860 the federal census already showed that of 317 households, 192 were headed by persons from German-speaking countries.[24] Here Lienhard had ample opportunity to retain and add to his already considerable High German vocabulary and to maintain his omnivorous reading habit.

Lienhard's Manuscript

By the time he commenced writing his autobiography in the latter part of 1873, Lienhard's formative and most eventful years were decades behind him. Doubtless his restless temperament could not have been completely fulfilled by life as a gentleman farmer and family man. The vivid and accurate detail that characterize his narrative reveal a person who had long and frequently relived in his mind the memories of which he wrote. By the end of 1877,[25] he had completed his manuscript, written in closely packed lines in the German script of his time, on 238 once-folded folio sheets, or 932 pages, a total of well over half a million words. A singular feature of the manuscript is that there are no chapter headings or indications of paragraph beginnings; indeed entirely new subjects are introduced within single lines.

What audience did Lienhard anticipate would be interested in his autobiography? On the basis of conversations with Mary Lienhard, the only one of his nine children still alive in 1941, Marguerite Eyer Wilbur reports that the children grew up on tales of California, learning popular ballads sung on the trail, and of the wonders of pioneer life in California. "A favorite son, John Henry, begged his father to write his memoirs for his family."[26]

In the opening sentences of the autobiography, Lienhard describes his intentions and expectations:

> I have often considered writing down my past experiences, insofar as I can remember them, since I assume that such a record might be of some interest, at least to my children and perhaps to their children. I make no presumption in so doing that they would be of interest to the general public, because I know

only too well that it was not possible for me to gain the necessary higher education for such an undertaking. There will probably be unavoidable mistakes in sentence structure, as well as in orthography, which would need to be corrected. (Lienhard folio 1/1/10.)

While he includes a few stories that might have especially appealed to his children, the narrative as a whole is directed toward an adult audience. If Lienhard's modesty prevented him from envisioning a "general public" for his account, he nevertheless plainly felt a responsibility toward posterity, as well as some appreciation for the singularity of his experiences, especially in California.[27] However, his concerns regarding "sentence structure" and "orthography" were unwarranted. Erwin G. and Elisabeth K. Gudde, otherwise his severest critics, write that he "acquired an excellent style and wrote in almost faultless German."[28] Also, it is a truism that much of the flavor and impact of the original language simply does not come through in translation. Some indication of the extent to which this applies to Lienhard's text was brought home to the editor during time spent in Zurich reviewing portions of the text with Christa Landert. Often she would remark, "That's really funny in German, but it just doesn't translate." She further explained that Glarnese humor tends to be dry and gently disparaging, often depending as much upon the manner of expression as upon content. Toward the end of my stay, she took me to the old family homestead in Canton Glarus. Until she returned by train later in the evening, she was kept laughing by the remarks of Caspar Lienhard and other family members, all of which was, of course, lost on me.

It is unlikely that Lienhard expected, or even wanted, his manuscript to be published during his lifetime. He would have been well aware that portions would have been hurtful to persons still living. Then there are passages that editors of the time almost certainly would have found too indelicate for inclusion. In any event, within two years after completing it, he had to bear the burden of losing beloved family members: his oldest son, Caspar, died in 1879; daughter Dora died in 1884, followed within a few months by the children's mother; and in 1892 he lost his youngest, Adela. For many years his manuscript was known only through the drastically abridged and unreliable version of an old personal friend of Lienhard's years in Kilchberg, Caspar Leeman.[29] This version was a great disappointment to Lienhard, and for good reason. All who have compared it to the original manuscript have condemned it for its large-scale omissions, errors of transcription, and rewriting so extensive as to bear little resemblance to the original.

To Marguerite Eyer Wilbur goes the credit for locating the original manuscript, in the possession of Lienhard's son, Adam H. Lienhard of Minneapolis. Her translation, *A Pioneer at Sutter's Fort, 1846–1850*, adheres to Lienhard's original text. However, dealing as she did with over 65 percent of the total text, the task of translating the whole must have been daunting. A reasonably satisfactory translation as far as it went, it omits those portions that she found, as she states on page thirty-three, "to be of slight historic value." The largest omissions are the thirty-seven folios in which Lienhard describes his lengthy journey to Switzerland to bring to California Captain Sutter's family, and the concluding thirteen folios in which Lienhard describes his journey from California back to Switzerland in 1850. Wilbur also omits considerable other text of varying lengths. But as Christa Landert has observed, "Yet it is in such passages [omissions] that the various aspects of his character are reflected that are vital to a personal account of this kind."[30]

Another portion of Lienhard's manuscript appeared in 1951 in *West from Fort Bridger: The Pioneering of the Immigrant Trails across Utah, 1846–1850: Original Diaries and Journals Edited and with Introductions.* Lienhard's contribution, "The Lienhard Journal,"[31] describes the Hastings Cutoff taken by him and his party, a route to California by which, instead of proceeding northward to Fort Hall in present-day Idaho, they detoured south of the Great Salt Lake through difficult and often dangerous terrain.

The first unabridged book-length translation of a major portion of Lienhard's manuscript is *From St. Louis to Sutter's Fort, 1846,* translated and edited by Erwin G. and Elisabeth K. Gudde. Starting with folio 51/1/21, where the present book ends, it takes Lienhard's manuscript through the point in folio eighty-three where Wilbur's translation commences, that is from about April 21, 1846, to about the same date in October when Lienhard and his companions arrived at Sutter's Fort. Thus, with this book, about 35 percent of the manuscript will have appeared in unabridged English translation. Meanwhile, Christa Landert is completing for her doctoral dissertation at the University of Zurich the first full German transcript of folios 118–60, corresponding roughly to chapters five through fourteen of Wilbur's work. When published, Landert's work will consist of the first thoroughly reliable German transcript of any portion of the text, the principal part of which deals with one of Switzerland's most famous emigrants, Capt. John Sutter.

Assessments of Lienhard's Work

Evaluations of Lienhard's California narrative by those who have immersed themselves in the text are diverse and often contradictory. These conflicting assessments largely relate to how Lienhard describes Capt. John Sutter, not an easy task, but certainly not an impossible one. Marguerite Eyer Wilbur, the first to closely deal with a large portion of Lienhard's text, writes:

One of the charms of Lienhard's record proved to be the curious quality of detachment in his writings; he seemed more like a curious bystander than an active participant in the life of the times. To him events in early California were a grotesque pageant, enlivened by an endless chain of colorful episodes. If an almost Germanic passion for minutiae, blunt truth, and outspokenness appeared in his pioneer story, yet in many of his seemingly trivial revelations the web and woof of his day were clearly etched. It was this meticulous viewpoint, moreover, that made Lienhard's record so revealing, so concise, and so colored with the sham and glamour of the age.[32]

In a similar vein, Christa Landert evaluates his account of Sutter as follows:

By reflecting on his relationship to Sutter, by clearly recognizing and stating his own role in the disenchantment, Lienhard never gives the impression of wanting to settle an old account with his former employer. On the contrary: although they were hardly on speaking terms any more at the end of Lienhard's stay (due to the quarrel with Sutter, Jr.) all of Lienhard's comments on Sutter reveal ongoing respect, even affection, and express the loyalty with which he had worked for him.[33]

More ambivalent is historian Richard Dillon, writing in his *Fool's Gold: The Decline and Fall of Captain John Sutter of California*. At one point he writes, "Lienhard had a Teutonic ear for scandal and was always quick to deprecate the man who offered him protection, friendship and hospitality" (95). Elsewhere he comments, "Lienhard liked to hang about the place, sponging on the man whom he maligned so much in his memoirs" (328).

Despite his reputation as a sound historian, Dillon's statements clearly indicate that he was an inattentive reader of Wilbur's translation—and perhaps of the original German text. Although Lienhard certainly did have "an ear for scandal," we should be grateful to him for it, because he was thereby able to record whatever he learned, either by way of direct observation, or from sources that he had good reason to believe were reliable. Moreover, his statement that Lienhard "was always quick to deprecate the man who offered him protection, friendship and hospitality" suggests that Lienhard was giving vent to a hostility that is contradicted by the fair and balanced characterizations of Wilbur and Landert, and utterly fails to describe the person revealed by the book the reader has in his hands. Finally, Dillon's statement that Lienhard sponged off Sutter should be similarly dismissed. On the other hand, he is to be commended for his overall assessment of Lienhard's narrative. In his bibliographical reprise he states, "Far too much has been written about Sutter and far too little has been said. . . . Best of all sources on Sutter is probably Heinrich Lienhard's memoir. . . . This graphic, critical portrait of Sutter and his fortress should be translated, edited and published *in full*."[34]

The most severe criticism of Lienhard's California narrative comes from Erwin G. Gudde, who writes in a review of Wilbur's translation:

> An interesting though not very valuable source for California history during the years preceding and following the discovery of gold has finally been made available in an English version. . . . Lienhard's story offers intimate glimpses into the pioneer life of those years but is hardly of historical significance. The author's horizon is too limited; his own well-being and his relations with other pioneers are his only concern. The quality of detachment which the editor praises in Lienhard's account is nothing more than his abhorrence of the vices of frontier life: hard drinking, Indian squaws, gambling. Otherwise he shows no signs of objectivity or fairness. Men whom he disliked, such as Frémont and Sutter, he pursued with unrelenting hatred. The reliability of his narrative is open to grave doubts. Even when he writes from direct personal observation his statements are often confusing and misleading, as for instance in his account of the days following the discovery of gold (pp. 115 ff.). What is worse, Lienhard repeatedly tells incredible stories from hearsay.[35]

In view of what has already been said regarding Dillon's statements, it would be better—with a couple of exceptions—to draw the veil of silence over Gudde's allegations. One of these pertains to his statement that he pursued Gen. John C. Frémont "with unrelenting hatred." However, an examination of Wilbur's text, which in connection with omissions, describes the content of material left out, reveals that Lienhard's few observations regarding Frémont—whom he never knew—are in accord with the generally held opinions of historians. Finally, in a footnote to his retelling of the diaries of William Henry Bigler, Gudde states that Lienhard was later "anti-Mormon."[36] On this point it should be sufficient to quote Lienhard's own words, from the present book, which were written with regard to unfounded allegations of wrong-doing on the part of the Mormons during their Illinois period. "I later became acquainted with many of these Mormons in 1847 in California, and I cannot say that I found them any worse than other people."[37]

In contrast to Erwin G. Gudde's adverse criticism of Lienhard's California account, he and Mrs. Gudde are generally complimentary of the portion they translate, stating that it

> is one of the three classical reports of the great migration of 1846. . . . We find in it, to be sure, examples of Lienhard's self-righteousness and some long, tiring passages. Yet, this Lienhard as he travels over the wide-open spaces seems to be a different man from the Lienhard who is confined to the hornets' nest of lawlessness, gossip, and intrigue, which Sutter's Fort became in the wake of the discovery of gold and with which the lord of New Helvetia was unable to cope.[38]

As previously stated, a portion of his account of the journey from St. Louis to Sutter's Fort appeared in *West from Fort Bridger*. The result of intensive research and on-foot examination of the trails described, Lienhard's contribution was subjected to intensive critical scrutiny in relation to other written sources. In unqualified vein, A. R. Mortensen writes in the preface,

> Lienhard's account will eventually come to be regarded as one of the classic diaries of overland travel; it presents a wealth of new information about the Donner party on the Hastings Cutoff—of such character that every book about the Donner party ever written from 1848–1950 now requires to be rewritten; and it explores and identifies in detail the trails across Utah used by the Forty-Niners.[39]

The above citations tell us little about Lienhard's virtues as a writer; on that subject the following by Christa Landert is authoritative as well as eloquent:

> He himself was a passionate narrator. To him, recollecting was an active undertaking to which he remained committed with admirable and untiring devotion to detail. Given his unpretentious manner of expression, a result of his modest formal education, we cannot help being amazed at the rich vocabulary he had acquired by reading, traveling, and a wide range of interests. He was not only a subtle observer, but also knew how to describe what he had seen fluently and vividly. Despite the passage of time, he tells his story with great enthusiasm, evoking good times with joy, but not omitting the bad ones. Explicitly as well as between the lines we can always sense his satisfaction, sometimes even pride, with the path he had chosen. He brings to life the thoughts and feelings that had directed his steps and actions in those days; sometimes it is hard to say whether his dry sense of humor is of Glarnese origin or already American. All this gives color and vividness to his style—we feel that we are taking part in his wanderings![40]

To what extent was Lienhard's autobiography based upon journals or upon diary-like notes? Perhaps assuming that the detailed exactitude of his recollections must have had their source in a journal kept at the time, Marguerite Eyer Wilbur states unequivocally that Lienhard had kept a diary in California. She produces no evidence to prove her assertion, however, nor does examination of her abridged text reveal any indication that Lienhard had relied on anything like a diary. It is only in the Guddes' translation, describing his arduous journey from St. Louis to Sutter's Fort in California, that Lienhard explicitly states,

> From the first day on, I started writing a kind of daily journal. Unfortunately, a good part of the first section of this journal got lost, and probably for this reason I do not recall exactly the campsites, and cannot give the precise dates when we arrived at certain places and when we left them. As soon as I come to

that part of the narration which has to do with regions for which folios of the journal were preserved, I shall again be in a position to write in detail.

For those portions where he has no diary to fall back on his account is still full and graphic, mainly lacking in dates and locations of some campsites. But stylistically it is difficult to tell at what point in the narrative he again made use of his journal. Later he states that "unfortunately, I cannot give the exact date, since some of my notes are lacking." Finally he remarks, "My daily entries stopped here. The daily chores were so tiring that I was glad to get some rest in the evenings. I recall the route and our campsite exactly for the next few days. For several of the later days I am not quite certain. Still I remember most of it, and this I shall record now."[41]

As regards the present work, only at one point is there an ambiguous hint that could be taken to indicate that Lienhard was accustomed to keeping a journal or diary-like notes. Of his traveling through France, he tells us that, since he was not very competent in French, he "could not possibly note and remember the names of towns, except the largest ones."[42] However, an almost certain indication that he relied solely upon his memory—supplemented perhaps at times by the recollections of others—is the lack of any mention of his keeping a journal, except for explicit statements during the account of the journey to California where he is careful to state where and when he did rely on one. It seems likely that he did not keep a journal in his earlier period, covered by the present work, or later in California. Specific dates, the hallmark of one who relies on a journal, are rare in all his accounts, except for in the journey to California. Where they do appear they are usually connected with significant events, which he would be most likely to recall anyway. Also, he occasionally refers to some minor person or place, "whose name I cannot remember"—as if to say, "Now I should have recalled that!" In any event—journal or no journal—wherever Lienhard's narrative can be checked against known sources, it turns out to be, with trivial exceptions, an extraordinarily reliable reflection of what he witnessed, heard, or felt at the time.

The Heinrich Lienhard who arrived in America at age twenty-one brought with him certain characteristics and values that would be modified, but in essentials remain little changed. In addition to his abounding curiosity, he retained a scorn for deceitful persons and a distaste for those of unclean or intemperate habits. But he also took pleasure from the company of good companions, enjoyed music and singing, and was at times an ardent dancer.

However the reader may react to his revelations of himself, he or she must surely also see Lienhard as an eminently humane person. This quality is revealed by his empathy for those to whom fate had been unkind. This aspect of his personality has been eloquently conveyed by Christa Landert in her discerning portrait of Lienhard where she describes how, after getting to know the California natives quite intimately, and having learned their language, Lienhard came to appreciate their culture more fully, and became angry when he realized the calamitous inevitability of their fate.[43] His sympathy for and understanding of the Indians or Native Americans is also an important feature of the Guddes' translation, *From St. Louis to Sutter's Fort, 1846,* examples of which may be readily accessed through its index. Regarding the present work, Lienhard first encountered Indians in the then still largely unsettled country of the upper Mississippi Valley, where his initial unfavorable impressions soon gave way to admiration and sympathy, examples of which may also be found through the index.

Finally, a special value and interest of his narrative derives from the circumstance that Lienhard was a person of modest, even precarious means, living among those who in varying degrees were similarly situated. From intimate contact he describes persons and environments, which would not have come under scrutiny by unadventurous persons or those viewing America in relative comfort.

John C. Abbott

Notes

1. As was then common, he was always known by his middle name, Heinrich.

2. Bilten, combined with the Ussbuehl, had a population of less than seven hundred. Oswald Heer, *Der Kanton Glarus* (St. Gallen and Berne: Huber, 1846), 595.

3. A more developed version of a battle-ax, with a large axlike, steel cutting blade mounted at the top of the long shaft.

4. W. D. McCracken, *The Rise of the Swiss Republic* (1901; rev. and enl. reprint, New York: AMS Press, 1970), 1177–183.

5. Canton Glarus continues to be one of three cantons which still carry on this system of direct democracy. It was not, however, until 1971 that the franchise was extended to the women of Canton Glarus—and all of Switzerland.

6. Carol L. Schmid, *Conflict and Consensus in Switzerland* (Berkeley: University of California Press, 1981), 22–23.

7. Georg Thuerer, *Free and Swiss* (London: Oswald Wolff, 1970), 88–89.

8. Franz Winteler, *Beitraege zur Biltner Geschichte* (Niederurnen: Thomas and Co., 1973), 135; Christa Landert, "Johann Heinrich Lienhard (1822–1903) and His Manuscript: A Biographical Sketch," *Yearbook of German-American Studies* 25 (1990): 132.

9. Fritz Blaser, comp. *Bibliographie der Schweizer Presse,* vol. 1 (Basel: Birkhaeuser, 1956), 53, 458, 461.

10. Leo Schelbert, "On Becoming an Emigrant: A Structural View of Eighteenth- and Nineteenth-Century Swiss Data," *Perspectives in American History* 7 (1973): 453–55.

11. Lienhard folio 4/1/42–49, 4/2/16–17; Gottfried Heer, "Geschichte des glarnischen Volksschulwesens," vol. 18 of *Jahrbuch des historischen Vereins des Kantons Glarus* (Zurich and Glarus: Meyer and Zeller, 1881), 134.

12. Heer, 134–35.

13. Lienhard folio 3/3/35–3/4/4.

14. Lienhard folio 1/1/24–25.

15. Lienhard folio 2/1/27–2/2/27.

16. Lienhard folio 2/2/45.

17. Lienhard folio 6/2/41–6/3/2, 6/3/45–6/4/13.

18. Lienhard folio 4/3/8–19.

19. Lienhard folio 8/3/40–8/4/26.

20. Lienhard folio 12/3/13–16.

21. Lienhard folio 23/1/48–23/2/1.

22. Miriam B. Theiler, *New Glarus, First 100 Years* (Madison, Wisc.: Campus Publishing, 1946), 17, 18, 24; Adelrich Steinach, *Geschichte und Leben der Schweizer Kolonien in den Vereinigten Staaten von Nord-Amerika* (New York: C. Bryner, 1889), 293–94; Winteler, 10.

23. Landert, "Johann Heinrich Lienhard," 140.

24. Ida Blum, *Nauvoo, An American Heritage* (Carthage, Ill.: Journal Printing, 1969), 27; Robert Sutton, "Illinois River Towns: Economic Units or Melting Pots," *Western Illinois Regional Studies* 13 (fall 1990): 28.

25. Dates of composition supplied by Christa Landert in a letter to Abbott of April 1994.

26. Heinrich Lienhard, *A Pioneer at Sutter's Fort, 1846–1850, The Adventures of Heinrich Lienhard,* trans., ed., and annot. Marguerite Eyer Wilbur (Los Angeles: Calafía Society, 1941), xiii.

27. During his lifetime he did publish two accounts of his time there. The first appeared in the *Glarner-Zeitung,* Nos. 95–99, 28 Nov.–12 Dec. 1849, and translates as "Descriptions from California, The Discovery of the Wealth of Gold, and the Consequences Thereof" ("Schilderungen aus Kalifornien, die Entdeckung des Goldreichthums und dessen Folgen"). Much later he published in English an article. "The Early Days: Reminiscences of a Pioneer Settler of '46," San Francisco *Daily Examiner,* 8 March 1885, n.p.

28. Heinrich Lienhard, *From St. Louis to Sutter's Fort, 1846,* trans. and ed. Erwin G. Gudde and Elisabeth K. Gudde (Norman: University of Oklahoma Press, 1961), xvii.

29. Heinrich Lienhard, *Californien unmittelbar vor und nach der Entdeckung des Goldes* (California before and after the Discovery of Gold), trans. Caspar Leeman (Zurich: Fasi and Beer, 1898). It was popular enough to call for a second printing in 1900.

30. Landert, "Johann Heinrich Lienhard," 138.

31. *West from Fort Bridger* first appeared as the whole of volume nineteen (1951) of the *Utah Historical Quarterly* (Salt Lake City: Utah State Historical Society). In 1994 a revised edition appeared (Logan: Utah State University Press), but with Lienhard's contribution

still the same except for minor note changes. In the first edition "The Lienhard Journal" appears on pages 117–76, in the revised edition, on pages 127–84.

32. Lienhard, *A Pioneer at Sutter's Fort,* xv.

33. Landert, "Johann Heinrich Lienhard," 142–44.

34. Richard Dillon, *Fool's Gold: The Decline and Fall of Captain John Sutter of California* (New York: Coward-McCann, 1967), 95, 328, 357, 362.

35. Erwin G. Gudde, review of *A Pioneer at Sutter's Fort, 1846–1850,* trans., ed., and annot. Marguerite Eyer Wilbur, *Pacific Historical Review* 11, no. 2 (June 1942): 233.

36. Erwin G. Gudde, *Bigler's Chronicle of the West* (Berkeley: University of California Press, 1952), 75.

37. Lienhard folio 32/4/29.

38. Lienhard, *From St. Louis to Sutter's Fort,* ix–xi.

39. In the original, 1951 edition, of *West from Fort Bridger,* Mortensen's comment appears on page ix; in the 1994 edition it appears on page xviii.

40. Landert, "Johann Heinrich Lienhard," 145–46. The rest of her analysis commences with the last two lines of page 144 and extends through the point on page 145 where the already quoted passage begins.

Critical awareness, perceptiveness, and sound self-confidence characterized Heinrich Lienhard's personality. These traits derived from the influence of his family and schooling; it was there that he had also developed the clear moral principles that formed the basis for his keen sense of right and wrong. Insincerity, hypocrisy, and injustice of all kinds were among the qualities he appreciated least. Although on occasion his judgment was considered to be rather strict, most people respected his integrity. His objective way of looking at things was in any case so well known at Sutter's Fort that even people who knew him only from hearsay came up to him to ask his opinion.

An author's credibility is, of course, the crucial aspect of a manuscript. To report objectively and truthfully throughout was Lienhard's main concern, and this is expressed in various ways. First we may mention the spontaneous manner in which he, as a father, wished to tell a story to his family rather than to convey a particular message. He writes with frankness, hiding neither his strong points nor his weaknesses, which were no secret to his family anyway. In addition there is his precision: he spares no effort in dealing with a topic as comprehensively as possible and in controversial matters he is far too conscientious to present merely his own view. On occasion his tendency to justify himself adds clarity. That trait as well derived from his childhood when, to forestall unjust punishment by his father, he had often felt obliged to give a detailed account of an event. This remained a pattern above all in conflict situations, manifesting connections even where the reader may not wish to accept his arguments on a certain issue.

Another feature of Lienhard's narrative style that strengthens its credibility is his clear distinction between his own experiences and those of others. In the latter case he not only offers introductory remarks to that effect, but often himself weighs the credibility of the person involved. For the stories of others, furthermore, he uses indirect discourse leaving no doubt whatsoever as to their origin. This clear, often even repetitive distinction indicates two things: Lienhard's deeply rooted suspicion of rumors and exaggerations—he never liked braggarts—and his wish to maintain the necessary distance to his own experience, the authenticity of which cannot be doubted. Himself an interested listener, he never forgoes that distinction, even when weaving longer adventure stories of friends into his text. On such occasions he skillfully avoids narrative clumsiness by relinquishing the role of narrator to the other.

41. Lienhard, *From St. Louis to Sutter's Fort*, 16–17, 138, 169.

42. Lienhard folio 14/2/48–14/3/2. In a letter of July 31, 1993, to Abbott, Christa Landert points out that the word *nehmen,* meaning to take, seize, receive, etc., here translated as "to note," would not be used in German, as Lienhard does, and that he was possibly using the word in the English sense, "take a name," that is, "to write down."

43. Landert, "Johann Heinrich Lienhard," 143–44.

New Worlds to Seek

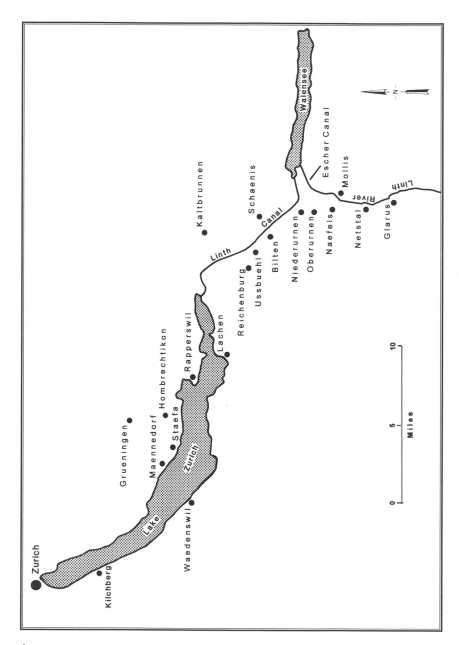

Portions of
Switzerland
Relating to
Lienhard's
Early Years

1

Growing Years in an Alpine Canton

1. Memories of My Earliest Childhood

I HAVE OFTEN CONSIDERED writing down my past experiences, insofar as I can remember them, since I assume that such a record might be of some interest, at least to my children and perhaps to their children. I make no presumption in so doing that they would be of interest to the general public, because I know only too well that it was not possible for me to gain the necessary higher education for such an undertaking. There will probably be unavoidable mistakes in sentence structure, as well as in orthography, which would need to be corrected.

I was born January 19, 1822, at the Ussbuehl,[1] near Bilten in Canton Glarus. My parents were upright, industrious farming people who, as far as I can recall, held us to strict rules and expected us to work hard. There were four of us siblings. My oldest brother [Peter] was nine, and my sister [Barbara] was about three years older than I, while my younger brother [Caspar] was almost three-and-a-half years younger.[2]

As far back as I can remember—and I can remember quite clearly—when I was about two-and-a-half years old the nearby village of Schaenis burned; and I remember just as clearly that almost at the same time a violent hailstorm[3] swept over our village, during which my mother was having me inoculated for smallpox by the village Doctor Burkhart; how frightened I initially was of the procedure; how they both tried their best to assure me that the procedure would be painless, and so on. I still remember exactly how I used to use a footstool to climb more easily up on chairs and benches in our living room, and how I used to draw, with a slate pencil, all sorts of pictures on the big slate table, which I often covered almost completely; how I used the footstools and chairs as horses, sliding them around the living room until finally, due to the terrible ear-splitting screeching noise, my mother, to my great regret, made me stop. She was slightly more accepting of my efforts at building churches at the roadside ditch,

3

using the available materials, street dirt, sand, water, and stones, coming home with what she called horribly filthy hands, face, and clothes.

At the end of my fifth year I was required to go to school, a good half-hour distance from my father's house. On the whole I enjoyed learning and school, although for a change I would have preferred to stay away and play in the street now and then if I had not been afraid of my parents' punishment. For this reason I played hooky but one time when, instead of going to school, I chose to spend the time at the home of a friendly neighbor woman who liked children and who treated me to tastes of honey. I left there only when the neighborhood children came home from school. But I was to be punished for my offense only too soon, because a neighbor girl four years older than I, Maria Hefte, had nothing better to do than to tattle to my mother, who happened to be baking a cake. Mother rewarded her with some cake, while I got none. Instead, I got what I would much rather have done without—which kept me from ever playing hooky again.

As early as my sixth year I had to begin tending cattle. A rope was tied around the horns of a cow that was not driven to the uplands during the summer. By this rope I had to keep her on our land. But I was barely a couple of years older when I had to herd ten to fifteen head of livestock, which generally went well enough for a short time, as long as the grass was still tall. Should this grass become sparse, however, and there was still good grass on the neighbor's pasture, I often had my work cut out for me, especially at the edges of the pasture where there were no hedges, fences or ditches, or where those that existed were ineffectual.

Despite the fact that my father regularly read newspapers, he held to the same principles as his fellow farmers: "Stay on the land and make an honest living." He believed that his sons should live the same kind of life as he had and his father and grandfather before him, and therefore he felt duty-bound to buy enough land so that each of us would be able to farm as he had. But since he could not pay for such a large quantity of land he had to go into debt, and thus each of us had all the more work to do.

I was now in my ninth year, and, as the herd of livestock grew, it fell to me to tend to the cattle, every spring and fall, Sundays as well as weekdays, on one or another of Father's pieces of land. Often I had my hands full with the livestock, especially when I was obliged to herd the cattle on the uplands, while also, at my older brother's instructions, gathering fir branches from our woodland, dragging them to the barn, and piling them up.

One warm, humid spring day in the following year, while I was dragging fir branches to the barn, the calves, severely tormented by flies and mosquitoes, began to grow restless and ran through the woods and brush, tails in the air.

Since I was aware that there were several dangerous so-called timber ravines nearby—a kind of timber slide used to slide whole trees to the valley below— which bypassed several steep precipices and cliffs, where logs shot downward at such unbelievable speed that at times they actually soared, I left off dragging branches, fearing the cattle might fall into one of these perilous slides, endangering their lives. Unfortunately my concern proved entirely justified. The cattle were able to run faster than I and, before I could prevent it, all of the livestock grazing there had reached the most dangerous of these ravines, called Lattenzug. This timber slide began right at a rocky outcrop some forty feet in height, with sides that ranged from steep to perpendicular. On the lower portion of this outcrop was a small level spot where a few blades of grass grew; between this small level spot and the ground adjacent to the timber slide was a steep rock ledge about fifteen to twenty feet in width. Through this moist rock ledge a fissure or crevice ran from the adjacent ground to the small level spot in the rock where some grass was growing. When I got there our largest young ox was already grazing in this fissure. The second ox, a beautiful animal, was already following his lead. It was impossible for the animals to turn around there safely. The first had already reached the small level spot, and the second had done the same as I arrived with a long hazelwood switch to drive them away from this dangerous spot. A careful assessment of the situation showed me there was no other means of escape except for the way they had come, which way I did not dare to follow.

Therefore I stood at the base of the rock, beating my switch against the rock in the direction of the young oxen, shouting "Hoi!" The larger steer turned back very carefully, setting his hooves into the fissure. The second, however, as he reached the middle of the rock ledge, with one of his forelegs on the ledge, slipped and slid past, within just a few feet of me, like a smooth log, toward the very high, nearly perpendicular cliff further down the mountain, plunged over it, and therewith disappeared from my sight.

Had I been a few years older I might have been able to leap forward quickly and hold him back, but not without endangering my own life. As it was, however, I was so frightened that I clutched with all my might to the sparse brush, fearing I would fall too. But the steer had hardly disappeared from my sight when I remembered the rest of the cattle, and I drove them away from the dangerous spot toward the barn.

From a thirty-foot high rock outcrop, barely sixty feet from the barn, I had a good view of the valley down to my father's house where, if I called loudly, I could be heard, which I then did to the extent that my strong, still young lungs permitted, sobbing all the while. And it was not long before my older brother (whom I soon had to fear as much as, or even more than, my father himself, for his authority was established by my father) was at hand. After I told him how

5

it had happened that the young ox had fallen, he went to the place, assuring me all the while that I could certainly expect to get a sound thrashing from Father.

2. Father's Thoughtless Words—Abuse from Brother Peter and Undeserved Punishment by Father

I knew only too well that it was my fate to serve as a kind of scapegoat at which they thought it their unquestionable right to vent their annoyance at will. Neighbors, drawn by my crying, helped me secure the rest of the cattle in the barn, comforting me by saying that when I told my father all that had happened the punishment would surely be less severe than I expected.

It was already dark when, very frightened, I reached our house. Father and Brother were still at the spot where the young ox had finally stopped tumbling. What Mother had to say about my father in regard to me was not particularly heartening. She told me to go into the living room where I waited, frightened almost to death behind the stove, for Father's arrival. Supper was already on the table; I heard Father and Brother come in; finally they came into the room, and I thought, "Now I'll get it!" Asked where I was, my younger siblings answered, "Behind the stove." "Come out here, you rascal!" I crawled out. "Sit down at the table and eat, but don't let anything like that happen again, for if I'd been there with you, I think I'd have thrown you down with the ox!" Naturally I was tremendously surprised, for that I should escape with only a few harsh words, without any blows, was almost beyond belief.

My father's words, that he would have thrown me after the ox if he had been there, had an impact on me that would not go away. To me it felt as though I were indeed careening down the rocks and the precipices of the Lattenzug, neck and bones breaking, and inevitably arriving at the bottom—dead. The fact that I did not receive further physical punishment was probably due to the fact that a few hours had passed and my dear mother had found time to discuss the matter sensibly with my father.

But the threat that he would have thrown me after the animal would not leave my mind, and about a year later this incident could have cost me my life. The same rocky outcrop which, as I have said, was scarcely sixty feet from the barn, extended to the vicinity of the spring where I watered the livestock. I had often noticed that our home cow and the two young steers, which I again had to herd, greedily tried to reach grass growing in several places at the outer edges of the rock, each time giving me no little fright. One day I had just watered the stock when, as I turned around, I saw the larger of the two steers again grazing at the very edge where a layer of sod extended precipitously past the end of the rock.

6

An old, rotten fir stump and some scraggly hazelnut bushes also leaned beyond the edge at this spot. The steer's front feet were almost at the edge of the precipice, and the rear portion of his body was considerably more elevated than the front. I called out to him immediately, but it seemed only to want to move still farther forward. The thought that, if this one dropped dead too, this time my father would most assuredly pitch me down as well, immediately awakened my resolve to risk my life in order to drive it away from this spot. I was certain that if the steer were to fall it would surely carry me down with it, resulting in instant death, for many huge jagged rocks that had broken off the mountain's face lay scattered below.

Calling the steer softly by name, I approached him. I succeeded in swinging myself over of the precipice in front of the animal by grasping some hazelnut bushes with my left hand; I set my left foot on the aforementioned, apparently completely rotten fir; at the same time my right leg was dangling rather freely over the precipice without any means of support. With my right hand I began gently hitting the steer's head, calling him by name all the while. My only fear was that, in his first move to turn around, he could easily make a misstep, and slip and fall forward. But this time everything went fairly well and the steer was saved. The danger having passed, I examined the spot more closely, shuddered and thought of the danger I had just escaped.

I began to take a profound dislike to our mountain uplands, feeling that I might some day not be so lucky up there. When my father came up to milk the cow, I begged him to build a fence as far as the rock extended, or even more of our livestock would be sure to fall to their death. I told him of my little adventure with the steer and showed him where it had taken place. His face became very serious and he said I should not have done that, that it was just lucky that both I and the steer had not fallen, for if we had, I would certainly now be quite dead. When I told him that if the steer had fallen to its death, he would have thrown me down there also, as he had said the previous time, he became still more serious and especially quiet. He told me that we would build a fence so that I would never again have to face such a danger.

After we arrived back home and he believed I did not hear him, he told my mother of the great danger I had survived, and said, "It was real folly on my part to tell the boy back then that, if I had been there when the other steer fell down the Lattenzug, I would have thrown him down after it. If the poor boy were now dead, I would blame myself for the rest of my life."

In school, as long as I was able to attend it, I made reasonably good progress. I was still in the lower school—I think it was in my second year of school—when one day we read about the creation of the world, of the animals, of Paradise, of the serpent in the tree, and of the Temptation of Adam and Eve, which for me was of enormous interest. The story made such an impression on me that I still remember it almost word for word, and I repeated it that same evening to my parents, who could hardly believe their ears.

It was also while I was still in the lower school in the old schoolhouse, cold in winter, that having completed my assignment, I went to warm myself a bit at the stove. Below the assignment, with just a few strokes, I had drawn a partridge, not dreaming that anyone would pay any attention to it. But while I was warming myself, our pastor, [Johann Rudolf] Schuler, who taught the upper school, which was in the same room, but who supervised the whole school, happened to pass my seat. He found my seat empty, my slate with the assignment done correctly, and the partridge below it. He wanted to know to whom the slate belonged. Naturally my name was given. The pastor picked up the slate and first said that we were not holding a drawing class here, and that such things were not permitted. He went on to say, "The bird is very accurate even though done with only a few strokes." He believed he had discovered a talent, and praised the bird even more.

Foolishly, on the other side of the slate, I had also drawn two generals with tall Napoleon hats, long sashes, as well as epaulets. Since the pastor was still looking at the bird and not scolding me at all, the girls sitting on the bench in front of me were talkative enough to tell the pastor that on the other side of the slate there were very beautiful pictures. But alas! Now I thought I would really get it, and if I had been able to, I believe I would have hidden in the stove. First he said, "Ei, ei, ei, I do believe that those are generals in conversation!" Thus it went, half jokingly, half seriously, and I expected most certainly to be punished for it, but it turned out to be only a gentle reprimand, and by noon he even gave me all kinds of drawing assignments to complete at home. He praised my talent, remarking that such should be encouraged. Naturally this increased my passion even more, especially since the copies seemed particularly to satisfy the pastor, and each time he gave me new, more difficult assignments, which, however, I completed without particular difficulty and was able to bring back quickly for him to examine. The assignments, or rather the pictures, he now gave me to copy consisted of various prophets and human figures. Had I been able to use leisure time, my progress would have increased correspondingly. I would have liked to use rainy days for drawing, but Father said, "Out with the lazy fellow. I'll teach him to draw in the middle of the day when there is so much work that needs to be done! Your drawing doesn't bring any bread into the house, and is completely useless for farming people." My father generally held to the view that a farmer, in addition to writing, reading and arithmetic, needed no further formal education. Under these circumstances I was left with no time for drawing other than in the evening after supper in the faint glow of an oil lamp, and anyone who has tried working this way knows whether it is possible to make progress under these conditions, and whether one's eyes can stand such strain for long. Mine soon became too inflamed and forced me to quit drawing completely for some time. Our pastor actually thought he could convince my parents to let me become a painter, designer, or a sculptor, arguing that it would be a sin not to develop such a fine talent by which I could expect to make a good living. But this was all in vain, and my father was not to be persuaded. "Stay on the land and make an honest living" was his motto, and if I were willing to work, I would also eat and live as he had done. When I dared declare that there was the greatest difference between one man's life and another's in that the poorest human being also lives, and that the rich man lives, but how differently they live, his answer usually was, "I suppose you know this better than I!"

Thus the years passed in much the same way. I had to help with the usual work. When I was only nine I had to help with the raking of the hay and plowing, and when my father felt I was not working hard enough my ears were soundly boxed, to the extent that one evening a neighbor reproached him for it. I can clearly remember having my ears boxed simply because a neighbor had dared to make some remarks about him that (in Father's opinion) were unjust. To be sure he was quite sorry about it right after, but that did not undo the punishment, and it was but poor consolation for me. But I had long since become accustomed to seeing myself as a kind of scapegoat, because in Father's view it almost always had to be me who was at fault when something did not go the way he wanted.

I was about fifteen years old when my brother Peter married, and since he bought out a neighboring family that was going to America, we had all the more work to do, and I therefore rarely had a moment in which I could have practiced drawing. My brother had been married for little more than a year when his wife and their child died and he came to live at our house again and to take his meals as before. But I cannot recall that he ever made any payment or did anything in return. On the contrary it seemed to me that he imagined he could do whatever he wished, and preferably if it benefited him personally. For example, I mention here that, without feeling it necessary to get permission from our parents, he began to blast rock in the so-called Grueth in order to build a new inn by the newly built main road that crossed a piece of my father's land and continued to the Canton Schwyz boundary. I do not know whether Father ever had the heart to tell Peter that he was not his only child, that he had three others. Nevertheless I did hear him discuss the matter several times with Mother, expressing his dissatisfaction with Peter's high-handed behavior. I do know that the construction of the inn was not carried out, but whether because of our parents' resistance, or because Brother gave it up on his own free will, I can no longer recall.

If my older brother was high-handed I believe it was primarily our parents' fault, especially Father's, for whatever he might do, it was in my father's eyes almost always the intelligent thing to do, and he usually got his approval. It is true Peter was an exceptionally industrious worker, usually of a cheerful disposition. He knew how to tackle every problem, and he was successful in everything that he undertook. These were qualities that my father valued more than anything, perhaps especially because my brother was often much more practical. However, my brother was not only high-handed but also selfish, and if we had had a law as in England which leaves the whole inheritance to the first-born, I am convinced that he would have taken the very fullest advantage of it.

One fine summer evening in my seventeenth year, as I was just coming home from the fields, and was about to take care of a certain need, my older brother was in the process of moving a heavy piece of rock he had blasted loose to use in building his planned house. Just as I was passing him he called to me to help him. I told him to wait just a little while and then I would help him. I hurried and do not think that I was gone more than five minutes; but as I came to help him, I found that, with the help of my younger brother, he had almost finished prying up the rock. Though I still wanted to help him, I was abruptly rebuffed, and even when I explained why I had not helped him right away, he continued to berate me. Although it was nothing new for me to be berated by him without real cause, I was quite indignant about this undeserved treatment as I left him and went back into the house, where the others were already seated at the table for supper. I sat down at my customary place, but had hardly sat down to eat when he came in and immediately claimed that I had not wanted to help him pry the rock out of the hole and had come only after he almost had it out. I replied I had wanted to help him, and said why I could not do so immediately. But my brother said that I was lying, whereupon I said that he was lying, not I. His next response was a blow to my face, which I returned; but, since he was of course much stronger than I, he seized me and threw me to the floor. I heard my sister say, "That is right." My mother urged reason, but my father grasped me less than gently and threw me out of the house! That was the treatment I got, the justice that came to me because I had had the courage to refute my brother's bald-faced lie, declaring it as such, and returning a blow with a blow, even though mine were the weaker. I was nearly overcome with despair, and I do not know what I would have done if I had not heard my dear, unforgettable mother urging reason and impartial examination of the affair.

I moved into the bushes, and from there to the upper house belonging to my father, my mind incessantly occupied with the most wretched thoughts. Soon I had the urge to hurry to the Linth [River] to end my miserable existence, or at least to run away, far away into the unknown world among strange, foreign people. I believed my lot could not be any worse anywhere else. My mind churned for some time; I was agitated and deeply hurt. Occasionally I would look up to the magnificent sky, illuminated by the moon and millions of stars. How glorious was the splendor and peace of nature; how very different from my own feelings! As I became somewhat calmer, I began to make plans as to how I would go about getting my best clothes and the little money I had out of the house, for I began to believe that I no longer had a home there, and that there I was completely superfluous. Moreover I was not willing to continue serving as a kind of scapegoat that could be beaten to one's heart's content whenever anyone felt displeased about anything, without troubling to consider whether it was just or unjust.

Then I thought I heard a sigh. I listened and thought it might be Mother looking for me because she feared I might do myself harm. I felt myself drawn in the direction from which I had heard the sound. I was heartbroken at the thought that Mother might be frightened because of me, for she was the only one who at least did not punish me without making certain whether or not I deserved it. Soon I could see a shadow coming toward the upper house; yes, it was Mother. She was looking for me; I clearly heard her say "Oh God!" Then I could no longer hold back. I hurried toward her, telling her, however, that I wanted never to return to the house, but would rather go away.

My mother was sensible and fair, a good caring mother who loved all of her children equally. She was much better able than Father to judge the qualities of her children. When she considered it necessary, she too could punish, and her punishment made an impression, but she also used kind words and admonitions, and they always had good results. Naturally Mother convinced me to come back into the house, and I attribute to her admonishing, sensible persuasiveness the fact that I did not leave my parents' home that night, and I still believe today that if it had not been for Mother, I would have quit my parents' home sooner. Only the thought of the great heartache I would cause my mother kept me from it.

My father was in many respects very narrow minded and dogmatic, although he did like to read newspapers. He did not believe in innovations, but kept to the old ways, whether appropriate or not, for that is the way he had done things, as had his father, and many other people, and after all, these people were no fools. These innovations were of little or no use. Working hard at a project, that was the right thing to do. That is the only way to make one's living. By the sweat of his brow man should earn his bread, and the person who worked especially hard could raise plenty of potatoes, wheat, hay, etc.; and that person would have food to eat and also have enough left over for clothing. My father never quite seemed to understand that man, whom God created with a healthy good sense, should use that gift to the best of his ability to improve his lot and that of his fellow men. My father was extremely strict, judicial in matters that he believed he understood. Perhaps he was seeking to follow the example of the Holy Book. He hated lying and deceit, was sober and sought to take himself and his family through life solely by honest means. But his somewhat stubborn nature and rather violent and rash character often caused him much difficulty, which he then later regretted, and for which he blamed himself. As a result, I am now convinced that he frequently and heartily regretted his earlier brusque and strict behavior toward me and asked both God and me for forgiveness. Regarding matters affecting me I have gladly forgiven him, and I hope that God has forgiven him his faults—forgiveness he so often and, in fact, sincerely prayed for.

3. Attending School—Failing to Be Truthful and the Resulting Punishment

I attended the village school according to the regulations of the time until I was over sixteen years old. Naturally my education was only that usually offered, which was available to every other pupil in the town. I generally got along well with my teachers, but I got along best with the village pastor, Johann Rudolf Schuler, by whom I was baptized, taught, confirmed, and later even married. Even before I began school other children had tried to frighten me; they said that the pastor would scrape my tongue if I misbehaved. But the pastor did not teach the lower classes which I initially attended. However these classes were also under his supervision. It was my first time at school. My presence had not yet been recorded. I sat timidly on one of the benches, and sure enough, there came the pastor. Although unaware of having done anything wrong, I was very apprehensive when I saw him striding toward me. But, as I half feared he was about to take out his pocket knife to shave my tongue, he began instead to speak to me, asking me my name. Then he drew the first three letters of the Latin alphabet on a slate for me and said I should see if I could draw them also. Naturally I did not dare disobey him, and since I had some drawing skill, it was not at all difficult for me to copy these three letters. My reward for this was definitely not having my tongue scraped, but instead he praised me and remarked that now I was able to write. I already liked this pastor whom I had feared so; nonetheless, I was still relieved when he walked away.

Until my eleventh year I remained in the lower school taught by the assistant teacher, Fridolin Blum, who was on the whole a good sensible man, except that like many people he had one weakness, and this was that he tended to favor his nephew, Caspar Schindler, which bothered me somewhat, but particularly annoyed another lad by the name of Caspar Zweifel. The teacher almost always considered his nephew to be right, even though we were of a vastly different opinion. Also he was almost always permitted to occupy the front seat, even when we were convinced that it rightfully belonged to one of us. One day Schindler, as usual, was in the front seat, with Zweifel in the next, and I behind him. The teacher and the pastor were nearby as my two neighboring Caspars began arguing about something. I noticed that the teacher and the pastor were watching them. I was afraid the teacher would come to take his nephew's part, but it did not happen. Instead the pastor suddenly took the ruler out of the teacher's hands, and first grasped Schindler's hand, whacking it six times with the broad ruler; then Zweifel received the same number in the same manner. Naturally they cried out, and I thought that I saw the color of the teacher's face change, and I confess I felt a kind of satisfaction, or a little malicious joy, not at Schindler's expense, but at the teacher's.

My years among the assistant teacher's pupils gradually passed without any noteworthy incidents. I believe it was the last year that Blum was my teacher; I was sitting as usual next to Caspar Zweifel, who was generally a cheerful friend. We were occupying the first places next to the windows; we were just working at some problem, during which I had laid my arm around his shoulders, when Zweifel moved, causing my arm to move involuntarily, which resulted in a sudden jerk of my elbow, breaking two panes of glass. The sound of the breaking window panes was loud enough to draw the attention of all the pupils, and our teacher, who was sitting in front of us and watching us had seen everything. He said to me, "Oh Heinrich, when dealing with fools, one often encounters foolishness. Now each of you can pay two batzen." I happened to have several batzen in my pocket with which I was supposed to buy some salt on the way home. Therefore I was ready to pay my part immediately, intending to pay for the salt later from my little bank. The teacher later gave my sister half of it back, explaining that he had seen that I had actually been quite innocent.

Not long thereafter Blum became ill, and after a short illness died. As a result the lower school had a number of substitute teachers, and, finally, as I had long hoped, I found myself in the upper school taught by the pastor. The pastor was known as a strict teacher, but I had no reason to be dissatisfied with him for I found that although he was a little strict, he never gave his pupils assignments which they were not capable of completing if they were willing to make an effort. I even found that he was very pleasant with those pupils who were conscientious in their work. He was sometimes a bit sharp, but only with pupils whose work was slipshod, or with the class buffoons who very likely deserved such treatment.

Among the pupils I was generally considered to be the most adept sketcher and was often asked by my classmates to draw caricatures. Naturally the pastor was not to know. I would sketch and draw various things at home which I would take to school to be admired by the other pupils. Once I had copied a drawing that showed a Turk on horseback, with a turban, wide baggy trousers, a short jacket, and his curved saber drawn, full of rage and fire, ferociously attacking a French infantryman, intending to slice him to pieces. The Frenchman, though, had prepared himself for the attack of the fanatical Turk and called to him, "Come on, you son of Mohammed and show your courage! My bayonet is thirsting for your tiger blood." I had used very bright colors, but I am not sure whether they were really those of the combatants' national uniforms. In any event, I still recall how very proud I was of this splendid picture and I was determined that it should be admired by my fellow pupils; so I took it to school, and since—as I had expected—it found many admirers, this picture also found a buyer among them; and I sold it to the happy buyer for the munificent sum of two batzen. Unfortunately the buyer was only too happy with his purchase. He did not even hide it between the pages of his school books as he should have. No, the stupid fellow laid it openly on top so that it could be more easily admired. Regardless of how much I would have liked to tell him to hide it, an opportunity failed to present itself, and the thought barely had crossed my mind when the pastor discovered the two-warrior picture. "What are you doing with that thing? Are you wasting your time admiring such things in school instead of doing your lessons? Ei, ei, just look at the kinds of things Ulrich Staub spends his time on!" And he set the picture where all the pupils could see it. I do not know exactly how I felt, but I definitely felt hot, and I would have been glad to crawl into the first available mouse hole if it had been possible. Ulrich was asked from whom he had gotten the drawing, whereupon he replied that he had bought it from me for two batzen. Again the pastor said, "Ei, ei," and since the pastor's gaze and that of all the pupils were turned to me, I seemed almost to lose my eyesight and hearing. My head burned and I lost my enthusiasm for the sale of homemade drawings in school.

On the whole I made reasonable, if not spectacular, progress in school, so that during my last two years, and particularly during my final year, I was almost always at the top of the pastor's pupils. I enjoyed geography, *Gegensaetze*[4] and compositions, and if for a change we studied natural history, I was absorbed body and soul. I admit that there were also subjects I did not enjoy studying, for which I even had an antipathy. One was learning to read music, a truly boring activity for me since I knew almost every melody by heart after hearing it a couple of times. Then there was orthographically correct spelling which I found downright disagreeable. To this day I do not know why I did not apply myself better in these two subjects, especially in the latter. It is so important at any time to be able to write grammatically and to spell correctly. I knew this quite well, but unfortunately my aversion to it was too strong for my common sense to overcome.

One day the pastor had given us some dictation from a book in the Swiss dialect. This we were to transcribe in proper German on our slates with as few errors as possible. Since I knew only too well that the rest of the boys of my age were, almost without exception, as indifferent as I about spelling, and I therefore did not need to fear that any of them would do better than I (for the pastor had said that whoever produced the best exercise would go to the head of the class), I did not make any particular effort to complete my work without errors. The girls worked very hard at spelling correctly. There was a sort of competition between them, and thus they became much more proficient than the boys. Taking advantage of this situation, some three or four of my closest neighbors looked at the slates of the girls in front of them, and the girls not only did not object but actually helped them. The pastor happened to be out of the room at the time, so everything went very well for them, for my warning that I would report them did not stop them, because they seemed to believe I would not do it. Finally the pastor returned. Since I was the pastor's top pupil, my slate was corrected first and sixteen writing errors were discovered. I had expected a good many, but not that many, and, knowing that the other boys had not done their work by themselves, I wrote "14" on my slate instead of "16," doing it quickly and at the same moment that the pastor took the slate from the boy who followed me. Having accomplished this great deed, I showed the slate to my closest neighbor. By now, however, his slate had also been corrected. He had several mistakes fewer than I; three or four of the other boys had fewer still.

When all of the slates had been corrected and the pastor came to me to ask how many mistakes I had made (for now the pupils were to exchange seats accordingly), unfortunately instead of saying "16," I said "14." "That is not the truth," he said. "Don't you have 16?" "I have 14, Herr Pastor," was my answer, for I reasoned that if one had sixteen errors, he must certainly have fourteen, and therefore one was not lying if he said that; but a slap on the face immediately taught me that the pastor regarded the matter differently than I did; and I was very angry, but even more, ashamed, and I immediately regretted having attempted such deceit. Even so I told him that several of my neighbors had not even done their assignments themselves, and that they, as well as I, deserved to be punished, for I had seen them laughing and was not inclined to remain silent. Whether the pastor was so wrought up about having been deceived by me, whom he had regarded highly, and from whom he had not expected such deceit, or whether he was simply doing it anyway, he not only did not punish the others, but to my shame, I had to leave my seat and stand in a place where the whole class could see me. I felt this humiliation only too greatly, even though I was convinced that I had amply deserved it, and I resolved to regain the pastor's good will in the future through good behavior, and hard work. On the following day, when I was to take my seat among my classmates, I declared forthrightly that I would much prefer to take the very lowest place of all, since others had only gained their places by cheating.

The pastor had introduced a certain procedure that enabled us to know in advance the next day's assignments. According to this procedure we did not expect to write a composition for several days yet. Naturally I hoped that day would come soon, for I hoped thereby to regain my lost position. I do not know whether the pastor may have decided that he had not been completely impartial in his handling of the situation on the previous day before. However, I do know that he made no objection to my taking the lowest position among the boys, as already mentioned. Instead of finding him still angry with me as I expected, I found not the slightest indication of anger, but instead he was very friendly toward me, which only strengthened my resolve never to misbehave in the future.

Contrary to my expectation, and to my great satisfaction, we were informed before the end of that same day that we would have a composition the next day, and he gave us the words he wanted us to use, pointing out various things about them in his customary way. I could scarcely conceal my pleasure at that, and I still well remember how the pastor smiled at me. He may well have known what I was thinking, and I believe I was thinking what he imagined I was thinking. I began working quite zealously at the composition in order to explain both the letter and the spirit of the topic as clearly and correctly as possible. And I took pains to make it as error-free as I could. The next day I waited anxiously for the moment when he would collect our assignments, and I could hardly contain my impatience until I received mine back from him, corrected and carrying his written judgment of it. My expectation not only was not dashed, but surpassed, for it received the best result I had received up to then, and it was particularly satisfying to me to be able, in this manner and so quickly, to resume my place as the top pupil. I could scarcely conceal a little jubilant smile. Even the pastor himself seemed to be somewhat pleased. From then on I remained at the top of the class, and I conducted myself in such a manner that I gave no further cause for dissatisfaction.

4. Unpleasantness with Teacher Grob — Evening Pranks of Boys — Military Drill, Etc.

The pupils in the lower school still had no regular teacher, but rather only a temporary one by the name of [Jacob] Grob, who would only too gladly have taken over the position as a regularly employed teacher, which would also have been the earnest wish of his father-in-law, Counselor Salmer. But the pastor knew that a good former pupil of his, Peter Lienhard, was soon to return to his hometown from a teacher training school, and he had it in mind to turn over the lower school to him. Teacher Grob and the pastor were therefore not on the best of terms. If Grob could do anything behind the pastor's back that he was not authorized to do, he was always ready to do so.

On Saturdays the pastor came to school only to examine our exercises, for he spent the rest of the day preparing his Sunday sermon. On one of these Saturdays, a neighbor's son was talking to one of his friends who was one of Grob's pupils. Grob saw this and told him to move away, which he immediately did, but smiled a little in doing so. But this infuriated Grob, and the spindly legged little teacher took hold of the left ear of my neighbor, who was much bigger and stronger than he, in order thus to lead him out of the school. But whenever Blum held onto a bench just a little, the strength of the skinny-legged teacher was insufficient to pull him further, until finally Blum's ear began to hurt a bit and he let the irate skinny-legged person have his way. And Grob had no authority to act in this way. He should have reported Blum to the pastor, who had the authority to mete out punishment. So it was a rude, high-handed action on Grob's part, and I confess that, as Mr. Skinny-Legs was pulling the much larger Blum past my seat, I had a good mind to intervene. But I remembered just in time that I had no right to do that either. However, I did think to myself that if I were in Blum's position I would not permit Grob to treat me in such a manner.

On another Saturday, a few weeks after this incident, the pastor gave us several bottles of ink and instructed us to have our compositions properly corrected by ten o'clock. Anyone who did not complete this assignment would have to stay after school. We all set to work at once. But I had to leave the class for a few minutes to obey a certain call of nature. When I returned, however, all of the pupils in our class were sitting there idly. I asked them, staring in astonishment, why they were not correcting their compositions. "Don't you know that if the pastor comes at ten o'clock and doesn't find the compositions finished you will be kept after school?" The pupils answered that while I had been gone Grob had all of the ink bottles taken away, saying that he needed them himself. I went up to him myself and said, "Teacher, we must have these ink bottles. You yourself heard that the pastor will return at ten o'clock, and if we do not have our work in order by then, we will be punished!" But teacher Grob told me that he needed them himself and intended to keep them; whereupon, however, I personally retrieved from his class, right before his eyes and very near him, as many bottles of ink as he had taken from us. And in so doing I observed that these bottles had been given to us by the pastor and therefore I would take them back; that he had no right to take any action in our class contrary to the pastor's instructions; and that if he did not agree we would immediately go to the pastor together, then we would see which one of us was right. The other pupils were extremely astounded at my audacity. No one would have dared to do as I had done. Grob did not attack me, but quietly let me proceed. But all could see his anger only too plainly. I had prepared myself; if he had attacked me I planned to really let him have it.

On Palm Sunday, 1838, after having completed religious instruction and passed the examination, I was confirmed in the church at Bilten, along with several of my classmates, and thereby embarked upon a new phase of my life. The school years were thus over, and with them a minor form of slavery, for wherever there is compulsory education, the pupil can never feel completely free. This thought was often of real annoyance to me; and yet I could easily comprehend the necessity of attending school; and in my final years I would gladly have attended school a few more years had there been higher level schools. Also, in my final years I believed I had learned a good deal more than in my early years, for I began to understand and appreciate the usefulness of a good education. I still remember very well envying the luck of youths of my age whose parents were able to send them to institutions of higher learning, who then happily returned to their homes during the holidays as so-called students, wearing bright colors around their caps or colorful sashes.

In accord with my father's wishes I was now to become a full-fledged farmer, for it never would have occurred to my father to ask me about my preferences, wishes, or talents. Of course this was something about which my father thought he "knew better" than I, and I had to put up with it, much as my thoughts might soar out into the big, wide world—and oh how often they did, especially when I was working on the mountain! The beautiful view of the broad valley in which our home stood; the mountains, valleys, rivers, and lakes of four bordering cantons,[5] and the magnificent view of Lake Zurich with its many splendid towns! Down there, over there, I always knew I too would have to go some day. But for the time being these were only idle, wishful dreams, and there seemed little likelihood that these dreams would ever be realized.

There were very few sensible ways for youths to entertain themselves back then. Roaming the alleys at night, playing all sorts of stupid pranks, such as distorting our voices and approaching each other in a stooped position, with jackets pulled over our heads, and then scuffling with one another, were the chief evening pastimes of these youths approaching manhood. Any sensible person will readily perceive that this accomplished nothing useful. For me this soon came to have little appeal. My second evening venture into the streets with the other boys disgusted me completely, and I could scarcely comprehend what enjoyment the other youths found in it. The first time I took part in this highly touted, time-honored activity, I sauntered about with a number of boys without any particular objective in mind beyond perhaps doing something silly. We were just going by a house whose owner, Johannes Zweifel, better known as the Standard Bearer,[6] was sitting with some of his family before some open windows. "Listen," someone said, "isn't that a strange fellow in there? He must be there because of Rosina [Zweifel's younger daughter]. Let's go into the vestibule to find out who it is!" So we all crowded into the dark vestibule. One of us opened the living room door, and we all peered into the dark room. Silence fell within. Finally the Standard Bearer's voice was heard to say, "Either come in or get out!" But no one paid attention to this directive. The Standard Bearer, in order to maintain control of his home, now came, in long hurried strides toward the door, from there to the vestibule. A noisy stampede ensued as each of us attempted to be the first to get through the door to freedom, almost allowing ourselves to be caught in the process. I clearly saw that the Standard Bearer was about to get hold of me, as being last I tried to squeeze my way out also. Knowing well that it was too dark for him to see me, and that he thought all of us were outside, I stood silently beside the living room door. I let the Standard Bearer lock the outside door and passing close by me, he closed the living room door as well. Outside they already had discovered that I was locked in, which they saw as a big joke. Since I knew that almost all house door locks were constructed alike, I quietly approached the door, felt for the lock, opened it without difficulty and was now back among my street fellows.

Since this event was declared the high point of the evening's amusement, in which I had found little that was amusing, I for one was satisfied and went home, not particularly convinced that this was such great fun; indeed I even believed I did not want to participate in any future evening entertainment of this kind. And yet our neighbor's son declared I would have to prowl the streets again in the evening, as the other boys all did, or I would be certainly labeled as an old-mannish fellow. So I let myself be persuaded to go along into the streets one more time. But I had not been there an hour before I was bored to death and explained to my neighbor that I was going home because I was not enjoying myself at all. He felt otherwise and let me leave, and thus fortunately my evening escapades with my fellows came to an end.

My brother's first wife had brought with her a stringed instrument called a zither. She played this instrument reasonably well, and soon my sister could play it too; but neither of them was able to tune the zither properly, so I did it for them after she showed me how. Naturally I soon began playing it myself, and in a short time I surpassed both my sister-in-law and my sister. And this zither relieved a good deal of my boredom.

On pleasant Sunday afternoons I would often take walks, now up into the mountains, or through the meadows, or along the Linth. I had a special desire to see something new. In particular, the ever-changing landscapes, which abound in our homeland mountains, held a special attraction for me.

I was in my eighteenth year when I learned that Colonel Schindler was offering to give voluntary military training to the young men of our town during evenings, if a sufficient number desired it. But I lived at the Ussbuehl and had to walk twenty to thirty minutes to get to the place where the exercises were held. For that reason I tried to persuade our neighbor's sons to come along, because I did not look forward to walking the long, isolated road along the Aschenwald[7] by myself at night, for back then the new road had not been completely finished. But my neighbor's sons were not interested in such things, so, since I wanted to take part in the training, I had to go alone. It was summertime, the evenings warm and pleasant. Each of us was outfitted with an old but shiny musket with bayonet affixed and an ammunition pouch. We made good progress since most of us participated enthusiastically. However, for me these nightly military exercises ended too soon.

5. The Black Man Affair and Its Resolution — Recruit Training in Oberurnen

At about this same time there was a rumor that three of my former schoolmates, returning home through the Aschenwald from the neighboring town on Sunday evening, suddenly were joined by a man dressed in black, without their having seen from where he had come. My friends were too afraid to ask their suddenly appearing companion where he came from or who he was. Thus they walked along together for an hour. Then he disappeared just as suddenly. This caused a good deal of discussion. Some believed it to be a ghost, others a prank, and soon every time one turned around someone claimed to have seen the man in black again.

One evening, during a pause in our military exercises, one of those who had claimed first to have seen the man in black approached me, asking me whether I was not afraid, walking through the Aschenwald all alone at night. I asked him about their man in black story, whether someone like that actually had joined them. He said it was all true, and said that they were all three so frightened that they did not dare to ask him any questions. Luchsinger—this was my friend's name—added that at no price would he walk through the sinister Aschenwald alone at night, and he speculated on just how terrified he would have been if he had encountered the man in black when he was alone! And he advised me to go home by the new road, even though it was not finished. I told him I simply believed someone was enjoying a prank at their expense and that, in any case, I had a bayonet affixed to my gun; if anyone got in my way I would challenge him, and if he did not respond, I would run him through. But he stated that I would undoubtedly be too frightened to make use of my bayonet. I believed only in flesh and blood spooks, and they had no business bothering me. If they tried it I was resolved to test my bayonet.

The night was beautiful, warm and moonlit. I came upon the place where the man in black had accompanied my friends, and since it was such a brightly lit night one could see everything, and I took a good look around but I could see nothing. I passed various spots at which superstitious, fearful people had claimed to have seen all kinds of ghosts, but I could find none. Finally I reached the center of the Aschenwald, where the oak trees grew, with tall oak trees to my left, a hedge with an adjoining meadow to my right, ahead of me (on both sides of the road) tall brush. And there, sure enough, I did see a black object off to the right by the brush; could this really be the feared man in black? I took the gun from my shoulder, holding it with fixed bayonet for any eventuality. Now I proceeded slowly but steadily. A few times I thought I saw the dark figure move, but the closer I came to it, the less it appeared to be a man, and finally I discovered to my satisfaction that it was only a large piece of wood, set upright by the side of the road, whose shadow fell, approximately to the height of a man, on the brush on the opposite side of the road. Thus my experience with the man in black came to a most peaceful conclusion.

Nevertheless this ghost story was not forgotten. A little evening adventure showed how the ghost story might have originated. My brother Peter, who was not the sort of man to be easily intimidated, wanted to go to Bilten one evening. It was almost dusk as he neared the above-mentioned oak woods. There he actually saw a man above the road near the edge of the woods slowly walking back and forth. Since my brother also had heard the story about the man in black he was determined to become better acquainted with the fellow. So he left the road and went toward the man. At first it did not seem as if the man intended to flee. But as he saw my brother coming ever nearer, he ran into a thicket of young trees. But my brother even followed him there, determined to get to know the ghost better. The man was by now convinced that my brother was not about to be frightened, and wishing above all not to be recognized, he attempted to elude my fast-approaching brother by means of some mighty leaps. But my brother was also a good jumper and quickly got hold of the would-be ghost. The man turned out to be a poor duffer who was in the process of stealing young ash trees from the community woods. He begged Brother not to tell anyone for he was a poor man, as my brother knew, and he promised not to play any more tricks in the future, a promise he probably kept.

But since many people were still afraid of the man in black, one evening Colonel Schindler, armed with a sword, Police Officer Elmer, with a rifle, joined also by Teacher Lienhard, determined to end this nuisance once and for all by arresting every suspicious-looking person who crossed their path. Teacher Lienhard was the son-in-law of Standard Bearer Zweifel and godfather to Jacob Lienhard, who was engaged to Standard Bearer Zweifel's younger daughter, Rosina. As Jacob came to the Standard Bearer's house one evening, he was told that the teacher, Colonel Schindler, and Elmer had gone to the Aschenwald to search for the man in black. My cousin, who greatly enjoyed any kind of fun, thought that if he could get hold of some kind of long, dark coat and an old, high hat, he would follow them and test their mettle. Help was at hand for he could easily find such things in the house; he soon found coat and hat and headed out after the three gentlemen. As soon as he caught sight of them, he carefully hid behind rocks, bushes and hedges until they came to a place where in earlier times a chapel known as St. Catherine's[8] had stood. Since this was pretty much the area where the man in black allegedly had been seen, the men looked around carefully. My cousin had just come to the meadow bordering the road. He had quickly put on the coat and hat, and strode in long measured steps across the so-called St. Catherine's meadow, in the direction of the new road. Suddenly he was discovered! "Look! There really is someone walking over there. Let's quickly catch up with him. This fraud shall finally be put to an end and the fellow punished for it!" In the meantime, while they were quickly approaching the man in black, he had reached the new road, and, disregarding his pursuers, continued along it deliberately toward the village. Colonel Schindler drew his sword and neared the man in black from one side, Police Officer Elmer, readying his weapon, ran toward the man from the other side. "Who goes there?" they called. No answer was given and the man in black did not walk one step faster. "For the second time, who goes there?" and again there was no response. Once more, "Who's there?" and now the men were ready to let the man in black get the payment he had earned. Then the fellow turned around, doubled with laughter, saying, "Why it's I, gentlemen. Don't you know me?" The gentlemen were not particularly inclined to laugh, for had my cousin waited to respond for just another moment he would have been shot and attacked with the sword, and the fun would have come to a very serious conclusion. Now my cousin explained how he had come to play the man in black, for they actually thought that he had been the ne'er-do-well person who had for some reason had been frightening upright citizens. His explanation proved, though, that he had simply from pure mischievousness had to have a little fun at their expense. Although the men were not at all pleased with the explanation, they had to content themselves, and they had in fact achieved their goal; the story of the man in black was thereby put to rest.

At the parish fair in Bilten in 1839 my brother Peter married for a second time. He married the youngest daughter [Dorothea] of old Peter Ackermann, who owned a couple of estates in Schaenis, Canton St. Gallen, which had once belonged to a convent that had since been dissolved. At the same time Ackermann's only son Jacob married my sister. It had been arranged by the relatives that Heinrich Blumer, also a son-in-law of old Ackermann, was to drive the coach for my brother and his bride. At the same time I was to serve as coachman for young Ackermann and my sister. Admittedly I had had little experience with horses till then, and therefore did not imagine myself to be a particularly good driver. The day promised to be a beautiful one, and at the appointed hour we left old Ackermann's home in Schaenis for where the marriage was to take place in the church at Bilten. Blumer drove in the lead, then came I with my prospective brother-in-law and my sister. Across the Linth, which flows very fast and is about two hundred feet wide, was a steep, narrow wooden bridge that served as the connection between Bilten and Schaenis. On the Bilten side the road made a sharp right-angle turn. Blumer already had his horse at a trot on the bridge; I personally did not intend to urge my horse to trot until I had passed this spot. My future brother-in-law however ordered me to speed my horse up as well. But as soon as I turned the sharp corner at this fast pace, the back end of our chaise turned over. Jacob and I naturally rolled with it a few feet away, but my sister fell under the vehicle, where she screamed loudly. But through our combined efforts we soon had the chaise lifted off my sister. My sister luckily was unhurt, but her silk wedding dress was torn. Now they set upon me; I naturally had to take the blame for this little accident although I had held to the center of the road. The horse was a docile animal. It had stopped immediately, and the front wheels had not tilted at all, and after some investigating it was found that the iron bolt connecting the rear part of the vehicle to the front had broken earlier, and no more than a half an inch of the bolt had been holding the front part of the chaise. So it was inevitable that, as a result of the quick, sharp turn I had been obliged to make at the curve, the bolt lifted, causing the back part to turn over. Even so, I continued to be blamed, for it is so convenient to blame someone else for one's own stupidity. Had Ackermann been a forthright person, had he wanted to give the matter fair consideration, he would easily have been persuaded that if the horse had taken the curve slowly the bolt would not have lifted from the front section, and as a result the rear would not have been overturned, and since he had ordered me to drive faster it was his fault and not mine. The discovery of the broken bolt was to some degree convenient because it actually removed all cause for putting the blame on me. Still Blumer felt, or rather still spoke that afternoon, as if it had been my fault, and my dear brother, Peter, was even willing to hire another coachman in my place. For my part I was in a less than pleasant mood. At first I considered tearing the flowers from my hat, throwing them into the Linth, and then running away; and it would have taken very little for me to follow through on that thought. Only the thought of the distress it would cause Mother kept me from it. As to Father I imagined that he would naturally believe I was entirely to blame for this incident. As it turned out another dress was quickly found for my sister, and since no one had been really injured we finally proceeded on to the church, after a forty-five minute delay, where the wedding took place. After the wedding we drove to Kaltbrunnen for a meal worthy of a wedding, and afterwards we drove back to Schaenis, and since the parish fair was underway and there was a dance at one of the inns we went there. But this gave me little pleasure. I soon left the inn. Due to the mortifying experience I had gone through that day I was in no mood to take part in the merriment. I went back to the house, then later that night back to our house.

In the spring of 1840 I, along with all young men of the two preceding age classes, had to take part as a recruit in military recruit exercises at the training grounds at Oberurnen. These exercises were required of boys of my age, along with the two other age groups, every spring in the last week of April. Upon reaching twenty-one, one would have completed the so-called recruitment stage and then have been assigned to companies, regiments, etc. I was assigned to the infantry, as were all who were required to train at Oberurnen. And since, after our initial assignment only a few applied for the commissioned or noncommissioned officer ranks, the law stipulated that the best qualified among the recruits were selected, and these were later trained for these positions at certain locations. Oberurnen was a good one-and-a-half-hour distance from my father's house. But at this time of the year the weather is usually pleasant — and it was thus during the three years I had to serve.

Instead of eating the noon meal at home as the boys could do who lived near the training ground, those of us from Bilten had to take our meals in one of the inns in Oberurnen. Since one of the recruits was the son of an innkeeper near the training field, we started taking the noon meal at his place. Because we were mostly served smoked meat, which was also used as a soup, with a lot of beans and barley, we soon left and transferred to the Double Golden Eagle.[9] Here we were at first most generously treated, because though none spent much money, there was something to be earned from fourteen or fifteen young people.

During our two-hour free period at midday we had enough time for all sorts of harmless pranks. But there was little opportunity for such. One noon—we had just eaten—the innkeeper's sister called our attention to two girls digging in the vicinity. "Those are real amusing girls," she said, which her brother confirmed. We should just go there, and that would convince us. We went and said that we wanted to dig for them; but the farce did not last long; we had hardly begun to speak to them when the two started to really pelt us with large clumps of earth. "You lazy good-for-nothings! You loafers! You think that just because you are wearing those monkey suits you have the right to insult decent people and disturb them in their work? You wait, we'll report you, so that you will leave people like us alone in the future!" Naturally we were very much disappointed. Instead of fun and games, we had received insults and scolding and our bodies had been pelted with large clumps of earth. Over in the inn everyone had seen it, and enjoyed it greatly. The girls had guessed correctly when they said, "You fools, those over there have led you on, right; but you'll be sorry, just like those over there." With that they shouldered their spades and left us behind. Everyone was busy cleaning the dirt with which we had been pelted from our clothes, which required some effort. Later we had opportunity to pay back the young innkeeper's sister with interest for her prank. During our second spring we Bilteners came to the conclusion that we were not being treated as well as we deserved by the keepers of the Double Golden Eagle. I, therefore, persuaded one of our fellow recruits, named Peter Elmer, to go with me to the Grape Inn.[10] There—so we had heard—were three lively young girls, the oldest of whom played the zither quite well. Arriving at the Grape Inn we ordered wine. And since the daughters happened to be there we were soon dancing with the two younger sisters while the eldest played the zither. A man who happened to be in the inn seemed to enjoy it and encouraged us to enjoy ourselves, saying, "That's right, boys. I like to see that. That's how I carried on when I was younger." We told the innkeeper that if they provided for us cheaply we could possibly bring along all the Bilteners. They promised to provide for us as cheaply as possible. From this time on the Grape Inn was for us Bilteners our inn during our training period. And since we let no noontime pass without dancing, several of our comrades from Mollis often came along to take part also. They really were very generous to us, and no one complained about being charged too much. Since dancing—except for church fairs, carnivals, and weddings—was forbidden in those days, we posted guards for safety so that should the policeman come we could stop in time, only to continue as soon as he was out of sight. Although we did not quite trust the boys from Niederurnen, they came in also, but not to drink or dance. Several times a little military strategy was required in order to get rid of them. Running past the inn was a nice, broad footpath which one used instead of the road because it was shorter. Not far behind the inn it took a rather sharp turn. It was agreed that when the Niederurners returned to spy, as we suspected, several of us would take our guns and rush outside the house crying, "Has the major already gone by? It's time for us to go!" (The major was our commander, or instructor.) Then we would run around the house quickly and come back into the house through a back door. With this maneuver we had dispatched them several times, and afterward they stayed away.

The training grounds were a source of pleasure for me. (Though in the beginning our backs were sore, that soon passed.) We were divided into detachments of sixteen to twenty boys to an instructor. Later when we had gotten a little further along with our exercises we often had to drill, march, load and shoot (of course without powder). For me these military exercises were a great pleasure, and I believed that there was hardly anyone present who had found more pleasure in our exercises than I. I learned a great deal, and I can say boldly, without bragging, that I was in the last year one of the most advanced. More than once I had commanded and executed drills that one of our young instructors had tried in vain to execute. Of course such could take place only when the major was not present; otherwise our young instructor would have been shown up.

These were the happiest days I spent in my old homeland, which unfortunately went by too fast. The major made it clear to me that I would be sent to the (cadets) officers' school at Thun, which, even if the cost were defrayed by the government, would still have meant significant extra expenses for me which, I, with my small means, would have found difficult to meet. The rather substantial expenses borne by officers in Switzerland are just the reason why so few applied for officer rank. For it was not only the greater expense of a better uniform and sword, but the little extra treats that soldiers expect of the officers which cost the officers quite a few extra francs.

6. Great Windstorm in July 1841 — Planting Trees

In the summer of 1841, on a beautiful Sunday morning, early at four o'clock, I got out of bed and set out at a brisk pace for Glarus, where I wanted to buy a book with the title of *The Well-Informed Farmer, Simon Struef,* edited by Johann Evangelist Fuerst,[11] which told all about horticulture, forestry, hop growing, farming, etc. The day remains clearly in my memory. Early in the morning the foehn,[12] or south wind, was blowing, first moderately, but slowly increasing in intensity. By the time I reached the *Alleweide*[13] between Netstal and Naefels, it was already blowing heavily and became stronger and stronger the closer I got to Glarus. I had hardly reached Glarus when I saw how the wind blew a number of flowerpots from a high window sill into the street, to the great distress of a housewife. I stayed in Glarus no longer than was necessary to buy my book. Then I started out on my way back, for I wanted to be home by ten o'clock. The wind had meanwhile turned into an extremely fierce storm. Going back through Netstal I found that window shutters, chimneys, and signs had already blown down, and a number of trees were uprooted or broken off. At Naefels I found many large pear and apple trees uprooted; but at Oberurnen and Niederurnen the damage was considerably greater. There I met a man who told me that the storm had caused even more damage in Bilten. The first house I saw on entering Bilten had its roof completely blown off, with its arbors torn off the house and blown away. On a nearby plot were lying some forty mostly large and old fruit trees, some broken off, but most of them uprooted. By one house lay the strongest and largest pear tree, as well as apple trees, some of them leaning against the house, or lying quite close to it, almost as if one wanted to barricade the house. Torn-off roofs, arbors, chimneys and shutters were to be seen everywhere, and the debris was strewn all around, together with uprooted and broken off trees. Also a few barns had been completely blown over. People stood alone or in groups in open meadows, and evidently it must have been quite difficult to escape the debris which was flying in all directions. In Bilten the storm seemed to have reached the peak of its fierceness because the indications of its destruction beyond there became less and less. When I arrived home at ten o'clock, in spite of its being Sunday, I found everyone at work repairing house and stable roofs, for a heavy rain was threatening. On one of our pieces of land, where we had hay and oats, we found little left, because most of it had been blown away. The leaves on the pear trees were black, as if they had been half burned, for the wind had been not only extremely fierce, but it was also hot — truly a sirocco. Even the oldest residents could scarcely remember one single storm similar to that just described, and that storm, my father said, took place when a sister and the mother of my mother lay dying inside the house, around the time I was seeing the light of the world for the first time. That storm was said even to have blown away the roof from our house.

I was now the fortunate owner of a good and useful book, and I made use of every opportunity to read and learn from it, for it dealt with almost every branch of agriculture. It told a great deal about growing fruit trees. I learned from it also several grafting methods. In the fall I scraped the pitch off of our ancient fruit trees. All the moss and the superfluous old bark had to come off and the excess, partly dry old branches were also sawed off. When we planted young trees I dug a trench four feet in diameter and two feet deep, placing the upper better soil on one side and the lower poorer soil on the other side of the trench.

If the soil was poor I tried to replace it partially with better soil, with which I made a hill in the center of the trench and set the tree to be planted on it. I spread out the roots as far as possible in the shape of a wheel, placed the best and finest soil between them, planted them only as deep as they had previously grown, added a straight stake, and put the poorer soil into the outer sides of the trench so that the outer poorer soil extended over the better soil by a few inches. When the roots were partially covered with soil I poured water over them with a sprinkling can until the finer soil had sunk in, and was close to the roots. If any roots became visible after the sprinkling, I covered them with more good, fine soil, then watered again and finally covered them with fine soil. Then the tree was tied to the stake. The ground was kept loose and free of weeds during the summer and I was thereby assured that healthy young trees planted thus would grow vigorously.

It was almost a miracle that my father let me have my own way in planting the trees, since he usually thought little of subjects which could be read in books. Books dealing with farming were in those days quite rare and since those books presented many ideas which departed from the long-established theories they were mostly rejected as not suitable.

My father had land which varied considerably in quality. The best was used for fruit trees. My oldest brother wanted to plant trees there, brother Caspar in a different meadow plot, and I in a meadow that had already proven that fruit trees would not thrive at all, or only poorly, because the land was wet and cold and poor. I was told that trees would not grow there, but I was confident that trees planted as my friend Simon Struef had instructed would be certain to grow. Brother Caspar, not quite sure that my method of planting would be right, followed my example only part way. But brother Peter planted as he always had by digging a few spadefuls of soil, putting in the roots of the tree, throwing the soil on top of them, and then stamping it on top of the roots. Our parents were, as were we all, curious to see the results.

Hardly a day passed when I did not examine my trees, and I soon had the great pleasure of seeing that the trees planted by me were not only alive, but before long began to grow vigorously, and most of them had by fall put out branches two to two-and-a-half feet long, while those planted by Caspar had put out branches of one to one-and-a-half feet long. On the contrary, those planted by Peter put out growth of only a few inches. Naturally it was not to be expected that trees planted in such unsuitable soil would do as well as those planted in suitable soil. It was to be expected that the vigorous growth would stop as soon as the roots of the trees planted by me reached the poor soil outside the trench, which however began to happen only a few years later. Had I planted them near the house, using the same procedure, those trees would have continued growing, and would have reached in about four years the size that the trees planted by Peter would have reached in six to eight years.

I would have liked to try different things which I read in *Simon Struef*, but my father would absolutely not hear of it. He kept saying that if one had a lot of money one could perform all sorts of experiments, and for those people book learning might perhaps be good, but would be of little value for our kind of folk. I took the *Simon Struef* book along with me a few years later to America, and still later to California, where it served me as a very useful gardening guide for horticulture, etc.

7. Carpentry Work at Home—A Trip down the Mountain with a Horn Sled, Which Might Have Ended Disastrously

In the last five or six years before leaving for America I fashioned all kinds of wooden articles. I had heard about a lathe without a wheel. I tried to figure out how I could possibly make one like it, using every rainy day to make or to repair something. I finally had an idea, and set out diligently to make a lathe without a wheel. I positioned a young ash tree above me as a kind of spring; to the end of this spring I tied a strong rope, which I then also attached to a treadle below. At chest height I positioned the object which I wanted to turn. I made latches and wedges to be used in turning the lathe to hold shorter or longer objects. A cord was tied around the piece of wood that was to be turned, and now it went up and down. On a board beside the piece I planned to turn I placed the instrument I needed to use, and with that my lathe was ready. Although this lathe was not exactly a work of art it was nevertheless serviceable. I could fashion with it quite well all sorts of things, such as crowbars, chisels, bowls, etc., especially when later I bought from my uncle a few instruments needed for turning.

The number of mice in our milk cellar had increased considerably, with the result that Mother was often obliged to feed the milk as well as the cream to the pigs. I set about making a mousetrap with which one could catch them alive. I soon had the satisfaction of having turned out a fine trap, and a few hours later had probably captured the entire mouse population. There were nine of them. Neither milk nor cream was afterward contaminated by the mice, and since the catch was so successful I had to make a few more for other people, for which I received four batzen apiece. Another boy, who used my trap as a model, soon provided competition.

The stairs from our living room to our cellar had one day been declared unsafe. I thought that making such stairs would not be difficult, and I wanted to make them when I had the time. I was given time to do it, and I believe that I made a quite adequate set of stairs. Father helped me carry them into the cellar, but alas, they stood a bit lopsided, which made me so angry that I immediately wanted to chop them to pieces with an axe, but my father ordered me not to do it, because the set of stairs was quite good and the small amount of crookedness was not important. Some eight or ten years later, when I came back one time from America, the stairs were still giving good service.

I may have been fourteen to sixteen years old when I got possession of a piece of bent wood which I felt could be used to make runners for a sled, a so-called *Geisse* [hornsled].[14] Utilizing every rainy day, I finally had the pleasure of seeing in front of me a quite decent sled, of which I was quite proud. I wanted to show it to my parents, when Uncle Jacob happened to arrive. "Did you make this sled?" he asked; to which I naturally responded affirmatively. Uncle made an offer for it which seemed to me quite low; and furthermore I would have preferred to use it for sledding myself. But my parents told me to let him have it for that price. I would be allowed to keep the money for myself, and after all I could make another one later.

When our so-called horn sled needed repair, I undertook it. The runners were often worn down, and then I had to make new ones because we used this kind of sled to bring home most of our firewood. The horn sleds were carried on our shoulders to the higher up woodlands, where one then loaded them with rather heavy loads, which with good snow and sled paths were easily brought down when the sled paths were in good condition. The handles, called horns, were about twenty-four to thirty inches in length, protruded above the sled, were attached in the front, bent backward somewhat, and gripped with both hands; one would position oneself between these horns, one's back to the sled, and pull it along behind. When the track is good and descends steeply, one takes the horns on both sides under one's armpits, holds the sled further down with both hands, lets the feet out in front as a sort of rudder. This act requires certain knowledge, skill and strength on a steep and curved track with a heavy load when one wants to stay on track and not capsize, because it often descends at considerable speed. Only seldom does one take these horn sleds up into the mountains, because in the winter when the ground is frozen, the logs, or parts of them, would be allowed to slide downhill on the already mentioned track, and they would shoot into the valley with almost unbelievable speed. If these thick logs had been cut into shorter lengths, they would often shoot with such terrific force into the valley that they would soar sixty feet or higher into the air, and when they then would hit a standing tree it would be broken like a blade of grass.

The mountain paths were used primarily to drag down tree branches, or also to walk or climb up and down on in winter. If one wanted to drive cattle over these paths in winter it often was necessary to hack steps into the ice with a pick in steep and slippery places, and then lead each animal over these places with a rope. If one had short logs, such as tree stumps, etc., one would then take the horn sleds, even when going higher up the mountain. Safety ropes would then be used to fasten chains underneath the front of each runner, so that, where it was too steep, they scraped the frozen snow and ice. In order to slow down the speed of the run, one would also fasten several fir branches behind the sled.

One day our neighbor's son, Emanuel Blum, about one-and-a-half years older than I, and I wanted to go with our sleds on our shoulders to get logs way up above the woodlots belonging to Father, into the mountain woods belonging to the community. I had carefully repaired our horn sled the day before. During the climb it became obvious that the path was very icy and slippery, and we realized right away that we would have to be careful on our way back; but there were two of us and we could help each other get over the difficult places.

From the community woods to my father's woodlot special care was not required since we mostly slid through untracked snow. But from here on the track was heavily used and for the most part very steep, and here I fastened a pile of fir branches behind my sled, even laying pieces of wood on them to make them heavier. Emanuel did likewise. We laid the chains underneath the sled runners at the most difficult places. I was in the lead and now we moved confidently downhill. In this way we proceeded quite fast and well without finding it necessary to ask each other for help. After we passed my father's woodlot, the path led again for a short stretch through community woods. Then one came again to a woodlot belonging to my father called the Blaenkli Woods. However, here came the most difficult stretch, from the so-called Rest Stone toward the Blaenkli Head, a rock of perhaps thirty or more feet high which was very precipitous on top, but vertical at its lower end. A long tree trunk had been attached for safety along the Blaenkli Head to minimize the danger of being driven over the Head. However the snow had completely filled the path and, as a result of being heavily used, the path was, especially on the steepest part between the Rest Stone and the Head, extremely slippery. In addition, on arriving on the Head from above one had to turn suddenly to the right, which ordinarily was easily accomplished when the tree trunk lay above the snow, and the track was not so slippery and icy. I inspected the spot, then looked back at my comrade, because I was inclined at first to wait for him, so that we could help each other over it. But since he was only following slowly I began to think that I could probably also pass over this by myself, and did so, thinking "Nothing ventured, nothing gained." I had placed the chains under the runners and taken every precaution. I did everything to ensure that the sled would not speed up too fast and, just as I was about to turn to the right, one foot slipped, and I felt my load slipping forward. I quickly swung myself around the right horn and tried to hold on after getting on my feet, but it was too late, for already the front end was over the rock. Immediately the sled, together with its logs and branches, plunged down the rock. By another route I was soon down, and found the sled broken, as I had expected, but I could still drag it home, naturally without wood. I was just about to leave the place when Emanuel appeared above. He came down without difficulty, but he believed that I must have been injured because he imagined that I must have fallen down together with my sled, and he was about to give forth with a small outcry. But when he saw me moving he hardly understood how I could have gotten down without bodily damage.

It was after two o'clock when I finally reached home. Father as well as Mother had already been watching out for me for two hours and thought that I might have had an accident. When they saw the broken sled, and I had told them the story, they were pleased that I had escaped with my skin intact.

8. The Course of Mother's Illness Which Ended in Her Death—Dividing the Inheritance among the Children—Our Father and Our Grandfather

In December 1841, we were just eating supper when a farmhand of my sister's father-in-law came from Schaenis. He started to tell us that my sister was not quite well. My mother said to him, "She's probably quite ill. Speak up freely and don't be afraid." The man then said that she really was quite ill and wished very much that Mother would come to her at Schaenis. Mother told him to let my sister know that she would be sure to come the following morning. Since Mother was not too strong, I was afraid that she herself could become sick because she surely would have to go through sleepless nights. So I tried to persuade her to come back home after a few days in order to recover. But Mother would not hear of it, and instead she said, "Barbara is my only daughter, and I won't leave her until she's better again." In my heart I already believed that she herself would become seriously ill, and perhaps even die.

Sister's illness turned out to be a stubborn case of nervous fever. Mother stayed more than two weeks, and said that in spite of her worries and nighttime care, she did not feel too bad. We visited her there several times, and I was surprised and at the same time quite pleased that my mother seemed so well. She finally came walking toward our house one evening as we were just eating. "Mother is coming!" we cried, and Father, Brother, and I ran like children out of the house toward her. She looked so healthy and well that we were quite surprised. She also explained that she felt absolutely no worse than when she had gone over there and that Barbara was now decidedly better and would soon be completely herself again.

On her way back she visited Jacob Blumer, who had been bedridden for a long time and was very emaciated and miserable. Jacob Blumer's oldest daughter, Elsbeth, would become my wife about nine-and-a-half years later [July 3, 1851]. Jacob lived until June of the following year, after he was supposed to have been so emaciated that his skin had become almost transparent.

After our mother's return, she was quite well for about a week until she started to complain about pain in her back, ligaments and head. Since we feared that she might herself end up with nervous fever, we soon sent for Dr. Zweifel. When he came our worst fears were confirmed, for she had a very serious case of it. We had a woman come in from the neighborhood (Reichenburg) who was to cook and care for Mother. But it soon became clear that the woman knew little about cooking — or much of anything else. When, early in her illness, Mother wanted bread soup or cooked sour apples, etc., everything was prepared so miserably that she could not enjoy it. Thereupon Mother said to me, "I think that if I tell you how bread soup or sour apples are supposed to be cooked you will be able to prepare them the way I would like to have them." I had her carefully explain how she wanted it done, and I am so happy that everything I cooked for her was prepared quite correctly. Unfortunately she soon lost all appetite, so there was little to cook for her except perhaps some tea. Her illness grew worse day by day. Neighbor women came to help. They wanted to make her bed and place her in another bed, but I saw how it caused her pain and made her weaker. Besides, she never seemed comfortable in the freshly made beds. I tried to make the bed myself, but with no better success.

I had become twenty years old during her illness and was a strong lad. Since having two women transfer her from one bed to another always caused my mother great pain, I took her in my arms as gently as possible and carried her from bed to bed each day myself, and I had the satisfaction of seeing that it saved her from a good deal of the pain she had previously endured. Her illness became ever worse. The doctor would not give his opinion, but he forbade us to give her fresh water, even though she asked for it repeatedly. The back pains and headaches became so bad that she could hardly remain lying down, and she found no rest or sleep, day or night. She was far too weak to sit up by herself or turn over in bed. For my part, I was far too concerned about her to entrust her to the women's care alone. I was determined to do everything within my power. I took to standing for hours beside her bed, now on one side and then on the other, with one hand holding her back and the other on her forehead, which seemed to give her some relief. I also stayed with her at night as well. I did not feel sleepy at all, for the thought that Mother might die allowed me to forget and overcome everything else; and I continued to do this for several days and nights. But then I also got a violent headache and was overtaken by exhaustion. Cool compresses were placed on my head as well, and I was urged to lie down. I began thinking I was getting the same illness as Mother, but I was not concerned about myself. My strong constitution and a little sleep soon brought me back to my feet so that I was again able to take on the primary care of good, dear Mother. But her illness would not let up. Mother only became more miserable every day. She was delirious more often; no let up in her fever was noticeable, and finally, after repeated questioning, the doctor explained that there was no longer any hope for her.

When occasionally Mother did regain consciousness, she implored us to bring her water from a sulfurous spring near one of our lower meadows, and we would gladly have carried out her wish if the doctor had allowed it. But why would he not permit it, since he had told us she was dying? Why did we not go and fetch her the water she so much wanted, despite the doctor's orders, and give her as much as she wanted of it since it could not have done any more harm? Yes, thus I have often since reproached myself. Good old Father particularly reproached himself with the knowledge that he did not grant her dying wishes, for he thought that by doing so we might even have been able to save her.

Sunday morning, January 30, 1842, the doctor came to visit Mother for the last time. As he stepped into the bedroom her words were, "What a coat!" I explained to her that it was the doctor coming to see her, but she seemed to feel that there was no point in his coming any longer, for he had barely turned toward the door when she said to me, "All the birds have flown," as if she were trying to say, "It's all for nothing!" On the same day sister Barbara was brought on a sled. She was still weak, and was especially devastated when she was brought to Mother's sickbed, and sobbingly called out to Mother several times. But at first she did not seem to recognize her. Finally she seemed to recognize Barbara, for she responded to her questions with a few kind words. This lucid moment was of short duration, however, and she fell back into a kind of slumber. Several more of our relatives were present. In the afternoon, at about four o'clock, they had a little coffee and something to eat. I was urged to go and eat to refresh myself a little because there were enough of them to stay with Mother until I returned, but I could not bring myself to do so. When I was alone in the room with Mother I asked, "Dear Mother, do you know me?" She opened her eyes, looked at me kindly and replied, "Yes, of course, you're my dear Heinrich!" I could hardly speak, but I wanted to ask her some more questions; however, those had been her last dear words, and she fell into a slumber again, and her pulse was very erratic. In an effort to make her more comfortable, I supported her back with my right hand and laid the left one on her forehead, and foolishly still had the vain hope that perhaps she would awaken from this slumber feeling better.

Father, my siblings, Brother's wife, and a few relatives had gathered around Mother's bed. I had momentarily taken my eyes off my mother, still supporting her, and glanced at the others, when Peter's exclamation, "Mother is going!" drew my eyes back to her; but after two or three long gasps her dear soul had departed its earthly shell!

34

I could scarcely control my feelings, for it seemed to me that everything in this world that mattered to me had disintegrated, and that from now on I could not go on living, and I believed that if at a word I had been able to accompany her into eternity, I would have done it. After my first agitation had subsided a bit, and I had regained my composure somewhat, my resolution was made. "I will travel to America," I said to myself; yes, I said it openly! My father was virtually inconsolable over the death of my mother, and declared, "If you go to America now you will also be as good as dead as far as I am concerned."

We kept Mother for two more days. Then we laid her to rest. It was a difficult proceeding, especially for Father and me, to attend the funeral, this final honor we bestowed upon our dear departed one, but one that had to be endured. My father was nearly uncontrollable. Regardless of how greatly I also suffered from our loss, I often had to comfort him. But it all helped very little, for soon he was unable to eat or sleep properly, and he even began to cough and become ill. On his behalf I went to Dr. Bamert, an intelligent old gentleman, to whom I described Father's illness as accurately as possible. He agreed with me completely and said that all of the symptoms I had described in my father indicated the onset of consumption, or its imminent development, unless immediate care and countermeasures were taken. Dr. Bamert gave me various roots and herbs, and told me how to gather several others. From these I was to prepare a tea, which Father was to drink two to three times a day, and this remedy was effective, so that in a short time Father was his old self again.

Since the inheritance laws in our canton at the time were such that the surviving spouse could coinherit only if he or she merged his or her estate with that of the deceased, and thus, being entitled to no more than a child's share, Father naturally preferred to keep his estate and left Mother's estate to us children. But because Mother's estate consisted of various parcels of land, my father decided to leave all of his land to us. A day was set on which the siblings gathered in our home to divide Mother's household possessions and the land holdings, as equally as possible, into four parts so that we could appraise each individual piece of land. Then we were to draw lots for the four shares. Whoever drew the home place was bound to provide Father with light, heat and free rent for the rest of his life, and to allow my younger brother, Caspar, and me free lodging as long as we remained unmarried. Although we appraised the home place somewhat lower because the lodging stipulation had to be considered, we still felt that whoever drew it would be the luckiest. But there was little we could do to make the division fairer, so we let the matter be decided by lot, and that turned out to my brother Peter's advantage. I received as my share the so-called upper place and a cultivated plot called the Zoggenbett. If the home place had fallen to me my future could have turned out differently. I offered to trade to Peter my share for his, according to the appraised value, plus two hundred gulden extra, but he wanted three hundred, which was higher than I wanted to go. A few years later he let brother Caspar have it for the price I had offered him.

It was totally clear that my staying at home any longer was hardly possible; yet Father would refuse to hear of it whenever I said anything about traveling to America. For even though I was his least favorite child, of which I became more convinced each day, he was fond of me in his own way, and I believe that he honestly felt he was acting in my best interests. But our concepts of life and living were very different, and because he was by far the elder he believed that his views of my future were the only right ones, and my plans were routinely discarded as worthless.

My father was above all an honest man, and he tried as much as possible to lead a Christian life, but unfortunately he had lost his mother when he was only ten or eleven. He was the oldest of his siblings, and as such he was expected by his somewhat unfeeling, hard-hearted father to take on all responsibilities, through thick and thin. He scarcely knew a milder maternal care and had experienced none of it himself.

Although his father tried to live strictly according to what was right and would have meted out the harshest punishment to dishonest persons if the authority to punish had rested with him, he was nonetheless himself a slave to several grave defects. The worst of his faults was that he loved to play cards, not for the sake of winning, but out of passion for the game. He was not a good player, but even when he lost, which unfortunately he did too often, he would leave his young children at home all night unattended; he was even said to have often played in the daytime. Knowing of his passion, there were always enough heartless individuals willing to take advantage of it, to the great detriment of Grandfather's family, for Grandfather was almost always the one who lost.

Another of his very great faults was that he was very stingy regarding living expenses. As a rule his family had to be satisfied with nothing but the poorest food. He himself lived as badly as his children. They seldom had meat to eat. The only thing he ever provided in ample quantity was bread. Likewise their clothes were no better than their food. But they were always allowed to wear good shoes. Whatever he lost playing cards, he tried to squeeze out of himself and his children. Bad food, bad clothing and a lot of hard work, that was the consequence of his vice. In addition to all that, he was also a very headstrong man. None of his children would ever have dared to ask him to give up gambling. Such a request would have been considered a serious offense, and might even have lead to punishment.

That was probably the reason why, having experienced such an unhappy childhood, our father did not truly understand what was required to foster a proper family life. He was hard without really wanting to be. He was prejudiced without really intending to be. But he was also somewhat pigheaded, vigorously defending his incorrect notions even after having been convinced of his errors. Naturally he usually regretted his mistakes later.

Our mother was much more clear-headed, possessed a much greater power of understanding, and her influence and perspective were a blessing for us all. Unfortunately Father often did not want to give in to her well-considered views because he believed that would cause him to lose his supposed masculine dignity. Therefore it sometimes happened that his projects failed to come out right, but when Mother pointed out his errors he preferred not to assume the blame. On such occasions there was considerable discord between the parents. Father could even be unfair and harsh toward Mother. If we children would take Mother's part, which was usually the case, because we generally believed her to be in the right, Father became even more bitter and would seldom listen to reason until his anger had abated.

9. An Appropriate Warning to Father—How Brother Peter Treated Me Deceitfully and Treacherously— How Apprentices Are Treated

One time my father, brother Caspar and I were haying. I was eighteen or nineteen years old. There was another exchange of words between our parents. Father's expressions were not only strong, but insulting toward Mother, and Mother, whose health had been more or less sickly since my birth, took this hurtful treatment very hard. What good was it to her when afterward he regretted his thoughtless behavior? Every time this happened Mother's health suffered, but what had happened could not be undone. I felt a great deal of pity for Mother and believed all the fault to be on Father's side. Therefore I planned to talk seriously with Father about the matter, which I did on another occasion when we were haying. I asked Father whether he intended to set a good example of how good parents got along with each other with his unfair and undeserved quarreling with Mother. He prayed much and every day tried to be a good Christian. But I could detect little Christian behavior in his squabbling with Mother. Or would he perhaps prefer that Mother should die? If that were so, I believed that he could easily achieve his goal, for a doctor had previously told him that if he wanted to see his wife dead soon he only needed to agitate her, and he would be half way to his goal. I was astonished that Father did not tell me to hold my tongue, which I expected. Instead he quietly accepted my rather blunt advice, although he seemed upset. To this day I am glad to be able to say that from then on my father never was either hard or insulting toward Mother; yes, he even told me after Mother's death that he had taken my warning very much to heart, and had determined to treat Mother better in the future, and he had held to it faithfully.

My wish to go to America became ever stronger. However, Father seemed to disapprove, and I was afraid that if I left while he was still feeling the death of my mother so deeply he could become ill. So I chose to learn a trade first. I decided to take my inherited upland holding to the auction to sell it to the highest bidder. The auction was to be held in late July or early August at a neighbor's inn—The Inn of the Horse.[15] Although just in my twenty-first year, I was of age, according to the laws of the time, and could dispose of my property as I pleased. But brother Caspar was only in his seventeenth year and was under our father's guardianship. I had no intention of trying to persuade Caspar to buy my upland holding because I knew that a transaction made with him would not be valid without Father's approval, and I was convinced that Father would not approve, because he correctly believed that once Caspar came of age, if he then wanted to buy or trade land, he could do as he wished. So I was not a little astonished when Father reproached me one day and admonished me for wanting to sell Caspar the upland holding without his knowledge and approval. I asked Father how he had come to this conclusion, and whether Caspar or anyone else had told him that I had such intentions. I said that the person who told him such things was a base liar.

On the morning of the day when my land was to be sold, at about three o'clock, I noticed Peter with Caspar, and it did not take me long to figure out that he wanted to sell Caspar the property he had bought from a family called Schneider so that he could buy my land, which would have been much more convenient for him since my land adjoined the home place, which he had acquired by lot. I brought it to Father's attention, because I also knew that it was Peter who had warned Father about a transaction between me and Caspar, of which there had never been any discussion. Now, since a trade between Peter and Caspar would have advantages for the former, it seemed hardly worth the effort to ask Father whether he would agree to such a trade or not. I was only too well aware of good Peter's sly ways. He probably believed that if he made a deal with Caspar so shortly before the auction I would then try to persuade Father to sanction it when he bid on my land. Whatever Peter might have thought, his underhanded behavior, which I had earlier come to know so well, was quite obvious and completely disgusted me. Not only did I advise Father not to approve the deal with Caspar, but I also pointed out Peter's intentions. But Father did not want to believe it. Nonetheless he did warn Peter, as well as Caspar, and said that he definitely would not approve any deal between them. But for my part I feared that as soon as my brother bid on my parcel, other potential bidders would hold back, and my fears proved to be well founded. In spite of

Father's warning that he would not approve the deal between Peter and Caspar, Peter bid on my land, whereupon a neighbor who had also bid on it stopped bidding. However he told me that he would have given two hundred gulden more for it had my brother Peter not been the other buyer. The auction was over and good brother Peter had no valid excuse; he probably did not even consider an explanation worth the effort. He said that Father either had to approve the deal between him and Caspar or he would not be able to pay for my land on which he had made the successful bid because that would cause him to go too deeply into debt, as though he had not known that beforehand. Although I was the one who would yet again be harmed by brother Peter's action, I advised Father that, since we had gotten into this predicament through Peter, he should himself take my plot for the price which Peter had bid, for, since the land was worth more, Father could only come out ahead. Father did as I had advised him. He took the land for the price that Peter bid for it, and a few years later he sold it to another neighbor, with some profit.

When Mother had still been alive, Peter had shown clearly on several occasions how brotherly and unselfish he was toward me, but Mother was not blind. She saw and recognized his selfishness and warned me more than once, saying, "Heinrich, when we will someday be gone, if I should die you all must be on your guard against him. Otherwise Peter will take advantage of you whenever he can." She gave me this advice because she was convinced of what she was saying. But I had sufficient reason to know brother Peter. I will give some small examples here.

When I was a boy of twelve I bought a beautiful candle at a market. Brother Peter had bought a candle at the same price just a year before. But his was not as beautiful as mine. In addition it was by now considerably used. Since he liked my new candle better than his old one, he proposed that I should give him my candle for his. But I told him that mine was beautiful and new compared to his, which was already old and not nearly so nice anymore. But brother Peter did not let up and asked repeatedly, until I finally thought that he really needed a nice new candle more than I did, and he was a grown man. I, on the other hand, was just a boy. So, in order to please my brother, I gave him my beautiful new candle for his old, battered one.

Another time I had bought an excellent pocket knife rather cheaply. When my brother found out he wanted to buy it from me at the same price I had paid for it. I did not want to agree at first, but he asked me repeatedly, until I finally could no longer resist his begging, comforting myself with the thought that after all he was my brother and that I could always buy a new one. Then there was the time Peter bought a dozen handkerchiefs from a peddler at a supposedly low price. I asked whether he would give me one of them at the same price, but brother Peter would not hear of it unless he could make a profit. My reminding him that I had not demanded a profit for the candle or the knife left him untouched, until our parents finally reproached him for his greedy behavior. He then threw one to me with a gesture that clearly showed how angry he was.

Peter was a good beekeeper and had success with them. I bought a swarm from him at the usual price. I already had three or four swarms which Peter was supposed to take care of for me, since he was able to take time for this purpose, and I was afraid of bee stings. It turned out that I received a so-called virgin swarm, that is a swarm which had formed the same summer by splitting from another. Brother Peter wanted to buy this swarm from me, but I told him I wanted to keep it for myself because, having so many swarms he did not need this one. That made him angry, and instead of placing my bees on supports or into the bee house near the house as he did with his, he carried my bees to an arbor at the upper house and left them to take care of themselves, and he could not hide his malicious pleasure when he was able to tell me one day that the mice had robbed my bees. Our parents reproached him for it, but that scarcely bothered Peter. I could give several more similar examples, but I think these suffice to show the selfishness of brother Peter.

As I have already mentioned, I was determined to learn a trade. This is easily said, but anyone who had to serve as an apprentice in Europe has certainly received a good foretaste of slavery. At least that is how it seemed to me. I was offered an opportunity to learn a trade with a cabinetmaker in Waedenswil, Canton Zurich. I was to have a three-week trial period. If both parties were satisfied then I was to stay (be a slave), if I am not mistaken for three years, and pay forty thaler in addition. But if I did not stay I was to pay three gulden for my keep. The business was the largest of its kind in the town, and it did turn out quite beautiful furniture. The master employed five or six journeymen and had two apprentices besides me. The first few days I was put to work painting in one of the rooms off the workshop. Then I moved to the workshop and was assigned to cutting boards length-wise with the rip saw, which I managed to do, sweating profusely. As a matter of self-respect I wanted to do a reasonably good job, but the unfamiliar work really tired me out. In addition I was the last one called to the table and the first one to leave.

The food was good. There was fresh meat every day, with soup and vegetables. But the soup was so hot that I always scalded my mouth so badly that I could remove whole patches of skin. One did not eat there; everything was devoured. I was expected gradually to take over all of the duties of the most recently hired apprentice. These duties were, first of all, to be available to assist the master in whatever he was doing; secondly, to carry water into the house; and thirdly, to help the master's wife by making the beds of all the journeymen; and also to help catch the many fleet-footed fleas, a task at which I was somewhat clumsy and slow. And finally, when the master was not there, I was to provide all kinds of services to the young Swabian rogues, who as journeymen considered themselves to be above me, and even to treat them to wine on Sundays. Had I been allowed to treat them according my inclination I would have been quite ready to do so, but instead of wine, with fists and heels. Even the two apprentices believed themselves to be somewhat above me, poor hungry devils that they were. I was tired of flea-catching and various other experiments even before I signed a contract, and I gladly left all of these little pleasures to my predecessor. But broad as his face was, he made a long face, and seemed not the least bit happy at the prospect of returning to his former duties. On the day after the three weeks had passed I paid the promised three gulden, took up my bundle, and said a very contented good-bye to the master, the master's wife, the journeymen, the apprentices, and the fleas, the whole kit and caboodle, and turned toward the valley of the matchless holy saints, Fridolin and Hilary, where the slates, slate pencils, green cheese,[16] and the good-for-all-ailments herb tea come from.

10. Into Slavery at Gunsmith Master Pfenniger's — The Ants' Nest of Pfenniger's Virtuous Young Sons[17]

When I got back home Father thought I would probably now stay home, but I had no such thought. Furthermore it was stupid of me not to learn the cabinet making trade in the neighboring town of Reichenburg with a very good-hearted man by the name of Voegeli, who always had enough work and knew how to turn out good products, but who had no journeymen. Unfortunately I had heard from two young people who had apprenticed with Voegeli that his wife, a woman from Wuerttemberg, was quite unsanitary, so that one often lost one's appetite at dinner.

I had always enjoyed shooting and beautiful firearms, and had learned that there was a gunsmith named Pfenniger in Staub on Lake Zurich. I set out for that place and inquired as to whether he would take on an apprentice. The answer was affirmative. There were no journeymen and no other apprentices except for the master's oldest son, Rudolf, clever and already somewhat advanced in this business, but also a very brash redhead. This redhead was the oldest of master Pfenniger's five sons. Before I signed a contract I again demanded a three-week trial period because I had made up my mind that if I did not like it I would rather pay three gulden again, then perhaps a larger part of the apprentice fee later.

Pfenniger's house stood on a hill next to a vineyard somewhat removed from other houses, and in this respect I liked it quite well. The three-week trial period was begun, and everyone—the master; the mistress; the daughter Elise, a friendly girl of sixteen; and from Rudolf down to the youngest of the boys—was without exception, pleasant and good to me during the probation period. I received wine to drink mornings and afternoons and had no complaint with the food. Under such conditions could I have hesitated to sign a contract? I was to remain with the master two and three-quarter years and pay an eleven doubloon apprentice fee. But I was not obliged to do any work other than that which related to learning the rifle-making business. The first half of the apprenticeship fee was paid immediately; the second half was to be paid when the apprenticeship period was half over. Now I had committed myself. Now I could not easily get away, and thus they thought that the morning, as well as the afternoon wine, might be replaced for the time being with cider, and then later gradually forgotten completely.

In the beginning I was often asked by the mistress or pretty Elise whether I would be so kind as to fetch them a bucket of water from the well, which I did not mind doing now and then for a change, because I wanted to gain the good will of the mistress and especially that of Elise, and in this I happily succeeded. But it soon became apparent that this was to be a small extra job for me which they left entirely to me as if it were part of the arrangement. The well was perhaps a hundred paces downhill, and it was understandable that I could carry water for household use more easily than the mistress or the friendly Elise, but I could not really understand why I should pay eleven doubloons as an apprentice fee for the two and three-quarter years I had to stay, and during this time also be considered as the water carrier for the Pfenniger family. However I tried to comfort myself and told myself that, as an apprentice, I had to put up with such a trifle. But now the second haying had to be done on a piece of land, and although the master did not directly order me to help, I could easily discern his expectation, and I did help. The grapes were ripe and needed to be picked. I was easily persuaded to help, although it was not part of the contract, and those few days of grape harvesting were my happiest at Pfenniger's, even though I was used more for carrying grapes than picking.

In the workshop I initially mostly cleaned firearms. One time about twenty old muskets were brought in and given to me for cleaning. The master usually stayed at home, although he occasionally had business to take care of, and on such occasions he gave me, as well as Rudolf, as much work as he thought we could finish during his absence. One day he had just left, and, as soon as his promising young sons knew that he was gone, it became exceedingly gay in the workshop. Redheaded Rudi seemed to have completely forgotten the work assigned to him. I, however, tried my best to complete my work, which of course was hardly possible, because not only Rudolf but also three of his younger brothers yelled, jumped, scuffled, cavorted around in the workshop, tearing down all sorts of things, shooting off blanks, disturbing and hindering me in my work, which I was making an effort to finish to the satisfaction of the master. The mistress came down a number of times, trying to put a stop to the noise, however, as it seemed to me, with little success. The daughter came and warned them, equally without success. I myself reminded Rudolf of his assignment, asking him what his father would say if he had not done his work; but it was all for nothing; I should just be quiet, for I was only the apprentice. Finally evening came; I had been able to complete my work, but only with difficulty. Rudolf had completed almost none of his assigned work. He had actually been the worst and the leader in the witch's dance. Now he was feeling a little uneasy. But he was accomplished at lying, and probably believed he could use that as an escape.

When the master finally came home late in the evening the mistress complained to him a great deal about their sons' misbehavior and about the atrocious noise they had made all day, which angered him greatly because he did not like to hear complaints about his promising young sons, and liked to believe them even less because he seemed to regard them as model boys. The next morning, even before the master came into the workshop, Rudolf was very busy; but the time was too short to accomplish anything. First the master came to me to see if I had finished my work to his satisfaction. He was wearing his glasses and examined everything very thoroughly, and I believe it might actually have pleased him to have found any sign of negligence in my work. But he found nothing and declared it good. Now he turned to his redhead with the request that he also show the work that had been assigned to him. But there was nothing to show except the little he had just hurriedly begun to do. He began babbling all kinds of senseless stuff. But this time nothing helped. The master was indeed convinced that his wife had told him the truth. He took a leather strap down from a nail, with which he began work on the good, virtuous Rudi. In response Rudi gave forth with a very high-pitched, dissonant song, timed to the beat of his father's leather strap; but whether the beat was too fast for him or whether he did not enjoy his own song, he did not retreat into the wings, but behind me, whereby a few of these beats of the leather strap intended for him fell on me. I had absolutely no desire to take this payment that the good Rudi had so richly earned, which the master perhaps would rather have preferred to give to me instead of Rudi; but I declared to the master that if he did it again, I was determined to relieve him of the strap in order, for a change, to try the experiment a little on him. The master looked at me for a moment through his glasses and may have decided that, if I suddenly changed from a mere spectator to an actor, this play might perhaps become unpleasant for him. With that this splendid comedy had reached its sudden conclusion.

Rudi, by the way, was anything but stupid, and he could, when he wanted, be of help to his father. And everything went tolerably well as long as the master himself was present. However, when he turned his back, the old mischief quickly started up again.

The next son after Rudi was named Caspar. This one was a lazy good-for-nothing and a mean fellow. When the master was not present it especially seemed to please him to annoy me, mostly when I was filing, by unexpectedly hitting my butt quite hard or disturbing me in other ways, or teasing me. At first I thought that if I warned him with pleasant words this teasing would let up. Later I threatened to tell the master, and I finally did tell him. But the master was more inclined to believe his infallible young son than me, and since my efforts were unsuccessful, and the teasing increased rather than decreased, I finally decided to demonstrate, when he did it again, that if need be I could stick up for my rights. But only too soon I had occasion to do so, for Caspar found it especially funny to begin teasing me even more. Of course the promising youngster again came into the workshop while the master was not there and played another new trick on me. I then seized him and made a small effort to shake the tricks out of his head. But I gave it up very quickly for he screamed so terribly that one could have believed that I was about to murder him by inches. I had barely let him go when he was already up in the house, and still howling terribly, which, as I expected, resulted in the appearance of my upright master, his glasses and all, over the top of which he shot me some very threatening looks. That I had dared mistreat the master's second son—who was goodness and harmlessness itself—so badly, was unheard of, for there was no doubt that I must have treated him abominably; otherwise the innocent Caspar would not have screamed so horribly. Naturally I was forbidden to ever again touch a hair on the head of any of his harmless sons. But I took the liberty of explaining that if this pestering did not stop I would nevertheless take care of myself. That was certainly very outspoken and a little daring for an apprentice!

Indeed, it began to dawn on me that it would be impossible to endure two and three-quarter years in this ants' nest. The master in Waedenswil had let me experience, during my three-week trial, what I had to expect as an apprentice; at least that was honest. But Master Pfenniger and his family had shown me the most charming side they could muster during the trial period, which, after the contract was signed, unfortunately was only too soon reversed, and this was not honest; it was a kind of deceit, because it had given me the impression that I would be treated quite well there, which they did not live up to.

Each month I had made considerable progress and, if the master had been amenable, my progress would have been even greater. But perhaps that was not quite in accord with the master's wish. He probably suspected that I would want my freedom sooner if he did not proceed rather slowly with my instruction. I often expressed a wish that I might be shown how to forge iron, but that was much too soon. "You want to forge already? Oh yes indeed!" The hardest jobs, such as pulling rifling into new gun barrels, renewing old rifling and pulling it deeper, cutting gun barrels, and such, demanding arduous exertion which left me drenched with sweat, came to be my entire job. Whenever I had finally finished a job, it aroused obvious envy in Rudi, which he made no effort to conceal whenever his papa turned his back. He then tried to belittle the work as much as possible. One time I was to make a half-dozen nipple wrenches[18] on the lathe, and, since I had done some lathe work on my homemade lathe, they turned out better than expected, although I was working with iron for the first time. The master expressed his satisfaction with them, which however, again aroused Rudi's envy. A short time later a few boys from the neighborhood came along and bought one or two of those nipple wrenches. They said they were quite good and asked Rudolf whether he had made them, to which he immediately responded affirmatively. However I told the boys that I had made them and not he, which naturally was another grievous error on my part!

For a change, now and then, I had to saw and split a little wood, and once the master even ordered me to ladle liquid manure from one container to another while he was occupied outside the workshop. But since these jobs had nothing to do with the business of rifle making, and since I was not willing to pay apprentice money to do them, after brief deliberation I left the manure where it was, and risked what might come of it. I was already at work in the workshop when the master came. When he found the assigned task unfinished he looked at me through the window and at the manure containers, and seemed quite angry. To get the worst of it over with at once I went to the window and calmly looked at him through it. I expected to be addressed about as pleasantly as he glared at me through his spectacles. But I calmly stared back at him and expected him to come into the workshop momentarily, but the master went into the house and did not say the slightest thing to me about it. Shortly thereafter the master's principal journeyman—Rudi by name—reproached me about it. Mr. Redhead also explained to me that in the spring I would have to help cultivate the vineyard with a mattock, spread liquid and solid manure, and do similar work. But I explained to my good master, through the same redhead, that those jobs were not part of my assignment and I would not do them. My situation did not improve by my refusal to be the hired slave, and I was determined to bring this whole business to an end as soon as possible. America now was definitely my goal, but for the time being I could not let anyone know of my intention.

I had a few acquaintances in the neighborhood and I knew that the master was known as a man who had poor control of his offspring. I was not envied by anybody for my position and people seemed surprised that I was able to put up with it for so long.

11. How Jacob Huber Attempted to Use Me as His Bodyguard— Trip with the Master to Bilten to Persuade Father and Siblings

One evening I was invited by a young man named Jacob Huber to go with him to the sexton's house. It was the first Sunday of the new year. I was not eager to go but I thought I would offend him if I did not go with him, thinking I would be back home by ten o'clock. But we had been at the sexton's only a short while when I found out that my two new friends were about to set out through the deep and very wet snow to go to Grueningen, a town an hour from the other side of Staefa Hill. I personally wanted to go back home again, for I did not know a soul in Grueningen. But that was not the intent of my friends. I was expected to go along, and I finally let myself be persuaded. The way to Grueningen was completely unfamiliar to me. It was night and it seemed to me very long and tiring, and I kept wishing I had stayed home. We finally got across the hill and were, I was told, in Grueningen.

We stopped at a large house with a mansard roof. We had undertaken this wearisome trip for Jacob, who now climbed up to one of the windows which showed a faint glow of light, and made some faces there, but the people in the house told him it was bedtime. This response was not what my companions wanted to hear, and Jacob wanted to go to another house, which we soon reached. In that house of course there was a girl, which was the magnet that had drawn us—or rather my friends—there. But, alas! There were five or six boys in the room who seemed to have been drawn by the very same magnet. My friends, especially Jacob, were very angry that we had made the long, difficult journey without having achieved our objective, that is without having called upon a girl. I, for my part, was quite satisfied, hoping we would start on our return journey without further adventures. But Jacob did not want to go back without having achieved his purpose, and he began berating the boys in the house in his night-street-fellow manner, even challenging them to a fight. I was to take a position next to the house door in order to throw anyone who might come out down into the cellar. But I heartily declined this honor, for I had not the slightest desire to beat boys who had never harmed me and whom I did not even know. I now thought I understood why I was lured into visiting the girls with him. I was to help him out of a predicament, if required, and he seemed inclined to bring about just such a predicament.

The girl seemed to know Jacob, because she looked out of the window of an upper room and immediately addressed him by name, imploring him not to start a fight; he should come back another time, etc. Since Jacob realized that I, on whom he had seemed to count the most, and who he seemed to think was a strong fellow, was not at all eager to fight, he finally let up, and we started on our way back. But the road led us past the house with the mansard roof. We were almost past the house when we heard repeated "Psts." We listened and Jacob looked up at the house. There he detected the head of the one whom he had wanted to visit in the first place. Jacob asked in an undertone whether we might come into the house. She said, "Yes, but you must be very quiet, otherwise my father could hear you."

We went quietly up a steep stairway; there the door was opened by a pretty girl. She closed it behind us and led the way down a hallway, opened another door, and we were in the warm living room. In the living room we sat down at a round table under which lay an enormous dog, who, however, seemed not especially pleased by this nocturnal disturbance, because while the girl was bringing up wine, we hardly dared move for fear he would instantly sink his teeth into our legs. But when the girl came back she let the dog out, and then there was peace. Jacob was naturally doing most of the conversing, which the sexton tried to do also. But his help did not appear to me to be particularly wanted. I of course remained a spectator, and I was ashamed even of that role, for our evening conversation seemed to me neither especially amusing nor instructive. To be sure, Jacob and the girl might have had a different opinion. By midnight I wanted to go home, but it became one o'clock, and finally the clock struck two. Then I explained to my friend that if they did not want to go back, I would find my own way, and I got up. That brought things to an end for this evening, to the disappointment of the others.

We now slogged our way homeward through night and snow, and had just reached the church at Staefa when the church clock struck three. All evening I had kept wondering what the master might say about my nocturnal adventures, for although I was almost twenty-one, I was after all only his apprentice. I expected to find the house door locked, but it was not. I opened it as silently as possible and closed it again. I sat down on the stairs and immediately took off my thoroughly soaked boots and stockings, went quietly up the steep stairs, opened my bedroom door in which slept three of the master's boys as well as myself, and since they were all sound asleep I was able to remove my Sunday clothes and put on my work clothes undisturbed. Then I lay down on my bed fully clothed.

A few weeks later I was called to Jacob Huber's house by one of his younger brothers. It was Sunday evening. Since the master was not at home, I asked the mistress whether she thought I should go there or not. She felt that it would be all right for me to go. When I arrived at Huber's Jacob soon let me know what he wanted, at which point I wanted to go right back. He wanted to take home a pretty girl from Hombrechtikon, and it was a good hour away. I understood right away that he wanted me along only for his own safety. I resolved that this would be the last time I would provide such services to the clever Jacob.

Of course, once again, Jacob was not at all in a hurry to get back home. When the living-room clock struck twelve I got up and said it was time for me to go home. This forced my clever friend to come too. When I arrived at the master's house the church clock was striking one. I found the door locked, and at first did not know what to do. But since the roof of the woodshed went down almost to the ground and reached up almost to my bedroom window, I crawled cat-like on my hands and feet through the deep snow across the roof, knocked on the window, and called to the boys to open the window for me. I noticed that Caspar was awake, but he was afraid to open it for me. So he called Rudolf, while I waited freezing on the roof in the snow. Rudolf finally opened it, but let me know right away that the master would likely give me a piece of his mind, and the master did so, showing me his displeasure with words and looks. Of course I thought he had a right to and I was willing to stay at home evenings, but still I resented his treating me as though I were just a boy of twelve to sixteen.

As I have said before, I increasingly felt the demeaning nature of my situation, the yoke which seemed to weigh me down. And more and more I came to feel that I had been tricked into signing the contract according to which I was only supposed to learn the gun smithing trade, but in violation of which I had been expected to do all kinds of other jobs, yes, quite often even ordered to do them. For some time now I had been pondering how I might leave without the master's being able to demand the whole apprenticeship fee. I was still inexperienced in those days, otherwise I would have packed my bundle and taken my departure feeling little guilt, and commended myself, because the contract was being violated by the master, not by me. But since I did not like to depend too much on the law in this matter, I had to devise and carry out some sort of scheme. If it worked, that would be good; if not, there was still time to employ other means.

Under the pretense that I was writing to a friend, I wrote my father that I had resolved to give up my apprenticeship with Pfenniger because I found that it was impossible for me to remain two to two and three-fourth years under the conditions that I described to him. I had thought about it, and it could work out quite well if he would help me get away without raising suspicion. My plan was this: He should write me that I would have to take over my upper land again; he had left his land to us children so that he would be relieved of it; however, were he to take my part back again then each of his other children would be able to return the land they had inherited if they did not like it. Therefore he could not make an exception for me, and he would therefore insist on my taking over the land myself.

My father was no friend of gun smithing, and in the beginning had tried strongly to dissuade me from learning this trade, for which he had about as much regard as for a tinker's. However, now when I tried to get his support, he seemed little inclined to give it. In his answer he said I should have given the matter more consideration before I signed the contract, especially since I had paid half the apprenticeship fee of five and a half doubloons. I should try to stay if possible. After all, two and a quarter years hardly seemed an eternity, etc. But I sent him another letter at once, secretly again, with the firm decision that even if, as he had indicated in his earlier letter, he did not intend to be helpful, I nevertheless was determined to leave the place, even though I might have to pay my entire apprenticeship fee. I wanted a definite response at once, and he should write his letter exactly in the style I used in my former letter so that I could let the master read it without his becoming suspicious that I had instigated the whole thing. During the interval I was very much in suspense as to what to expect, and hardly dared hope Father would comply. But finally a letter came from him to me, and its contents were entirely as I had wished. Of course I showed it to the master, whose expression changed slightly while reading the letter. Perhaps there was some unknown family problem; I patiently awaited the outcome, and thought I noticed a slight improvement in his treatment of me. However this time I could no longer be held back, even if my treatment had become a great deal better, because I had completely lost faith and trust in their sincerity and good will, and I would have considered this momentary improvement only as a kind of bait to get me to reconsider. I could sense that the master had such an intention, because he made the proposal that he and I would go to see Father on a certain Sunday. Then we would go over the matter once again, and it would be desirable to have my siblings present. It was his plan to persuade my siblings to keep the land inherited from my father, but that Father should not give my upland parcel back to me. He wanted me to write to Father, indicating the Sunday on which we would arrive, and suggesting that all my siblings be present on that occasion. Thereby the master anticipated, to his way of thinking, an advantageous result for me. I wrote the desired letter, which I read to the master, and which was in accord with his wish.

Naturally I had to seal and address it afterwards, and I took the opportunity to add a warning to Father and my siblings: "Be firm and do not let the master persuade you otherwise, even if, in his presence, I should pretend to be in complete agreement with him! Remember that you can cause me to lose or to save half the apprentice fee!" I posted the letter myself to ensure that my father would receive it.

The Sunday set by the master had come. It was still dark when we set out for Bilten. It was a frosty February morning. There were still many patches of snow and crusty ice on the road. The master walked very quickly, and was almost always one or two paces ahead of me, and fell a few times, hurting himself a little, which, had I been inclined to be a bit superstitious, I might have taken as a good omen for me. Since the distance between Staefa and the Ussbuehl was roughly five hours, it was noon when we reached Father's house. The sky had cleared and the sun was pleasant and warm. Shortly after noon my siblings had all finally arrived and I had already received a sign that my prospects were not unfavorable.

The decisive moment arrived. The master presented his proposal, intending to persuade Father as well as my siblings that they ought to permit me to complete my training in the gunsmith trade, in which I had already made considerable progress, because he was convinced that I would become quite a good gunsmith. My father should keep my land, or perhaps he could sell it, and my siblings should make no difficulty for me or Father over this, adding that it would be a pity if I were to have to leave this trade now.

My father told me that he had warned me from the first and had told me that I would have to take back the land; besides he was already rather old and did not want to concern himself with land anymore, except that which belonged to Caspar, Caspar being still a minor, and that was enough for both of them. The siblings were all steadfast, and did not show any sign of changing their minds, so the master was convinced that all of his good words and exhortations on my behalf had been in vain.

The next day we set out on our return trip. We did not utter a single word about our mutual concern until we were already quite close to the town of Staefa. Suddenly the master spoke to me. "Heinrich, at first I did not believe that what you told me about having to take back your land could have been serious, but I admit that yesterday I became completely convinced of the accuracy of what you had told me. I would not have believed that I would find your father and siblings so obstinate. But of course it's only to your disadvantage. If I wanted to be as unyielding towards you as your family is, then I could still make you pay the other half of the apprenticeship fee!" But I believe that if the master had been as sure of himself as he pretended his compassion toward me would not have stood in the way at all, because I had had the opportunity to get to know his humane feelings, and he would definitely not have been inclined to promise me something advantageous unless he could foresee a larger profit for himself. He had the audacity to say that he would suffer a great loss because I had to leave him! "You're suffering loss because of me? Haven't I more than earned my keep through my work, and haven't you received five and a half doubloons from me in addition?" "I have to reckon differently. I must take into account how valuable you might now have become to me, and then there's the other half of the apprentice fee that I'm losing!" With these words the master had spoken the truth, but he himself had been entirely to blame for the outcome. Had he kept better control of his spoiled boys, not permitting them to tease me at will for their pleasure and amusement, or, as soon as he left the workshop, they had not removed everything from its usual place without thinking to put it back, and then, when he could not find those things where they belonged, had he not automatically tried to blame me, as though I had not put those things back in place when picking up on Saturday evenings, etc., etc., this misfortune would not have befallen him. I had been patient long enough in the hope that things would improve, but instead I could only see my condition getting worse, and the neighbors marveled that I could bear it for so long. There simply was no one, or at least very few, who knew master Pfenniger, as well as his young sons, who would have testified favorably regarding the exemplary discipline of his promising young sons.

Since this unselfish, sensitive master now fully realized that I was not going to stay any longer, he wanted to get a bit more work out of me. He had a pile of wood in his woodshed; this I was supposed to saw and split for him. To avoid the displeasure any refusal would bring I set to work briskly and sawed with doubled effort, and the large pile was done by evening, to the astonishment of the entire family, for no one would have expected that I could accomplish so much in one day, and I think that they would still have been satisfied if I had done this work in two days. As for eating and drinking, that day I was treated as I had been during my trial weeks. The next morning I quickly bundled up my clothes, and finally cheerfully took my leave; that is to say, I cheerfully said good-bye, and like a bird in the air I reached my father's house soon after midday.

12. My Plans for America Cause Discord with Father — Uncle Peter — Preparing for the Trip and Departure

I could not bear it at home any longer. My thoughts and my longings roamed far away across the ocean. But at first I could not allow myself to show it because Father did not want to hear about it. Only bit by bit did I want to let my intentions be known, and that is what I did. But unfortunately our household tranquility suffered considerably as a result. Although I believed quite strongly that my father loved me at that time the least of his children (and I am still of that opinion), I believe that because he loved me too, he did not want me to be so far away from him and the homeland. The thought of what might happen if I became ill among foreign people seemed to torment him considerably, and my failure to consider such concerns seemed almost too puzzling for him to understand. Equally difficult for my good father to comprehend was that I did not heed his well-meant advice, that is: "Stay on the land and make an honest living," as well as "You too will have food and live as I have if you remain here." It was his view that, being much older and therefore the more experienced, he was bound to have a better, more practical and mature outlook upon things than I, and the fact that I did not want to heed his well-meant advice, which he seriously intended for my best interests, angered and annoyed him very much. As soon as Father finally realized that my intention to go to America was quite serious our household tranquility unfortunately was no longer the best. I believe if had he known for certain that I wanted to go to America, he would hardly have helped me get away from my master, and it sometimes appeared to me that he felt I had tricked him.

Our quarrels were almost always about America, and as he became increasingly convinced of my determination to leave the homeland he even proposed that, if I really wanted to leave, I should travel instead to Algiers. There one would receive a certain amount of land from the French and it was not nearly so far from the homeland. I could easily return, should I not like it. My view that the living conditions, the climate and social conditions there were too different from ours, and that these differences were much less in America, he absolutely did not want to accept. Soon thereafter we received the Glarus newspaper in which there was an article about emigration to America and Algiers, and the great difference between them for Germanic people. Father was pleased to find such an article in his newspaper just at that moment, but this article proved me, and not him, right. It stated that in America Germans could always find enough people of the same culture, that the climate was much more similar to ours than the African, and that one could buy excellent land for very cheap prices, while the African climate was probably healthful for South Europeans, but not for Swiss. In America one could go about one's business unmolested, while in Algiers one had to be armed to protect oneself against sudden attacks by the native inhabitants, which still often occurred, etc.

If Father was cured of his Algiers notion by this newspaper article, it did not make him one whit more receptive to my America plan. Weary of our continuing conflict, on one occasion I attempted to scare Father and perhaps make him more receptive to my America plan by proposing that if I could not go to America I would marry. But this was grist for Father's mill, for he at once agreed to it. "Do so!" he said. "It's the smartest thing you can do!" I realized my mistake at once, and replied I was still much too young.

After this incident Father's younger brother, Peter, came for a visit. Uncle Peter's eldest son had been in America since 1836. Also the eldest son of Father's second brother, Jacob, had been in America since 1837, and both uncles did not seem to have any regrets. After Uncle Peter had sat down and spoken a few words with us, he suddenly turned to Father, remarking, "Brother, you keep fighting with your boy just because he wants to go to America! Let him have his way and let him go! If he makes something out of himself once he is there, you should be glad. But if he should turn out to be a good-for-nothing, you can be glad that he's so far away from you! He's good with his hands. He surely will make his way there, just as other young people have. Brother Jacob and I both have a son in America, and we're satisfied. Why are you so set on refusing the same for your Heinrich?" These words from Uncle Peter were just what I might have wished.

I agreed fully with my uncle, and remarked that if I were forced to stay at home against my wishes I did not know what would become of me. For the moment Father was defeated, and so half defiantly, half unwillingly, he said, "Well, if you absolutely want to go to America, then go in God's name. If you do well there, I'll be satisfied!" Overjoyed at Father's sudden change of mind, I called out, "That's it! You've heard, Uncle, that Father has nothing against it anymore! Now I'll begin making preparations for the trip right away!"

My father was a man who did not like to break his word, but I believe that in this instance he regretted having given his permission. But it was too late to go back on it. He said, "Once you are so far away from us you will not be much better for me than if you had died, for I won't be able to see you or talk with you anymore." "But," I remarked, "I can still write to you, which the dead cannot do; also we might see one another again if we both still live a few more years, and we are in good health."

In our neighborhood lived a young man, a distant relative of ours, by the name of Jacob Aebli, eight years older than I, who had also been wanting for some time to travel to America, provided that someone he knew well would want to make the trip with him. Naturally this was ideal for both of us since we knew each other well, and, since such a great journey could not be taken lightly, we could count on each other should the need arise.

Jacob Aebli had a brother, Caspar, who practiced law. He wrote for information to an emigration agent named Rufli, in Sisseln, Canton Aargau. He was willing to take us to Le Havre[19] in France for a not exactly cheap amount; that is, us and our luggage; and if we wanted to pay a certain amount more, he would also provide meals. We preferred to see to our own food because we half-guessed that the meals might turn out to be of less than the best quality. I was in those days, as are most first-timers or greenhorns, still very inexperienced. We found out later that we could have made the journey from home to Le Havre every bit as cheaply, in a much shorter time, and much more pleasantly, by mail coach.

Our departure was definitely set for August 24, 1843, because by then we hoped to have completed our outfitting. Outfitting for a trip to America was no small matter in those days. This outfitting, if it were to be adequate according to the thinking of the day, considering the space on the boat and provisions for meals, called for thirty to sixty pounds of cheese, dried prunes and dried cherries from home. The cheese would then be sealed at the French border. Such sealed cheese could not be opened until we were at sea. Everyone had to provide his own feather bed for the ocean trip. Also a copper cooking pan was required. Considered as absolutely necessary were two to four complete outfits of clothing, one or two dozen shirts, one or two dozen handkerchiefs, and if possible thick cotton and woolen stockings, besides a gun, and a pistol, and perhaps a rifle, in order, after our arrival in America, to be able to send into eternity the many deer, bears, panthers and buffalo. Taking all these objects in one trunk required something which quite certainly must have resembled a miniature Noah's Ark, and required at least two sturdy porters to manage between them. With these nice iron-bound little trunks, on which our first class names were painted in yellow paint, we were then well outfitted.

Shortly before our departure we went to the government office in Glarus to pick up our passports. It was a splendid August day. We had been measured and our descriptions had been recorded, and the passports had been prepared, when one of the gentlemen remembered that if the passports were prepared for America we would be required to present and pay the money for our sea passage as soon as we arrived in Bourglibre,[20] necessitating unnecessary expense and trouble. Passports made out for Le Havre would be just as good, and from there we would have complete freedom to travel wherever we wished. With that our just-finished passports were torn up and others prepared for us. We later had occasion to be convinced of the accuracy of this information. This saved us considerable unnecessary trouble and expense, and we were thankful to our obliging government clerk of Canton Glarus, which stands under the special protection of the holy Saints Fridolin and Hilary. Who knows, perhaps this happy idea had been suggested to our official by these saints.

On the way back home from Glarus by way of Mollis we saw our romantic Glarus mountains once more, and they rose so majestically and yet looked so peaceful on this pleasant and sunny August day. "Will we ever see these magnificent mountains again?" we asked ourselves. "It really is quite beautiful here!"

2

By Land, Sea and Upriver to St. Louis

13. Taking Leave of Father and Siblings —
Travel by Water to Laufenburg and Then Sisseln

THE TWENTY-FOURTH DAY of August had finally arrived. I hardly know how I really felt now that the long wished for time had come. The thought of leaving my closest relatives for a long time, perhaps forever, awoke in me a strange feeling. Was it a kind of homesickness? I could not say. On this day one of our distant relatives, Jacob Lienhard, was buried. Brother Peter's second wife, Dorothea, wanted to attend the burial, but she still came by our house to say good-bye to me. This woman was one of those people whom I believed, then and now, to have had just cause to dislike. She did not behave as a close relative should. At one time she had caused our dear, blessed mother much vexation, without real cause, and had recently been unable to hide from us, especially me, her petty, envious, and self-seeking character. And could I believe this woman tearfully paying good-bye to me; could I believe her tears were sincere? I would have been just as satisfied had she not come; in fact, I was angry at her because I considered her sobbing hypocritical. She has now long since gone to eternity, and with all my heart I forgive her the wrongs she may have committed. Perhaps her tears were genuine; perhaps she guessed that she was seeing me for the last time, for she died five years later.

Down on the road my traveling companion, Jacob Aebli, accompanied by some of his siblings, was waiting for me. While my brothers, Peter and Caspar, fastened my baggage to the back of the little chaise for me, my father and I were alone in the house. We drank a little wine together and forgave each other any mistake or wrong that we might have done. Suddenly Father said, "Heinrich, stay here. I'll gladly repay all your expenses if you'll stay here." By that I finally clearly saw that Father loved me after all, which I had doubted so often in the past. Naturally I could not agree to his wish, and I told him that even if I really wanted to, I would not dare to do it because I would be ridiculed forever.

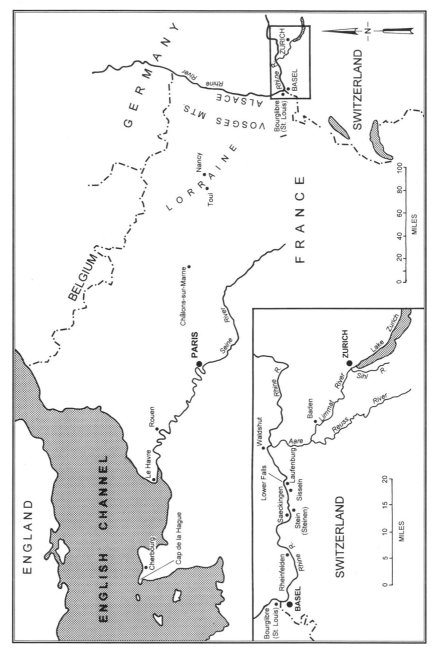

Portions of
Switzerland
and France
Relating to
Lienhard's
Travels

Now everything was ready below. Father was going to accompany me as far as Lachen.[1] Leaving my paternal home, in which I saw the light of day for the first time, in which I had spent my childhood and grown up with the kind care and attention of my parents, especially that of my unforgettable mother, now moldering, whose eyes I had pressed shut, well it did hurt after all, even though I tried to resist.

The day was calm, but a little rainy. By eleven o'clock we had arrived in Lachen, and had gone to Doctor Diethelm's Bear's Inn,[2] where we took our mid-day meal. It had cleared up splendidly, and everything was as peaceful and as beautiful as one could have wished. At the landing lay a so-called mail ship[3] on which we would have to make the trip from Lachen on Lake Zurich to Zurich, a vessel that may have been good for hauling freight but which left a lot to be desired in the way of passenger comforts.

We had finally left the inn, for the time of departure had come. We were accompanied to the boat, and now I said farewell to Father. Father remained standing at the landing for a long time. Probably he believed that he had seen me for the last time. I periodically waved my handkerchief at him until he finally left.

Now that we had left our birthplace, siblings, and father, we finally really grasped that our journey to America was under way. We looked over our vessel. It was an ordinary, medium-sized sailing boat with a single, large four-cornered sail, which could not be used, however, because there was no wind. The place in which the not very numerous but rather motley group was to spend the night was a kind of low cabin hardly three to four feet high, in which, instead of beds, there was a quantity of straw and hay on which the passengers could settle as well as circumstances permitted. I lay down between my travel companion and the keeper of a Glarus slate and slate pencil shop. Across from us were several men, women, and girls. Since I did not especially care for this community bedroom, I was not in a hurry to return to my evening quarters, once I had located them. We proceeded—by rowing rather than sail under the bridge at Rapperswil—and then past the shores of Hombrechtikon and Staefa. Here I pointed out to Aebli the house of Master Pfenniger, the place of my travail as an apprentice.

We stopped at Maennedorf and took our evening meal. It had already become dark, so that little more than lights were visible on both shores of the lake. I had recently suffered a good deal from a toothache, and my face was somewhat swollen. The air was cool, and since the others had all gone to their sleeping quarters, I finally felt compelled to crawl into my place also. The person across from me was, as I finally noticed, a resolute girl from Lachen for whom these nocturnal boat trips seemed nothing new. I pulled back as far as possible toward the ship's wall, and she moved so close to me that I had to pull my legs, or feet, ever more tightly against my body, and my feet thereby became so warm—I had already taken off my boots—and the numerous fleas seemed quite lively, biting me enthusiastically, making it impossible for me to sleep. I crawled back out of my sleeping quarters, took off my stockings, and tried to beat off the fleas. I tried to stay up for good, but the cool night air and a stomachache forced me to seek out my sleeping spot again. But the girl and the incorrigible fleas seemed inclined to spoil my every attempt. At any rate, it was long after midnight before I finally got to sleep.

I was the first one up very early in the morning. The cool air refreshed me. The sun was already lighting up the top of the Uetliberg.[4] The air seemed rose-violet and all of nature, as well as both shores of the lake, appeared to be competing to outdo one another in beauty. We had hardly left the flea boat and reached the sailboat landing as the sun rose. I, for my part, had had quite a fore-taste of boat travel. I hoped to find only better voyages from there on, and I did find some.

In Zurich we first had breakfast, and then bought a few more supplies. I bought a so-called German-English dictionary,[5] and Aebli soon returned with the information that he had found passage on a boat to Laufenburg, and for a cheap price. These boats were very narrowly built, long barges which were managed by two or three men with long poles or oars. Our luggage, some heavy pieces of iron, and a number of fat calves for the shops in Baden made up the principal freight of these barges, which seemed to us a more than ample load. Aebli and I were the only passengers. The barge was untied, the oars and poles taken in hand, and now our long pointed boat shot swift as an arrow through the foaming waves of the Limmat [River] out of Zurich and past the mouth of the Sihl, as if we were trying to escape from some threatening danger. By early afternoon we had already reached Baden, where most of the fat calves were unloaded, lightening our barge a good bit. Now we went even faster. But we passed a few rocky, dangerous places on the Limmat, where the water literally foamed and boiled about us. At the most dangerous spot the barge swung around in a circle, causing the man at the helm to scold the other. The barge was soon brought into the calmer channel, and our continued progress was a real pleasure. But instead of our making forward progress it seemed to us that the banks were rapidly receding. Passing the mouth of the Limmat we found ourselves suddenly in the combined waters of the Limmat, the Reuss, and the Aare. The Aare was a major river whose waters shot along quite rapidly, and it was no longer the clear water of the Limmat, but looked more like the water of the Missouri River. Under the barge we could hear a strange hissing. The boatmen explained that it came from all the sand mixed with the water.

Evening finally came, and after arriving at a rather large inn and some thatched-roof houses, the name of which place I have forgotten, we stopped for the night. Here I saw a ferry over the Aare, the likes of which I have not seen since. In the middle of the river were some dinghies over which a strong iron chain was fastened, which chain extended its entire length downstream, the lower end being attached to a strong flat-bottomed boat. At the rear of this flat-boat was a rudder, and merely by manipulating this rudder the boat could be swung back and forth, from one bank to the other.

In the inn we were surprised to meet a close neighbor of ours, Fridolin Streif, who dealt in green cheese, and was going to Zurzach the next day, which supposedly was not far from there, between the Aare and the Rhine. By way of Streif we once more sent greetings to our relatives back home.

We set out the following morning by ferry across the Aare/Limmat to where our barge lay, which we boarded, and again danced gaily down the river. In the afternoon we came to the waters of the Rhine, which at this point was little—if at all—larger than the Aare. But while the waters of the Aare were turbid and dirty, those of the Rhine were as clear as those of the Limmat, and one could observe for quite some time the struggle and gradual mixing of the waters of the two rivers. This bore a good deal of similarity to the waters of the Mississippi and the muddy Missouri at their confluence.

Not far below the union of the Aare and the Rhine, on the right bank lies Waldshut, an old town in Baden with a beautiful view up and down the Rhine and over into Switzerland. Here we made a short stop so that we had enough time to look around the town a bit, and with that we actually stood on German soil for the first time. After about half an hour we were seated in the barge again and headed straight for the ultimate goal of our Rhine trip, Laufenburg, which we reached fairly early in the afternoon. Here we encountered the so-called Lower Falls. However, they are more like rapids than actual falls. The foaming water shoots through the many boulders, creating a continual noisy din. For the boatmen these falls present an insurmountable obstacle. While Aebli looked around for a vehicle to take us to Sisseln, I enjoyed watching the logs coming down the Rhine, making all kinds of leaps over the falls. Sooner than expected Aebli brought back a light wagon on which we loaded our baggage. A half-hour later we had arrived in Sisseln. On our arrival, we found only a lone passenger from St. Gallen, Jacob Behler, who, like us, considered Highland as the ultimate goal of his journey to America. Behler had read, like us, the same small book by Salomon Koepfli about New Helvetia in New Switzerland, and he and his two brothers had become as enthused as Aebli and I about the new Promised Land, which, according to this description, we considered Highland to be.[6] We regarded each other much like old acquaintances, and had, if I remember rightly, no reason to regret this acquaintanceship.

Rufli did not expect most of the passengers he was to lead to Le Havre, coming mostly from Kuettigen, Erlinsbach, Frick, etc., for a few days yet. Since there was little of interest to see at Sisseln except Rufli's inn and stables, which were large solid buildings, and consisted of a few old plain houses near the Rhine River bank, we were perfectly willing the next day to help Rufli's workers with the haying in a meadow almost halfway to Steinen.[7] It was quite a warm day, and I sweated profusely unloading the warm hay, which made me thirsty, a thirst Rufli's pretty young wife quenched with lemonade made from raspberry syrup and cool water.

The following day was Sunday, and since the weather was so pleasant Aebli and I went to Saeckingen, half an hour away on the Baden side of the Rhine, which was connected on the Swiss side with Stein, or Steinen, by a wooden bridge built on solid, stone columns. Saeckingen is, I believe, entirely Catholic, and seems to be quite an old place of some importance. It boasts a large church, with very heavy, large bells in the two towers. There we admired several Black Forest beauties (?)[8] in their Sunday finery, consisting of heavy shoes, red stockings, short skirts, with even shorter bodices with no sleeves, instead of which they displayed clean, white shirt sleeves, and huge black-ribboned headgear, that almost made us believe they wanted to represent the ears of a mule.

By noon we were back at Rufli's inn. Soon after midday a young, pretty, well-dressed female, perhaps twenty or twenty-one years old, approached me asking whether I also was traveling to America, which I naturally confirmed. She told me that she was also about to travel to America, and was going with Rufli to Le Havre for that purpose. I found the conversation engaging with this small, seemingly intelligent girl, which I still took her to be, and we soon felt ourselves to be on friendly terms. I was glad to find such respectable people among my traveling companions. As I talked with the supposed young miss, there were several other people in the room; but I had hardly left my place for a moment, and passed by a handsome young man, when he addressed me in an undertone, saying that the supposed young miss was a married woman, who apparently was about to run away from her husband. I was advised to watch out for her. I did not forget this warning, and I did take care.

Among the travelers for America who straggled in were two brothers named Knobel who were going to Brazil, one a boy of sixteen to eighteen and his brother who was about ten years older. This older Knobel soon became acquainted with the unfaithful young woman and became so friendly with her, and so persistently acted as her protector that one could have assumed he was her rightful husband.

Toward evening, a wagon load of our future fellow travelers from Aargau finally arrived. For the most part they were families with still young children, but there were also a few young adults. However, most failed to measure up as fellow travelers. We had higher hopes for the wagon load of people that was to arrive the next morning. The next morning came and the other wagon with our fellow passengers arrived as well. How did they look? This much I can say. We were not at all pleased when the living contents began to pour out of the wagon, and one of the first, a half-grown, idiotic boy, who, in the presence of all—without much ado—relieved himself right out in the open, without being hindered by any of his relatives, or taken aside a little.

14. Traveling from Sisseln to Rouen, France— Pacifying Our Friend Fricker

The two wagons with which we were to make the land journey to Le Havre consisted of two huge covered wagons, very wide, with benches fastened lengthwise along the inside like omnibuses, scarcely capable of accommodating many more passengers. In the rear, two steps were fastened to the door opening for convenience. Each wagon was drawn by four or five strong horses. The driver sat on one of these horses. It took some time before all of the baggage and passengers had found suitable spots. The families with small children were required to take the places in the front, while the young adults placed themselves near the wagon door. We had thought the passengers were already too many for the two wagons, but we gained nine or ten more emigrants from Bern before we reached Basel. Finally the baggage, as well as the passengers, had been packed into this wheeled ark. The drivers cracked their whips, and we were underway. We arrived at Rheinfelden fairly early in the afternoon.

There we made an unscheduled stop. It came to light that one of the emigrants from Aargau, by the name of Fricker, had signed a contract with a Basel emigration agent for transportation to Le Havre. This emigration agent, whose name I have forgotten, would not permit us to proceed any further until Fricker had paid him a certain compensation. This Fricker, although married and the father of three children, had nothing visibly masculine about him other than a huge pair of feet. Otherwise his size was that of an ordinary twelve-year-old boy; his voice was high-pitched, like that of a child. Even so, Fricker was a man. He had a wife of normal size. Furthermore it was said that Fricker had money. Yes, he had—if I am not mistaken—supported with quite a bit of money two other families who traveled with us. They were to repay him in America! Poor Fricker, I am afraid you got very little of it back. Since Rufli himself had stayed a bit behind, we waited for him to arrive. He soon came and went with Fricker to the justice of the peace, and after Fricker had been plucked to the satisfaction of all involved we were permitted to proceed.

Rheinfelden is still an old small town, enclosed by moats and high walls and reminiscent of highway robber times. We stopped in Basel-Land[9] for the first night, and then entered the old, unattractive, but, nevertheless, very wealthy city of Basel around noon of the following day. We did not spend any time in Basel, but while driving through, I noted that Basel was still enclosed by walls and moats. The most outstanding of the buildings was the twin-spired cathedral built in Gothic style. Among the inns the foremost was the Three Kings.[10]

Only a short distance past Basel, we came to Bourglibre, in those days still a French border town, where we stopped to have our baggage inspected so that no contraband could be smuggled into French territory. The examination of our baggage took most of the day, and it was decided that we would spend the night there. Tiny Switzerland, our beloved, little free country, land of our birth, now lay behind us. Aebli and I took a room in an inn, but we soon found that, besides us, several other people were spending the night in that same room. Outside in the open a dance floor had been erected, festooned with green boughs and branches. We tried, with little success, to get some sleep, but at first the loud music, the dancing, loud talking, singing and laughter kept us awake. Only toward morning, when it became a little quieter outside, did we get a little sleep.

I had almost forgotten that Aebli and I would be required to make a travel deposit at the police station. "Aren't you going to America, as well?" we were asked. We answered, "Perhaps yes, perhaps no. First we want to go to Le Havre. If we like it there, we'll stay. But if we feel like traveling to America, then we will." Since the young official could not get anywhere with us, he scolded us to his heart's content in the French manner. He could not do anything, for our passports were not made out to America but to Le Havre. Visas were entered in our passports, and we were permitted to go.

We remained only a short time in Alsatian territory and soon entered Lorraine. Aebli and I bought our food at every place we stopped, and as long as we could speak German with the people everything went well enough. Rufli had already asked us repeatedly to let him provide our food for a certain price, but the scorched gruel which he fed to his emigrants had little attraction for us, and we preferred to buy what we needed ourselves. When we left the German part of France behind us the situation changed considerably, for although I asked the innkeepers for cheese, sausages, bread, soup, or wine, in their language and showed them money for payment, we were politely told "Oui, oui," and received no further response, and we had the pleasure of continuing the trip with empty stomachs. Rufli, who was with us a few times, and whom I asked to tell the people for us that they should bring us food for the money, did not do it, but smiled gloatingly, and we could easily guess who was responsible for their not heeding our wishes. With that he succeeded in forcing us to partake of his diet of scorched gruel. At first, to the extent we could find them, Aebli and I took beds for the night in private homes. But soon we did not fare any better than with the food, and we were obliged to bed down in straw in large stables, as did the others.

Since I was not really competent in French, it was impossible for me to note and remember the names of every hamlet, village, or town. I only have a clear recollection of a few of the larger cities, such as Toul, Nancy, Châlons-sur-Marne[11] and Rouen. We moved steadily ahead each day, but not very rapidly. Sometimes we single people preferred to walk for a while because the odors drifting from the front of the wagons, where lazy, dirty women and filthy children rode, often were not the best. As we walked, one or the other of us would tell all kinds of stories. For a change, once in a while the older girls also joined us on our walks. Tired of walking, one would get back into the wagons.

We numbered twelve young men altogether. Of these, eight were from Canton Aargau. One had the quite inappropriate name of Frei,[12] for there could hardly have been a more offensive and quarrelsome fellow; then there were two of his cousins, Johannes and Jacob Bircher, stupid, arrogant blockheads whose talk and stories always showed indications of being lies; and then there was a slender eighteen-year-old youth called Heinrich from Erlinsbach who considered himself especially clever, handsome, learned, strong, and more, which is often the case with brash youths in their awkward years. On the whole, however, he was not mean-spirited. Then there were the two Knobel brothers, the younger a calm and quiet lad and the older carrying on in the most tender manner with the runaway beauty. Finally there was a young man of my age, Jacob Amsler, a peaceful and agreeable man who liked to read, with whom one could have a sensible conversation on any subject. And then there was his friend, Rudolf Prat. He had a crippled leg, but he was an amusing and entertaining fellow. Then there was another youth, about nineteen, from Canton Bern, who did not exactly exude brilliance, but on the whole was not a bad fellow.

One Sunday, as we were just crossing the Vosges Mountains, we came upon a small inn at the top of a mountain where we stopped for a drink. Soon a slender, young Frenchman who understood no German joined us. While we were driving down the mountain, our Frei, his Bircher cousins, and Erlinsbacher Heinrich, tried to make themselves understood by the young Frenchmen through gestures and some snatches of bad French. Then our young, know-it-all Erlinsbacher made a gesture with his cane as though he wanted to engage in a sword fight. The Frenchman understood this gesture and requested a cane from someone who obliged him. He and Heinrich crossed their imaginary swords, and, whack, he took a blow from Heinrich's cane. But because this hit violated fencing rules the young Frenchman became very angry and, greatly agitated, babbled away at Heinrich, who naturally understood as little as the bystanders, Birchers and Frei. Our Heinrich was quite ready to demonstrate his pride in his fencing skill when, to the amazement of the young Frenchman, he was scolded harshly by his companions, Bircher and Frei. To show the Frenchman that we Swiss did not travel through their country to start a war with them, the conceited Hans Bircher ran toward the brash Heinrich, trying to knock him down. Heinrich, who saw what was coming, stepped aside and our Hans fell plump in the road, tearing his clothes, and bruising his face and hands, and we could not help laughing!

We were favored the entire time with the most splendid weather. We had a little rain only once or twice, but not enough to make our journey unpleasant. But sleeping quarters were nothing more than straw bedding in stables; however, this sometimes provided a little excitement, or even fun. Generally these stables contained a number of horses, usually huge Norman stallions whose screaming often awakened us from our soundest sleep. But sometimes not only did they scream, but they would also engage in a little scuffling, trying to kick and bite each other. However, their scuffling usually ran its course without serious consequences.

I remember one time when deep in the night we were all awakened suddenly by a frightful trampling of hooves and screaming, made all the more alarming because we thought we clearly heard the screaming of a child. There was a lantern in the stable which partially illuminated the huge room. By its light we could clearly see a little boy in nothing but a shirt running back and forth, almost beside himself with fear. However, our excitement quickly changed to general laughter when we discovered that no one was at all hurt, and what we had taken for a screaming child came from none other than scared little Fricker, who, frightened by the trampling and screaming of the horses, thought he was about to perish. After we had calmed Fricker down, and had proven to him that, in spite of the racket made by the horses, we were in no danger, he finally dared to lie down again. I hope that, like the rest of us, he was able to get some rest.

Nancy is a beautiful city in a splendid region of vineyards in Lorraine. However, we stayed only long enough to eat our noon meal. Châlons-sur-Marne is a large and beautiful city. We saw Paris to our left. We reached Rouen about four in the afternoon. It took us two full hours to pass this city. Afterward we bedded down for the night in a large stable. Rouen is on the Seine. Smaller steamboats come that far. The landing resembles a seaport, with the smells of tar, the huge ropes, anchors and sailors; all in all there was much life and a great deal of commercial activity.

That evening, as we were about to go to bed, our Fricker became angry with his wife about something, and declared that he did not want to spend the night with her. I had just come to the stable door when I met Fricker, who shouted a few furious words at his better half in his boylike voice. "What's the matter and where are you going?" I asked him. "Don't you see that it is dark outside?" "Away!" was his enraged answer. I tried to advise him to return to his wife. But Fricker apparently wanted to give his wife a little scare. I took him by the hand and tried to lead him to the place where his wife and children and the rest of us were to spend the night. But the gentler I spoke to him the more he resisted. Then I picked him up in my right arm, spoke to him soothingly, and carried him through the stable door to where his family was, but Fricker flailed his arms and legs like a really unruly boy, even pulling my hair, berating me royally. But now I had him back with his family and I told him he had to stay there. Everybody around burst out laughing, even his wife laughed a bit, and Fricker stayed where he was. I hoped that he bore me no grudge, for his wife could not say that he had come back to her willingly. The next morning he seemed to be quite happy and even laughed a little himself when he saw me.

15. Arrival and Short Stay in Le Havre—Herr Schmied, Legler and Koehler—Booking Passage on the *Narragansett* and Departure

We were rapidly nearing Le Havre where we intended to embark, and indeed all went well. On Sunday, September 14, we suddenly came to some heights from which we got our first view of the ocean. It was a magnificent view. The sea glistened like a silver mirror and aroused an indescribable feeling within us. A short distance further our road led downhill. The roads became busier and the houses more numerous. We crossed a bridge and found ourselves in Le Havre de Grâce,[13] next to the harbor, where many large three-masters lay tied to the bank.

Had we made the trip through France by mail coach we would have reached Le Havre in less than half the time and it also would not have cost us nearly so much. Traveling as we did [only by day] we naturally had a good opportunity to see France—the part we traveled—better, and I was delighted with the mostly beautiful, well-cultivated, and fertile regions. We traveled through only one region where the soil seemed to consist for quite a distance of gypsum or chalk, and the vegetation grew only sparsely. The remaining areas seemed to be thriving and densely settled.

On the journey up to now there had often been bickering among the people from Aargau, or much grumbling about Rufli, the scoundrel. There was talk of writing home about what kind of a fellow he was. People also wanted to expose him in the newspapers so that all the world would know how he treated us, etc. But Rufli never seemed to be especially concerned about such talk. He seemed to understand such people well, and also knew a cheap way to appease everyone once and for all. We took our last meal from Rufli in an inn next to the harbor. It was the best meal of the entire journey, and probably he counted on it to make his clients view him favorably. But an even better one was promised. However, Aebli and I took no part in that much better meal.

We had been at our midday meal only a short time when a man appeared and asked us whether there were also natives of Glarus among us, which both of us naturally confirmed. "I'm from Glarus, too." he said. "My name is Legler. I'm well acquainted here and am free until next Thursday. However, then I have to go to work in a brewery for a fellow countryman by the name of Schmied. If I can be useful to you during this time I will be glad to do so, which might be helpful to you since you don't speak French." We were really glad to meet a man from Glarus who seemed to know his way around so well and who was even about to go to work for Mr. Schmied, whom we were intending to look up. We soon finished our meal and followed Legler directly to Mr. Schmied's house, where we were immediately introduced to Mr. and Mrs. Schmied as newly arrived natives of Glarus. Schmied at once advised us to take our baggage to another inn, which was run by an Alsatian named Koehler, and which happened to be the very one to which we had intended to go. We found Koehler's quite plain, but well kept and inexpensive, and we had no complaint, whereas the house to which Rufli had taken us was not regarded as one of the most praiseworthy. When we returned to that place to get our baggage a sort of letter of thanks and recommendation was being passed around for signing, and it was surprising to see how ready all were to sign this paper in which Rufli's services as an emigrant agent were praised to the heavens. The good meal that still was to come silenced even the loudest complainers completely. We were also asked to sign. As far as I was concerned, I explained that I would not sign such a paper since I was of a decidedly different opinion. I stated that it seemed to me that that last good meal appeared to have produced a considerable change of mind in those who had been so vocally dissatisfied with Rufli and had wanted to have his conduct printed in Swiss newspapers. Aebli told me that he too had not signed the paper.

Mr. Wild and Mr. Koehler accompanied us to the shipping office the next day, and we arranged a passage from Le Havre to New Orleans for exactly half the price Rufli had had to pay for the other passengers. The ship was a medium-sized three-master which proved to be a solid, fast, sailing vessel, commanded by an older French captain, bore the Indian name *Narragansett*,[14] and had a crew of sixteen to twenty men. Second class, or steerage, passengers all had to provide for their own food. So we set out to buy a supply of butter, ham [?],[15] bread, ship's biscuit, potatoes, dried meat, vinegar and wine. We also bought the dishes we would be using, as well as mattresses. All of this had to be on board the *Narragansett* early Thursday, September 18. That was the day set for departure.

Before I describe the sea voyage further, I have a few words to add. Le Havre lies near the mouth of the Seine on the English Channel. It has a so-called man-made harbor, enclosed by solid rounded walls, with locks at each end and crossed by two or three movable bridges. At high tide the ships are easily towed in by steam-powered tugboats, and they are towed out just as easily. Formerly the towing in and out was accomplished by means of a number of long ropes. Near the mouth of the harbor canal is a market. Here one can find all kinds of shells and various articles made from them; also all kinds of colorful birds from southern lands, especially a variety of turtledoves and parrots and monkeys, etc. This place appealed to me the most; I found many new things there which I had never seen before. It appeared to me that important trade with overseas countries was carried on there, and I found it all bustle and life.

16. The Ocean Voyage—How Well Frei Knew How to Behave—How I Tried to Bathe with Salt Water

On the morning our ship was to depart Mr. Schmied accompanied us to it. We thanked him once more for the favors he had done for us, said a heart-felt farewell and climbed on board, as the ship crept through the locks. A large number of laborers towed our ship toward the mouth of the harbor. The ropes were pulled in and we found ourselves in the open waters of the English Channel. The ship had only a few passengers in first class. There were two ladies and five or six gentlemen. Steerage passengers numbered about eighty, of which some fifty were from Switzerland, the rest being from Baden and other parts of Germany, and some Frenchmen.

The accommodations for the steerage passengers were plain. Along the sides of the ship, fastened lengthwise, were rows of three-tiered bunks. Each bunk was intended for three to four persons. As for myself, I was soon convinced that I would probably sleep rather poorly in these bunks as soon as the consequences of seasickness made their appearance. Therefore I preferred to move further toward the cabin where there was still open space on which I could place my mattress on the deck, and I never regretted it. Quite close to me were two Frenchmen, each one on a small bunk. Up on deck, between the fore- and main-masts, there were two cooking stoves for the steerage passengers. Farther back was the longboat, the chicken coops, some large water casks, some stalls for the cows, and finally the kitchen for the cabin passengers and crew. In the hold was the freight, as well as most of the water barrels, firewood, the various provisions for the passengers, etc. The passengers' baggage was stored in steerage for the most part. According to ship rules, every morning the upper deck was washed clean by the sailors, the steerage by the passengers, quite a good rule for preventing illness. As soon as the cleaning of the ship was completed the steerage passengers were allowed to make a fire for cooking their meals (each side of the ship had its own stove); until then no fire was permitted on deck.

At first the weather was splendid. With a favorable easterly wind, which allowed us to maintain a direct course southwest, we sailed along the coast of France, out of the English Channel toward the Atlantic. It was not long before

Le Havre had disappeared from our sight. We sailed past Cherbourg and Cap de la Hague, and England came into view; the coast of France was now completely out of sight. The following day we passed so close to England that one could make out the landscape of the coast with its bays and cliffs with the naked eye.

The favorable wind continued from the same direction, but on the third day became considerably stronger. Almost all of the sails were hoisted and filled out splendidly, so that our ship tilted slightly toward the right. That morning, from the ship's various quarters, one could hear a little wailing, interrupted now and then by strange gurgling sounds. One could almost have believed that the people had been into their cups on the previous day, and as a result were suffering hangovers. The tarry smell below deck revolted me. I felt dizzy; my mouth watered, but not from thirst. I went on deck into the fresh air where I hoped to feel better. I looked all around at the ocean. All land had disappeared, while at the bow the waves splashed and foamed. The ship plowed through them at a fine clip. If only I had felt just a little better. I was completely lost in my thoughts, watching the play of the waves, the sea birds, the clouds, the horizon and the movement of the sails and the masts, when suddenly here came two, three, four of my fellow passengers, and the vomiting began all around me. There were so many different looking substances splashed on the deck about my feet that I felt nauseated myself. I fled to another spot on the deck, because now I also had urgent business overboard, which I proceeded to take care of. Seasickness now seemed to be the norm, and the various characters of the passengers soon became evident; while some sought to remove themselves as much as possible when they became nauseated, others often were indifferent as to where they unloaded their filth. Such persons seemed, either by nature or by habit, to have much in common with certain four-legged long-nosed grunters, to whom it hardly makes a difference whether they soil someone else or roll in their own filth. Not everyone is equally subject to seasickness. It seemed to me that those of irritable or excitable temperament were affected the most, whereas others were hardly touched by it.

Aebli and I had jointly purchased our provisions in Le Havre. Unfortunately we both took sick at the same time, so that we were unable to cook for ourselves. It is good to have friends, but when these friends steal from you, then it is not so pleasant. When we were both down with seasickness, along came a fellow traveler, a family man from Bern called Erbi. He had a wife and a child. "If you wish I'll cook for you until you feel better again," he said. We happily accepted his offer and we were quite grateful to him, because he occasionally prepared a little soup or coffee. After several days we felt better and did our own cooking again. We looked for our butter supply, but could not find it. So we asked Erbi where our butter was. Then it turned out that he had annexed it for his own use, and for his wife, and child, and had already used it up completely. That left us in a nice fix. We had hardly even begun the sea journey and were already without lard and butter. We confronted Erbi about it, but what can be done with people who know nothing of honor and shame? Erbi only laughed, and in the end we could do nothing but laugh ourselves. But from then on our soup was seldom very rich.

When the worst of the seasickness was over we could begin to look around a little. Those with some common bond were drawn to one another. Some found pleasure in singing merry songs, and others told amusing and entertaining stories, which I liked best. There were others who also sang a lot, yes even knew a great many songs by heart. However the songs that were sung were not especially choice, and the different sounds that were uttered had many similarities to a bunch of Irish sailors, or Shanghai and bantam roosters, all trying to outdo one another with crowing and yelling. The harmonizing certainly left a lot to be desired, but this seemed unimportant.

I remember well a handsome, old Wuerttemberg tailor [called Heinrich], who declared with special pride that he had fought Napoleon for his emperor. This tailor knew every old folk song, and joined in the singing whether he was invited or not, and he set himself apart from everyone else because he sang almost every song to the same melody, and his voice sounded like small stones being thrown into deep water.

One day I was singing with our Badeners when our Swabian[16] tailor appeared and immediately joined in heartily. But my friends from Baden seemed to feel that we could do without his loud vocal assistance, and immediately began to sing a different song that went something like, "Three times ninety-nine tailors sitting on a goat," and ended with the bleating of a billy goat. This billy goat song worked like magic. Our tailor immediately stopped singing, his face became completely red, he stuttered a few words, spun around, and marched off. In my opinion that should have been enough, but for some passengers the poor devil's anger seemed to offer an opportunity for some diversion, so whenever he was near they immediately started the tailor song, or bleated. Our tailor completely lost his patience. He scolded like a magpie, but since this did not help, the old Napoleon warrior began to weep, went to the captain and complained. And the captain ordered his tormenters to leave him alone, and it helped, which was only right.

Since our Frei from Aargau did not seem to have a voice for singing, because it was much too grating, he tried to use it in other ways, namely for quarreling, scolding, or bickering. He seemed to pay most of his attention to our Erlinsbacher friends, our serene highness Heinrich and his father, although he did not mind starting a fight with anyone if the opportunity presented itself, or should it not offer itself, he was not beyond finding an opportunity somehow. With favorable winds and our fast-moving ship we had already come into considerably warmer waters, and some of us preferred to sleep on the upper deck at night, weather permitting. So in the morning we were up early and enjoyed the fresh morning air. One morning—it was still early—several of us were already on deck. The lovable Frei was there also; the old Erlinsbacher appeared on deck to get something, dressed only in a shirt. That offered Frei a marvelous opportunity to play a prank on the old timer. Quickly he took an empty water bucket standing nearby and filled it up with sea water from a tub and poured it over the head of the unsuspecting old man as he was about to go below. This big heroic act, which Frei considered a splendid joke, was not taken as quite so funny by the Erlinsbacher, for our serene highness quickly jumped up to the deck scolding and gesticulating violently, thereby providing only more amusement for the sensitive Frei, who seemed happy only when other people suffered harm or any kind of annoyance. What else was he there for?

But Frei did not restrict his acts of kindness to only the Erlinsbachers, but soon shared them with the French, then the Badeners, the other Swiss, and if nothing else presented itself, even the like-minded Birchers, his own relatives. He showed a particular interest in Barbara Bircher, his cousin. If anyone spoke to her in a somewhat friendly manner, this daring action immediately brought forth some kind of retaliation. To be sure, this cousin might have seemed to him the epitome of youth, beauty and virtue, for she was only twenty-four or twenty-five years old; her figure had grown as beautiful as a bean stalk; her tanned soft face was very freckled but still very pleasing; her manners were so fine and decorous; her mien so delicate, although her dainty mouth was a little too broad; and her laughter, oh, how beautiful it was when she let out her loud, drawn-out, high-pitched "Hee, hee, hee." Who would not have been enchanted by her? But that this did not happen, despite all her great charm, is certainly a miracle, one which no doubt fanned the hope of her charming cousin Frei that he might after all realize his much longed-for goal.

I will give only two small examples of just how ready Frei was to retaliate against any young man who exchanged a friendly word with his cousin. Rudolf Prat, whom I have previously mentioned, was an entertaining and jolly fellow. He enjoyed pretending to court the charming Miss Bircher. But this aroused a little of what one might call jealousy in the eyes of Frei, who was always guarding over her. Instead of sleeping on the bunk, Prat and his friend Amsler preferred to sleep nearby on the floor. Not far from them several women and some girls also slept on the floor; and among them was Barbara Bircher. Frei might have imagined that Prat could easily encroach upon forbidden territory in the dark of night. One evening, soon after the steerage lights had been put out, Prat softly spoke to Amsler. Frei hears something and becomes suspicious. Finally he cannot control himself any longer and says loudly, so everyone can hear, "Oh, I do believe you will soon be lying next to Baebi!" Prat takes advantage of this suspicion and says just loud enough to be heard, "Baebi, move back a bit and be very quiet, otherwise the fellow will hear us." Frei is now even more taken aback, and says, "By Jove, you are lying next to Baebi!" But Prat is heard to say very softly, "Back up a little more, Baebi, and be very quiet, or he'll end up coming over here." And that is too much for our Frei. He quickly jumps up from his bunk, strikes a light, and comes to where Prat and Amsler are sleeping. But Baebi is not near them, but some distance away. Frei's jealous behavior resulted in loud, general laughter, and nearly everyone was glad and felt he deserved his being taken for such a fool, since he was considered the most disagreeable of all passengers.

But this did not make Frei change for the better, for some time later, one fine afternoon, he saw me talking with his cousin Baebi, on deck where most of the passengers were. Noting the jealous look Frei was shooting in my direction, I conversed even more cordially with his cousin, and occasionally pretended to tell her a secret, after which Baebi's lovely soft voice was heard and her "hee, hee, hee" rang out again and again. Now Frei was determined to get back at me for this amorous intimate conversation with the apple of his eye, and I expected there would soon be consequences. Very early the next morning—it was hardly dawn—I saw Frei slinking to where I was sleeping. "He's up to something," I thought, and pretended to be fast asleep. And he was certain of it. Soon, sick with jealousy, he came down the steps with a pail of water and began to splash the deck, pretending to wash it, but while doing so came quite close to me, and, as I expected, splashed water on me too. "Frei, just stop that, and go splash where no one is lying," I said to him quietly. "Oh, oh, you are there? I didn't know you were sleeping there!" "But you were here just a little while ago to make certain that I was sleeping, and now you come and lie, saying that you didn't know I was lying here? Go away and don't come back or we'll settle this another way." The two Frenchmen who were sleeping nearby called something to me, and when I turned around to look at them, they made signs with their fists, which were easily comprehended; they indicated that I should beat up Frei!

As we neared the West Indies the favorable easterly breeze had stopped blowing. Often the sea was completely calm. This became really wearisome, especially when large waves rocked our ship from side to side. For variety we had an occasional thunderstorm, naturally with wind, often of only short duration. Every gust was utilized as much as possible to make some forward progress. Once—it was a very humid day—black thunder clouds suddenly appeared on the horizon and bore down on us very rapidly. The passengers were ordered to go into steerage, which all obeyed except for me, because I found that the nauseating air in the hot steerage quarters was quite unbearable. The two deck hatches leading to steerage were sealed with fitted covers and then covered with oil cloth. The thunderstorm was soon upon us. By order of the captain only a few sails had been pulled in or reefed. The wind blew fiercely and the rain came down in torrents. I was wearing only pants and a shirt and, since more sails had to be taken in, I pitched in also. I did not have a stitch of dry clothing left on my body, but because it was warm I did not feel at all uncomfortable. The captain looked at me and smiled a little, but did not seem angry that I had not obeyed his order to go down into steerage.

Since the thunderstorm lasted for some time, and the waves splashed up wildly over the bow of our ship, the hatches were kept closed and I began to imagine, "What a stench there must be in the hold!" I was soon convinced that it had to be a little unpleasant down there, because people began to cry out for the hatches to be opened, and to show that they really meant business hammered on them. However, they were only opened after the wind and waves had calmed down a bit. But when the hatches were opened, the passengers poured onto the deck like a swarm of bees, and the air that streamed out with them was almost enough to make me seasick again.

One fine Sunday morning, near the island of Santo Domingo[17] — but not yet in sight of it — I decided to really wash my entire body with sea water. Aebli also intended to bathe himself. We agreed that I should be the first to climb over the bow of the ship down to where there was a pump. I intended to stand on the ropes that connected the bowsprit with the ship, holding onto some ropes tied to the ship. Aebli was to begin pumping as soon as I called to him, very slowly at first, and then somewhat faster when I called up to him again. I had barely climbed down and had positioned myself under the pump spout, and was about to call, when the water was pumped upon me so forcefully that it got into my ears and eyes and mouth, so that I forgot where I was and let go of my hold with both hands. But immediately, remembering where I was, I grabbed the rope again with my right hand and leaned aside a little, letting the water run down my left side. Of course I looked up, intending to shout to my comrade to ask what he had in mind, when I saw — instead of him — the fiery red, very disagreeable face of a big Irish sailor, the most repulsive of all the sailors. It turned out that this red human animal had pushed Aebli away from the pump as soon as he knew I was below, and had then pumped water down upon me with all his might, so that I had almost fallen into the ocean because, not expecting such a volume of water, I had lost my grip. To be sure the ocean was quite calm, almost like a mirror, but since I did not know how to swim I do not know what would have happened to me if I had fallen. We knew this red sailor by the name "Nickety, Nackety, Bow Wow Wow," because these were the only words he used when he tried to sing with a voice that would have done credit to an alligator.

This fellow and another Irishman and a German sailor once had a hand-to-hand fight with an American sailor from Buffalo, but because the captain came along they had to break off. This redhead was involved another time when the sailors beat up the ship's cook, and it was this redhead's brownish red-haired dog, which he kept on the ship without permission, who had bitten a piece of flesh more than a half-inch wide and an inch long from the cheek of a handsome six-year-old French boy. Left hanging by a piece of skin, it left an ugly red scar that must have disfigured the boy for life. Supposedly the captain had ordered him to throw the dog overboard, to which Nickety, Nackety was said to have responded that he would do so only if the captain would pay him for the dog, which did not happen, and the dog came along to New Orleans.

The above-mentioned sailor from Buffalo, a fine-looking, slender man, took it into his head to make a sailor of me, and tried to explain to me the names of the various parts of the ship. But he had to give it up because I did not understand enough English.

One day a young man from Baden, also called Heinrich, climbed hand over hand ten to twelve feet up a strong rope hanging from the foremast, and said when he came down again, "Let anyone match this if he can." Being a bit of a showoff myself, I seized the dangling rope and like him climbed the rope, almost to the first crow's nest. I looked down and called to him, "Let anyone match this if he can!" Then I saw several sailors quickly approaching. I shot quickly back to the deck, and immediately let go of the rope; otherwise they would have tied me up and extorted a ransom before releasing me. It is said that such is a custom of sailors, and later I have seen it done more than once to other inexperienced travelers.

17. Our Trip Close to and Between the Islands of Santo Domingo and Cuba, Then Through the Gulf to the Mouth of the Mississippi

By the time we neared the West Indies we had seen only a few ships. When we did see some on the same course as ours our ship usually turned out to be the faster. One morning we saw a two-master brigantine just to the right of us, which was almost on the same course as we, only a little more to the south. All day the two ships sailed without one or the other gaining a noticeable advantage. But finally, when evening came the two-master came closer and closer, and also a little ahead of us, but so close that we feared we might run into each other, and we could have easily hailed one another. The brigantine now crossed our course, hardly a cable's length in front of us. The next morning we could see it to our left. But by evening it had put considerable distance between us, and the following morning it was no longer visible.

Our captain now more and more often took up his telescope, looking especially off to the right where he probably reckoned the southernmost of the Bahama Islands lay. We also began to see more and more sails. They appeared to belong to small vessels rather than to large ones. Finally we heard the cry "Land!" And soon we could make out off to our left above the water, on the horizon, a misty-looking mass which gradually became more distinct. It was indeed land; in fact it was the eastern edge or tip of the island of Santo Domingo. We came closer and closer, and I would have liked to have been nearer still, not only to make out the coast lines, but also to be able to see its plant life, palm trees, and such.

Unfortunately we often made no progress at all. Sometimes the ship would turn almost completely around, and we could hardly comprehend how some tip of land that shortly before had been ahead of us suddenly reappeared behind the ship's stern. If I had had a really good big telescope to examine more closely the beautiful island's landscape, I think time would have seemed to pass less slowly. I felt somewhat like a hungry man who sees a table covered with good food but is not able to reach it.

We got little steady wind. It would let up as suddenly as it appeared, so we did not progress as fast as we would have liked. To our right, land at last appeared. It was the eastern part of the island of Cuba, and as we held slowly to our westerly course, the landscape of the two islands revealed their various bays and elevations. To the left we saw a small point of land. It was one of the peninsulas of Santo Domingo, of which we gradually lost sight. We had seen high mountains on Santo Domingo. Moving further and further west we finally lost all sight of land. But to our right Cuba was often quite close.

These waters sometimes swarmed with fish, the large blackfish belonging to the whale species, which appeared near us on the water's surface with brown backs as broad as those of horses. Now and then dolphins and other fish also were seen.[18] We had earlier become acquainted with dolphins. Also another kind of a reddish shimmering fish, about two feet long, had accompanied us for quite a long time. The sailors made futile attempts to harpoon some of them. Flying fish often appeared in great numbers above the water, scattering in all directions. They appeared to be pursued by some other kind of fish, and often flew quite far from the spots at which they emerged. The largest seemed to be little more than a foot long. As for sea birds, they became less and less rare as we neared the islands, and among the islands we saw many different kinds circling above the water, then suddenly shooting down almost as swift as an arrow, immediately rising up again with a fish.

A few days after losing sight of Santo Domingo we again saw, to our left, a low, flat island. We were told that it was one of the Tortugas Islands,[19] inhabited only by some Negroes who caught giant sea turtles. The side of the island facing us seemed to form a vertical wall. On top it was flat and seemed to fall off toward the ocean on the other side. We soon passed this island and approached Cape San Antonio, the western tip of the island of Cuba. The days had been quite lively with sails of all kinds, from the smallest sailboat to the largest three-master, sailing in various directions. We expected that we would shortly sail out of the Caribbean into the Gulf of Mexico.

Portions of the West Indies and Midwestern United States Relating to Lienhard's Travels

One morning when I awoke I found, stretched right next to me, a wall made from a sheet of bed linen. At first I was puzzled as to why it had been done. But I did not remain ignorant for long, for behind the linen sheet I heard women's voices and the voice of a small child could also be heard. The young citizen-of-the-world, so it was said, was the offspring of the first love of the attractive young couple from Baden. The young man, whose father was well-to-do, had fallen in love with a pretty but poor girl whom he wanted to marry, but his father had not permitted it. But since the couple's love had flourished to the point beyond which it was impossible for the young man to give up the girl, the father gave him money and told him to leave. The young man did as his father ordered, made the girl his wife, and set out with her on the *Narragansett* for America. The little one, who had seen the light of day for the first time on the *Narragansett,* was their firstborn son. It was said that we had passed Cuba's Cape San Antonio during the night. The Captain's name was Anton, and the name of the happy young husband and father was Anton, so it was understandable that our new fellow citizen must also be named Anton.

The waters of the Gulf of Mexico were not as calm as those we had encountered among the islands. The wind was in our face, the water was turbulent, and we had to tack. Although we frequently met various vessels, no land was in sight. If I am not mistaken, we had already been sailing around in the Gulf for six days, and no one could or would tell us how much longer it would be before we reached the mouth of the Mississippi. We were told that we might easily run onto a sandbank if the wind drove us too far to the west, etc. I for my part had long since had more than enough of the sea journey. The constant quarreling of some of the Aargauers, among themselves or with others, had long since totally disgusted me. The day had been gloomy, and we could only move forward by tacking, but had no idea how much progress we made toward our goal. For the first time I felt something a little like homesickness.

The next morning when I came up on deck the sky was still cloudy. But the water had lost its deep blue color and appeared to have a greenish cast. The captain took his telescope in his hand and peered through it in various directions. Several ships passed by. The cabin passengers were also looking in all directions. I took this to mean that they were expecting to see land or something else. The water lost more and more of its dark color, and I learned that they were looking for a tugboat. I had always had a sharp eye and, since I was now certain that we could not be far from land, I became very alert and looked in all directions. Suddenly, toward the southwest I saw a small white speck hardly more than an inch tall. I called this speck to the attention of one of the cabin passengers, and he pointed it out to the captain, who raised his glass to his eye and immediately declared that it was one of the tugboats. The tiny white speck became visibly larger. We could soon make out that the white was no sail but steam from a boat. Finally we could see the smoke stack and the hull. It came speedily toward us, and our captain signaled that he wished to be towed. Our sails were lowered, a strong rope was tied from the bow of our ship to the tugboat's stern, and we then headed directly toward one of the mouths of the Mississippi. The boat was called the *Black Star,* considered one of the best and fastest tugboats.

The color of the water became ever lighter, not clear but murkier and murkier, and the closer we came to land the cloudier and yellower the water became. The clouds dispersed, the sun began to break through again, and by about ten o'clock the sky was completely clear and blue, smiling upon the low banks of the Mississippi Delta. There were remnants of trees floating everywhere. On the larger ones numerous birds often sat, as though on a pleasure cruise. Numerous fish swarmed around the ship. Blackfish, dolphins and others carried on as if they shared our high spirits, for now there was general excitement and gaiety among the passengers. The tugboat towed us over the river bar and a short distance inside it. We dropped a heavy anchor. Then the *Black Star* immediately departed and soon disappeared from sight. A rowboat rowed by four dark, fat Negroes, came toward us with a doctor from the police station and came to rest next to our ship. The doctor found all in order, since no one on board was ill, and soon left.

There is little to see at the mouth of the Mississippi except low banks that have formed gradually over thousands of years from floating tree trunks and mud, among which very abundant coarse grasses now grow, as well as all kinds of bulrushes and reeds, inhabited by alligators, turtles, crabs and all kinds of sea and swamp birds. Several of the passengers claimed to have seen alligators. Personally, I could not claim such glory, much as I looked. I came, therefore, to the conclusion that the alleged alligators might have been only old mud-covered pieces of wood.

Our sea journey had taken exactly forty-seven days[20] and was, despite Frei and his associates, short and successful. The *Black Star* was out of sight all day. She finally reappeared at dusk, by which time she had three small two-masted schooners alongside. She drew up to our left side, our ship was tied to her, the anchor was drawn up, and we headed upstream toward New Orleans. The small schooners were from the islands and coasts of Central America and Yucatan and were carrying mostly tropical fruit. One of our sailors, who was from Hamburg, had brought aboard several plantains[21] from one of these vessels, and he gave me one. That was the first fruit of this kind I had ever eaten, and I was delighted by its delicious flavor. But the sailor from Hamburg later gave me an orange peel and said that in tropical lands there were all kinds of even better fruit than those I had tasted and smelled. I immediately felt a great longing to visit those countries someday to see for myself the truth of his claim.

18. Travel to New Orleans and from There
on the Steamboat *Meridian*

We moved quite rapidly up the river toward New Orleans despite the four vessels the *Black Star* had in tow. I stayed on deck until long after midnight hoping to see something interesting, for the moon was shining and it was warm. But since the river was so broad and the banks so low, there was little to be seen. Whenever we happened to come close to the banks I heard a horrible, gutteral, hoarse roar. I was told the roar came from a startled alligator, and it is easy to imagine that voice being associated with the ugliness of such a repulsive monster.

By the light of the moon I had only been able to make out tall bulrushes and reeds along the banks. I was on deck again by four in the morning and found that I was one of the first persons up in spite of having stayed up so late. Soon more and more came up to take a look at America. In certain respects the countryside had changed considerably. The banks, although still low, were no longer only bulrushes and reeds. Instead we saw large plantations and here and there a large two-story mansion surrounded by gardens and trees; and not far from them were straight single or double rows of little cabins, all looking the same, standing side by side. Often there would be one or several white, proud-looking men with wide-brimmed hats riding about on their horses. Negroes drove mules ahead of them down to the river bank, or drove teams hither and yon. Short-haired Negresses, with bright cloths wound about their curly heads like turbans, often accompanied by half-naked little, black, woolly headed children, fetched water or seemed to be otherwise occupied. The whole scene made a special impression on me. I hardly found time to wash up and almost forgot to eat breakfast. In the course of the morning we observed large fields of sugar cane and whole rows of Negroes busy cutting it down. Others were moving it to sugar houses which were not far from other kinds of buildings, identifiable by their high chimneys. Most of the trees and bushes seemed still to be in leaf, although it was already November.

In the air I thought I saw a large number of chicken hawks. But they were only carrion vultures, so-called turkey buzzards or turkey vultures, because, like turkeys, their necks are naked. These birds are considered very useful, especially in southern climes, because they do away with all carrion and filth, making the air less contaminated. Still farther south are two species. Besides the brown ones found here there is a black kind that differs from its northern relatives only in its black color. They are very numerous in Mexico and Central and South America, and so lazy or tame one can often touch them with one's foot. There they are called gallinazo[22] and no one harms them. If one were to shoot one of these birds, one would be committing a serious crime in the eyes of the natives, for they regard them as benefactors of mankind, because they make short work of so much filth. If one gets too close to them they usually just rise to the nearest rooftop where one can often see several of these birds sitting next to one another with outspread wings, as if trying to dry them. The brown, or northern ones, do the same thing, only they seldom fly to the tops of buildings, but prefer any old dry tree for the purpose.

The closer we came to New Orleans the livelier it became on both banks of the river, as well as on the river itself. From the river bank the land fell away more than it rose up. We often saw reeds and dense woods. This whole region, or Mississippi Delta, grew from the trees and mud that have floated down from the interior of the country over thousands of years, and, in order to protect these properties from annual floods, levees were built along the river bank, beginning hundreds of miles above New Orleans.

We finally reached New Orleans fairly early in the afternoon. No passengers were permitted ashore until customs officials had inspected their baggage. They did not take long, and it was often amusing to see how they turned up their noses when they had to inspect the steerage passengers' laundry, soiled from the journey and not particularly aromatic. They usually finished quickly, and did not seem too thorough, and I know of no passengers who would disagree. Of course it was very lively on our ship. There was general confusion. Many cleaned themselves up a little and put on better clothes to go to see a little of the city, to buy something, or to investigate how and where one could find transportation up the river to St. Louis.

Aebli and I also went ashore. In order to reach the shore we had to make our way over two other vessels, from which one crossed to the shore over a strong plank. We found a number of people gathered there. One of them held a rope in his hand, to the other end of which was tied the leg of a well-dressed drowned man in sailor's clothes. The water would have carried him away had he not been held by the rope, for he was floating on the surface. This sight was very disagreeable to me, and I wondered how the people could appear so indifferent.

We also entered a market hall where all kinds of vegetables, fruits, fish, meat, etc. were being sold. It was almost closing time, so many of the stands were already empty. The market hall was being swept and washed by a number of people, but what kind of people were these? A mulatto woman was cleaning and had an iron band around her neck with three six- to eight-inch long spikes bent outward. A Negress had an iron band around one of her hands which was connected to another band on her ankle by a chain. A Negro had one of his ankles held to a heavy block or piece of iron by a welded chain. Others appeared to be fettered in various ways, and it was under these conditions that they had to do their work. But they did not seem to take it too hard, because they laughed and talked

79

quite cheerfully. But it made a disgusting impression on us. Surely these were criminals, and therefore were devoid of any sense of dignity.

Outside the market hall there were still many market stands where we could have bought magnificent apples, melons and such, and our mouths watered. But the vendors all seemed to be ugly Negroes to whom, at the time, we had an utter aversion. Even so, I wanted to buy some of the beautiful apples, thinking that after all I could peel them. But Aebli said he did not want to buy the slightest thing to eat from these disgusting creatures, and so I did not. At that time we did not know about watermelons, and were surprised to see how some of the people, without a thought, ate whole chunks of these green-skinned, red-fleshed pumpkins, which we took to be raw. Had we known more about them I almost believe I would have bought some, even if the seller had been a Negro.

By evening many of the passengers had already left the ship. Others—especially the Frenchmen—left the ship well-adorned to partake of an evening's entertainment. One of the Frenchmen, a still young dancing master, also came out on deck intending to find a little amusement in the city. His hair was combed. He wore a top hat and carried a pretty little cane. But he was married, and his wife, a big person, was in a condition in which no wife wants to be without her husband. Therefore she followed her husband to the deck, and seemed to beseech him to stay with her and not leave her alone. Our dancing master sought to comfort and coax her, but it seemed difficult for him to accept that he should be denied the opportunity for a little amusement in the city with several of his countrymen. There the two spouses stood right beside me. She pleaded with him to stay and he pleaded that she should let him go. But she held him by the hand and was close to tears. Then he seemed to propose to her that I should decide whether he might go or not. He probably expected a result in his favor because I too was young and fun-loving. But he was mistaken. Although I only had an imperfect understanding of French, I thought I thoroughly understood what it was all about, since both spouses were looking at me expectantly. Since the condition of the sorrowful, entreating woman appeared clear enough, and touched my heart, it did not take me long to gesture to the man that he should go back down into the steerage with his wife. The poor woman nodded at me happily and smiled cordially because of the scarcely expected result of my decision, but seemed to worry whether he would stay. The dancing master seemed disappointed over this unforeseen decision and stood as if undecided for a few moments. Then he looked at me, looked back again at his wife, took her by the hand, and went back down with her. The next morning we learned that the dancing master was the happy papa of a young French girl, and that wife as well as daughter were doing well.

The next day we finally found a steamboat which was to set out that evening upriver to St. Louis. It was an old, rather small boat named the *Meridian.* The fares were, if I am not mistaken, ten dollars for cabin passengers, two-and-a-half or three dollars per person in steerage. The French all stayed behind, but almost all the Swiss and Germans ended up on that same boat, and unfortunately our charming Frei and his relatives were not left behind either. Most, or all, had bought steerage tickets, and since there was not enough space behind the engine rooms, accommodations were found in front of the cabin, between and next to the smoke stacks, on the so-called hurricane deck. Our baggage, beds, and food boxes were stacked at the very front of this deck, forming a sort of protective wall against the wind blowing in our faces. Among the passengers housed there, besides Prat, Amsler, Behler, Aebli and me, was a family of five from Baden, including the above-mentioned Heinrich, who had climbed up the ship's rope. I had found them to be harmless people on the whole. Unfortunately, there were also the Birchers and the well-known angel Frei, as well as a few other families. One of these honorable fathers was also named Frei, and was a tailor by profession. Evening was coming on, the sky was clear, and there was a brisk north wind blowing directly toward us. As darkness fell, we all tried to find a little place to sleep. Behler, Aebli, Prat, Amsler, and I were sleeping very near each other; not far from us was the family from Baden. But the Birchers, and the noble Frei also were not far away. The Heinrich from Baden was somewhat delayed. When he arrived there it was rather dark. In the darkness he tried to find a spot near his parents, but there was no room except for a small space between his parents and the extremely sensitive Baebi Bircher. The young man wanted to lie down there, not realizing who the other person was. Baebi, probably in the knowledge that the spotless purity and chastity of her respectable person might suffer harm, had no intention of allowing Heinrich from Baden to lie down there, but scolded and carried on wildly, making a rather hellish racket. Heinrich, although also angry, behaved much more reasonably. He said, "We paid our passage just like you, and like you have been assigned to sleep here. I have not the least desire to sleep near you and didn't even know you were there." The noble Bircher brothers and their jealous Frei now spoke up to show that they were also present. There was soon an unholy magpie squabbling back and forth, and it seemed they would ultimately come to blows. Our family from Baden naturally took their relatives' part. But since they were not nearly so practiced in the art of quarreling and scolding as the Birchers and their group, and were not so inclined, they began to be a little intimidated.

The captain of the ship came to see what was causing this caterwauling, but could not understand a word, and no one was able to explain it to him, so since neither could understand the other's language, he soon left. Heinrich's parents had moved apart a little to make a small space for him, but the ire of the Birchers and company had not yet subsided, and they continued to make a scene. We had long since grown weary of their awful behavior, and expressed our feelings among ourselves. Finally I tried to convince these people that, since the others had paid their passage just like us and had been assigned this place to sleep, they should be reasonable and accept Heinrich's right to be there. They immediately turned on me, saying, "Oh! You're taking their side?" "No, I'm not taking their side; I am impartial. However, you seem to have lost all common sense, otherwise you'd finally stop spewing out abuse so the rest of us could finally get some sleep." From then on we, and especially I, once again found ourselves the object of Frei and company's ill will for having had the temerity to set them straight a little bit.

That night we suffered greatly from the cold. All the blankets and huddling together helped but little. We had been in a tropical climate until the last few days. Tonight the area was hit with a hard frost, so we felt it all the more. The next morning everything was white. If our sailing ship was one of the fastest on the ocean, then our steamboat was one of the slowest, if not the very slowest on the river, for almost every boat behind us passed us without effort. Some shot by us as if we were standing still, a frequent annoyance to me.

For two days above New Orleans we saw only flat land, with large plantations on both sides of the river. The larger towns at that time, to our right—on the left bank—were Baton Rouge, Natchez, Vicksburg, and Memphis. Scattered between them were smaller towns, often consisting of only a few houses. Since we rarely stopped anywhere for more than a short time we had little opportunity to take a closer look at the small towns. We were kept busy buying the most necessary provisions and generally we brought them straight back on board. Most land bordering the river was low-lying, covered with dense woods in which the trees were often overgrown with wild grapes or other kinds of vines, often making the woods almost impenetrable. On the trees of the lower Mississippi hung long festoons of gray moss, moved to and fro by the slightest breeze. The ground was covered with masses of horsetails, as well as other coarse grasses and weeds. The trees were mostly varieties of oak, black and white walnut, ash, Kentucky coffee trees, poplar, swamp cypress, beech, cedar, and various hickories, while pecan, hackberry, persimmon, and many others could also be found there.

Most of the shoreline is very low. There is a good deal of land which is under water most of the year and cannot be cultivated. At places such as Baton Rouge, Grand Gulf,[23] Natchez, Vicksburg and Memphis, up to the mouth of the Ohio, where there are high bluffs, the earth is a reddish, brick-like color. Near Baton Rouge one finds large white-flowering, waxlike evergreen magnolias.

We often landed to take on wood. One such time we found a single, low log cabin. Outside it, beside some pieces of wood, lay an ax with a bent handle, the first implement of its kind I had seen in America. As I was admiring the ax and its handle, I saw several of our fellow passengers enter the cabin. Thinking perhaps Negroes lived in it, I stepped in too, but was surprised to find, instead of dirty ragged Negroes, two attractive, well and spotlessly dressed white women, probably mother and daughter, busily sewing. A couple of clean beds, some chairs, a mirror, a clock, and a table comprised the furniture, but though there was no wooden floor, everything was nonetheless clean, and I felt quite ashamed at having barged into this poor-looking cabin. The women looked at us calmly, and I began to think that they must have found our presence most unpleasant. Therefore I went to the open door, tried to say, "Adieu," to the women, and once again found myself outside. Just then a fine-looking, slender young man came out of the woods toward the cabin. Probably he was a newcomer and the husband of the younger woman. I vowed to myself to be more careful in the future about entering a house in this way again.

Soon after leaving New Orleans I had observed a pale youth of eighteen to twenty lying on a pile of sacks of wood in the engine room. The youth seemed to have no blankets or much of anything else, except the poor clothing he wore. It was obvious that the poor fellow was ill, but no one seemed to pay any attention to him, much less to be concerned for him. We were unable to communicate with the poor youth. Our attempts to question him were unsuccessful; he did not understand us. If we offered him something, he apparently could not appreciate it. One evening I tried again to give him something to eat. He held it in his emaciated hand but did not try to enjoy it, staring at me so vacantly that it actually physically startled me. The next morning I found the poor fellow in almost the same position as I had seen him the night before, but he was stiff and dead, and hardly a soul seemed to have cared about him. When we landed a few hours later at a lonely spot he was brought ashore in a box made of unplaned boards and given over to some Negroes. Might his parents ever have learned what had happened to their son? I doubt it, and I still cannot think of that poor youth without an odd sense of sadness.

19. Traveling up the River and Arrival in St. Louis

Most of us passengers had brought from Le Havre little chests in which we kept dishes, vinegar, and also some provisions. They all were equipped with similar locks. They looked alike and a single key would open practically every one of them. One day I saw tailor Frei open my food chest. He looked inside, looked around, and seeing me, locked it back up and said that he had made a mistake;

he had thought the chest was his own. Since I had myself once made a like mistake I was willing to believe him. In this chest I had a little pistol; its cock had fallen off, and I kept it somewhere else. The pistol lay on top in a side compartment. It was visible as soon as one opened the chest. The tailor must have seen it. When shortly afterwards my pistol was gone my suspicion fell on tailor Frei. I told our friend Amsler about it and we agreed to put the question to Frei unexpectedly. If he had the pistol, Amsler thought, there would surely be a change in the color of his face. If that did not happen, he probably did not take it after all. As agreed, we questioned the tailor, but could detect no change in his complexion, and he was even able to look quite innocent. Amsler was of the opinion that Frei definitely was not the pistol thief, otherwise he would not have been able to look so innocent. Since this matter did not remain a secret, the other Frei and his friends immediately let it be known that, according to them, a sixteen-year-old member of the Baden family had to be the thief, because allegedly he had been seen fiddling about my chest. Frei was very free with his insinuations that these people were guilty of thievery. Besides which, it served me right for having taken their side, and this was the thanks I got, etc. Nevertheless I did not believe the youth was the thief; rather I had not given up my suspicion of tailor Frei. And I said as much to Amsler. Belligerent Frei and his relatives now believed themselves even more justified in squabbling with the Baden family to their hearts' content, and they threatened to have Heinrich, the older son, arrested as soon as we got to St. Louis for having struck delicate Baebi, for in America men were not allowed to strike women; generally they were jailed! According to him, women would have had the right to strike men as they pleased. As soon as a man struck back, however, he would have immediately landed in jail. At least that was the fine theory. If Heinrich had one time laid a hand on Barbara, she had pounded him at least a half-dozen times in her fury, but—according to their theory—that made no difference. They insisted that Heinrich of Baden was going to jail. I do not know whether the Baden family was weary of the constant bickering or if they were truly afraid, but this is certain, they left the boat below St. Louis, although they had paid for passage to St. Louis. Frei and his colleagues were accordingly jubilant and gloatingly taunted me. "See there, your friends and their pistol thief son are afraid to come to St. Louis. They know why all right. Admit it, they have shown their thanks for your having taken their side by taking off with your pistol. It serves you right, etc." Still, I held to the view that it was not the boy from Baden, but rather another who was the thief and, in spite of everything, I did not regret having spoken up for the family from Baden, for I believed them to be innocent.

About a year after our arrival in St. Louis I again met Amsler by chance. We had barely exchanged greetings when he said to me, "Heinrich, I've seen your pistol again. Tailor Frei took it after all and not the Baden family. I came into his workshop one time," he continued, "and I saw the pistol hanging there, and I recognized it immediately. He had it fitted with a new cock. I told him right away that it was your lost pistol." By chance, a short time thereafter, the tailor passed near where I was, together with some other Swiss. I said, "Well, just look. There comes tailor Frei, the man who stole my pistol!" Frei had nothing to say. He was in a great hurry to get away from us. I saw him again by chance in Galena in the summer of 1845. "Why there comes my pistol thief again!" I called out to him. "What are you up to here? How often have you stolen again?" Frei acted as though he did not know or hear me and hurried away as fast as his scoundrel tailor's feet would carry him. I met Frei, the squabbler, in St. Louis in the spring of 1846. My friend [Heinrich] Thomman[24] was with me when I saw Frei approach. Frei was unexpectedly friendly, or at least pretended to be, and insisted on standing Thomman and me to drinks. He told me a good deal about his experiences in America, and wanted to know about my experiences also. I gave him as brief an account as possible, only telling him the pistol story in greater detail, thereby letting him know that the Baden family, whom he had suspected, had been completely innocent. On the contrary, just as I had always believed, it had become evident that the pistol thief had really been his name-sake, Frei the tailor.

The trip up the river offered little of interest. Occasionally, now and then, we saw great numbers of wild geese, which however flew away before we came within shooting range. When we stopped to take on wood I often went into the brush or the forest to see whatever there was to see. Once I believed that I had discovered a kind of wild orange. But its odor was too similar to that of a walnut, which is what it turned out to be. Another time we discovered a tree draped with wild vines from which hung clusters of little grapes. I took some back to the boat, and was about to eat my fill of them, when one of our Swiss mid-wives — we had three of them — saw me, and they immediately raised a hue and cry, much as if I had been about to poison myself, because a terrible fever would have been the certain result of my enjoyment of this fruit. I was actually fool-ish enough to believe them, and was about to throw them into the river. There-upon one of the cabin passengers motioned to me and, giving them all to him, he ate them without any concern, and yet he seemed to know full well what he was doing. I had also found some hickory nuts. The gentleman however said, "No good," and made a grunting noise like a pig to indicate that only pigs ate them.

Still another time we landed at a place where a plot of land had been cleared. Toward the rear stood a good log cabin inhabited by clean, attractive white peo-ple, surrounded by several Negroes, presumably their slaves. At the front, near the river bank, stood several fine trees covered with yellowish-brown fruit. Many picked some and ate them, and from their greedy expressions I assumed they were delicious. Since these fruits seemed to be free for the picking, and I took them for some sort of overripe pear, I also took a number of them, and expected to find them enjoyable. I had only eaten a few, however, when I felt an uncontrollable puckering on the inside of my mouth. This terrified me, and I threw away the remaining fruit, convinced that I had been poisoned. I soon discovered that others who seemed familiar with the fruit ate them without fear and since the strange puckering effect finally disappeared, I lost my fear as well.

During the night we often passed burning woods, which made a spectacular sight in the dark. It was said that this was the best way to clear wooded land so that corn and cotton later could be planted on it. One time we landed on the left bank, where I saw ripe cotton for the first time. The bolls were just opening and the white emerging cotton seemed similar to a small snowball. Near the cotton were several buildings. One of them seemed to be a nice home. When I saw several people entering it I went in too, a little more carefully than before. I came into a couple of neat rooms and found in one of them a nice looking couple and a girl, presumably their daughter. Again I was surprised and was about to draw back. But the gentleman and everyone seemed so friendly, and even offered me a bottle containing a light, yellow liquid and a beautiful glass. I thought I understood him and, thinking it was wine, I poured myself a little. However it proved to be a kind of brandy, which I later learned was called whiskey, but which, fortunately, I never came to consider a good drink for temperate people, but one fit only for intemperate swine!

The weather was almost invariably dreary during the trip up river, and the sky was covered with threatening clouds. There was little that would have made this river trip pleasant, especially in such company. We were glad to learn that we had arrived at the mouth of the Ohio and that the greatest part of the distance to St. Louis lay behind us. We landed on the right bank of the mouth of the Ohio, near an unusable old steamboat. Only a few huts were still visible in the darkness. Adjoining these lay much swamp and mud, and this was Cairo, a place which was later destined to achieve great importance. After the necessary business was completed our extremely slow speedboat again turned its prow up the Mississippi. The river bank, especially on our right, was at first low, but later often became very steep and high. One might have been tempted to call them mountains had not we, living in Switzerland, become accustomed to using that term to designate entirely different elevations. Also on the left bank—the Missouri side of the river—there were more considerable elevations. The towns we passed were of little importance. Cape Girardeau may have been the most important town in Missouri, but back then it was insignificant enough. In this town I saw two young, very black American bears chained to a post, which was the most interesting thing found at that place. The only other interesting place I recall was on the Illinois side, not far below St. Louis, where we landed, which had only a few houses, and where the muck in the street was extremely deep.

Finally—this evening marked exactly ten days since we had left New Orleans—in the distance directly in front of us we caught sight of the end of our long journey, namely St. Louis. Naturally that again caused some excitement among us. Everyone again packed up his belongings. I certainly was glad finally to be getting away from the many disagreeable persons I had had to put up with. First I offered to sell my jug of vinegar cheaply. Many wanted it, but gave nothing for it. So it splashed into the river. Number two was my Le Havre food chest. "Who'll give me something for it?" "Give it to me! Give it to me!" was heard from several directions. "Who will give something for it?" But they wanted it for nothing. Splash! There it was swimming back toward New Orleans. Number three my mattress, covered on both sides with tar from the *Narragansett*. Otherwise I would have kept it. "Who'll give me something for it?" "Oh, what a pity," I heard. "Give it to me!" "No, give it to me!" from another direction. "Who'll give me something for it?" and saying that I made a motion toward the river. Mrs. Zobrist hurriedly bid "Five cents." "Give me the five cents!" I received it and Mrs. Zobrist got her mattress. This was the end of my auction. Two articles I had consigned to the Father of Waters for permitting me to ride upon his back. The net proceeds consisted of the munificent total sum of five cents, and thereby everything was well disposed of!

On our arrival in St. Louis we found a lively and thriving community, with much running hither and yon, shouting and complaining, a veritable chaos. The *Meridian*—that was the name of our boat—slow as it had been, had nonetheless brought all of us here safe and sound. Aebli looked around for a conveyance, and soon came back with a so-called drayman. We wanted to go to the main street to the Switzerland Boarding House, run by a certain Mrs. Werkmeister. The drayman said he knew where she lived and took our baggage there for twenty-five cents.

While Aebli had been looking for a drayman, many of the passengers had spruced themselves up. Among them I discovered Miss Bircher, looking much too refined to be called Baebi. At first I believed I was in the presence of a fine American lady. But, as she turned toward me, it was the Bircher girl. As I recognized my error she let out an especially gracious "Hee, hee, hee." But it was not only the better clothes she was wearing that set her apart. No, she was already speaking English to the many young dressed-up fellows who seemed to have come on board only to admire her and pay her all kinds of compliments. You could pick out her meltingly sweet voice every few seconds murmuring,

"Yes, No," and her even more frequent "Hee, hee, hee." What her poor cousin Frei, burning with jealousy, may have been thinking and going through only he alone could know, for it was easy to see that his cousin, idolized in this fashion, would soon end up being snatched from the steamboat by one of many attractive, well-dressed young gentlemen.

Having arrived at the Switzerland Boarding House [at 51 South Second Street] which we had been told was patronized mostly by Swiss from New Helvetia visiting St. Louis, we asked how we could find a way to reach our final destination, the paradise of New Helvetia. We were reassured that usually farmers came from there every day and that we would probably soon find an opportunity to get there. Our reference to paradise as the town of our destination, which was known actually as Highland,[25] caused a good many persons to shrug their shoulders a little as they stifled a smile.

On the fourth day two farmers finally arrived in a wagon drawn by two yoke of oxen. Both were Swiss; the older was a Mr. [Joseph] Buchmann, a man of about fifty, tall and well-built, with pleasant features, an enlightened, well-read man from Canton Lucerne; the other, Mr. [Johann] Iberg [from Kuettigen, Canton Aargau], father of many children, was rather tall, quiet, and as was proven later, a good, hard-working man. We were to be ready to go the next day. That was when they planned to begin the return journey to Highland. Since Highland was thirty miles east of St. Louis in the state of Illinois, two days were usually allowed with an ox-drawn vehicle.

Before I go on I must make some additional comments about St. Louis. It was the largest city on the Mississippi, with the possible exception of New Orleans. Daily steamboats headed up the river from St. Louis, either to Galena or sometimes to St. Peter's [Minnesota]; others steamed up the Missouri to Independence or to St. Joseph; larger ones to New Orleans, and others up the Ohio to Louisville, Cincinnati, and even Pittsburgh. It had a population at that time of between 25,000 and 30,000.[26] The older citizens, especially the city's founders, were French. Now the greater part were already Americans, with many Irish and Germans. There were already iron foundries, oil and grain mills, ropewalks, breweries, and hog slaughter houses. Leather goods such as saddles, trunks, harnesses, and various kinds of footwear, were produced. Steamboats were also built. English, German, and French newspapers were published. In short, St. Louis at that time was already the principal commercial and business center on the Mississippi. A short distance below St. Louis were the Arsenal and Jefferson Barracks. A little further was Carondolet, or Vide Poche, now incorporated into St. Louis.[27] St. Louis was, not only for Missouri, but also for a large part of Illinois the chief center of commerce, as well as for Iowa and those places accessible by river beyond.

3

Becoming More or Less American

20. Travel to Highland Where We Arrived on the Evening of the Second Day at the House of the Schneider Family

THE NEXT DAY BUCHMANN AND IBERG came to load up our baggage, that is Aebli's, Behler's, and mine. The wagon was so overloaded that it was not even remotely possible for a passenger to ride in it. It had become afternoon before we crossed the river by ferry to Illinoistown.[1] On the advice of our driver we had of course taken some provisions with us, for we were told that we would not be spending the night in an inn, but in the woods.

The road proved rather muddy, but was good enough as we proceeded through the so-called American Bottom[2] that stretches nine miles to the bluffs at Collinsville. The bottom consists of an extraordinarily rich alluvial soil, as is true of all Mississippi Valley bottom land. The greater part of the land at that time however was not under cultivation; only around Illinoistown did one see fenced and cultivated land.

Several miles west of the bluffs were a couple of small elevations, but there was also a large one. These were well known as the so-called Indian mounds. The whole bottom area is quite flat, except for these hills. Near these hills are depressions, perhaps the places from which the soil for the construction of the hills was taken. One of these hills is very high and broad in circumference, perhaps fifty feet or more in height, and may well cover several acres of land. On the top of the hill was a little house, and later I found it fenced in and planted with fruit trees.[3] The bottom was all open land here, with the exception of places where there were wooded streams.

Late in the afternoon we reached the bluff, at the very base of which was a spring, and near it a little farm house. The bluff here was high, and in my opinion it would have taken a good deal of effort for us to ascend it with the heavily laden wagon. The bluff seemed mostly to consist of pale yellow sand. Having reached the top of the bluff we found the area to be wooded, but we still came

Portions of South-
western Illinois and
Eastern Missouri
Relating to Lienhard's
Early Years in the
United States

across an occasional small farm. Here the soil was no longer sandy, but more like clay.

About two miles east of the bluffs we came to the small town, or rather the small village, of Collinsville. We stopped here no longer than was needed to water the oxen and to take on some water for our own use. We drove a short distance farther until we arrived at a thick stand of young trees. It was now evening. The sky had been overcast all day, and it looked like rain. The leaves in the woods were all dry, and most had fallen. There was no room for us to sleep in the wagon. If both Buchmann and Iberg hoped to sleep, there was only a little space for one in the wagon. The others, as did we, had to find space for the night outside. The oxen were tethered and had been fed. We had started a small fire by which we warmed ourselves a little. Our prospects for the night were not encouraging, for the ground was so damp that none of us would have wanted to lie on it. Then it also began to rain. We had no woolen blankets, nor was there any cover under which we could have protected ourselves from the rain. We had gotten out our umbrellas and cowered, sometimes here, sometimes there, as if forsaken by the entire world.

Old Buchmann told Iberg to hand out the jug of whiskey, which he did, after first taking a good swig for himself. Then Buchmann followed his example, and they handed it to us, saying "Here, take it. It's good for times like these." I was astounded that people in this country drank something like that, for I associated the name "wiski" only with whitewash,[4] and therefore felt that this could neither be good to drink, nor healthy. I soon learned that here whiskey does not refer to lime and water (whitewash), but rather to corn whiskey. For sure this was something different. Although I was not ordinarily a drinker of hard liquor, I thought that a little alcohol could do no harm in this unpleasant weather, so after my two traveling companions had taken their turn at the jug I followed suit.

Minnesota is the Indian name for firewater, or in German, simply *Schnaps* (spirits). Whiskey completely deserves this name, and the Indian who first uttered it was certainly no fool. The name was given to one of the states, probably because the gentlemen in Congress were for the most part very fond of firewater and considered it a worthy name for a large state.[5] This is not so long ago and proponents of cold water and firewater are yet at loggerheads with one another. Over thirty years have passed since that evening, and, although whiskey is regarded by many as their best friend, and by others as their worst enemy, for me it has been neither a friend nor an enemy.

It was a good thing that Buchmann, like us, also found his quarters for the night too uncomfortable to permit sleep. Like us he stayed awake. He told me how immigrants made their way to Oregon and California, taking five to six months, over plains and mountains with their oxen and mule-drawn vehicles;

how they outfitted themselves with provisions, tents, and weapons; how they met various Indian tribes; and about the buffalo, antelope, deer, etc. He said that for the past two or three years people had banded together in the spring in larger groups, and he told many other details about the mysterious regions. Thus I had not even arrived at the goal of my travels and I already was feeling a desire to perhaps risk the same kind of trip.

After it became day and we had eaten a little, we continued our journey on foot, the greater part through woods, occasionally interspersed with solitary homes and farms, until, nearing Troy, we came to the open prairie, where the earth alternated between yellow clay and deep black vegetative soil. This prairie was an arm of the excellent Looking Glass Prairie, known as one of the most fruitful in the entire state.[6] After walking through this area—still at that time partially open prairie—we arrived at Troy, a settlement of perhaps one to two hundred people. The road forked here, one way leading to the so-called Marine Settlement, the other, which we followed, leading toward Silver Creek and Highland.[7] As before, the greatest part was woodland, with farms at intervals; the road was more bad than good; the trees here were, with some exceptions, small, that is still young, until we finally came to the Silver Creek bottom land woods, where the soil was deep and black. Here we found a heavy growth of woods.

After passing these woods, through which Silver Creek flows, we again found ourselves in the open country making up Looking Glass Prairie. A short time later we stopped at the log cabin of a young German settler. Again, there was a light rain. We entered the house, and, as a matter of course, the whiskey jug was passed around, of which, by the way, I felt no desire to partake. This German was Joseph Mueller from Baden, his wife was a pretty girl from Bern, and he was the father of two daughters.

We did not stay long and soon were driving through another isolated stand of woods; then we found ourselves on the vast, undulating, rich Looking Glass Prairie. From here it was said to be another six English miles to Highland. To get there we would have had to set our course somewhat more to the left. Buchmann and Iberg lived one-and-a-half to two miles beyond Highland, near Sugar Creek. The closest route now led over a long high ridge stretching from Highland to the southeast, which the Koepfli gentlemen had named the Jura.[8] On the prairie we found a solitary little, newly built frame house, where a man from Canton Aargau called Leutwiler lived with his wife and sister.[9]

We had now come to a bend in the so-called Jura Ridge. A Berner family by the name of Gilomen lived here.[10] There we found a large peach orchard. From here Buchmann and Iberg pointed out their log cabins and to the northwest that of the Schneider family, next to a new, two-story frame house that was not yet finished.

We had now arrived at the house of our old, good-natured Buchmann, but he found his only son Wilhelm, a fine looking young man of about twenty-two, in bed in great pain from a broken leg. The bad news about this incident was brought to the old man in St. Louis on the very day we were preparing to leave for Highland. Wilhelm Buchmann, astride a spirited young horse, had wanted to take some steel scales somewhere or other. The jingling frightened the horse, throwing him and breaking his leg.

21. Short Stay at Schneider's — Going to Mollet's Where I Am Fed Three Times Daily for a Period of Nine Weeks Bad Cornbread, Oversalted Bacon, and Wheat Slop

Behler had already left us on the west side of the Jura to head for Highland. Aebli and I now set out on foot for Schneider's home, about two miles to the west, which we reached just before dark.[11] On our arrival at Schneider's farm we found Margaret Kundert outside the house. She recognized her cousin Jacob Aebli immediately; me she called Peter, for I had, of course, grown during the last six and a half years. Old Caspar Schneider also appeared. He had aged markedly, seemed pale, and had his head bandaged. Fridolin Kundert did not live in the house. It seemed to me as if his wife Margaret no longer really cared for him, which already had been the case earlier. Margaret indicated that, according to law, she could divorce him after seven years, for if a married couple lived apart for seven years this was sufficient grounds for divorce. She could not find anything bad to say about Kundert, as far as I know.

We were cordially received, and naturally we were asked many questions about old acquaintances and relatives in the old homeland. But we also had many questions to ask. It seemed that times back then were favorable for those who had a lot of money, because everything could be bought cheaply.

By the way, I have more to tell about the Schneider family. The eldest son, Caspar, lived with his wife and two children in a small new frame house, somewhat to the north of his father's house. The second son, Gallus, I learned, had married a poor but respectable German girl [Sophia Klug]. He had an established occupation and was a quite intelligent and good-natured man. But he was not a favorite of the rest of the family because he went his own way without allowing himself to be influenced by anyone. Balthasar was living at home and seemed to be on his way to becoming the leading male of the family. Fridolin, the youngest, likewise still lived at home, but he naturally had to toe the line. Kundert's children were also there. They were Magdalene and Heinrich, born in Switzerland, and a little boy three or four years old. The main person and guiding spirit seemed to me to be Margaret, still using the name Kundert but later planning to change her name to Schneider, which I believe she did.[12] During the two weeks I spent at Schneider's I found that the relationship of the Schneider and Kundert families had in general changed little.

One day I wanted to buy myself a fur cap. Margaret offered to come along because I would probably have to pay more if I went alone than if she were with me. We went to Highland the next day. I bought a winter cap for myself. Since I had no other purchases to make and since Highland could be explored in a quarter of an hour, I would have been ready to return immediately to the farm. Margaret, however, had a lot of visiting to do here and there, and it was not until evening was approaching, and I had asked her a number of times if we could not head home, that she was finally done, and as a result darkness had fallen by the time we arrived home. I had absolutely no idea that I had done anything wrong, but I found Balthasar acting very reserved and barely speaking to me. Of course I asked Aebli what Balthasar could have against me that he was suddenly so cool toward me. He laughed and said, "Probably it was because of you and Margaret not returning home until dark." So apparently it was nothing more than jealousy, and I determined to leave Schneider as soon as possible so that Balthasar would no longer have the slightest grounds for jealousy.

On the day after our arrival the Schneiders hauled our baggage from Buchmann's. Buchmann had sent a request through them that Aebli and I might be so kind as to help get his son Wilhelm to Highland where he would do better under the excellent care of his brother Anton and wife, and also be close to a doctor. I had seen Wilhelm only for a few minutes upon our arrival, but he had impressed me favorably. Aebli and I were glad to offer the requested assistance. Shortly after we arrived at Buchmann's several other men had gathered for the same purpose. Under a doctor's direction we placed Wilhelm on a featherbed, and carried him in this fashion to the home of Anton Buchmann in Highland where, with the best of care, he soon recovered completely! I visited young Buchmann often and grew very fond of him, for he was a handsome, friendly youth, and not dull.

While I was still at Schneider's I got to know a Swiss from Canton Solothurn by the name of [Michael] Mollet. He was, he said, a wagon maker by trade who also did carpentry on the side.[13] I had decided to leave Schneider's and was looking for other lodging, even if it meant working for only room, board, and laundry. At Schneider's, after all, I also had to work without pay. Mollet had married an American woman [Rebecca] and was the father of two handsome boys. He promised good accommodations and laundry and wages as soon as he felt I had earned them. He also spoke of how well one lived in America as compared to those back home. Of course I was very pleased about this excellent opportunity, for it would make it possible for me to learn carpentry, and probably English as well.

The house in which Mollet lived had two sections and was outfitted with jalousies. Only the two ground floor rooms had doors and windows. The upper floor was probably intended to have two rooms, but at this time was far from completed, for it had neither windows nor doors. It also was not plastered, and the winds, regardless of their direction, blew through it freely, almost totally unobstructed, especially from the west. My bed was here and it would have been clean and good enough had I had more and warmer bed covers. I learned during the first night that the covers were insufficient in such a drafty room, contrary to the paradise Koepfli promised. Fortunately I had a feather blanket of my own in my large trunk. I laid this over the other thin covers, and now the wind could blow through the room to its heart's content; thus I could now sleep.

Insofar as food was concerned, I had found it really very good at Schneider's and expected it, based upon the little he told me, to be at least as good at Mollet's. But I was soon to be persuaded of how very wrong I was. If one considers good food to be three meals a day consisting of very salty bacon, scorched to a crisp, corn bread prepared without salt or lard, served with bad wheat-coffee with a maximum of ten drops of milk which barely changed its pitch-black color, then I would hardly disagree. Despite my best efforts, it was not possible for me to decide whether the best part of the meal was the bone-dry bacon, the unsalted and unlarded cornbread, or the black wheat slop they called coffee. But Mollet really knew how it was done. He taught me to cut up the corn bread and pour gravy over it, which is what he called the grease that had been fried out of the bacon. This more than replaced any salt and lard lacking from the cornbread; and the dark, fried bacon was then crunched between the teeth as a side dish, which of course gave indescribable joy. To heighten the enjoyment of these splendid, delectable meals even more we washed the mush down our throats with slop grandly designated as "mocha"! When I add that such delicacies remained the same three times a day the whole week long, Sundays included, who would not have envied me?

Naturally Mollet, kind soul that he was, assumed that, having made available to me such a well-ventilated room and having provided me with such delightful meals, I should provide him with a little labor. My tasks started by getting up at the break of dawn, quickly chopping some wood, and then building a good fire in the room used for cooking and eating, where he, his wife, and children slept. Secondly, I was to bring in a bucket or two of water to his better half, for doing so put women in a better mood. Apparently he thought this would result in the bacon being burned even more thoroughly. And finally, probably in order that I would earn his special praise even more, I was to feed his horse, cow, and the several head of young livestock. Of course after that I was permitted to partake of the luxurious breakfast.

After breakfast we would go into the workshop where we labored all day. Looking out for my welfare, Mollet tried to keep me from becoming too fat by having me work for him until nine in the evening, whenever possible. But since I differed with him somewhat on this score, this did not entirely become the rule.

Thus the weeks passed by. I often had a bad taste in my mouth. Mollet frequently proclaimed how well one lived in America since people are fatter here than elsewhere. But I ventured to suggest that I preferred a little less fat and a slightly greater variety, and that I found the food I had enjoyed in the old country better and definitely more healthful.

One day I found that a number of young American girls had come to Mollet's to stitch a so-called quilt. Mrs. Mollet and other "ladies"[14] kept themselves very busy baking all kinds of pastry dishes (pies) and such. In the evening a good many young American youths arrived. One even had a fiddle (violin). The inner room (parlor) was cleared for dancing. In the other room a long table was set, abounding with all kinds of baked goods that literally made my mouth water, although I could find none of the daily scorched bacon or corn bread there. Even the coffee smelled totally different; or did my nose deceive me?

Several of the young men tried to talk with me, but I would have understood a flock of geese as easily. When I asked Mollet to explain what they were saying to me he made a face, and I soon got the impression that he was ashamed of me. But I must have been mistaken, for he gave me proof of his good intentions toward me by saying, before the food was served, "Heinrich, if you wish to go to bed, you'll find it made up." I would have had to have been thickheaded not to understand his good intentions, but I chose not to understand, deciding that there was time enough for that later, and that since I had helped him get rid of so much scorched bacon and cornbread, it was only right and proper that I also help dispose of a few of the delicacies. But I made sure to note that, if someone begrudging another such could spoil one's enjoyment of fine food, I would have had the worst of stomach cramps that night.

Following the refreshments, the mosquito dancing again commenced—or that is what these strange dances appeared to be. There were all kinds of games whose primary purpose seemed to give as much opportunity as possible for kissing. A Mr. [Garrett] Crownover[15] appeared to be leading the way in this activity. He was by far the oldest among those present and doubtless was the most experienced. Since I could not carry on a conversation intelligibly with anyone, I finally got bored. I especially wanted to while away some time at the Helvetia Hotel run by Durer, but everyone was just going to bed. I turned around and went back, only to find the same, boring to me, festivities in progress. Now I thought that the best thing for me to do was to go to bed, although I had little hope that I would be able to sleep, for the mosquito dance had begun again, and the fiddler was scraping on his instrument for dear life, and the steady muffled tum-tum-tum-tum beat of the dancing shoes was irritating enough to make one believe that perpetual motion had finally been invented and was in full swing here.

I finally retired to my well-ventilated room, and found the bed, of which the good Mollet had spoken, not made up, but rather was just as I had left it that morning. I lay down on it, but did not bother about getting undressed. There was no question of sleeping; the interminable tum-tum-tum-tum, accompanied by the screeching fiddle, drove away the slightest possibility of sleep. It was bright daylight when I heard the last guest say "Good morning," and that was also my signal to get up. There was no sign of leftovers from the previous evening's many delicacies. Instead something totally new appeared: bad cornbread, ditto the bacon, and black liquid manure. And this new fare was held to as rigidly as if a strict law prohibited any other.

I was certainly not fool enough to believe that Mollet and his better half restricted their food intake to the bacon, cornbread, and watered-down coffee served me regularly twenty-one times a week, for all too often I had caught them working their jaws when they thought I was not watching. Furthermore, I had never believed that all of the food remained from the quilting and dancing party had been thrown away.

Naturally I did not feel exactly fortunate to be in the paradise of New Helvetia in New Switzerland portrayed so glowingly by Salomon Koepfli, because up to now I had seen only the dark side, unless I wanted to regard the time when I smashed my half-paralyzed fingers working on the roof of Suppiger's mill during damp, cold weather as a sunny side, bathed in the glory emanating from Mollet.

For some time now I had been weighing a plan to look around for something better, for it seemed that my stomach was not at its best. I was not superstitious enough to believe the cause to be those sweets that had been begrudged me. On the contrary, I assigned much more of the blame to Mollet's highly prized cuisine—so laden with grease. One day I went over to Schneider's and took several kinds of medicine. Even so it was clear that medicine would do little to help if I continued on the same diet.

Ever since I had moved in with Mollet his wife had never once washed anything for me. I had six to eight shirts that badly needed laundering, and finally I dared to ask Mollet if his wife could wash them. This did not appear to be done very willingly, but it was done, although I certainly could not have bragged about the cleanliness of the shirts when they were finished.

22. Stay in Highland—Mollet's Shameless Conduct

Soon thereafter Mollet had a young man haul corn from the field where it still stood. The drayman was named John Johns, and he had a black medium-sized dog. The corn still stood in so-called shocks in Kaempfli's field,[16] from where we were to haul it. The northwest wind blew quite ferociously and, since I had no gloves, my fingers were very cold. We had hauled the greatest part of his fodder. As we returned to the field we found several hogs helping themselves to a little of one of the shocks. Thereupon Mollet set John's dog at them, and it turned out that the dog was well-suited to this purpose, for it had soon seized one of the pigs by an ear. But Mollet was not satisfied with this. He ran to the pig and kicked the poor animal until I feared he would kill it. I called to him to finally let the poor animal go. Instead he got the dog still more excited and again trampled upon the poor animal himself, causing the dog to go half-mad and to tear the pig's ear off, which was still in his mouth. At that, I called to him again to finally stop, but instead once more he egged the dog on, who then seized the other ear of the poor, bleeding, screaming pig. At that I jumped into the fray, intending to let Mollet experience a little pain. When he saw me coming he quit, but just when I thought I would be able to free the pig, the dog ripped off its other ear. When I returned to the wagon I made remarks which were not of a flattering nature. He had to endure being called "an abominable, low-down, animal torturer," and several other similar names. And I had decided that I would give him proper payment, too, if he tried to come back at me!

Mollet had responded more tamely than I had expected, and more quietly than I wanted at that moment. I called him a man devoid of all human feeling, and demanded that he lend me a pair of gloves if he wished me to help with any more feed hauling. He offered to give me a pair without fingers. I would soon tear up the new pair he had at home, and he was not willing to give up the ones he had on. "Good," I said. "In that case I will consider my hands too good to be ruined by your corn feed." We now had a full load on the wagon, and since it was getting late he decided it would be the last load of the day.

That evening I bought material for trousers and underpants, and, since Mollet often had bragged about his wife's sewing ability, I decided to test him. I asked him whether he would have his wife make these clothes for me. I believed I knew the reply in advance, and, although I still understood far too little English, I could easily tell by their facial expressions what the answer would be. And it was the response I expected; she did not trust herself to make clothes for someone else for fear they might not turn out right. That was just what I wanted. I thereupon took the material to Mrs. Buchmann in Highland, who was an experienced seamstress and not expensive.

The next morning, when it was time to get up, I was in no hurry to do so. Mollet probably believed that I was sleeping especially soundly that day. Although I heard him get up and make an extraordinary amount of noise with his wood-soled shoes, I just stayed in bed. He was particularly noisy today, and while chopping wood, a task he had completely left to me during the nine weeks I had been with him, he also made more noise than seemed necessary. And I knew the noise was intended to wake me, but I was determined to let him do his own work for a change. He fetched water, but I continued to lie comfortably in bed. He was going to feed his cattle and, to ensure that I was now awakened, he came tramping loudly up several steps of the stairway, and then loudly stamped his feet there a few more times, while watching my face. But I had my eyes almost completely closed, although they were sufficiently open to observe. I pretended, however, to be sleeping peacefully. Thereupon he stamped again, but nothing was effective today. I do not know whether or not he suspected my intention, but he finally left. And as soon as I believed he had left the house, I jumped out of bed, packed all of my belongings in my trunk, shouldered my rifle, went downstairs, said "Good morning" to Mrs. Mollet, and left the house.

Across from Mollet's house lived a man from Bern named [John] Zimmermann.[17] I had learned that he took in boarders, when he could get them. I went to see him, asking if it would be possible to board with him if I behaved myself and paid promptly, to which he readily agreed. Zimmermann was no longer very young, but was still quite robust. If I am not mistaken this was his second wife. Her eldest son may have been about twelve years old. There were, however, as far as I remember, two younger ones as well. Another inhabitant of the room, besides the wife and children, was a goat, whose bleating, combined with the children's racket, made for quite a concert. But there was something else the goat and children had in common. There were a great many bean-like droppings all over the floor. They were definitely not coffee beans. I believe they were called sheep beans. Though not belonging to a genus of beings that spontaneously produce such beans, the children sought, in cooperation with the goat, to decorate the room and create a "confiture" by adding certain liquids of their own, thereby increasing the already noticeable pungent odor.

Breakfast had just been prepared when I discovered the aforementioned floor decorations cooperatively provided by the children and the goat. Breakfast consisted, as I remember, of fried eggs, butter, bread and coffee. I really should have dug right in, but I felt that my appetite had already been taken care of by the combination of decorations and odors. When breakfast had been successfully survived and the table was cleared, I sat down on the decorated settle, lost in a variety of thoughts. Zimmermann, after all, was Swiss, and why should he not have had a decorated settle? Since, coincidentally, there was no sign of fragrant liquid or of other forms of decoration upon it, I sat down on it, letting the northwest wind blow at will outside.

It was at least an hour past Mollet's usual breakfast time when he came over to borrow a fork from Zimmermann, and, since he just happened to notice me, the good man said, "Heinrich, come and eat. It is ready." I told him that I could well believe it, but that I already had had more than enough.

After breakfast Zimmermann wanted to go about four miles west into the woods to a tannery run by a Frenchman. He invited me to go along, and since I was convinced that if I stayed in the room until noon the strong perfume would permeate my being to such an extent that I would not even know myself, I was ready to accept his friendly invitation. When we returned at noon we found fewer decorations, but still more than necessary. Having survived the meal, I paid, thanked my host, shouldered my rifle, and strode out onto the streets of the town of New Helvetia.

Before I continue I have a few more comments about Mollet; I could say— that is I could write—a great deal more about him. I had been at his place only a few days when he told me about a Johannes Blattner,[18] according to him about my age, whose parents lived to the west of Sugar Creek, Blattner spent much of his time praying with a Methodist family from Bavaria, even though his parents tried their best to discourage him. It seemed to me that Mollet took the young Johannes's side, and, since I had no prior knowledge of Methodism, he was very willing to give me all kinds of information about it. It also seemed to me that he himself had a desire to become a Methodist. We were not in agreement about young Blattner, for I believed he should have listened to his parents rather than to strangers, whose language he might not even properly understand. Since I later learned from Mollet that the family with whom Blattner spent so much time, instead of staying at home and helping his parents, had several daughters who were beyond their childhood years, I began to have serious doubts about the genuineness of the young man's piety.

Mollet however seemed to think that I would certainly change my mind if I would participate in several Methodist gatherings. He also told me how people wishing to become Methodists prayed so fervently that they often appeared to go raving mad, leaping to their feet, falling down, screaming, laughing, crying, and, in short, conducting themselves, when they had accepted the Holy Spirit, just like the disciples in the temple at Jerusalem when the Holy Spirit entered them at Pentecost. From what he told me, I did not get a good impression of Methodism. Nonetheless, I let myself be persuaded to plan to attend the next meeting, which was to be the following Sunday evening. Sunday evening came. But I had left several belongings at Schneider's, which I first had to pick up before I joined the meeting. Mollet, with wife and children, had gone immediately after supper. The meeting was being held in the schoolhouse, in which direction I headed as soon as I had put my belongings in the room that had been assigned to me. The schoolhouse windows may have been four feet above the ground. They were only, I believe, on the west and east sides. As soon as I neared the schoolhouse I could hear loud, dissonant singing, but at the same time, from another side of the building, I at first believed I could hear preaching. Before entering I wanted to look in to see whether I could find anyone I knew. I first looked in from the west side and there I could see a number of people earnestly engaged in singing. Naturally I could not understand the words. As for the melody, however, I cannot say that I found it pleasing. It was a very monotonous, as it seemed to me, unharmonious melody, with most of the singers repulsively screeching, reminding me very much of several people with long wood saws busily sawing wooden blocks in unison.

Through the window I soon discovered another group on the far side of the room; several men were resting their heads on their arms on a table around which some women were sitting. Another was screaming into their ears. Naturally I could not tell whether he was preaching, praying, or scolding them, but it seemed the latter, for the men were moaning as if they were suffering from the colic. The entire scene made a repugnant impression upon me. I could not understand how such singing and carrying-on could be pleasing to our Creator. I felt an antipathy toward this heathenish conduct and could not accept that such behavior, lamenting and screaming, should please Our Heavenly Father. I thought, "I will not go in there," and was about to retreat, when Salomon Koepfli and a Mr. Fischer came out of the schoolhouse. I asked them whether persons other than Methodists were in the building, to which they answered in the affirmative, and they invited me to come in also. In the north end of the room I found about a third of those present not taking an active part in the religious activities. They were only spectators, and I joined them.

The dissonant singing was followed by a sudden silence. Now a woman of about forty entered, knelt down and, as I was told, began to pray, and she kept at it so long, so loudly, and so fervently that she literally foamed at the mouth; finally she stopped, apparently from sheer exhaustion. But her place was now taken by a pretty, slender girl of about eighteen, well-dressed, with hat and veil. The poor girl knelt down, prayed, wept, and rolled around on the floor. Two or three young fellows screamed right into her ears like madmen, at the same time clapping their hands as hard as they could. I felt as if I had stumbled into an assembly of demented persons and began to believe that they would drive the girl out of her senses. I confess that, if I had had the courage, the two or three clapping bellowers would have received a punishment from me that ultimately would have knocked their barbarous yelling from their heads.

What I saw on this evening had filled me with abhorrence and disgust, and I was shocked that Mollet had represented this kind of religious meeting as especially beneficial. I thought to myself that this kind of religious activity was really offensive. "Thou shalt not give offense, and it were better to have a millstone tied about thy neck and be sunk into the deepest sea. Woe unto him who gives offense!" On the way home I sought out Mollet and told him that this had been a scandal and that these events I had witnessed on that evening were nothing short of detestable. The following day Gallus Schneider came by and we discussed Methodism with Mollet at such length that he finally ended the discussion. He said, "You are two against one."

That evening remained so fresh in my memory, and disgust had been so deeply driven into me that it just seems to have happened yesterday. I confess that it was sufficient for a lifetime. Later I learned that Mollet had actually become a Methodist. But since he was fond of brandy, and the drinking of spirits was not permitted by the Methodists, he later left them. I do not know whether or not Mollet is still alive, but if I am not mistaken, neither his wife nor the two boys of that time are living.[19] He was not known either as a good husband or as a good father.

23. How Inexperienced Youths Were Taken Advantage of in Highland—I Go to Leder's Family on the Rigi

I now feel obliged to present a small example of how they often tried to put young people to work here. I believe that I had scarcely been living in the area four weeks when I was called upon to perform road work.[20] Towards Pocahontas, on the prairie, about four miles northwest of Highland, a new bridge was to be built. A man named Durer, who ran the Helvetia Hotel, was supervisor of roads. Squire Joseph Suppiger was on the job as well, and among others there was a little man named Jacob Schuetz. I was handed a large, two-inch drill and was expected to get busy drilling, without being allowed an occasional rest. I felt that being called upon to do this kind of work so soon after my arrival in the area was somewhat presumptuous and premature. The fact that I was expected to work without being allowed to rest seemed to me to be unreasonable. Durer had apparently believed that he, Mr. Supervisor Durer, could take advantage of me. I had drilled a good many holes when I began to tire, so I rested a few times. Durer, who set his own work schedule to suit himself, made it a habit to tell me to get to work each time I tried to take a little rest. Several times I let him get away with it, but, since I found that he seemed to have selected me as his particular target, I took the liberty of telling him that, if he did not feel I was working hard enough, I would quit entirely, and that I had accomplished more than he himself had and as much as anyone else present; that it seemed to me very presumptuous to demand that persons who owned no land and had just barely arrived should have to labor on the roads.

Of course Mister Supervisor of Roads had not expected such an answer from a young greenhorn, and he became very angry over my remarks. Squire Suppiger also felt compelled to take the side of his friend Durer, and said some things that were not especially flattering. I was almost at the point of throwing away the big drill, and I suggested to the dissatisfied gentlemen that they themselves try working with the drill to show how long they could last without resting. This they did not feel obliged to do, and that made the two of them still angrier.

The little man, who had been listening quietly until now got up, and I thought that he also was going to attack me. But I hardly dared believe my ears when I heard him say that it was downright unreasonable to demand that just because I was a fit young man I could work continuously without being allowed a little rest after having drilled holes in the oak with a two-inch drill. He suggested that they try it themselves sometime; they would soon find out whether or not they would need to rest. These few words from the plain farmer, Jacob Schuetz, had a remarkably calming effect on the two over-bearing gentlemen, Squire Suppiger and Helvetia Hotel Innkeeper Durer, for they immediately stopped their grumbling, and afterward did not have a single complaint about my work. As for me, I could have embraced Schuetz and kissed him because he was the only one with the courage to tell the two over-bearing gentlemen the truth. Naturally this man found a warm place in my heart. But at the time I had no inkling that I was to come to regard him with even greater affection and respect.

I had quickly become convinced that Koepfli had portrayed the Highland area as too much of a paradise. Also, the letters written by Schneider's family encouraged one to expect everything to be much better than it turned out to be. There was enough food, but very little money was in circulation. Produce had little value. Eggs brought three to four cents a dozen, butter four to five cents, pork two to three cents a pound; good cows could be bought for seven to nine dollars a head. Farmers paid five to seven dollars a month for hired men, seldom more, and often were hard put to raise even this paltry wage. I had too little money to start a farm of my own, and, had I had enough, I would still have been too inexperienced to be successful. In addition, I found myself very disillusioned, for, after all I had read about the region I had expected much better conditions.

While at Mollet's I became acquainted with a genial young man named Bernhard Suppiger[21] who was training to become a blacksmith under a man from Hannover named [John] Lang. In addition to him, I came to know another young man by the name of Jacob Leder, whose father was known as Rigi Leder because his farm, south of Highland, was at the northern slope of a beautiful large hill, which bore a slight similarity to the Rigi,[22] after which it had been named by the Koepflis.

The Koepflis were land speculators who owned much federal land,[23] and needed people on it to make it valuable. This made it necessary for them to publish their pamphlets. Naturally they had to provide, especially for the Swiss, warm reminders of their old homeland, such as the Jura and Rigi mountains, and everything also had to be embellished and described as a veritable paradise.

One must admit that the Koepflis knew how to describe, or actually glorify the area. They achieved their purpose, luring settlers and selling their federal land, but of course not at the federal price of $1.25 an acre. That could hardly have been expected of land speculators. All in all the Koepflis were quite obliging. If a beloved countryman did not have enough money to pay cash for the land, they gave him time, charging ten percent interest[24] on the balance. And new arrivals who had money considered it a special honor to be driven around the beautiful farms by the Messrs. Koepfli in their chaise and have them describe the advantages of particular parcels of land. And since, after all, they could have time to pay, and they were told in detail what a short time it would take them to pay off the balance, what good, credulous Swiss souls could have had any further doubts? It was all perfectly clear. Everyone must surely understand, for the esteemed Messrs. Koepfli certainly would not have advised their countrymen thus if matters had not just been as they said!

At that time there was still plenty of fine federal land that anyone could buy for $1.25 per acre. One would have thought that reasonable men would have purchased such rather than pay the Koepflis double, triple, four-fold, and five-fold as much for similar land and thereby plunge themselves into debt. Back then the bilious fever and ague [malaria] were almost as certain as day and night. Newcomers could be assured that they would be stricken and, once infected, entire families suffered dreadfully, so that even the most necessary work was sometimes left undone. Quite a few persons died of the malady, and others suffered from it for months. Under those conditions it was particularly difficult and distressing for families that had become heavily indebted and who, following severe illness, could neither pay interest nor scarcely provide for the necessities.

But again the Messrs. Koepfli found a way to help, for the old gentleman and one of the brothers were physicians, and it was understandable that when people were ill they needed a doctor. However, if the people had no cash, that could be settled later. It was not uncommon, though, for this debilitating fever to afflict the same person for several consecutive years. What then? The Messrs. Koepfli believed themselves entirely justified, and so they were according to the law, to demand payment of the interest and the outstanding principal for medical services, etc., and so the debt continually multiplied. He who had once been blinded by flattery and fine words, sat sick, depressed, and impoverished, waiting to be driven from the paradise of his dreams; and along with wife and children, with no money and diminished physical strength, he was forced to find the means to continue his life. Similar sufferings were experienced by many in the paradise of New Helvetia in New Switzerland. Since I had neither land nor family at that time, matters were not so bad for me in this respect, although I suffered enough from the fever, as you will learn.

I now return to the moment when, coming from the noon meal at Zimmermann's, I stepped out onto the road. At first I hardly knew what to do, but I decided to look for another temporary job, for the housekeeping at Zimmermann's was not exactly to my taste, and I felt that I definitely could not spend a night there. As I wandered about aimlessly, I saw a boy riding toward me who immediately called out to me in his child's voice. Since this voice sounded familiar, I looked at the apparent child more closely and found to my surprise that it was no lad, but my former traveling companion, little Fricker.

"Where are you going?" I asked him, to which he replied, "To Leder's on the Rigi. Don't you want to come along?" Although I had never cared much for Fricker's company, I was nevertheless ready to go along, that is, I on foot and he riding. As we headed in the direction of the Rigi he told me he had bought a farm on Sugar Creek. "I have had this horse only a short time, but it seems to understand no German. I can hardly make it move forward. If only I knew what to say to make a horse go." Although I also did not know much English as yet, I did know that one had to say "Get up!" or "Go along!" to horses if one wanted them to go, and this I shared with the little man. He chose "Go along!" as the easier, and he soon was convinced that his horse actually understood it, for it already seemed to be moving more quickly. In any event, he crowed out "Go along!" often enough until we arrived at Leder's house.

24. My Stay at Mr. Leder's — I Go to Work for Jacob Schuetz

Having arrived there we found only a little boy named Anton Abeck[25] who told us that the Leder family was threshing in the northwest corner of the farm. We went in that direction and found them. In Switzerland I had often helped thresh with a flail. The method of threshing, as I encountered it here, was new to me. I found my young friend Jacob Leder and his sister Susanne on horseback, riding around upon the spread-out wheat, usually at a moderate trot, and I thought that this method of threshing could not be very difficult. Jacob was immediately willing to let me take his place, leaping from his horse and, if I thought it was so much fun, inviting me to try it. I did not wait to be asked a second time, but had already laid aside my rifle and mounted the horse. Now I rode behind the little but fairly good rider, Susanne, and found that I was enjoying it. It was a lot of fun. Of course I had to be careful not to tumble off. I soon learned that one could do a substantial amount of threshing fairly easily in half a day with two horses, and I concluded that this method was an improvement upon flail threshing.

As evening fell I prepared to return to Highland, but the entire Leder family told me that, since I did not want to return to Mollet's anyway, I should remain with them. Jacob had told me earlier, "If you don't like it at Mollet's, you can come here any time and work for us as much as you like, and as for the food I think you'll find it better than at Mollet's." It took me only a moment to make up my mind. I stayed. Jacob's view that I would find the food with them better than at Mollet's was correct. Cornbread was not served often. Instead there was good, genuine wheat bread. Rather than scorched bacon we had good pork chops, coffee with milk, cooked dried peaches, eggs, and butter. In short, the food was good and sufficient.

I slept in the same bed as Jacob, getting up in the morning when he did and helping him feed the horses, etc. Of course I was given work, for I did not want to be a sponger, because I would have been ashamed to accept anyone's board and room unless I knew that I had really earned it by the sweat of my brow. I was treated so well that I soon felt at home, and evenings were often quite entertaining. Since old Mr. Leder was a good clarinet and trumpet player, we even tried dancing once, with me in the role of instructor. While I could certainly see that they were pleased to see me working as though I were earning a wage, they definitely did not make me feel, as Mollet had, that they were only trying to exploit me.

One day old Mr. Leder said to Jacob, "You're my only son, and yet you don't try to beautify the place by planting trees." But Jacob had no interest in doing so, although in general he was an industrious and good-natured youth. Since we happened to be talking about planting trees, I offered to try to graft tree stock onto the so-called crab apple trees, if he furnished the grafting stock. Father Leder immediately agreed, and shortly thereafter the grafting stock I had asked for arrived. I grafted them to young wild apple trees, which I transplanted into the garden and banked with earth, so that a few buds of the twigs were covered. I had planted all of them in a corner of the new garden, and then I had the pleasure of watching them all thrive.

But one time, one Sunday, when I came to visit the Leders, I found all of them apparently cut off, some high up, and others close to the ground. This made me angry, so I went into the house to ask who could have done such a stupid thing. But no one would admit to having done it, and I was told that wild rabbits must have been the culprits, of which I became convinced only after they had shown me their footprints and droppings. Since those trees were grafted, in the year 1844, thirty years have passed. A few years ago, during a visit, father Leder showed me several of those that had survived. They had become beautiful tall trees, and I was glad that I could consider myself, at least in part, their author. But I also felt some sadness looking at them. I was reminded that everything in this world comes into being and fades away; how an unimportant seed or bud, be it man, animal or plant, in a relatively short time achieves maturity, exists, and then gradually declines, dies, and finally is practically forgotten, as if it had never existed.

One time Mr. Leder wanted to get boards from a sawmill on the so-called Shoal Creek,[26] about fourteen miles northwest of his farm. For this purpose he took his two wagons. Of course Jacob also had to go along, and I went also. We took the shortest route over the Jura to Sugar Creek and its woods. Then we came to Shoal Creek Prairie,[27] a beautiful, undulating, and treeless landscape, with deep, rich soil. This prairie stretched from the northwest to the southeast, and was ten English miles wide. At that time there were only solitary, scattered settlements near the wooded areas, seldom in the middle of the prairie, and generally they were situated on particularly beautiful rises. Most of the land still awaited the plow, and the greatest portion was still federal land that could be purchased for $1.25 an acre. Anyone visiting that prairie today would find thriving farms with neat homes, orchards, and fields. Back then, standing in the center of the prairie, we could barely see woods bordering it on both sides, and it almost seemed to me as though we had chanced upon the open ocean. The woods along Shoal Creek still contained magnificent hardwoods, among which the black walnut was one of the most prominent. Similarly the area was not lacking back then in wildlife; in the woods there were many deer, and turkey were very plentiful.

The sawmill owner was a Berner. But we stayed no longer than was required to load the boards, and it was already getting dark as we crossed Sugar Creek and reached the edge of the woods on the southwest bank. It was uphill from the creek to the woods. Since the load was heavy and the ground somewhat soft, in addition to the horses being tired, we got stuck at the steepest spot. As we attempted to urge the horses to pull, one of them reared high into the air, very nearly breaking my leg. It only grazed me, but caused me considerable pain. The elder Leder was a little ahead of our wagon, and having searched in vain for him, so that he could hitch his team to ours to help pull our wagon up the incline, we found his wagon, but he and his horses had disappeared. Jacob decided to leave our wagon there also and come back for it the next day when the horses were rested.

It was four miles from here to Leder's home by the shortest route over the Jura. Without removing the horses' harnesses, Jacob mounted one of them and told me to do the same. Then he rode off at a brisk trot. Naturally my horse tried to stay right beside or directly behind his. Since I had seldom been on horseback before then, and the ride was over uneven ground, I soon found the rapid pace uncomfortable, and quickly became very sore, and it was all I could do to keep from being thrown, since I was not then a very good rider. Finally we arrived home, worn out and hungry; the elder Mr. Leder had already arrived sometime earlier. He reproached his son, and I could not be entirely certain whether some of his comments were meant for me as well.

The next day, when we rode back to get the wagons with their load of boards, we took the road through Highland and passed the farm of an American named [Seneca] Gale. Gale may have been fifty years old, had an attractive, healthy appearance, was of medium height, and was fairly stockily built. He of course spoke English with Jacob, of which I could understand very little. Because he, as well as Jacob, kept glancing at me as they spoke, I believed that their conversation concerned me, a fact which Jacob confirmed after I had asked him about it. After we left Mr. Gale, Jacob told me that Mr. Gale, a well-educated man who had formerly taught school, wanted to hire a newly arrived immigrant who would work for low wages. As partial pay, he was willing to give the worker instruction in English. The idea appealed to me, and I inquired more about the man. What Jacob told me, namely that Mr. Gale was a strict taskmaster and probably would be referring to me soon as a "God-damned Dutchman," was enough to immediately banish any interest in the position with Mr. Gale that I might have had. As I was to learn later, I discovered that this man was much better than he had been described to me.

Along with Jacob, I had gotten my clothes one evening from Mollet's, who, since he was convinced that I had no desire to serve him any longer as a kind of slave, was not especially friendly. I had now been at Leder's for more than two months, and, although I was satisfied with them, my good sense told me that I could not go on this way. Up to then, as had my friends, I had occasionally visited the taverns on Sundays, and also had attended a few dances, all of which took money, of which I had as yet earned none. Whenever I removed one of my twenty-franc pieces, with some guilt, from the money belt I always kept on me, it made me feel like a spendthrift, although I certainly was not one. In addition, I realized that I could not survive for long this way, and, that, as much as I hated having to take such a step, I should look for a paying job, for I knew that it was not prudent to wait until all of my twenty-franc pieces had been used up.

The Leders told me of two farms looking for workers. The first was that of two brothers by the name of Ambuehl from Canton Graubuenden, hard-working but hard-driving farmers who owned a lot of land and paid good wages for that time, but who also worked until all hours of the night. The other was already favorably known to me, Jacob Schuetz, the man who had taken my part during the bridge construction episode, getting the self-important Durer and his friend Squire Suppiger so quickly and effectively to hold their tongues. Schuetz, so I was told, did not pay much money, but he treated a good worker more like a son than as a hired man, and since the designation "hired man" impressed me unfavorably, and since I had a lot to learn about farming, namely handling horses, plowing, etc., I immediately decided to ask at Schuetz's first.

On a bleak Sunday afternoon in March, Jacob Leder and I made our way to the Waldecke, or so-called Ruef farm[28] where Schuetz was then living. When we arrived Schuetz was in the midst of discussing something with another man. We held back for quite awhile waiting for the discussion to end. Since it did not appear to be drawing to a close, my friend suggested that I ask Schuetz about a job. I could not bring myself to do it, for I felt it demeaning, and I persuaded him to ask Schuetz for me. My friend did as I wanted, and Schuetz replied that he would soon be finished with the man he was talking to, and would then speak with me afterwards. We may have waited another half hour for the conversation to end and, when he showed no sign of finishing, I began to feel that if Schuetz really wanted to hire me he had plenty of time to say so. Feeling like a beggar, I was weary of waiting any longer. My friend, who understood my feelings, tried to reassure me that the conversation would end soon. I felt, though, that Schuetz had had plenty of time to let me know whether he had any intention of hiring me. We started to walk away in the direction of Highland, and had gone several hundred steps when we heard Schuetz call to us, and when we turned he was waving to us. When we had come back Schuetz' first words were that he had thought that I was looking to work for him, which I confirmed. "Then why are you leaving so soon?" "Because I felt that if you really wanted to hire me you had plenty of time to say so." At that he looked at me in amazement. He told me to return the following Wednesday, by which time he would have discussed the matter with his wife. I believed, though, that it was more likely that he wanted time to make inquiries about me.

25. My Stay with Good Old Jacob Schuetz

On the specified Wednesday I reported to Schuetz before noon. He asked me how much I knew about farm work and finally told me I could begin on the fifteenth of March, but that he could not pay me more than $4.50 the first month. If he found that he could use me he would pay me $5 a month after that. I had worked without wages up to now and knew how much had been expected of me. How much more would be asked of me if I worked for pay? This question weighed on my mind for some time, and although the pay that had been offered was small for the time, I was quite anxious about my upcoming employment.

On the evening of March fourteenth my friend drove me and my belongings to Jacob Schuetz's. As I sat on the wagon I was overcome with the feeling that I was going directly into slavery, and I felt very degraded. Early in the morning of March fifteenth, while it was still quite dark, I woke up. Fearing that I had overslept, I leaped out of bed to get dressed. Schuetz did not sleep with his wife, but in the same room in which I slept. My leaping awakened him, and he asked me what I expected to do so early. I replied that I was going to feed the livestock and the horses. Schuetz simply laughed and told me to go back to bed; sunrise would be early enough to get up. I would have been able to sleep for fully two more hours after that, but I was afraid that he would get up and begin working, while I might oversleep. Therefore I preferred to remain awake. But I soon became accustomed to waking quite regularly at sunrise and I cannot recall that Schuetz ever needed to wake me.

Schuetz's livestock consisted of a team of very good workhorses, some foals, six to eight milk cows, some young cattle, quite a few hogs, a large number of chickens, geese, etc. Milking the cows was easy for me since I already knew how, and, since I soon learned how to feed the horses and pigs, I encountered little difficulty in satisfying Schuetz. After breakfast on the first day I had to chop off corn stalks in the field; several days later I chopped a little firewood and eventually hauled it home. Everything seemed to satisfy Schuetz, and that meant much to me. The food was good and always plentiful; a bottle of whiskey, smoked meat, and bread were available at any time of the day if I desired them. In a short time I felt very much at home. There was no longer any thought of the abasement I had dreaded.

Soon after my arrival at Schuetz's — it was still March — there was an overnight snowfall of several inches. The following morning Schuetz told me that I could take my gun and go hunting, for there might be wild turkeys. At first I could not believe that I had heard correctly, but Schuetz added that there really was not anything else that could be accomplished. Since I realized that this was Schuetz's wish, I was naturally glad to get started, for what young man does not enjoy hunting?

I headed into the woods and was soon lucky enough to find the fresh tracks of a turkey, which I followed for some time, until I suddenly lost them. Down to the left was Silver Creek. I went that way until I lost sight of the turkey's trail. On its opposite bank I heard the repeated barking of a hunting dog. If only I could take something home with me, even if it was not a turkey; as long as I did not have to return empty handed, that was my objective. I crossed Silver Creek with the help of some driftwood that had collected, and, as though guided by fate, turned downstream. But I had gone only a short distance when an animal suddenly sprang from the bank of the creek toward some nearby brush, but stopped barely twenty-five steps from me, apparently quite surprised by my unexpected appearance. If the animal was surprised, I was possibly even more so. It was without question a deer, but it had no horns. I was in no danger, for of course it was not a predatory animal, but I had to shoot the stag (or doe, or whatever it was). I took aim, but in my eagerness I was so excited that I could simply not hold my gun steady. But I was certainly a fairly good shot. Why should I not be able to shoot this deer which was so quietly presenting its side to me? I tried to breathe calmly, aimed and aimed again, but my excitement would not subside, and, when I felt that the deer was losing patience with my strange behavior, I pulled the trigger and missed! The report of my gun had somewhat frightened the animal. It took a few graceful leaps, stood still, repeated the leaps; then standing still again, looked toward me again and again. Several moments passed in this way while I anxiously busied myself with reloading my gun. Now all that remained was to cap the charge, but at that very moment the deer had disappeared into brush. I can hardly tell how I felt. I do know that I suddenly came to have a poor opinion of my marksmanship.

Now I went back, and a short distance upstream I saw several ducks on a little island. But thinking they were of the smallest kind I decided not to shoot at them. Near this spot I saw a red squirrel sitting in a tree. I aimed at it and shot, and, as expected, it fell to the ground dead, for my hand had become so steady that I was able to hit this tiny animal high up in the tree without missing, though I had just missed a beautiful deer only twenty-five steps away on level ground.

I had no sooner fired the shot when my attention was drawn to a chorus of quacking from the departing ducks, which, to my disgust, turned out to be five or six beautiful large green necks [mallards], not the small ducks I had taken them for. Discouraged, I set out for home, and was soon back on the right path. It was one o'clock when I finally got home. Jacob Schuetz was about to come looking for me because he feared I might have become lost in the woods. I told of my bad luck, which gave him a good laugh. He put my gun on his shoulder, determined to try shooting something himself. "Go and eat your noon meal," he said. "After that you can go hunting again and you can take a couple dogs with you if you wish."

I soon finished my meal and headed back to Silver Creek. But this time I walked through some fairly open country known as Hudson's Prairie. This was the shortest route to the creek, about two miles away. Here the creek made a sharp bend, turning from a southerly direction to the west. There was a swift current here, and the water was muddy and seemed deep. Here the trunk of a one-and-a-half-foot thick sycamore tree had fallen across the creek, serving as a kind of bridge. It was very slippery, but I crossed it easily. Since my dogs were not really trained for hunting, I soon began to feel that it would have been better if they had not come along, for they paid no attention to my commands, but rather rushed ahead upstream, frightening away everything on the water before I could come close enough to shoot.

I had followed the creek upstream about a half mile to a point where it took a sharp turn from the west when I suddenly heard the dogs begin barking and saw that they were eagerly tracking something upstream along the right bank. Naturally I did not remain rooted to the spot, but ran as fast as my legs would carry me to see what the dogs were actually chasing. I suddenly saw a young deer trying to outrun the dogs. But one of them was close behind it while the other one cut off the escape on the high bank. Since the creek took another ninety degree turn to the north at this point, the poor young animal was forced to jump into the creek. But the dogs did the same, and I saw that they quickly caught up with the deer. Finally one of them seized it from behind, and then the other immediately seized it by an ear. The efforts of the little animal to free itself were in vain, and it began to cry out pitifully. Gasping for breath, I had finally reached the high bank next to most of the swimming animals. I tried to shoot, but again I was too excited. I was also sorry for the poor little animal.

But my eagerness finally to shoot a deer drove out all thoughts of pity, and since the dogs had just given me an opportunity for a clean shot at the animal's left breast, I shot it, whereupon the poor thing immediately gave up its life, for I had hit it in the heart. I now tried to induce the dogs to pull the young deer to the bank. But they did not understand me, and the young animal remained lying in a shallow place more than halfway across the creek.

Lying near the spot was the broken-off top of an oak tree. But although I tried with all my might, I could not budge it. I intended to make a sort of bridge from it. Therefore I used several big branches for this purpose. But the structure to which I now entrusted my body was of questionable construction. I had carefully made my way across the branches, and had almost reached the middle of the creek when the entire structure gave way, and I found myself about four feet deep in the cold rushing stream. Since I was wet anyway, I tore loose the remaining branches so that they could float away, seized the dead animal by its long ears, and dragged it toward the right bank. I had quite a time getting up the steep bank, but finally managed it.

The animal was a year-old male deer, and it was covered with wood ticks. But after brief reflection I tied its four legs together, and bearing it on my shoulders, I headed toward the spot where the sycamore lay across the creek. While crossing on this tree I feared at every step that I might plunge into the water. But I finally reached the opposite bank and rested a moment on a large tree stump. Despite the unpleasant sensation of the cold water in my boots and clothes, I was so overjoyed at having today shot a deer after all, even if it was a small one, that I carried it the two miles home without resting a single time. This was my first deer hunt, and, as far as I can remember, I have shot but one other since then, and that was in California. Although I often went hunting after that, the game I bagged usually consisted of only a few ducks, muskrats, squirrels, wild rabbits, and the like. So it turned out that my first day of hunting had been the most successful.

The weather had turned delightful with April, so all of the farmers began to plow. As I had long since cut off all the cornstalks and chopped them into pieces, Schuetz also decided one day to start plowing. He said he would show me how it was done, and then, as soon as he felt I was able, I would plow alone. On a beautiful April morning we went to the lower end of the field. Since the horses were plowing for the first time this year, I had to lead them the entire length of the eighty-rod wide field several times. But after only the third round Schuetz told me to hold the plow while he led the horses. I had never plowed before, and, since the cornstalks that had been chopped into three or four pieces kept getting in my way, the work did not turn out very well. I assumed that Schuetz would take at least until noon to teach me to plow. How surprised I was when, after my guiding the plow for two rounds, he announced that I would now be able to carry on by myself. I was completely taken aback at his declaration and wanted to tell him that I was not nearly ready. But he left without a word, leaving me behind with the horses and plow. At first I almost felt like running away. But after reflecting a bit to the effect that I surely could learn what, by my reckoning, stupider fellows than I had already learned, I determined to at least give it a try. I guided the horses as best as I could, and of course it did not go very well because I felt that I could not keep my eyes on both the plow and the horses at the same time. Moreover, the plow was constantly being forced up out of the furrow by the masses of cornstalks. It was some mess, for the tangled cornstalks mixed with the soil, and the plow was often down into the earth up to its handle, or in the next moment rose completely above ground, while the furrows — if they even deserved the name — veered sometimes right, sometimes left.

Completely covered with sweat, I finally finished the first round, and I almost believed that I could detect some slight improvement. The second round followed, and now I was convinced it was going better. With every round the furrows became better, and with every improvement my zeal increased and my feeling of inadequacy shrank. And even before the horn called me to the noonday meal I had concluded that I could probably plow as well as almost anyone, and plowing had almost become a pleasure, rather than hard labor. When Schuetz asked, I told him about my morning experiences, whereupon he laughed heartily, saying that he had known very well that I would soon be able to do the work alone if left to myself.

The month of April was very pleasant and agreeable, and I, plowing with my two excellent horses, felt as happy as only a young person with a clear conscience and full of hope for the future could feel. I competed with the larks of the field in singing and whistling, all the while plowing joyfully. Even the horses seemed to share my mood. All Nature was filled with joyous activity. The plowed area grew quickly, and I could show my work to anyone without being ashamed of it.

One noon Schuetz told me that it would be better not to work the horses so hard, that they needed at least an hour's longer rest, and that I need not go back to work until two or three o'clock, etc. I asked him what I should do during the time when the horses were resting. Whereupon he again laughed and replied that I could do whatever I liked, read, sleep, or whatever appealed to me, and that working was the only thing I did not need to do during that time. Plowing two acres a day was enough for a man and two horses; he asked no more. I naturally abided by these new rules without debate, and, since the Ambuehl brothers had loaned me some short stories by [Johann Heinrich Daniel] Zschokke, the midday hours flew by like brief seconds. I also often used the evening for reading, as long as daylight allowed after the evening meal.

During the winter, especially while I was still a recipient of Mollet's hospitality, including the salty, scorched bacon and the unsalted cornbread without fat, washed down three times a day with that black, terrible tasting wheat slop that passed for coffee, I had come close to leaving New Helvetia in New Switzerland, so highly praised by the Messrs. Koepfli. I would return to Le Havre de Grâce, staying there until I had learned the French language, while waiting for a favorable opportunity to go to Brazil. These warm spring days, with their choruses of singing birds returned from the South, echoing above field and woods, combined with the entirely different treatment I now enjoyed, had driven all such thoughts from me, and I was determined to stay in America for at least a couple of years.

I should have described earlier in somewhat more detail Jacob Schuetz and his family. Since I have neglected to do so, I shall do it here. Schuetz was of a bit less than medium height. The openness of his facial features reflected his whole character. He may have been fifty-two to fifty-four years old.[29] His face was furrowed by wrinkles that gave him a serious appearance. He wore his beard fairly full and he had a head of thick, somewhat curly hair, in which there were some gray hairs. He was known as quite a good farmer and kind to his animals, which he fed well and treated with care, so that his horses, cattle, and pigs were generally among the best in the area.

He was quite experienced in treating horses and cattle, and had acquired significant knowledge thereof, so that he was often called away from his own pressing work to save some other farmer's animal from dying. He never turned down the request of a neighbor or acquaintance, and always helped if help was still possible. Unfortunately few showed appreciation for such emergency services, so that he told me more than once that he was glad to help his friends and neighbors if only they would at least remember that he had laid out his own money for the medicines he used, and that they should try to repay him.

Schuetz was a man of upright character. He despised bearers of falsehoods, swindlers, userers, arrogant and deceitful persons generally. He was glad to help the poor and needy as much as his circumstances permitted, and anyone who was treated badly or unjustly by another person could count on finding a defender in Schuetz.

26. Schuetz's Unpleasant Experience at the Beginning of His Marriage — Helping Out at Ambuehls'

At the time I first knew him, Schuetz had been married only three or four years to a widow, who, like himself, was from Canton Bern.[30] Her name was Maria, and at the time Schuetz married her she had a six- to eight-year-old son from an earlier marriage. Before he married her Schuetz had bought an eighty-acre farm where the little village of St. Jacob is now, as well as sixty acres of good timber near Silver Creek, paying for it largely with money he had earned himself.[31] But when I came to work for him he had rented this farm to an American and he and a [Moritz] Huegi family from Canton Lucerne lived in two separate houses on a farm belonging to a Mr. Ruef, about a mile west of Highland.

Since his wife, Maria, was close to forty years of age, and moreover the daughter of a farmer, Schuetz believed he had founded a happy home for his old age. But although he had achieved his purpose in some respects, he was soon to make a bitter and unpleasant discovery, which was to upset him for many years, and which he probably found hard to forget as long as he lived, although this unexpected calamity did finally turn out to his advantage.

His young stepson, Fritz, was a half-idiot boy, half-wild, and afraid of people. Jacob was unable to do much with him. He hid whenever he wished to talk with him and watched him with the distrust of a half-wild animal which comes near only when it considers itself unobserved, but quickly disappears as soon as it fears one might approach it. Later, in California, I suddenly often came upon Indians who rarely had contact with whites and observed a similar timid, distrustful look that reminded me of Fritz, especially among the women and children. Maria, instead of trying to increase the boy's trust in her husband, apparently had far too little insight to attempt to do so, and it soon came to be an almost daily occurrence that when Schuetz came upon the timid boy, talking in a half-whisper with his mother, he would immediately flee and hide somewhere as soon as he noticed Schuetz nearby. Schuetz kept hoping that this would change with time, but the opposite happened. He realized that all his efforts to turn the boy into a useful human being were in vain, and with that he lost the joy and hope he had originally had for the boy.

Schuetz had not known that his wife had been engaged to another man, a Hannoverian in poor circumstances. He thought that she was free. But after only a few months his wife could no longer conceal the consequence of her intimacy with the Hannoverian, and about four or five months after the wedding she gave birth to a little girl. As can be easily imagined, Schuetz was not at all pleased regarding the disgrace and deception that had been perpetrated upon him. At first he found it almost inconceivable that his honest, docile-appearing wife was capable of such cunning deceit and betrayal, but the naked truth was undeniable. Under ordinary circumstances a clear-thinking and considerate man, Schuetz was outraged over the disgraceful thing that had been done to him, and his first impulse was to drive his deceitful wife and her brood out of his home immediately. However, his wife solemnly declared that she had been promised to the Hannoverian and that she had been planning to marry him, but that her own father had advised and ordered her to send the poor Hannoverian packing and to choose the well-to-do compatriot instead, even though she had told him about her condition. He had said that even if Schuetz initially became angry he would not cast her out, and that he would eventually accept her. Such advice from a father to his daughter was indicative of a person who valued money and security above honor and a good name.

Schuetz finally took pity on this woman, who was now so miserable. He did not drive her away as he had intended in his first flush of anger. He let himself be moved by her very real tears and her entreaties. She was allowed to stay, but she really could no longer regard herself as his wife. The innocent little daughter had to be removed from the vicinity, and Schuetz lived under one roof with his wife for many years—in some respects divorced from one another. Mrs. Schuetz was in every other way an industrious, quiet, peaceable person who performed her household duties faithfully, giving her husband no cause for dissatisfaction in this respect. I even believe that Schuetz often felt sorry for her and appeared instead to blame her father much more than her, and to regard him as the principal offender, and I cannot remember ever seeing the father-in-law in Schuetz's home.

About three years had passed since the innocent little Maria had been brought into the world and had been given to a Low-German[32] family that lived in a little log house near where St. Jacob is now. In March 1844, good Jacob Schuetz happened to ride past the small cabin where the little Maria lived. There he saw the lively little thing at play. He spoke to her, and the child, who was not bashful, responded in a friendly manner, which apparently pleased the old man greatly. Schuetz took pity on the friendly, innocent, little child. He decided to take her into his home, and he soon turned resolve into action; as a result, the child came to live there on the very day before the one on which Jacob Leder and I had asked Schuetz about my employment. We found the child almost constantly at the side of old Schuetz, who was barely able to answer her many questions. But he looked happy, laughed often, and was obviously pleased to have finally found a child. It was almost as if the little girl wanted to make good the wrong her mother had done Schuetz. She was always there, ready to be of help to her fatherly benefactor, and she showed not the slightest shyness or fear of strangers or horses or cattle; thus the sight of this lively little thing was particularly suited to brighten the countenance of father Schuetz. Schuetz was always drawn to people who were not easily frightened, especially in the handling of horses and cattle.

He himself was not the kind of man who could be intimidated by domestic animals. He proved this one day by capturing a large boar that had become wild. Chased by our dogs, the boar tried to flee into the same hazel bushes where Schuetz happened to be. He seized the boar and held it until the dogs got hold of it, and some men rushing up to help were able to tie it up. As testimony of his fearlessness in this battle, Schuetz came away with a three-inch-long wound on his shin made by the boar's huge fangs, a wound that did not entirely heal for almost three months.

His total lack of fear around horses eventually cost him his life many years later, in his seventy-sixth year, May 9, 1865,[33] when disregarding all warnings and his neighbors' offers to help, he tried to break in two spirited young horses all by himself. The fiery animals had barely been hitched up when he jumped on the front of the wagon, which had no seat, whereupon the horses immediately tore off with the wagon and crashed it against a cherry tree with such terrible force that both the poor old man's legs were broken. During the amputation of one of his legs, which was being done by three doctors, he had not been given enough chloroform. He said, "Don't murder me so abominably. Hurry up and cut off the limb, or bring me a hatchet and I will chop it off myself." Soon after that the limb was amputated, but, as the final stitch completing the operation was put in place, the last spark of life deserted that courageous man.

In the month of May, in the year 1844, the weather became very rainy. The Mississippi rose to a level that had never been known and has not since been equaled. The entire so-called American Bottom stood under water, up to the bluffs. Only the so-called Indian mounds rose above the surface of the vast expanse of water, and people, animals, and even wildlife sought refuge there. Many people and animals went to their deaths in the flood waters, and the water caused a tremendous amount of damage. In numerous newly planted corn fields the seeds rotted in the ground, forcing farmers to replant, often two or three times.[34]

Jacob Schuetz was always ready to help friends whenever he could, and although our own field work had been hindered by the recurring rains, thereby putting more work on us, nevertheless one day he said to me, "Heinrich, my friends, the Ambuehls, have fallen way behind in their field work because of all the rain. They have to plant a thirty-acre field for the second time. Will you help them for two or three days?" I answered that if he wished me to I would do as he ordered. Jacob said that he was not ordering me to do so, that it was solely up to me, and that it would not be done for pay, but rather out of friendship. "If you want to go," he said, "you may take Bub—the name of the better of his horses—and you can help them out for two or three days." Since I saw that it was what he wanted, I was ready to provide the needed help the following day. To get to Ambuehls' farm I had to travel at least some four miles, mainly through woods and brush.

I got off to a good start, so it was still early when I arrived at the Ambuehl farm. We immediately got to work, the two Ambuehls and I, each with a horse and plow, laying out the thirty-acre field in furrows that crossed the old furrows at four-foot intervals. I had laid out a field before, and I no longer feared that I would be unable to learn how it was done. Moreover, I had an excellent horse. Paul Ambuehl was my teacher. He showed me how to set my plow guides, and, like his brother Nikolaus, plowed beautiful, straight rows. Despite my best efforts, several of my first furrows were not as straight as those of the Ambuehls'. But I was able to plow a fairly acceptable furrow. Although I was allowed little time to keep up, I did not want to fall behind the others. Furrow after furrow was plowed, almost as though we were in a competition, so that by evening the thirty acres were ready to be planted.

The next day Paul and I did the covering while several children laid the seed corn in the places where the furrows crossed one another. Paul walked in front of me with his hoe, covering a carefully placed seed with each stroke. Of course I did not want to be left behind by little stooped Paul—being the much larger, heftier, and stronger fellow—and I kept up with him, but I confess that it became very difficult. I was already feeling the effects by noon. As evening fell, by which time, according to Paul, he and I had covered about twelve acres of kernels, I slowly began to think that, if I were to work like this one more day with those two small stooped fellows, I would probably be as bent and stooped as they by the next evening. Whenever I tried to relieve my aching back by straightening up, it would cost me a good deal of effort, as well as considerable pain. The food was ample and good, but by the evening of the second day I was so exhausted that I lay awake, due to my aching back and limbs. If I ever prayed fervently, it happened that night, praying that it might rain the next day; for had it not rained, my pride would not have permitted me to return home without finishing the third day as well.

But I finally fell asleep. I do not know how long I had slept, for I was suddenly awakened—and what was that? I heard a loud noise, and sure enough it was a downpour that made field work out of the question, and although I was in a sense sorry, I was ever so thankful, for now I could return home without embarrassment. But I would never have wanted to work at Ambuehls permanently! On the ride home I was soon soaked by the wet leaves of the bushes and trees. But having arrived I was able to change into dry clothes, and soon all was right with the world again.

27. How Schuetz Buys a Claybank Mare and Finally Trades Her—The Trouble That We and Others Had with Her

One day Schuetz brought home a claybank mare, so-called because of its yellowish color.[35] This mare may have been five to six years old, was well-proportioned and appeared quite spirited. Jacob may have thought that he had made a good buy because of her low price, but we still had something to learn about the animal! Since I now had almost the sole care of the horses, I also had to take care of the Claybank, which is what he had named her. The next day Claybank was harnessed next to Bub in order to do some plowing. In general she did not pull badly going forward, but when I had to turn at the end of each row she soon showed her true disposition. No matter how careful I was, Claybank managed at almost every turn to step out of the traces with one or both hind feet, and then she kicked out to the rear so quickly with both feet that it was dangerous for me to approach her in order to loosen the traces, put the mare into her proper position, and then reposition the traces. In order to avoid her hitting me while I replaced the traces, I got as low to the ground as possible, but even then her hooves often came so close to my head that I could feel the air movement caused by her kicking. Several times her hooves actually grazed my hair. Not satisfied with mere kicking, she often squirted my eyes full as if she also wished to blind me. All the patience in the world could not have controlled her. She was determined to make herself as objectionable as possible. She was virtually a devil disguised as a horse! I told Jacob several times that he would probably find me lying dead in the field with a smashed head some day. But he only laughed, for it was his view that a man should be able to handle any horse, provided that he knew how.

The reins we used for guiding the horses were very worn, and I mentioned this to him more than once. He felt, however, that they were strong enough. One day he asked me to get a wagon load of corn as rent from the tenant on his farm six miles away. The initial stretch of road, a short distance south of his house, led slightly downhill. Since heavy rains had made the road uneven by creating several small ruts, the old wagon bed made quite a clatter as I drove along. This racket did not particularly frighten Bub, but Claybank, suddenly, wildly, threw herself into the harness and repeatedly kicked out violently to the rear. At the foot of the grade I had to make a sharp turn to the left through a gate, and since I was unable to hold the horses as firmly as I would have preferred—because of the worn rein—I was afraid I would hit one or the other side of the gate. But I managed to get through it successfully and soon reached the open prairie.

Calling "whoa!" had no effect on Claybank. She did her best to act as wild as possible. The wagon seat had broken beneath me, and I was sitting in the wagon bed, but since the prairie was quite flat at this point, I decided to let the horses tire themselves a bit rather than risking breaking the reins by keeping a firm hold. But now the mare's bridle threatened to come off, and that would have made any idea of ever getting her to stop out of the question. After the horses had been racing along for a mile or so, I thought I detected a slight slackening of the wild pace, and I called "whoa!" a few times very loudly. This time Claybank suddenly obeyed, but she was shivering all over and snorting like a little steamboat, while the other horse, Bub, was relatively quiet and seemed almost unaware of the threat of a runaway. After I had straightened out Claybank's bridle, I drove in the direction of Jacob's farm at present day St. Jacob, where I filled the wagon bed with corn, and eventually we arrived back home without further incident. Jacob, who had watched as I drove away from the house, had had no idea that I would be able to return without some damage to the horses, harness, or wagon. But when I was able to report that nothing was missing, he was overjoyed, and he praised the way I had handled myself. I told him again that if the reins had been reliable I would have been able to stop the horses much sooner. But he insisted again that they were strong enough, and, since I saw that he was not going to be convinced otherwise, I considered it useless to belabor the point, thinking that time would after all be the best teacher.

Soon after this incident Jacob wanted to get one of his hams from his brother-in-law, Schmied's[36] in Highland, where he had them smoked. It was a cloudy day, with rain threatening. Claybank had not behaved badly that day until we came to the gate and were going up the bumpy lane approaching the house, where the wagon rattled a bit as we passed over the washed out spots in the lane. At this point she suddenly struck out behind her, threw herself into the harness, and showed just exactly how devilish she could be. This was a good opportunity to show Jacob whether he or I was right. So I drew in the reins firmly, for we were now close to the house entrance. It only took a few seconds for the right rein to break, and since, as usual, no amount of calling had any effect as she madly tore off, I had only the left rein to control her. Then the shaft broke, although it was of excellent wood, and continued to hang together by several fibers. The mare came to a halt on the left side of the wagon, facing backward, and I was able to grasp her nose with my left hand and her left ear with the right. Holding her in this manner, I shook her head for some time, not too gently, and soon had her almost completely under my control, for she stopped struggling and blood ran out of her nose where I was grasping it. Jacob had got hold of an ox tail, and after we had unharnessed her, he beat her with it until she was completely covered with sweat and foam, and with this he believed he had thoroughly driven the devil out of her.

The next day Jacob brought a good new rein home from Highland, and I was determined to show Claybank that I was now her master. We had the new reins only a short time when we had an opportunity to see the difference between a good and a bad harness. We were driving together through a flat wheat field, and there was really nothing there to frighten a horse. But suddenly Claybank took it into her head, just as a diversion, to display some of her deviltry. But this time she miscalculated badly, for, after one terrific backward thrust, she got her right hind leg caught in the traces and fell on her back, from where she tried every means to get back on her feet, but I held her back and let her struggle in vain. Jacob had to laugh heartily, for he had come to realize that Claybank was a worse than ordinary animal. But he was far from convinced that he would not be able to gain complete mastery over her. After the mare had fruitlessly tired herself out on the ground, we let her stand up again, and for the rest of the day she was really cured, for she made no further attempts of that kind.

But the mare had displayed her nasty qualities not solely in pulling a plow or wagon, but also when under saddle, and especially in the morning when I tried to harness her. She refused to let herself be caught. She threw herself into the fence and kicked as hard as she could with her hind legs when she was approached. Next to the big yard was a little one in which the cows were milked.

It was connected to the large one by a little rail gate. As I had long since realized that it was useless to try to catch Claybank in the large yard, I drove her into the smaller one, which afforded her no room to escape. But here she would strike out so quickly at me, to both front and rear, when I approached her with a halter that it was really dangerous to get close to her. But since it was my job to harness her I had to find a way to become her master.

I went to the nearby woods and cut three long, thin hickory switches, and beat her fairly hard. But at first this did little good. Later she let me get closer to her after a good beating, but she turned quick as a flash and kicked at me, or struck at me with her forelegs. Sometimes she did not miss me by much, but I paid her back with the hickory switch every time. Finally, after many attempts, I got her to the point where, as soon as I came after her with the halter and called her by name, she would stand still. After she had convinced herself that escape was not possible, she quietly allowed me to harness her, for the hickory switches had clearly driven some respect into her.

She created similar difficulties for me when I first attempted to ride her. She threw me every time I mounted her. However I did not give in, but instead tried over and over again, and then by clamping my legs to her sides, holding on to her mane with the left hand, and grasping the reins in the other, I managed to get the better of her. But I rarely trusted her, always holding her carefully in check, and as long as she felt I had control she did not try to throw me.

One time — it was toward dusk — we had been in the field, and Jacob was riding Bub, and he told me to ride Claybank. I had been unwell the entire day and had been intending to walk. But I mounted her. We had come quite near the yard, Jacob preceding me. I had been holding the reins loosely. I had no idea that Claybank might throw me. Suddenly she kicked and I hit the ground so hard that it at first knocked the breath out of me. Gasping for air I leapt to my feet. Claybank, as though enjoying having played a malicious trick, turned to look back at me, and then quickly trotted off after the other horses. All of this had happened so fast and quietly that Jacob was not at all aware of it until he dismounted and saw me following on foot. He remarked, "I thought you were riding the mare." But I told him how it happened that I was on foot.

When the corn was big enough to cultivate I plowed day in and day out with Bub and came to think of this horse as a halfway sensible creature. I really became fond of him, and it seemed to me that he understood when I spoke to him.

One fine morning Jacob suddenly appeared in the field with Claybank and a cultivator. We were close to the top of the field, near the apple orchard. He had pieced together the remnants of the old rotten harness. "Surely you're not going to cultivate corn with Claybank?" I called to him. "That is just what I am going to do," he replied! In response to my observation that he would have no success with this animal and this rotten harness, he responded that he had never seen a horse he could not master. But I was of the opinion that perhaps Claybank was that horse, whereupon Jacob actually became angry. "Tie up Bub and come lead the mare back and forth a few furrows for me. Then everything will be all right." I immediately carried out this request, and, as long as I led her by the bridle, she went along fairly well. "You can go now," Jacob said. "I can manage." And I went, but I had hardly reached my horse when I heard him yelling loudly, "whoa! whoa!" and when I turned I saw that one of the reins had broken and that Claybank was galloping around in circles, with Jacob holding the remaining piece of rein in one hand, while holding the cultivator in the other, trying desperately to prevent her from wounding herself. I was quickly back in front of the animal and called to her with the already familiar "whoa, Claybank!" whereupon she suddenly came to a quiet halt before me, just as she had when I approached her in the yard with a halter.

Jacob was not the sort of man to easily give up on something he had set his mind to. He knotted the torn ends of the rein together, and again I led Claybank up and down several rows, all the while Claybank performing quite satisfactorily. "Now you can leave again; it is going well," Schuetz suggested; although I was of a different opinion, I did not comment. But this time I had not reached my horse and cultivator when I noticed that something had already gone wrong again. I saw Claybank, just as before, running around in circles as if she were trying deliberately to ruin as much of the succulent, three-foot-high corn as possible, and I believe she actually did ruin almost a quarter acre of it.

Just as before, she stood still when I came near and called to her. "Do you want to try it with her again? Hasn't she ruined enough corn?" Schuetz was wild, but he no longer wanted to work with her. "I will trade the beast as soon as I can!" was his answer this time, and was I glad! He traded her a short time later for a young, black mare with a foal. The previous owner of the black mare believed he had driven a good bargain, but she soon almost succeeded in costing him his life. I need only note that the mare had four different owners after us within the space of one month.

28. Schuetz's Horse Bub Seems to Possess Understanding— How Stepson Fritz Behaved and Angered the Good-Natured Schuetz

Since a large part of the area was at that time still open prairie, one generally allowed horses to run free during the night, just like cattle. As a result it often happened that I had to search the next day for the horses for miles about on the prairie. As a rule I was soaked through to well above my knees. I did not change my clothes after I got back, but simply let them dry on my body. One can easily see how good this was for my health.

More than once I found our horses beyond Highland, near Sugar Creek, almost four miles from our house. I usually took a halter or bridle with me. But since I could usually ride and guide Bub without a bridle—for the intelligent animal seemed to fully understand my intent—I often went without bridle or halter. And if I was really wet, walking on the road felt better than riding.

One morning I had again found our horses a mile beyond Highland and was about to drive them through the village toward our farm when Claybank suddenly took it upon herself, probably to annoy me, to turn around and gallop back, in spite of my attempts to head her off. She paid not the slightest attention to my calls. She shook her mane as if in sheer exuberance, and to anger me more. I could easily see that I would have a hard time getting her home, but Bub, who came to know my intent completely, quite unexpectedly came to my aide. Claybank was not yet very far away when, to my shock, he dashed after her. But imagine my surprise when I saw that he was not running away to prolong his freedom, but ran after Claybank at a dead run, and, with ears laid back, bit and struck out at her. In short, he forced her to come back, and did not allow her to run off again. Is not that more than mere instinct? It seemed to me proof of a fair amount of understanding. Bub knew they were supposed to go home. He saw and understood that I could not catch up with Claybank. So he did it for me, and he did it without being asked—an act of friendship for me!

But occasionally Bub also seemed inclined to enjoy having a little fun at my expense, which again appeared to me more than mere instinct. One time I had again located the horses beyond Highland, and, without the aid of either bridle or halter, mounted Bub and serenely ridden toward the farm. In Highland, as I was passing by a livestock enclosure, I suddenly noticed that Bub was carrying me away from the other horses toward the enclosure, and without the slightest hesitation was proceeding through the small wooden gate. The opening would have been almost too narrow to permit passage of both horse and rider. I placed my feet on the fence at each side of the opening and let him walk out from under me into the enclosure. He looked back at me from within the enclosure as if to see what I would do now. I climbed down from the fence and led him out of the yard by his long mane, back close to the other horses, climbed onto his back, preparing to move on again. But my Bub paid no attention to what I was telling him, and, when I tried to guide him with my hands, he turned back to the yard with me aboard and repeated his prank. Of course I did not remain on the fence for long, but brought him back out again, and led him back by his mane for a short distance, driving the other horses ahead of me. Finally I got up on his back, and then headed home, without any further tricks.

Another time, if I remember correctly it was a Sunday, our horses were grazing in a meadow ordinarily only used for young calves. Bub did not seem even to notice that I was approaching him, and without speaking to him, as I usually did, I grabbed his mane, and with a mighty leap flung myself over his back, landing on the ground on the other side. For Bub this was totally unexpected. Startled, he turned quickly and planted a solid kick from his rear hoof just a little to the left of my stomach. By coincidence I happened to have my left arm partly over this part of my body so that it took a bit more of the blow than my stomach. But for a short time the breath was knocked out of me, and I writhed about wildly on the ground in terrible pain, gasping for air. I thought I was done for. But I finally got my breath back, and although I ached for some time afterward it soon enough got better. Bub had turned around and had probably recognized me as I lay writhing on the ground. He did not resume his grazing until I got to my feet again. When I approached him later he edged away. He probably feared that he would be punished. But the whole thing had been my fault, and I had no intention of punishing him. Only after quite a bit of coaxing did he permit me to catch him. Then I mounted him, and he carried me up into the meadow where I let him go again.

As my probationary month with Jacob had ended, and he'd uttered not a syllable as to whether or not I was to stay, I finally asked him whether he thought he would be willing to pay me five dollars a month. He laughed loudly and said he did believe that I deserved it. With that I knew I had a job for at least the summer and, although the pay was little enough, I was nonetheless satisfied, for I felt very much at home with Schuetz. Schuetz had told me that I need not worry about feeding and milking the cows on Sunday evenings, for he assumed that I would not want to leave the company of my friends in Highland. I was glad to take advantage of this privilege now and then, for I naturally spent most of my time in Highland on Sunday, generally in the company of young people, wherever there were tales to be told and laughter to be shared.

One Sunday Jacob set out with his wife and children to pay a visit to his brother-in-law, Joseph Mueller, a short distance west of present-day St. Jacob. Since it was a good six miles away, I thought that it might well be late before he got back home. Although Jacob did not say anything to me, I considered it my duty to feed the livestock and milk the cows that evening, since I assumed it might be late before Schuetz and his family could get back. I had already milked most of the cows when Schuetz suddenly came back. Seeing me at home and busy feeding and milking, he laughed, saying that he had not realized I would be coming home to do the feeding. Had he known that he would have stayed a few hours longer, etc. But he obviously was pleased to find that his animals would have received their customary care, even though he had been away.

At corn plowing time it rained a good deal, and it was not always enjoyable because the ground was often almost too wet for plowing, and the plow threw the earth up quite high. As a result uncovering the buried seedlings took a good deal of effort. Schuetz told Fritz to follow me to help uncover the buried corn. But I often had trouble with this strange and also lazy boy.

Fritz was not only lazy, but had his own peculiar quirks, and at times was especially determined to annoy me. If there was buried corn that he could plainly see, but which he ignored and failed to uncover, and I called his attention to it, he asked, "What did you say?" with his incessant, long drawn out and repeated, "Hee, hee, hee, hees." I tried to control my anger as much as I could, but his constant, "Hee, hee, hee, hee, what did you say?" finally got to be too much, and since politeness seemed useless, I thought it was finally time to talk to him seriously. "Fritz," I said, "Stop your continual foolishness and do your work properly or I will deal with you more directly." But Fritz was beyond redemption. He may have even gotten worse. So I finally seized him by his long ears, lifted him into the air, and shook him less than gently. Then I ordered him to get to work if he did not want me to provide that kind of persuasion again.

Fritz momentarily appeared transformed. He stopped his "Hee, hee, hees" completely and began doing a much better job of clearing the soil from the corn. But I had to go through the same exercise with him twice more, not during plowing but at milking time. Fritz was supposed to let each cow's calf join its mother as soon as I was ready to begin milking the next one. Instead, he seated himself like a monkey on the tall rail fence and, neglecting his part of the work completely, he practiced his "Hee, hee, hee." He told me, "I want to put on my monkey act again," (because at one time I had told him, "Fritz, be sensible and quit acting like a monkey."). I warned him at length and threatened to tell Schuetz. But this only made him behave worse, until I reached the end of my patience, seized him by the ears, and gave him a good shaking. Fritz screeched like cats fighting. However, I refused to quit until he promised to behave. After this Fritz was a fairly good boy for quite some time, and I believed that I had him under control.

But one evening, as I went to milk the cows, and it was time for him to do his chores, Fritz suddenly declared, as he again seated himself on the fence, "Now you may not touch me. I will do my monkeyshines as much as I like." And he pointed to the porch where Schuetz and his wife happened to be. "You see, Father and Mother are both there, and you cannot touch me anymore." And he immediately resumed his endless laughing "hee, hee, hee." Completely disregarding my advice that he quit his foolishness and get down to doing his work, he seemed determined to act even sillier than ever before. I decided to risk losing my job rather than allow myself to be tormented like this at every milking by this half-idiot. And although I could plainly see the old folks on the porch, I seized Fritz by his ears again, and this time I shook him especially hard, with him letting out howls in tempo with my shaking. When I let him go I told him to go and complain to his father and mother. But Fritz preferred to get on with his work, and from then on he conducted himself fairly well toward me. Schuetz seemed not to have seen or heard anything. But Fritz's mother was quite cool to me for several days.

When I told Schuetz about the affair in detail he seemed satisfied and laughed agreeably. But he said, "If I had done that my wife would not have spoken to me for a long time, but she is half-afraid of you, so it is a good thing that you gave a little direction to that good-for-nothing boy."

Jacob had often tried to make the strange Fritz into a useful human being, but he seemed to completely misconstrue the intentions of his stepfather and benefactor. Just as before, he remained the strange, timid, half-wild boy who only dared to give the old man sidelong glances and would have much rather hidden from him entirely had that been possible. The old woman simply did not have sufficient insight, and so she failed to convince the stupid boy to develop a trusting relationship with the upright old man. She and Fritz usually spoke to each other softly, almost furtively, whenever she believed Schuetz might be near, and then quickly separated, as though startled to find themselves observed, which always angered the good old man.

I will give here only one more example concerning Fritz and Mrs. Schuetz. In the spring of 1845 Schuetz had left the farm he rented from Mr. Ruef near Highland and moved to his own farm six miles to the southwest, where St. Jacob is now. Not long afterward I had gone there also, because I considered my home to be wherever Schuetz might live. Schuetz had an iron-gray, three-year-old colt, an extremely gentle animal with which one could do whatever one wanted. Since Fritz was a slender lad, almost thirteen years old, Jacob wished to have him learn to ride, so that, if it ever became necessary, he could send him off on horseback. One day he told Fritz to get up on the gray colt in order to get some riding practice. But Fritz resisted this order as if mad with fear, and struggled ferociously. Even the old lady chimed in fearfully at this unreasonable demand. Most annoyed at this foolish fear and obstinance, Schuetz lifted the struggling and pitifully weeping Fritz onto the back of the calm colt, put the bridle reins in his hands, told him to sit tight and urge the animal to move forward. The colt made not the slightest effort to unseat the boy as it moved forward at a moderate pace. Screaming frightfully, Fritz threw his arms around the colt's neck and back, crying repeatedly, "I am going to die, I am going to die!" The old woman now, through her tears, reproached Schuetz, saying, "If he is hurt and dies, it will be your fault!" "Now I have had enough," Schuetz said. "I have finally become convinced that all of my attempts to make a decent man of Fritz are in vain. My wife, like her son, is too foolish to recognize my good intentions regarding this boy. I will make no more attempts to help him, but he also cannot expect ever to get anything from me."[37] But Fritz had gradually come to trust me. I succeeded in getting him to comb his almost white hair daily and I awakened in him an interest in books and maps.

Sunday pleasures in those times were very limited for young people in Highland. Often one went to Mr. Durer's so-called Helvetia House. At Durer's one drank, usually cider, sat at a table, as in Switzerland, and discussed many subjects, while the innkeeper provided everyone with a bad cigar to smoke. I had never been much of a smoker. But since everyone else was smoking I, of course, thought I must too, although I must confess I never found it enjoyable.

One humid Sunday afternoon in June we had been at Durer's, drunk cider, and each of us had received three cigars. I had smoked barely an inch of mine when I felt as though I were getting seasick. We were going to Mr. Buchmann's house where there were several young girls, including a couple of Mrs. Buchmann's sisters, and one of my friends, Bernhard Suppiger. Various things were discussed, amidst much laughter, but I felt uncomfortable as a result of my cigar smoking, so I gave some kind of excuse and left, for I felt really bad. I lay down on the ground in a clump of hazel bushes, oblivious of my clean Sunday clothes, and almost became unconscious, for the sun burned down on me and the humid air was suffocating. Finally, after writhing around on the ground, I began to sweat. A slight breeze came up. I arose and felt as if I were waking from a dream. I cleaned my somewhat disheveled clothes, and looked around for my friends. My friends had missed me and had been looking for me, and had not known the reason for my sudden disappearance. I had had enough of tobacco smoking, and from that hour on I rarely smoked again, and I do not to this day regret it.

29. Taking Part in Theatre—Making Hay, Threshing, and Coming Down with Bilious Fever—Extremely Severe Cold Fever

Another pastime, one that was seldom indulged in, was small theatrical productions, in which I also took part a few times. I was only too happy to participate in dances; yes, it was my passion, so much so that I still believe today that my health suffered as a result. I could hardly bear to let a single dance pass without taking part. Consequently I would sweat profusely, and then after the dance, I would go home in the cool night air, with my clothes soaked, and get into my cold bed. So I usually ended up with a cold as a result of my impulsive behavior.

On July 4, 1844, I had taken an active part in a theatrical production and in the ball following it. It was close to three in the morning before I headed home. At five Schuetz awakened me, for we had made arrangements to have some men come early on the fifth to mow timothy grass. Four or five young people showed up, and, as often happened, each one wished to outdo his neighbor, so we had a kind of mowing competition, which only let up somewhat after one of them had established himself as the best worker. After that each one took a position he believed he could maintain. Then the work progressed at a more moderate tempo. It was a very humid day and by ten o'clock we were already really beginning to feel the heat. We were brought some wine made from wild grapes, which, while sour, was also very strong. Although I drank only a little of it, I was nevertheless overcome by severe dizziness. The whole world seemed to be spinning around me. At the same time I was extremely hot and felt very faint. But I did not wish to give up my hard-earned rank to any of the others, so I held out until finally the horn called us to the noonday meal.

I almost had made it to the house when my headache and dizziness became so severe that I had to lie down in the shade of a tree. Afraid I would lose consciousness, I did not just lie there passively. I kept turning constantly, until finally Schuetz came looking for me and called to me to get up, saying that it would be better for me to come to the house and recover in bed. However, even then I was unable to rest. Not until I went to lie down in the shade of a leafy tree did I find temporary peace and sleep, after which I awoke and felt much better.

Two or three days later, while stacking hay, I had a similar attack. It was an extremely hot day, and, since none of the day laborers wanted to bundle the hay, I got angry and decided that I would do it, and all by myself. But I had undertaken too much, for the wagons came at too fast a rate and too many men were busy loading for me to have been able to do the bundling alone. Exhausted and again overcome by dizziness, I finally fell to the ground, into the tall weeds. Gathering and stacking the hay could not be put off just for me. Others had to take turns in my place.

Toward the end of July, I prepared a site for threshing wheat in a flat part of the field, and by the beginning of August, Schuetz wanted to begin threshing. The threshing was done by spreading the wheat in a round circle. I stood in the center of this circle, holding the horses on long leads, each one individually—not next to one another, but rather one behind the other—and let them trot at a moderate speed over the wheat. When the stalks were sufficiently threshed, the straw, as well as the wheat, was removed, and a fresh load was spread. For several days the threshing went quite well. But ever since the haying had begun I had had frequent severe headaches, and now I was starting to have a backache, and finally I even developed a peculiar weakness in my limbs.

On the eighth of August I finally felt so bad that I could hardly stand upright. Schuetz, who could see this only too well, did not want me to continue to help while I was ill, but told me to go home and take care of myself. Although I tried to cure my condition myself with Brandrith's pills,[38] my condition continued to deteriorate. On the second or third day—it was a Sunday—I felt thoroughly miserable, and I thought I had the dread bilious fever. On this day Joseph Mueller came to pick me up to work for him, for I was to go into his employ, because Schuetz, now that the threshing was over, had no more work for me until corn harvesting time. Although I liked Mr. Mueller, and he promised to take good care of me during my illness, I could not, under the circumstances, leave Schuetz's employ.

Two of my friends, Christian Wenger and Jacob Leder, came by to pick me up for a Sunday outing. But nothing came of that either. Jacob Leder, in the belief that fresh peaches would be good for me, rode three or four miles to a Mrs. Iberg's to get some, but they also did not help. I wanted a doctor and I asked my friend Leder to ride to Highland to fetch Dr. Ryhiner;[39] Jacob promised to do so right away, but it seemed to me that it took all day for the doctor to arrive. Finally he arrived, and it seemed as though just hearing he was there made me feel somewhat better, as he cheerfully reassured me and explained that things were not as bad as I thought.

Even so, I had a hard time, and for ten days I could only take medicines and weak lindenblossom tea. My strength had deserted me. For several days I could not sit up in bed by myself. Sometimes I was not completely lucid and I dreamed continually about unpleasant, stupid things. Schuetz, who slept near me, offered to bring me the necessary medicines, or tea, at any time during the night. I only needed to call him at any hour in the night and he would be sure to hear me. But he had all kinds of work to do during the day and was tired in the evening, so it happened several times that I could hardly wake him, even after repeated calling, for my voice had become so weak. Then, when he finally did wake up and learned that I had hardly been able to wake him, he truly felt sorry for me.

After two weeks I began to feel decidedly better, and a light diet would now have hit the spot. During the day, when Schuetz was working, Mrs. Schuetz had taken good care of me. She was a good, well-intentioned person. But unfortunately she seemed to understand little, if anything, about helping someone convalescing from a serious illness. Light nourishment would have helped to stimulate my shrunken, still weak stomach. This will illustrate Mrs. Schuetz's thinking: I wanted a thin bread soup, with little fat and salt. The woman obligingly set about her work and soon told me that the soup was ready, and that I should go ahead and dig in; then I would soon be better. But the soup was so filled with pieces of bread that one might say that a spoon could have stood upright in it. Of course it was impossible for me to bring myself to eat as much as a spoonful, much as Mrs. Schuetz urged me to do so. I was finally forced to tell her that the soup might be good for a strong, healthy working man, but that it was too thick and hearty for me. Obligingly, she declared herself ready to prepare any other kind of soup if only I could tell her how. I told her to use far less bread, adding just a little onion instead. Mrs. Schuetz, completely willing to oblige me, immediately went to work and soon returned with a large bowl of soup that indeed had less bread than the first. Instead it was so full of onions that they fairly overflowed. Of course I could enjoy none of that either. Involuntarily I shuddered and, much as I hated to do it, since I feared I would offend the well-meaning woman, I had no choice but to tell her that the soup was much too thick for me. As I had expected, Mrs. Schuetz was hurt. She was very sorry that her good soup failed to please me, and said that she had absolutely no idea what to cook that I might enjoy.

By chance, a squirrel had ventured too close to our house, and, when Schuetz and two other men happened by, the squirrel fled up a small sassafras tree scarcely six feet tall. Schuetz had learned of his wife's disappointment in cooking her soup and, since such a convenient opportunity presented itself, he quickly seized the frightened squirrel by its back and squeezed the poor little animal so hard that it was utterly unable to defend itself. He killed it and gutted it, declaring, as he brought it to me, that this would make a good soup for me. Although I was still very weak, I decided that I would myself supervise the cooking of the squirrel and the preparation of the soup. Mrs. Schuetz was curious to see what kind of soup it would be. But she followed my directions willingly. When I believed that the soup had cooked long enough, I asked Mrs. Schuetz to bring me a little bread, a knife, a bowl, and also a bit of salt. I cut a few thin pieces of bread into the bowl, poured the boiling soup over them, mixed in a tiny bit of salt, and told Mrs. Schuetz that the soup was ready, and that it tasted wonderful to me! Mrs. Schuetz could not believe her senses when she heard me say this and saw with her own eyes how spoonful after spoonful disappeared between my eager lips.

"You call that soup! Why, goodness gracious, that's only a little water and even less bread and almost no fat at all! That can give you no strength at all. Eating such weak stuff will do nothing for you!" And so on. But I explained to her that this kind of soup was much better for a dehydrated stomach than a thicker one, at which she shook her head doubtfully. By the way, I will gladly admit that Mrs. Schuetz made excellent egg biscuits and the best cornbread I have ever eaten. Above all, the dishes she prepared were healthful, nourishing, and always plentiful. Furthermore, she was on the whole good-natured and did her housework diligently and punctually.

After I was finally able to leave my sickbed, and as soon as I could carry my gun, I kept a constant watch for the squirrels that daily visited the hickory trees at the edge of the woods bordering our house, and for several days I was able to shoot one of them almost daily. This made it possible for me to prepare fresh squirrel soup for myself daily, which soon restored me to my usual strength.

Dr. Ryhiner advised me to drink a little wine every day. But in order to get it I had to go down to Highland, which was more than a mile distant. I finally undertook the walk, allowing myself plenty of time, stopping to rest when I felt like it, and eventually I reached the tavern of shoemaker Schmied (a brother-in-law of Schuetz's), the only tavern at which one could get wine at that time.

The first day I drank three glasses of red wine, and felt no ill effects. The second day I drank two glasses, thinking that I should not drink more. On the third day I drank only one glass, and I soon felt its effects. On the way home I again experienced a certain weakness in my limbs, and lightheadedness, and when I reached home I felt exhausted and shaken. The next day I felt really ill and had to send for the doctor again. I had a kind of relapse, or rather I had a severe attack of intermittent fever. Although my condition did not become as bad as when I had the bilious fever, I often felt dreadfully miserable.

My intermittent fever manifested itself in all kinds of ways; first it began with particularly severe chills that often shook me terribly for two to three hours and from which the best fire in the fireplace and no quantity of covers and feather comforters brought relief. When the chills had passed, they were usually followed by severe headaches that became worse with every attack of chills, and finally grew so severe that one evening I nearly went insane, the condition becoming so bad that I thought I was going to die. Like a mad man, I ran about in the dark, outside the house, trying everything I could think of to stop the terrible pain, but without success. I honestly do not know what would have become of me if there had not soon been a change in my condition. Driven by pain, wandering frantically about the yard, I came upon the haystacks. A ladder was leaning against one of them. The thought occurred to me, "How would it be if I wrapped myself in my buffalo robe, with my head uncovered, and lay down on top of the haystack?" My body would be warm, but my forehead would be cool. Taking little time to make up my mind, I got my warm buffalo robe, climbed upon the haystack, wrapped myself tightly in the robe, leaving my head uncovered, and lay down up there, just like that. This had been a good idea, for I had lain there only a short time when I fell asleep and did not wake until the following morning—as I thought in my confused state—completely cured.

Schuetz told me the next morning that he had heard me moaning for a long time, but since there was sudden silence the thought occurred to him that I might have done myself harm. Concerned, he had gotten up and searched for me in the yard, around the house, and even in the well, without hearing or finding another sign of me. Then he had come near the haystack, and since the ladder leaned against it, he had looked up, seen something on top, and, climbing up there himself, he had found me sleeping quietly. Of course, he had not wanted to wake me.

Unfortunately this was just the beginning of the intermittent fever, which I was to come to know in its many variations. For a while the chills came every second day, then two days in a row, with one day's respite, then three days at a time, at first one hour later each day, with one day's interval. Then the chills rarely came less than one-and-a-half-hour later, often lasting three hours.

Fortunately the headaches were never again so severe. Instead, after the chills had abated, I initially experienced a terrific, feverish heat, after which I sweated horribly; I would soak five, six, up to seven shirts in a night, until there wasn't a dry thread, and my hands looked like those of a woman who had been washing in hot suds for days on end. After such bouts of fever I was completely exhausted; for quite awhile I had no appetite. Then after awhile I would have a ravenous appetite. Almost three months passed in this way, from the time I became ill until I finally regained my health. Jacob Schuetz had paid me my full wages, although I had taken ill eight days before the end of the fifth month. But I gave him back a dollar, for not only had I missed by eight days working through the fifth month, but I had given him and his wife a lot of trouble.

30. Harvesting Corn at Schuetz's—I Go to St. Louis and Stay with a Man Named Christ Who Tried to Use Me for Thievery

The time for harvesting corn had at last come. I helped Schuetz harvest his corn, some twenty acres, and haul it home. The weather was perfect for it, and we were soon finished. Schuetz wanted to pay me for my having helped him. However I regarded myself as being still in his debt and therefore accepted no payment. I felt at home there, and Schuetz had become a kind of father to me. Seeing that I was thankful, his affection for me grew even greater, and he offered to let me stay with him the entire winter, going to school, hunting, or doing anything I wanted. His wife would do my laundry as before, and I would receive the same meals, but need not work for him unless I wished to help him feed the livestock, mornings and evenings. But even this I would not have to do if I did not want to. Although I was touched by this kind offer, and thereby became completely convinced that I had a home with Schuetz, I did not accept it.

I had an idea that I probably would be able to do better in St. Louis, so I had a Swiss, named Grass, from Canton Graubuenden, take me there. In St. Louis I took a room in the Switzerland Boarding House, with the so-called Mrs. Werkmeister, or actually with Strasser, a Thurgauer who had come between her and her former husband.

I looked in vain for any kind of employment. Everyone else was also looking, money was very scarce, and therefore there were few jobs. In addition to me, there were other young unemployed Swiss at Strasser's. Everyone wanted employment, and several had no money.

One day we heard that a raft of logs had arrived and that one could earn half a dollar per cord chopping it up. Two poor devils, one from St. Gallen and the other a Berner, declared that, if only they had money, they would buy axes and go to work. Feeling sorry for them, I gave the one from St. Gallen a twenty franc piece, telling him to have it changed, but he brought back about fifteen to twenty cents too little. Even so, I bought a good ax for him, one for the Berner, and one for myself. Both had promised to repay me for the axes from the first money they earned.

We set to work cheerfully. But none of us was good at chopping. Moreover, we found that almost all of the trees were dead cottonwood that had been in the water for a long time and had become water-logged. Even when we chopped the logs into cord lengths, it was virtually impossible to split them, for even when we drove almost the entire head of the ax into the wood it would not split. Only too soon we found that it would scarcely be possible for us even to earn our board. We chopped and piled up only a few cords, and then gave up. Obviously my friends could not repay me for the axes. The man from St. Gallen gave me back the ax; the Berner said he would pay me later if I would be willing to wait. The St. Gallen's ax I sold to another Swiss somewhat over a year later, but got twenty-five cents less than I had paid.

With the help of a Lucerne man named Guggenbuehl I looked for an opportunity to learn a trade, be it making furniture, harness, or trunks; but all positions were taken, and no one needed apprentices. After further useless efforts, one day I learned from Mrs. Werkmeister (Strasser) that a butcher named Christ was looking to employ a young man. Christ, whom I soon got to know, was a Swabian. He was a large, rather abrasive man. Christ told me that he would try me for a month. If he liked me, then he would pay me four dollars a month. He told me that he butchered every week and that he mostly made sausages, which he sold in Vide Poche (Carondelet). The pay seemed paltry, but I thought that, if I could learn how to be a butcher, it might prove useful to me in the future. So I decided to at least give it a try.

Christ lived outside of the old St. Louis Brewery, near a hog slaughterhouse and between the main street and the Mississippi. He was married, had a small, skinny, one-eyed, but resolute wife, who had had an eye scratched out in New Orleans while trying to fight off a bear that was tearing one of her children to pieces. She, herself, was almost torn apart herself in the process, without having been able to rescue her child. Of course the bear was slaughtered soon after. They had only one remaining child. In addition, the house occupants included a wench, nearly thirty, fairly good-looking and fat, and by the second day I already thought I had seen something that made me believe Christ must be very intimate with this person.

In the morning I was supposed to get up at three o'clock to feed his horse and pigs. During the day I was to get rid of several little dead pigs, chop meat for sausage, and help make the sausage. At mealtime we had collared pork and liver sausage, and pickled pigs' feet; this three times a day, and, during the entire time I was there, it was the same daily fare.

From the good Christ's talk I soon gathered that he was not a fancy butcher. I also found that he thought he could treat me as though I were a stupid boy. Furthermore I soon learned that he rarely did his own butchering, but picked up the pigs' heads, feet, lungs, livers, and hearts that were otherwise discarded by the nearby slaughterhouse, for which he paid some of the employees there a trifle, and from which he made his sausages. The unfamiliar diet I suffered resulted in severe stomachaches and diarrhea. In addition, I began to have doubts about the good character of the residents in the house.

On the fourth day I had to accompany him to Vide Poche, according to Christ to get to know his customers in order that I would later be able to deliver the sausages without him. We had delivered all of the sausages and were on the way home. Beyond the town was a small partially cleared stand of trees, some of whose trunks were scattered around the ground. Christ stopped his wagon and told me to help him put a small load on the wagon. "Does this wood belong to you?" was my question. "Yes, indeed!" he said. When the load was of sufficient size, and we were again driving away—sitting on the logs—Christ said, "This wood actually belongs to a rich widow. So it doesn't do any harm if we take a little load of wood with us once in a while." "I thought you said this wood belonged to you. If that is not true, it is an injustice, a theft to take this wood." But Christ cut me off so forcefully that I felt it best to hold my tongue. "I'm telling you to bring some of this wood home with you each time."

We had not driven far when we met several men who, knowing Christ, asked where he had gotten the wood. He answered quite brazenly that he had traded sausages for it. This audacity was despicable, and I turned away from him involuntarily, feeling that he was a base, dishonorable fellow. The men were scarcely beyond our hearing when Christ turned to me and asked why I did not tell the men that we had traded sausages for the wood. I replied that he did not trade them, and, therefore, I would have had to lie. Christ cut me off again.

But I had already made up my mind, and had decided to leave this wood thief the next morning. I have since only regretted that I did not do it right after our arrival in St. Louis. The next morning I had packed all of my things and headed out into the street to find a so-called drayman, and I actually found one going by. I immediately came to an agreement whereby he would take my baggage to the Switzerland Hotel for twenty-five cents. After the driver had left his vehicle in front of the door, we went to my room, and we took all my belongings in one trip. We had to take them through the dining and living rooms, and although Christ had not been there a moment earlier, now, in addition to him and his wife, there was also a very loutish fellow, apparently a sailor of exceedingly strong build, who immediately called me several vulgar names, seeking to provoke me into a fight. But I motioned to my drayman to go ahead and to disregard him. My baggage was loaded on the dray and we soon arrived at the Switzerland Boarding House. With that my career as a butcher and sausage-maker came to an end, and I felt that I had escaped from a dangerous clique. During my stay in St. Louis, which was about a month, I had nothing but unpleasant experiences, and had also spent about ten dollars.

31. How Hans Blattner as a Failed Candidate for a Higher Position Became a Detractor of the Methodists—How He Tricked His Clockmaker-Partner—I Go to Mr. Gale's

Thinking that the best thing I could do would be to return to Highland, I sought out the first good opportunity to do so, and one soon turned up. Christian Gilomen, a native of Bern, who had a farm on the Highland Jura, was in St. Louis with a four-horse team and was leaving the next day for Highland. In addition to me there were two passengers from Bern and a Johannes Blattner from Canton Aargau. The latter made himself out to be very pious, and although still a young man—he was about my age—he was nevertheless a kind of Methodist preacher.

It was customary at that time to take something along to eat on the way. I had taken a so-called gingerbread cake. Near the bluffs at Collinsville, on the American Bottom, was a spring where the draft animals customarily were watered and one then enjoyed the food one had brought along. Gilomen, as it appeared, had nothing with him. So I offered him my cake, of which I had eaten only a little, expecting him to break off a piece and return the rest to me. But Gilomen kept the whole cake, remarking, "This cake is choking me. I believe you begrudge giving it to me."

Blattner asked Gilomen—purely from piety—whether he might drive the team, because he found our merry singing and story telling too sinful. Gilomen was happy to let him, if he knew how to drive. Blattner climbed onto one of the rear horses and energetically set about driving. We—the three Berners and I—kept up our merry singing, and the time passed quite pleasantly. We had put Collinsville and Trenton behind us. The horses were stepping out quite briskly, and we four were singing a very merry song, when we started down a little hill, and the front pair of horses suddenly turned to the right, causing the shaft to break. Of course our singing also came to a halt when the wagon came to a stop. Gilomen asked Blattner, "Did you do that deliberately?" But Blattner denied it. I, however, still believe that it was done deliberately, despite the denials of the pious young Blattner. We had an ax and a piece of rope in the wagon. Quickly we chopped down a young hickory tree and fastened it to the broken shaft, and off we went again. Blattner was permitted to continue driving, only he was supposed to be more careful, and the four of us resumed our song where we had left off when the shaft broke. Because the farm where Schuetz lived lay a mile to the left of Gilomen's route, I had my baggage taken off at Mr. Leder's farm on the Rigi, for I felt more than a little at home there also.

I will get a little ahead of myself here in order to tell something about the pious young itinerant preacher, Hans Blattner. Though I had never discussed religion with Hans, or even associated with him very much, I had heard a good deal about his apparent piety. Hans was said to have felt certain that he, or rather his soul, would go straight to heaven when he died. Blattner's piety appeared at that time to be universally acknowledged and admired by his Methodist brothers and sisters, and the salvation of his flock, especially that of mature young girls, seemed to be close to his heart; and, moreover he was assured of receiving good meals everywhere, which certainly lay close to his heart as well. So it came about that for some time Hans had considered himself one of the leading Methodists in his district, and that he aspired to a higher position. At last he had reason to hope that the time for a promotion might have arrived; the highest position a Methodist clergyman could attain became vacant. The district elders had invited the lower clergy to apply for the vacant position. Our Hans had actually become a candidate for the more lucrative position, naturally not for the material advantages involved. God forbid! No, only to be better able to enhance and care for the spiritual welfare of his little sheep, the brothers and, especially, the sisters.

As the individual who had served as an ordinary preacher longer than anyone else in the district, he was also most certainly figuring on the promotion—in fact was counting on the fact that he, the exceptionally pious Hans, would be assigned to the position. But as it unfortunately happens all too often in this sinful world, and Methodists are no exception, it turned out that the wise church elders, in whose hands lay the disposition of this somewhat better position, did not bestow this position, which was owed him, upon our Hans, but rather upon another who had the temerity to apply for it, even though he had not worked in the district nearly as long.

Since our pious Hans was so convinced that his pure soul would ascend to heaven immediately upon his demise, it does seem that this unfortunate development, aside from the inexcusable, mean ingratitude it showed on the part of the all-wise Methodist elders, caused such unwavering faith as his to be shaken. But our Hans must after all also have inherited a bit of wickedness from our forefather Adam, who was quick to eat the ripe fruit when his wishes were denied; for he had barely learned of the elders' choice, when he, the pious proselytizer, full of righteous (?) indignation at such a rejection, renounced Methodism entirely and apparently become one its most vicious detractors.

As the story goes, after Hans gave up preaching he became a watchmaker (a clever person, of course, can learn anything). But, since in the beginning he did not know much about that business, he took on a partner. Another capable man, an actual watchmaker, a bachelor—also Swiss—was the lucky man who joined the company of this former saint.

Hans had a pretty young wife. On the other side of the ledger, Hans needed to borrow three to five hundred dollars from his partner in order to establish a proper watch-making business. Hans' better half made a favorable impression upon his partner, so much so that one day she was able to report to her ex-pastor, "Hans, our associate has his eye on me." Hans probably thought, "What is the point in being a clever person if one does not make use of it?" And upon making this glorious discovery, he immediately decided to derive some practical benefit from it. Thereupon he discussed with his sweet, partner-enchanting little wife how they might most easily be able to get the partner to cancel the debt of three to five hundred dollars. He and his other half hit upon a good, promising idea. The idea became a plan to lure the adoring, love-sick partner into a trap whereby they could get the note for the borrowed money into their hands without paying him back. The infatuated partner naturally had no inkling of what the object of his affection and her Hans had in store for him. He felt so safe and secure that he had no premonition of danger. Soon after this plan was hatched Hans told his partner about some kind of personal business, saying that it required him to go away for several days; thereupon Hans indeed did say goodbye to his partner and to his good little wife, and left the house. By chance, however, something else occurred to him, causing him to sneak back into his house by another route, hiding in an adjoining room, keeping quiet as a mouse. Hans' wife had been sweet and enchanting before and now her demeanor toward him was even more so, causing him to fall utterly under the spell of her loveliness. The partner thought Hans was away; he had seen him go himself. How could he continue to resist this extraordinary charm any longer? The object of his affection suddenly grew very loving toward her husband's partner, and he probably entertained the thought that one should harvest while the fruit is ripe. Our watchmaker-partner, who earlier had an eye for the ex-preacher's wife, believed that the long-awaited time had finally arrived when he might cast both eyes upon the woman he adored; and, oh! how overjoyed he now felt he had reason to be. Then the door opened, and the spouse-partner appeared in the same, to the partner's complete consternation, destroying his short-lived joy. "So! So! You treacherously dare to usurp my sacred conjugal rights! To destroy my happy marriage! Just you wait fellow, I'll send you to the government courthouse at Alton![40] I have distrusted you for a long time; now I have you dead to rights, and you are going to pay for it!" Naturally the good watchmaker must have felt utterly miserable, for up to this time he had been seen and regarded as a good, respectable man. What would people think and say about him now, especially if he were to end up in jail for such a thing!

After prolonged entreaty the former pious Methodist finally allowed himself to be moved to listen to the sinner as he proposed conditions which might compensate for this serious violation. But, since the watchmaker was unable to come up with a suitable proposal, the compassionate Hans helped him out, and the guilty party was all ears. The affair finally was settled, with the result that the watchmaker returned to his partner the note for the money Hans had borrowed from him, without any compensation; and, moreover, he promised immediately to leave Blattner's house, as well as the area, and never show his face there again! The watchmaker was relieved to avoid jail, and the fox of an ex-minister and his charming vixen doubtless had a hearty laugh at the success of their trick! That Hans apparently was proud of this accomplishment was demonstrated by the fact that he evidently was not ashamed to tell the story himself. But some people speculated that if the watchmaker had heard that it was a contrived affair, and had lodged a complaint, it might well have happened that the crafty Hans would have ended up in the place to which he threatened to send his partner. Hans is said to have become some kind of a lawyer later. Perhaps he thought, "Try everything and settle on what pays best."

32. The Gale Family—I Study English

I stayed at Mr. Leder's only a few weeks. What I wanted was to live with an American family where I would be forced to speak only English. A year before, an American named [Seneca] Gale, who lived northeast of Highland, near Sugar

Creek, had wanted to hire me. But Jacob Leder had scared me off at the time by saying that Gale was a hard worker and that if on occasion I did not understand him right away he would before long call me a "Goddamn Dutchman!" I was not at all pleased by the translation into German. Since then, however, I had found that Mr. Gale was to be sure hard-working, but nevertheless a decent man.

Jacob Leder finally went to Mr. Gale's with me, and we soon came to terms. I was to come to his place for two months and help him feed his cattle (about eighteen head) and three or four horses; kindle two fires in the morning; carry some water into the house; help him chop firewood in the woods during the day; and in the evening carry enough wood into the house to stoke two large fireplaces. In return Mr. Gale promised to give me English lessons after supper and to pay me a monthly wage of two dollars, hardly enough to keep me in shoes. Of course I was also to receive room, board, and laundry.

I wanted to begin my new job in January. Since it was around Christmas the Leders had baked all kinds of good cakes and cookies, and we would spend a joyous Christmas Eve in Highland with Jacob Leder, the mason. Mr. Johann Leder, my friend's father, was a musician. He played the trumpet, but also played the clarinet, the latter quite well. Of course Mr. Leder did not forget to bring his clarinet, and since several neighbors were present, as well as several young people, Mr. Leder played his clarinet, and we danced merrily.

Up at shoemaker Schmied's there was also a gay gathering. Included in that group were my friend Schuetz, young [Wilhelm] Buchmann, the Berner Schlurp, and many others. When we got there and Schuetz saw me he urged me to stay and take part in the merrymaking. He also was not entirely pleased with me for having stopped at Leder's after returning from St. Louis, rather than at his place, as he had expected. But after I explained the matter to him he was satisfied. And he also approved of my wanting to stay with an American family to learn English. But he would have liked me to spend the entire evening in his company.

In January, Jacob Leder took me to Mr. Gale's farm. His family—besides him and his wife—consisted of a daughter, Mariet, and a son John, the former about twenty-three and the latter about twenty. Since I had learned very little English up to this time, it often was difficult for me to understand everything accurately, and it happened not infrequently that I carried out the instructions intended for me incorrectly. I also believed that when the family members were together and laughing that it was at my expense. But when I learned to speak a little and began to understand English more, I decided that I must have been mistaken about their making fun of me. But often I was somewhat embarrassed when, after I had begun speaking a little and they asked me about something or other, I found that I was suddenly brought up short, unable to fully express myself. At those times I got very hot and I must have become quite red in the face. If they laughed I knew it was at what I had said. But they were decent people and had patience with me.

When the day's work was done and supper was over, I would begin working on the English A, B, C's, which I completely mastered the first evening. By the next evening I was already working on "ba, be, bo." The third evening we did some reviewing before continuing. At first old Mr. Gale was my teacher. He had, as he told me, often done some teaching in the past, and he certainly seemed to me to be well qualified, for he appeared to be an enlightened and well-read man. Later on I more frequently received my evening instruction from Mariet, to which I did not at all object, for she was quite pretty and had a pleasant personality, and I came to know and regard her as an admirable girl and one whom I learned to respect. Mariet Gale was not like so many American girls of today, concerned only with coloring and powdering themselves, sitting in a rocking chair, or going for walks, etc. She did most of the housework, prepared good meals, always turned out good, white, well-ironed laundry, sewed for herself, her mother, father and brother, did the milking, fed the many chickens and a number of turkeys and only rarely went visiting. In short, I considered her an ideal girl.

The son, though, was very different from his sister. Working was not his favorite activity; to stay at home and help his father with the farm work did not appeal to him at all, one moment wanting to study one thing, and the next moment something else. He scarcely listened to his father's sensible advice, which was based on experience, much less followed it. Indeed he often used such expressions when speaking of his father behind his back that I would have gladly hit him in his impudent mouth. In general, John was not a bad boy, but he was frivolous, careless and inconsiderate.

One time he went away; I no longer remember just what he wanted to study. He came back a few weeks later, having come down with the measles. But he had barely recovered when he left again, although his father owned much land and had plenty of work for him to do. When he was at home he rarely picked up a newspaper or a book; instead he popped popcorn and amused himself eating it before the fireplace. Mr. Gale often tried to get him to change his boyish behavior, and then, by way of comparison, pointed to Mariet and me. "Look here," he said, "Mariet and Henry occupy themselves with something useful, reading newspapers or books. But you seem to think only of silly things, if you think at all!" But John turned a deaf ear to all of his father's remonstrances, and Mr. Gale now often considered disinheriting John. Later, when Mr. Gale died, it turned out that he had left a third more to Mariet than to John.[41]

My duties at Gales remained as I have described them. There certainly was not time for me to do any loafing. Mornings, when it was still quite dark, I was called to get up. John, if he was at home, peacefully slept on. It took more than a little effort for the old man to get him out of his warm bed. As for me, I got a good fire going, first in the bedroom, and then a much larger one in the big kitchen hearth; then I fetched a few buckets of water, and by that time the daughter usually had appeared in the kitchen to prepare breakfast. After I had fed the cattle out in the yard, I went to the kitchen where I washed up and combed my hair. By then breakfast was usually ready, after which Mr. Gale and I, taking our lunch with us, went to the woods about two miles distant. Back then I had attained my twenty-third year and I had become husky and strong again, and was confident that I was up to almost any task. But my first day in the woods alongside Mr. Gale, who was perhaps about fifty, soon taught me how little I knew about wielding an ax compared to Mr. Gale. While it seemed child's play to him to work steadily, and his pile of wood grew noticeably in a short time, I sweated and puffed with all my might, but still my wood pile did not reach half the size of his. I took off my coat and vest and tried my best, but I could not match Mr. Gale's performance. Mr. Gale had probably noticed my embarrassment. He laughed and often tried to cheer me up when I was in the dumps. The chips flew from his ax in all directions, so that it almost seemed dangerous to get near him, but, in spite of my best efforts to match him, I was still unsuccessful.

Exhausted and soaked with sweat, I finally sat down on a tree stump. Mr. Gale also rested a little. At this point a woodpecker in one of the neighboring oak trees seemed to be mocking me, as he cried out, "hee, hee, hee, hee." Mr. Gale had been watching me sympathetically. I now called his attention to the bird's "hee, hee, hee," saying, "Bird laugh at me." Smiling up to this point, Mr. Gale now laughed heartily. That evening at the table he told about it. And he also reassured me by telling me that he was not exactly a novice at chopping wood and that I would improve and become faster with practice. Then he showed me how to guide the ax and how to chop.

We stopped chopping early enough to reach home a little before sundown, where we fed the livestock, and then I brought in enough wood and stacked it in both rooms so that there might be enough for the next day. After the evening meal I practiced spelling in English for an hour and after that I then read a book I had bought in St. Louis with the title *The Hundred Wonders of the World and the Three Realms of Nature.*[42] From this book I learned much that was then new and to me interesting. It described Fingal's Cave in Ireland [actually in western Scotland on Staffa Island], Mammoth Cave in Kentucky, what caused tides to ebb and flow, earthquakes and volcanoes, prehistoric animals, Egypt's pyramids, the Colossus at Rhodes, the buried cities of Palmyra and Pompeii, and many other things worth knowing, which interested me tremendously. Mrs. Gale was of the opinion that such reading of German would muddle my English and make me forget it. I agreed that I was concentrating too much on new things that interested me, but Mariet told me that even so I was making good progress in English.

Time passed very pleasantly and quickly at Gale's despite all the work. I felt no need to go to Highland on Sunday or to look up my friends. I had gradually become better at chopping wood and Mr. Gale was satisfied with me; and, because he thought that he had enough wood for the summer, we turned to other, but in no way easier, work. Mr. Gale still had about eighty acres of unfenced land upon which patches of dense hazelnut bushes grew. He wished to chop these down and then later burn them in order to be able to plow that piece of land. We used a so-called shrub scythe, work that required skill and is by no means easy. At first I was quite stiff by evening, but after a few days I got better at it, so that before long we cleared a large area.

I could already read a little English, and Mr. Gale, as well as Mariet, assured me that if I stayed with them a year they would have taught me to speak English so well that I would be able to converse with any stranger in Highland. Should I stay two years I would be speaking English so well that it would be difficult even for an American to tell whether or not I was American born.

While I was at Gale's young men came to visit several times, and among them was a teacher. I thought I knew at whom their visits were directed and on the whole I was seldom wrong. Mariet did not seem to favor any of these visitors, and I admit that pleased me. Then she herself told me what I thought I had observed; so, when she praised my beautiful fires and also did more favors for me, I found myself increasingly drawn to her. And it seemed to me this feeling was reciprocated. But back then I was still a poor fellow, and the thought of becoming more involved with a girl before being fully in a position to support a wife kept me from becoming too friendly, and so I always maintained a little reserve.

Mr. Gale wanted to hire me for the coming summer and promised me a wage of six dollars a month, good pay for the times. However in the previous fall I had made an agreement with a good (?) friend. His name was Christian Wenger, a Berner, about six years older than I, and since he formerly had also worked for Schuetz, who regarded him as an industrious worker and a fairly good hunter, I felt myself fortunate to strike up a friendship with him. Nonetheless I had had ample opportunity to observe that, just as he boasted about his superior shooting and his hunting, so also he was not always especially particular about the truth. However I considered this merely an unfortunate but harmless habit.

Wenger had traveled to Galena in the fall of 1844 and had promised me, as his best friend and comrade, that if he found wages to be higher there he would write me. I actually got a letter from him saying that in the lead mines at Galena one could earn ten to twenty dollars a month. The river traffic on the Mississippi now being open, Christian seemed to be counting on my joining him. Of course I read the letter to the Gale family and told them as well as I could what the letter said. Mr. Gale sought to dissuade me from my plan, saying that if I went up there I would not only not make a lot of money, but more likely would have to spend thirty to forty dollars and be only too glad to return to Highland in the late fall. Mariet was not in favor of my going either and seemed to feel that I did lack fidelity, and I admit that I was not really glad to leave. It seemed to me that I was not doing right to leave this family that had treated me so well. For these reasons I could hardly decide what to do. But when I thought about the ten to twenty dollars per month, compared to six dollars, I believed that I would be able to earn much more there in six months than in Highland. Furthermore, I would get to see more of the world.

Although reluctant, I nevertheless finally decided to leave, and I believe I hurt the Gales, especially Mariet, by my decision. I took my belongings to Jacob Schuetz's. He was already living on his farm, where St. Jacob is now, and a few days later I went to St. Louis where I found the steamboat *Iowa*, which was leaving the very next day for Galena. The next day, at the appointed hour, I left as a cabin passenger. The boat was not one of the best and was very slow. The banks along the river were still dreary. It was early March. River traffic had only just resumed and the vegetation had not yet come back to life.

Nauvoo, of the towns above St. Louis, was the most important at that time, but it was almost exclusively inhabited by Mormons, and people spoke of this religious sect as though it consisted of nothing but bandits, thieves, and murderers. The Temple was under construction and nearly finished, and yet no one knew how soon these people might be driven away, for the gentiles, that is to say the non-Mormons, were very angry at these people because it was there, it was said, that most of the thefts and villains of all kinds were planned and carried out. The farmers in the adjoining counties were especially stirred up and ready to take up arms against the Mormons at a moment's notice. In that year Joseph Smith, the Mormon prophet, would soon be, or already had been, targeted by six or seven bullets, and had been shot to death at the courthouse in Carthage by an enraged mob.[43] Then in the following year, 1846, the Mormons were forced to leave Nauvoo. Many settled in Iowa. A number of them volunteered to serve under Col. [Stephen W.] Kearney to fight the Mexicans in California. Others went to California by ship, around Cape Horn. But most of them crossed the wilderness to the Salt Lake in what was then the Territory of California,[44] which has since become the Territory of Utah. But, as can be imagined, many thefts were carried out by persons who were not Mormons. As for me, I later be-

Portions of the Upper Mississippi Valley Relating to Lienhard's Travels

came acquainted with many of these Mormons in 1847 in California, and I cannot say that I found them any worse than other people.

Above Nauvoo the main landing places at that time were Fort Madison, Burlington, Bloomington (which is the present-day Muscatine), Davenport, and Rock Island. But these were then still small, and, compared to now, unimportant. Galena lies on the so-called Fever River, about six miles from where it flows into the Mississippi.[45] Although the Fever River is really only a creek, at that time, because its waters were augmented by the Mississippi, the largest steamboats were able to proceed up it as far as Galena. Because the Fever River is in places so crooked, boats often have difficulty making headway. Because the ship's bows would often bump into one bank, while the stern almost touched the other, it was very difficult to turn steamboats around there. In those days Galena was for most boats the end of their journey, and only a few proceeded as far as Fort Snelling, some miles above present-day St. Paul.[46]

4

To See More of the World

33. I Go to Galena—A Gambling Bank in Galena—Experiences in Lead Mine in Hearts Gravel—Return to Galena— We Make Preparations to Go to the Pineries

GALENA WAS THEN SAID TO BOAST a population of about five thousand, a figure which was probably somewhat exaggerated. But, people came there, not for the beauty of its location; on the contrary, Galena owed its existence to the substantial quantities of lead ores in the surrounding area. Galena had only three proper streets. Main Street was the business street. Along it lay storehouses, hotels, etc. Above this, along the bluff, was a street on which were most of the residences. Off Main Street, at a right angle, Liberty [actually Hill] Street[1] extended as far as the heights. Behind the steep bluff there was a little valley through which a small creek flowed, emptying into the Fever River, below the boat landing. In this little valley [Spring Street] were one or two breweries, slaughterhouses, and also several private homes. On the left bank of the river there were many nice homes, some of them expensive, having quite beautiful green lawns and numerous shade trees. Here lived the more well-to-do inhabitants, some of the more successful lead mine owners. The two banks were connected by a solid, wooden bridge.[2] At various locations, not far from Galena, were the lead mineral smelters where the lead was melted into seventy-five pound bars and then carried away, almost daily, by departing steamboats.

For a place of its size, Galena was quite lively, especially on Saturdays. That was when the miners flocked in, for this was payday. The miners felt that they were obligated to make up for their partial abstention from hard liquors during the week. Since a great many of the miners were Irish, whiskey was in great demand on that particular day, and since an Irishman is not happy without fighting or boxing, rows were not uncommon.

But there was also a so-called bank, that is to say not a financial bank, but a gambling bank, to which foolhardy men flocked, intending to win money without having to work for it; however, most of them returned as losers. A friend

147

of mine, of whom I will have more to say later, persuaded me to go to this place one evening in the company of another man from Canton Graubuenden, a confectioner by trade, and an extremely powerfully built man. I went, not to try my luck, but out of curiosity and to give in to the urging of Christian Teuss. Dierolf —I believe that was the name of our large Graubuender—had apparently been there fairly often, and had, as Teuss enthusiastically told me, often won a great deal. That Teuss did not play was, as I believe, due to one reason only, a good one; he lacked money.

The gambling "office" consisted of a large room, or hall. There were a good many tables, small and large, each of them surrounded by greedy fortune seekers; the spacious hall was almost full. Each player—for so I must designate them—would choose a number which he hoped would give him his best chance of winning. In an apparatus—a rotating drum resembling a Swiss butter churn —were corresponding numbers, of which a certain quantity appeared to be winners. The owner of the establishment, a good looking, tall, fat, well-dressed gentleman—in America anyone who wears good clothes, expensive rings, a good watch, and the like, is thereby termed gentleman—gave the drum a few turns. Then he pulled out a number. If none of the players held the corresponding number, he gave the drum another turn, stopped again, drew out another number, and called it out, etc. If one of the players held the corresponding number he would call "Halt!" or he would repeat the number, and then he would pay an appropriate amount.

Although I did not completely understand how the game was played, clearly the entire business was a kind of lottery. Our big Graubuender was a winner again this evening, and he seemed to think that it was impossible for him to lose. As soon as all the winnings had been distributed the gambling was over for the evening, and everyone left the place with the exception of the handsome, well-nourished "bank" manager.

Teuss was fascinated by this game of luck and seemed surprised that I did not share his enthusiasm. I was of the opinion that there was only one sure winner and that was the good-looking, large gentleman "bank" manager. Certainly there were more losers than winners.

Wenger finally came to Galena from his lead mine—actually a pit—in Hearts Gravel.[3] He informed me that I could get work with a neighboring mine owner, a man called Buehler, also a Graubuender, and with his partner, a small, cold, dry Englishman. Christian Teuss had already been employed by these men, and planned to return. Hearts Gravel lay southeast of Galena, about fifteen miles away. The road to it led over hill and dale, and was nearly treeless.

One fine morning a wagon picked up my baggage, various mining tools, provisions, etc. Wenger, Teuss, and I accompanied the oxen-drawn vehicle on foot. We arrived at our destination early in the afternoon. It lay in a little valley one hundred and fifty to two hundred paces wide, through which a little, spring-fed brook snaked. Our employers' mine was on the eastern slope, not far from the cabin, our living quarters, which was located in the little valley at the foot of the slope. The cabin had only one room, but it was fairly large. Beside Buehler and his wife, the Englishman, Teuss and I all slept in this room. The cooking was done there also. Buehler was a large, husky man of about thirty. As long as I was there I could find nothing bad to say about him; his wife, a small, rather pretty compatriot of his was several years younger than her husband. She was a cheerful and fairly industrious woman.

The lead mine, belonging to the Englishman and Buehler, had already been sunk to a depth of about sixty feet, mostly through solid rock. Halfway down the mine shaft there was a side gallery, or tunnel, and, down below, another was about to be blasted out of the rock, both of them going in an easterly direction. If I am not mistaken, they had found some lead ore. But I believe that it was not very rewarding. At the moment they were finding only rock, with no ore. The Englishman seemed to be in charge of the mining, and as long as I was there Buehler, to the best of my knowledge, never set foot in the mine.

When I first looked down into the dark pit, which was supposedly sixty feet deep, it made me shudder, and I declared that I did not want to go down there. So they let me work at the hoist, around which was wound a long, thick rope, fastened to a sturdy tub that was lowered into the mine. The Englishman and Teuss, along with the necessary drills and other blasting apparatus, were then lowered one after the other into the mine. They disappeared into the darkness, and it required careful attention on my part to understand their shouted instructions. Although it was very strenuous work hoisting up out of the sixty-foot mine the rock which the workmen had blasted loose down below, I had no desire to trade jobs with Teuss, whose job it was to help the Englishman in the mine.

However, one day Teuss became ill and declared that he was unable to work in the mine, because, as I understood it, he had taken some medicine. So, whether I wanted to go down or not, there was no alternative. Therefore, the Englishman needed a helper, and I had to change places with Teuss. I cautioned Teuss to be very careful not to lower me too fast. I stepped into the tub, held on to the rope with both hands, and then began the slow descent into the dark bowels of the earth. When I arrived below I was dizzy. I fell against the side of the hole and felt like a drunkard colliding with a stone wall on a dark night. I was awakened from my half-conscious state by the Englishman, who called to me to come toward him, cautioning me to stoop so that I would not hit my head on the rock. It was only then that I looked around and finally saw, at some distance, a faint gleam of light. In a half-crouch, I approached it. The tunnel may have been four to four-and-a-half feet high and perhaps as wide. The Englishman now positioned his steel stone borer, and I had to start beating on it from a most uncomfortable position, with the heavy, iron hammer. When the hole was sufficiently deep it was immediately loaded with dynamite. I got into the tub, grasped the rope, and then called "Up!" Very slowly, I began to rise. When, halfway up, I reached the old tunnel, I swung myself into it and released the rope and tub, which were immediately let back down to the bottom of the mine. By this time the Englishman had usually finished loading, had lit the fuse, had also gotten into the tub, giving the sign to ascend to those at the surface, and soon found himself at my side. Usually it was not long before there was an explosion below, often shaking the rock around us, followed by a few minutes of dense smoke from the blasting powder. As the smoke began to clear, the Englishman and then I were again lowered. Having arrived at the bottom, we cleared away the rock loosened by the blast, and the man at the hoist had to start all over again.

We—Teuss and I—were to be paid ten dollars a month, but I thought this seemed little enough for such dangerous work, and I began to regret having come there. Our employers had not hauled out a single pound during the time I was there, and it was unlikely that they would be able to continue to pay us much longer.

Christian Wenger and his partner, a somewhat older man by the name of Tufly, also from Canton Graubuenden, whose son George and son-in-law, a conceited little Hessian, kept the Washington Hotel in Galena,[4] had also been looking for lead in a mine not far from our cabin, on the other side of the valley. But it seemed to me that their trouble, work, and money were all for nothing.

After spending a few weeks in this lonely area so riddled with holes, I remarked to my friend (?) Wenger one day that I liked neither the area nor the work, and that I could think of other things I would rather do than to be in this sixty-foot hole in the ground. Wenger also seemed to have become fed up with the nonproducing mine, and started to tell how much we three, he, Teuss, and I, could make if we went together to the so-called pineries, constructed a raft of rough-cut logs, and then floated it down the river to St. Louis. Each of us would surely make several hundred dollars.

After closer questioning on my part as to whether he was completely certain that it would be a success, he was quite positive. He had made sufficient inquiries and knew what he was talking about. We would travel up to the Black River,[5] to where the pine forests were; then chop down trees, saw them into rough cut logs, roll them into the river, lash them together into a raft, and down the river we would go. If we did not sell them along the way to St. Louis, we could certainly get rid of them there.

I believed that I had a reliable friend in Wenger; how could I have doubted his very positive words and reassurances? Our tentative plan soon became a firm resolve. Our employers, the Englishman and Buehler, seemed not at all upset that we wanted to leave. Perhaps they were secretly relieved, which would apply to anyone who has to pay a salary without anything coming in.

One pleasant spring morning, with our baggage on an oxen-drawn wagon, we strode back to Galena, through the same country we had crossed a few weeks earlier on our way to the glorious mines at Hearts Gravel. Having arrived in Galena, at the Washington Hotel of George Tufly and Co., we inquired as to how long it might take for us to catch a steamboat up to the mouth of the Black River. Connections to places on the Mississippi beyond Galena were not then reliable. From Galena a small steamboat, called the *Otter,* belonging to the Harris Brothers in Galena, went as far as Fort Snelling, at the mouth of the St. Peter's River, now called the Minnesota (Firewater) River, and then continued up the St. Croix River to its falls. It was said that the *Otter* was to leave for the upper regions in a few days. It behooved us to get ready.

We had to buy a large supply of flour, ham, lard, potatoes, etc. I had already brought a supply of dried apples from St. Louis, and I still do not know why I did that. We needed axes, a large wood-saw, a whetstone, a drawknife, a shingle knife, and iron wedges, and the like, all of which we finally assembled at the Washington Hotel. At first I believed that each of us would pay his share of the food stuffs and tools, but only too soon it became obvious that Teuss could contribute a total of two dollars and thirty cents, and Wenger, whom I had believed in the best shape financially, had some sixteen dollars, while the amount I had to lay out for Teuss ran into the upper twenty dollar range. Our combined total came to about thirty dollars apiece.

While we were still in Galena, our former employer, Buehler, came to see Tufly. He was somewhat tipsy and showed quite a different side to his character. He appeared to me to be somewhat quarrelsome, and it would not have taken much for him to get into a fight with young Tufly. Teuss told me that Buehler had often had little squabbles with his wife. Once she had become so upset by his behavior that she had threatened to kill herself. Whereupon Buehler had quickly given her a pistol, with the comment that she could go ahead and use it to achieve what she wanted. At that Mrs. Buehler had immediately lost interest.

34. Traveling to the Pineries — How Wenger and Teuss Played Cards, Ignoring Our Impending Departure — Our Trip to the Stillwater Sawmill

Christian Wenger and Teuss did not appear to be the least bit concerned about the departure of the *Otter.* Much to my dismay, they found costly amusement in playing cards with young Tufly. The *Otter* was at the landing. I had told the mate that two men would be seeking passage besides me, etc. On a sunny pleasant afternoon, after twelve o'clock, the mate told me that we were to bring our baggage on board because they intended to leave promptly at one o'clock. My two wonderful partners were, as usual, still busy playing cards with Tufly. I immediately went from the *Otter* to the hotel and told them what the mate had just said. This interruption did not please my good friends. Tufly said, "I'll take an oath that it's not true. The *Otter* will still be there at this time tomorrow." And so my pinery partners played on.

I dragged one thing after another on board the *Otter*. After about a half hour the mate asked me again whether I had not said that the two other men would be accompanying me. I answered in the affirmative. "Well then, inform your friends that we will be leaving in five minutes." I hurried back to the hotel where I found my good business partners still playing cards. "So, you are still playing and the boat is going to be leaving in five minutes." This time it worked. They moved like lightening. But Teuss still had to get some bedding somewhere. We carried the rest of our things on board. I went back to the hotel to make certain that we had not forgotten anything, and I found my dried apples.

Having returned to the boat, I turned to Wenger, and asked if we now had everything. "Yes, yes," was his answer. At this point the mate interrupted us again, asking if I had not told him there were three of us who wanted to go. I answered yes. "Then where is the third person?" "He will be here right away," I answered. "We will have to go without him," he remarked. But at that moment I saw Teuss quickly running toward us with his bundle of bedding on his back. And it was high time, for the boat was about to shove off and Teuss had to take a few steps through the water to reach the boarding plank.

I was extremely cross about the ungodly lack of concern of my companions and commented that it would not surprise me at all to find that we had forgotten something. We checked, and sure enough, our whetstone was missing! It seemed to me that our undertaking was completely doomed, and I heartily regretted having gotten involved with those fellows. And I made no secret about how I felt either, reproaching them for their unpardonable carelessness, and I recited an old adage, "If one has to carry hunting dogs on a hunt, it will be a bad hunt." Fortunately we were able to buy the boat's whetstone, but had to pay almost twice the price of our lost one.

Finally we were on our way up the Mississippi on the little *Otter,* as I thought toward the mouth of the Black River. The first settlement on the right bank, on the Iowa side, was Dubuque,[6] about eighteen miles by water from Galena. It already boasted several good, brick houses. Even so, its inhabitants could only have numbered a few hundred.

On the Wisconsin side, either on or near the river, were Snake Hollow[7] and Cassville. About eight miles above Cassville, on the Iowa side, was Prairie la

Porte, which was just being surveyed as a town site and was to be named Guttenberg[8] in honor of the inventor of printing.

Not far above Prairie la Porte is the wide mouth of the Wisconsin River, where
it empties into the Mississippi. Beyond the mouth, on the right bank of the Wisconsin, is Prairie du Chien.[9] At the time that place was the last small outpost
of civilization and of white settlers, was largely inhabited by Frenchmen, and had
the appearance of a French village. Behind the little town, or up on the bluffs,
there was a military post, or fort, not yet fallen into disuse. From this point on,
at varying distances from the river, there were frequent rocky elevations (bluffs)
or hills, which at various places attained considerable height. Indeed there were,
between Galena and Prairie du Chien, several of considerable height that fell off
very steeply.

The water of the Mississippi had taken on a dark, brown color. It was said that
the water of the Black River was the source of this dark color. However I later
learned that the waters of the Chippewa,[10] and especially those of the St. Croix,
were just as dark as those of the Black River. At last we reached Prairie la
Crosse.[11] At that time there was no town there, nothing but a Frenchman who
owned a small log cabin and carried on a modest trade with the Indians.

Not far upstream from there was the mouth of the Black River. This then was
the place where we had planned to leave the steamboat in order to continue our
journey later by canoe. But the boat proceeded leisurely on its way, and, when
I at last asked Wenger if we had reached the mouth of the Black River, he replied
that we had already gone a mile past it. To my question as to why we had not
landed, he responded that he had learned along the way that the pine trees had
already been felled for a long distance upstream and that further up the river presented many problems for the floating of rafts. But now, he said, we would go
up the Chippewa River, where, he had been told, one could still easily find pine
woods close to the river and where there would be no difficulty floating rafts
of logs out to the Mississippi.[12]

Opposite the mouth of the Chippewa River, where it flows into the Mississippi at the lower end of Lake Pepin,[13] on the right bank, there was a small settlement of several houses. It seemed to me that its sole function was trade with
the Indians. Here I encountered my first savages, three or four of them. They
were the so-called Sioux Indians,[14] to this day the most numerous tribe of natives still surviving in the United States. Two of them were squatting close to the
river bank, and at first we could not tell whether they were men or women. Both
had large coarse faces with coarse features and seemed, according to my thinking at that time, very scantily clothed. Finally they rose and began to speak with
one another; thus we could tell, by the difference in their voices, that one must
be a man and the other a woman.

At the mouth of the Chippewa there was also a log cabin that served as a trading post. Here I thought we would finally unload our equipment and continue our journey by canoe. Imagine my surprise when Wenger told us that he had been advised not to go up the Chippewa because the Indians upstream were very hostile toward whites. But then I wanted to know just where we intended to go, because there would be Indians everywhere up there. But Wenger claimed that he had made detailed inquiries and that he had been told that we would find just what we were looking for on the St. Croix: many beautiful evergreen forests, growing right by the river bank, and no hostile Indians.

I became quite angry and resentful about our undertaking, about our totally unplanned foray out into the world, or rather into the wilderness. Teuss did not seem unduly concerned. Why should he be? He only had two dollars and thirty cents invested in the entire venture. What did he have to lose? Wenger, our leader and the chief organizer of our grand pinery undertaking, had at most ten to fourteen dollars at stake, and since he was well aware that our venture had developed as it had, primarily due to his great vision and speculative spirit, and as a result of the confidence we had placed in him, he remained silent, and would have been satisfied if I had held my tongue.

Unfortunately I still understood too little English at that time to be able to make sensible inquiries on any subject in that language. Since Wenger had been in the country much longer, the language was much more familiar to him, and, as a result, we had to rely mainly on him. Initially, having been foolish enough to have placed too much trust in Wenger, I had in the beginning believed that each of us would be able to pay his full share of the cost of the necessary provisions, tools, passage, and freight. But I would learn soon enough how mistaken I had been. In addition to my share of our expenses, I had advanced some thirty dollars to my companions. From the Black River to this point I had to pay the passage for everyone, since I was the only one who still had a little money, and oh how reluctantly did I take these 20-franc pieces, brought from my homeland, out of my belt! And so we continued our random travels on the *Otter,* through Lake Pepin, from whose interesting shores very high, rocky hills (or bluffs), often rose. Except for the valleys through which little streams flowed into the lake, the land seemed very thin and barren. One saw only sparse woodland, or none at all, and the few trees that did grow there were stunted and deformed.

Above Lake Pepin, if I am not mistaken, was the Indian village of Red Wing.[15] It consisted of a number of fairly large log buildings whose roofs were covered with bark. It seemed at that time to be uninhabited, and it lay at the upper end of a broad stretch of so-called bottom land. At the mouth of the St. Croix River there were, on both banks, a couple of small houses, or rather huts, posts where trading was carried on with the Indians. We did not disembark there.

Wenger said that he had spoken to the boat clerk, who told him that he would not ask us to pay passage for the trip from there to Fort Snelling. For the remainder, from the mouth of the Chippewa to the falls of St. Croix, we could help load lumber, until we reached the Stillwater Sawmill at the upper end of Lake St. Croix. I was glad not to have to pay for passage again and thought that the clerk must surely be a really good man and that we had been treated generously. Just how accurate I was in this assessment will be seen below.

About ten miles above the mouth of the St. Croix, on the left bank, we found a single log cabin, an Indian trading post. A handsome, slender Indian was there. He may have been twenty to twenty-two years old. He had a kind of flute or clarinet from which he was coaxing several melancholy sounds. He seemed to be quite proud of his music. He probably considered himself a true virtuoso. He was dressed in good buckskin breeches with a good deal of fringe, and was wearing glass beads and other adornments; on his face were several red stripes; and he even had some of the same color in his hair. He was the owner of a long-barreled rifle decorated with a great many brass nails, the stock and barrel of which were held together by a pair of shiny brass clamps. In short, the fellow seemed to be quite a character, a real dandy. Since then that place has grown to be a city of many thousands of white inhabitants, known today as St. Paul.

After our boat had proceeded up the river for a short time more it landed at the foot of a high, soft white sandstone hill on whose back Fort Snelling lay. The Stars and Stripes fluttered from the flag staff of the fort, around which one could see soldiers wearing light blue pants, some of them busy, and others lolling about. Here was the confluence of the St. Peter's and the Mississippi rivers, but while the water of the latter was fast-flowing and quite clear, the St. Peter's (now known as the Minnesota River) flowed considerably slower, was muddy, and had a yellowish cast. At this point the Mississippi seemed no more than one hundred to one hundred and fifty yards wide, and the St. Peter's seemed to be nearly as wide. The white sandstone cliff, on whose back the fort stands, is so soft that it can be readily cut with a dull knife. Little pieces of this cliff can easily be crumbled into a fine blotting sand.

On the right bank of the St. Peter's River and the Mississippi lay St. Peter's,[16] consisting of a small Catholic mission church and several small houses, where it was said that six Catholic clerics were busy trying to convert the Indians to the only faith that could save them.

The *Otter's* freight for St. Peter's and Fort Snelling was soon unloaded, and it had consisted mostly of gunpowder. The *Otter* now turned its bow downstream, and before long we entered the mouth of the St. Croix, and soon after that we found ourselves on Lake St. Croix,[17] or as it was perhaps more frequently called, Stillwater Lake, with its wealth of fish. This lake is said to be twenty to almost thirty miles long, but is not wide. From the boat the land seemed rocky and poor.

During the night the boat ran aground, and we had some difficulty getting it back afloat. The next day we reached the so-called Stillwater Sawmill[18] at the upper end, or head, of the lake. Here a good many men were working with saws and at putting together plank rafts, etc. It was here that we three Swiss were to help load lumber into the boat in payment for our passage from the Chippewa. From the way space was being made for loading the boards on to the boat, I began to fear that they did not intend to take on a small load. As soon as everything was ready for loading, someone shouted, "Hurry up, Dutchmen!" And I must say that all of us came to know the meaning of that expression very well before the next day dawned.

Other words that we got to know well during the night were "Look out below!" which we had to call down into the hold every time we let the boards slide down. We had been foolish enough to expect that we would at least be permitted some rest after midnight, but that never entered the mate's mind. "Hurry up, hurry up!" was the call whenever, overcome by exhaustion, our loading of the lumber slacked off.

Wenger never complained, or uttered a word of dissatisfaction, but Teuss and I made up for him. At one point Teuss suggested that we tan Wenger's hide, but we knew well enough that the mate would probably take a dim view of such activity. So we carried boards the entire night, until day had dawned again. By then the hold was fully loaded.

The boat started up again, but docked again a short distance upstream; and there we were required to carry six cords of firewood to the boat. Fortunately, the wood pile was not too large, otherwise we might have broken out in open rebellion. But we made it quite clear to the mate that we were not particularly enthusiastic. We told Wenger in no uncertain terms what we thought of the barter arrangement he had made for us to pay for our passage, which sentiments he probably did not find especially edifying. Finally they left us alone, and we found ourselves headed upstream through the black, or rather dark brown, waters of the St. Croix, encountering scattered remnants of winter ice along the way.

35. Our Pointless Wanderings—Returning to a Mississippi Island—Chopping Cordwood for Minter and Getting to Know the Indians a Little

For some days now I had been surprised to find almost no sign of pine forests. It was seldom that we saw a tree from which it would have been possible to cut lumber. In fact we rarely saw a single pine, large or small, or any other evergreen trees. Heavily wooded stands were to be found only in the river valley. On the high banks we could mainly see only small, often even deformed, stands.[19]

Now we were rapidly approaching the final destination of our steamboat journey, for the St. Croix Falls, fifty miles above the Stillwater Sawmill, were as far
as our boat went. Finally there appeared directly ahead of us high, grayish-brown
rock walls, rising almost perpendicular from the water, crowned by low shrubs.
At the foot of these cliffs, directly in front of the bow of the boat, was a kind
of warehouse, narrow but tall. Next to this building was a steep wooden stairway, leading up to a recess in the rock wall, and here was the last landing on
the St. Croix. This place was ill-suited to put already out-of-sorts persons into
a good mood. I climbed the high stairs and found a wagon, which, though not
heavily laden, four mules were having difficulty pulling.

When I arrived below again, the boat's crew was busy unloading our provisions, tools, and bags. I saw a pale young man watching our activity and, although I did not speak English all that well, I immediately spoke to him, asking
if he lived here and where one would find the pineries. The young man instantly
realized that I was German, and since he himself was also a German immigrant,
I was thus much better able to ask him what we needed to know. The man told
me that if we wanted to go up the St. Croix River, until we found pine trees that
could be cut into boards, we would have to go at least sixty miles farther upstream. But he could not advise us to do so because a rabble band of lawless Indians, that had been expelled from various tribes, were roving about up there.
He was of the opinion that very few whites would be safe in their vicinity. We
would be robbed and perhaps even murdered. "And how are you going to get all
of the things up there since there are no roads and no wagons available to take
you there? If you had oxen, you would not need to go more than twenty miles
upriver. You could use them to drag the logs to the river." Scouting around for
pine woods closer would be a waste of time because the large sawmill near the
St. Croix Falls, where we stood, had already thoroughly cleared out the entire
area. He thought that we would have to overcome considerable difficulties if we
went further afield by trying to take our many belongings upstream by canoe.

I do not believe the young man had any reason to try to frighten us, and,
when I reviewed our situation, I could only regard our entire undertaking as
thoroughly ill-considered, a total failure. I was thoroughly discouraged, and since
Teuss did not look much happier than I, and, because the boat was soon to set
out on its return trip, I quickly decided to have our things taken back on board,
although I really had no idea where we would go next.

Teuss, to whom I related what the young German had said about our situation, had, like me, lost all enthusiasm for our undertaking, and was glad when
our things were again brought back on deck. Wenger, despite the fact that we
had been there almost half an hour unloading and reloading our things, finally
appeared with an ax in his hand. All the while he had been looking for his ax,

which he could not find, and therefore took the ax belonging to the boat, for he believed that his had been intentionally misappropriated because it was better. Naturally he thought our things had been unloaded, because he had seen them being carried off. He was therefore more than a little surprised to find everything back on board. The situation was soon explained to him. "You're crazy," he said. We were of the opinion that our whole enterprise—ill-considered and rashly undertaken—was much crazier, and we had his craziness to thank for it all, to which our clever leader had no reply.

When all the freight from this place had been loaded, the boat was again turned around, and we were headed back downstream. Our relations with Wenger had become somewhat cool. Teuss and I considered various plans as to what to do next, and we finally decided to go ashore on some island in the Mississippi, with a lot of fine timber, and stay there as long as our provisions held out. There we would work away, cutting up cordwood and sell it to the first steamboat that came along. This idea was probably a bit quixotic, but we could not accept the thought of returning to Galena with all of our provisions. And we had to do something. Teuss suggested that we enter military service. I would not hear of it because I felt that peacetime military service was suitable only for loafers and ne'er-do-wells. I still had too much self-respect to want to join such company.

Wenger had been keeping to himself, in another part of the boat. We had seen him talking with a large American. Now he suddenly came toward us, bringing the American with him. Wenger reported that the American had told him he was working stands of timber in two different places on islands below the mouth of the St. Croix. If we would be willing to cut up cordwood for him and to provide our own food, he would pay us fifty cents per cord. If one has few prospects one cannot pick and choose, and we certainly were no exception to that rule. We welcomed this timely opportunity to put to use our well-traveled provisions, and soon came to terms with Mr. John Minter, for that was the American's name. Before we left the boat I had to pay the passage again for all three of us, for my companions had long since run out of money.

The timbering operation to which Minter took us was on an island off to the right bank, about four miles below Prescott and Point Douglas.[20] There we found a very low log cabin of the simplest construction, with doors about four foot high. At the far end of this cabin was a kind of platform on which, if necessary, six men could lie. To one side was the hearth, and the furniture consisted of but one roughhewn bench. The cabin was perhaps a hundred yards from the bank, and had been constructed on a rather low spot.

We found that the best timber for cutting and splitting had already been removed. For the most part the only trees left were those that were either very difficult to split, or were much too large—trees that previous woodcutters had seen fit to let stand. In order that he would not be by himself, Minter requested that one of us go with him to his upper timber site. This was about two miles above the one that we were working. Teuss went up with him, but left his trunk with us.

So now Wenger and I remained by ourselves on the island, and we set to work with a will. But despite the fact that Wenger was an experienced woodcutter, he was not able to get much done because the best trees had already been cut. As for me, of course I did my best, but my pile of wood did not seem to grow at all. Each of us had cut only a few cords when the sky darkened and the weather turned rainy.

36. How Wenger Showed His Cowardice—Fleeing to the Upper Cabin Because of High Water

Wenger had earlier spent some time in Texas, and claimed that he had come to know wild Indians there, on one occasion even having had to fight them off for an entire night. He referred to them as the deaf people. By this he implied that they were little more than idiots, and he acted as though he had not the slightest fear of them. At first, of course, I thought that I had found quite a man in Wenger, for since he was familiar with Indians, at least he would not be afraid of the savages. But soon—one evening, after a rainy day—I was to see what kind of man my partner really was.

We had just finished our evening meal, the few utensils had been washed, I had put aside enough leftovers, in a tin dish so that we would only need to warm them up for breakfast the next morning, and I had just lain down on our platform, when the little doorway darkened. Thinking it was Wenger entering, I was about to speak to him. But it was not Wenger. It was a slender Indian; behind him was another, and behind this one yet another. Lastly Wenger entered. I was startled at first, but did not want to show it to the Indians, instead positioning myself before them with an expression that was far from friendly. The Indians stared at me at first, but then held out their hands to me, and said "Howdy do?" Having discerned that they were not hostile, I naturally tried to be friendly as well.

Because it was rainy, and also a bit cool, the Indians squatted before the fire, especially the female, for one of them was a woman. Wenger, who usually referred to Indians as the deaf people, had become quite pale, and said, as he placed more wood on the fire, "The Indians are cold and probably hungry. We ought to give them something to eat." As he spoke he had already taken our next morning's breakfast and offered it to them. This did not please me, for the Indians had not even asked for something to eat. But I let him have his way. The food consisted of boiled potatoes, dried baked apples, and several slices of fried bacon. The Indians seemed satisfied; they rummaged through the proffered food with their dark, dirty fingers, fishing out the bacon and the apples, but leaving the potatoes. The apples tasted especially good to them. This they demonstrated in various ways, often saying "Washteido," which was supposed to mean "very good."

Wenger, the fool, seemed, from outright fear, to have lost his senses, for when he saw that the Indians especially enjoyed the apples, he was stupid enough to show them that we had a sackful. They lost no time holding out their woolen blankets, and gestured that he should give them some, and Wenger gave each of them as much as he could scoop out with his two hands. But the Indians were not satisfied with that. They demanded even more, and Wenger actually wanted to give them even more, but I ordered him to stop, for the apples belonged to me. I was infuriated by Wenger's cowardly behavior. It appeared to me that the Indians must have noticed his fear and had decided to take advantage of it.

As soon as the Indians realized that I was taking charge, they directed their requests for more dried apples to me. They called me "Captain," perhaps to encourage my generosity. But that did not alter my resolve. Wenger had sat down on our bench. The larger Indian sat down beside him, while I remained near the other Indian and the squaw. The larger Indian had looked all around, had discovered salt, flour, sugar, etc., and wanted some of each. I gave him a little salt, since we could best spare some of that, but he wanted some of everything, and I thought the time had come to show him that he could not have his way in everything. I gave him nothing more, and should he try to help himself, I would attempt to keep his hands off our goods. Then the fellow seemed to realize that there had to be something to drink in the coffeepot, and, after he picked it up, he noticed that there was something in it, and he lifted it to his large mouth, intending to gulp the coffee down. In the next moment he coughed up a large quantity of coffee grounds. It was comical to see the face he made. I could not keep from laughing, and finally everyone else laughed too. As soon as he had managed to spit the grounds out of his mouth, he laughed also.

Wenger, from the moment I had taken charge, had become as quiet as a timid boy. I think that he would have let the Indians have whatever they wanted, for he never dared deny them anything. My Indian neighbor had sat down on an empty powder keg. He seemed to believe that it might be filled with whiskey; uttering a word that sounded like whiskey, he pointed upstream. Perhaps he thought he could buy it at the little trading post, present-day Prescott.

The Indian woman now arose and went out the door, with my neighbor following her; but as he stood up, he started to carry under his arm the cask on which he had been sitting, intending to make off with it. But I was right on his heels, and outside the cabin, seized the cask, and threw it back, through the open door, almost hitting the large Indian, who had been following us and was, at that moment, coming out. The Indians seemed astounded at my audacity. The fellow, from whom I had taken the keg, angrily grunted a few unintelligible words. The large one just stared at me in surprise, but seemed to be halfway amused. I wanted to follow them to the little stream. However, they all protested vigorously, and my frightened Wenger desperately begged me not to follow them to the river, for they had guns in their canoe and might yet shoot me dead. I had let myself be persuaded, and have reproached myself for it ever since, for it surely must have given the Indians the impression that I had come to fear them after all. But I really read the riot act to Wenger for his cowardly behavior, he who habitually referred to Indians as simply deaf people. I bluntly told him that I could no longer have any respect for him.

The rainy weather continued; the river rose higher. Finally a considerable current ran between us and the high river bank, across the island, closer to our cabin, and, since we had no canoe, and the water kept rising ever higher, our situation began to cause some concern. By felling trees we tried to make a kind of makeshift bridge, up to the high river bank. But the small trees were immediately swept away, and, since the only other trees were very large ones that would require a great deal of work, and probably would not have served our purpose anyway. So we gave up that idea. I tried using our cabin door as a raft, but it sank under me. So there was nothing to do but wait patiently, and, if necessary, take refuge with our possessions on the low roof of our cabin, for the flood waters would have to rise almost two to three feet more before the cabin itself would be in danger of being swept away.

Early the next morning we found, as I got up from my bed, one to two feet of water in the cabin, in which our clothes trunks and other belongings were floating about; and the cabin was completely surrounded by fast flowing water, which was rising ever higher. We knew Minter had a large, heavy canoe, and, since our situation was becoming more serious by the hour, we hoped that he or Teuss would come to our rescue. If they did not come, then we would surely perish. From the roof of our cabin we kept looking in the direction from which we expected help. Then Minter arrived with his canoe. He guided it through the open door, into the cabin. In order to get everything onto dry land, we first took everything to the high river bank. Then we packed the canoe with our provisions and tools, leaving our trunks and some other things behind.

Minter told me to get into the canoe, which was very heavily laden. It was the first time in my life I had been in a craft of that kind, and I found that, due to the added weight of myself and Minter, the canoe sank considerably deeper, barely three to four inches above the water. The waters of the Mississippi tore by, and, because I was a complete newcomer to this kind of craft, it rocked so precariously that I expected the canoe to capsize at any moment. I tried as hard as I could to just stay upright and perfectly still. But since I had to help paddle, which I had never done before, the rocking continued, to the extent that Minter called out, every few minutes, "Look out, or we'll capsize!" I don't believe that I have ever been so frightened in my whole life as I was during that first canoe trip. The sweat streamed down my face, and I did not even dare wipe it off because I feared the effect of any undue movement. At the same time we simply had to paddle strenuously against the current in the heavily laden canoe, and, even so, we made but slow progress. After about a half hour of constant hard paddling I had learned how to paddle better. I could also move, without putting the canoe in constant danger of capsizing. But I believe that it must have taken us at least two hours to cover the two miles to the upper cabin. At the upper logging area the wood that had already been chopped lay strewn about in the forest, and the rapidly rising waters were threatening to wash it all away. Minter said, "If you want me to go back for your trunks and for Wenger, you will have to help me save some of this wood."

He showed us that, if we felled two adjacent trees going in the same direction, we could pile a good bit of the wood on them, thereby possibly saving it from being swept away. Teuss and I were willing, and went to work immediately, but Minter soon had to return to the lower cabin to get Wenger and our baggage. While Minter was gone we cooked our midday meal, including a portion for Wenger. Then we set about saving as much wood as we could for Minter.

Several hours had passed and we were still waiting for the canoe to return with all our worldly goods, but we saw and heard nothing. Then we heard a rifle shot and assumed that Wenger had perhaps shot at a duck. In the area from which the shot had been fired a canoe did come into view, and we thought it was Minter and Wenger, but then another canoe came, and then another and another; indeed there were many of them. They were Indians. But Wenger and Minter were not to be seen. We did not know what to make of it. We were afraid that Wenger and Minter had ended up being killed and robbed and that perhaps we were to be attacked next. So there was no time to lose.

I quickly readied my rifle and placed it behind the door, and I concealed my large, sharp butcher knife on my body, should it be necessary to use it. Teuss, unfortunately, was still without a firearm. Like me, however, he had armed himself with a knife, and he also had an ax with which he could defend himself, if necessary. We stayed outside the cabin, for I felt that we should show no unnecessary fear, although some of the Indians had begun a strange, jubilant shouting. One of the canoes came paddling up a sidearm of the river, toward our cabin. Its occupants were only a full-grown Indian, a woman, a boy of about twelve, and a little boy of perhaps two. The Indian apparently thought he could get between the tree trunk and then back into the mainstream. He landed at our cabin, and they entered it. All were well dressed for Indians and wore various decorations, especially the little boy, who seemed to be everyone's special favorite.

Teuss had his large tobacco pipe in his mouth. I noticed that the Indian looked at him frequently, as if expecting that Teuss would offer it to him as a peace gesture so that he could take a few puffs too. But, since Teuss made no move to do so, the Indian said something to the older boy, who left but returned right away with a long-stemmed pipe and a bag of tobacco. He filled the pipe, lit it, and then handed it to the Indian, who took a few puffs and then handed it to me. I naturally did the same, for I assumed that this was a sign of peace, and I then handed it to the boy, who followed our example exactly, and then gave it back to the elder Indian. Teuss was thereby denied the peace pipe, probably because he had not offered his pipe as a gesture of peace and good intentions. Perhaps he wanted thereby to teach Teuss better manners.

Since the Indian saw that we had salt he asked us for a little, which I gladly gave him. These people had not been rude or demanding, but were quite decent, with the result that I already had a much higher opinion of Indians than after our first encounter on the lower island. The canoe was full of various items. Among other things, there were two rifles decorated with a great deal of brass, one of which he indicated could shoot quite a distance. They got in and followed the others, who had already moved on upstream.

We still had not seen a sign of Wenger and Minter. We had only seen an Indian canoe, with several persons in it, way out in the mainstream, just prior to the Indian family's arrival at our cabin, but we were at a loss to understand how it happened that it had completely disappeared so soon afterward. We half-feared the canoe might have sunk, along with its passengers. Then soon afterwards we heard human sounds again, and when we looked downstream we saw, quite close, our Christian Wenger in a canoe, along with three Indian women, who actually seemed to be managing the canoe quite easily.

Wenger came ashore, and so did the Indian women. We gave each one five cents and a tin cup of flour for their having brought Wenger; Minter had found that even without Wenger, the canoe was almost too low in the water; and Wenger told us that Minter would follow and should be arriving soon. But, even before the Indian women left us, we heard my name being called, and saw our Minter, on the crest of the eastern bank, calling out to me to kill the Indians because they had killed Wenger. Wenger answered that he was not dead and that everything was all right. Minter did not cross to our island that day; he had left our trunks on the Wisconsin side of the river, where he had taken them the day before. We feared that perhaps everything, at least a part of our clothing, would be lost. Teuss was furious with Minter, and declared that, if he did not bring us our trunks and everything in them, he would break his neck at the first opportunity.

The next day was Sunday. Not having to work, we had all the more time to mull things over. We called out to Minter again. He let us know that he was going down to the place where he had left our things, including the canoe, the evening before, and to our pleasant surprise he brought everything with him. That is, Teuss and I found nothing missing. Wenger, on the other hand, claimed that his silver pocket watch had been taken from his trunk. We felt that Minter would probably know best what had happened to it, for if someone else had been the thief, especially the Indians, they would not have been satisfied with only the watch.

During the following days we tried to save as much of the chopped wood as possible from being washed away, and we often waded up to our hips in the cold Mississippi waters. That was rather stupid of us. It was an even greater stupidity to wade into the cold river water three to four feet deep to fell trees, which we cut into cordwood as soon as we had dragged them to higher land. The first morning, after our work in the water, my left arm was so stiff from rheumatism that at first I could hardly move it. But when my associates went right back to work I did not want to be the only one who was not working. So I took up my ax and, despite the cold water, I chopped wood like the others, although at first it caused considerable pain in my arm. On the morning of the following day my left arm still hurt very badly. But again the others went to work, so naturally I felt I had to be there too. Though initially still extremely painful, strangely enough I was not bothered by it afterwards, though, like the others, I worked in water two or three more days.

The water had gradually risen to such a level that the greater part of the island was flooded, and it would have been utter insanity to have tried to work in that icy cold water any longer. In addition, there was no room left on which we could cut and stack wood. Our log cabin stood on the highest spot of land, and this was scarcely eight or nine inches above water. The water had risen right up to the back of the cabin, and it now stood on an island scarcely thirty feet in diameter. We now had quite a lot of idle time. To pass the time, or partly out of necessity, so that we would not entirely run out of food we tried to fish, to which end we set out large fishing hooks at likely places in the river. We caught a good many. They were all large catfish, but, though they tasted rather good to us at first, we gradually tired of them.

One day Minter offered to show us his so-called claim on the Wisconsin side. We set off across the river in our canoe, secured it, and then walked downstream along the river bank for about four miles, until we came to the place Minter had told us about. Although too hilly to suit me, a good deal of it did seem of average quality. Also there were some moderately good oak stands. Minter planned to settle on his land later, and then to begin a modest trade with the Indians.

Another time Wenger and I set off for the Wisconsin side in the hope of shooting some game. I had my rifle and Wenger brought along his long-barreled gun. Since he considered himself to be the chief hunter, he suggested that I lend him my rifle, to which I did not agree. We arrived on a rise, partially overgrown by a thicket. "There is a deer in there!" he called to me. "Chase it out of there!" I did so, sending the deer leaping mightily, out on Wenger's side of the thicket. "Crack" went the rifle, and "Aha, I got him!" Wenger yelled. Quickly I hurried around the thicket, expecting to see the deer in its death throes. But there was nothing there. "So where is your deer?" I asked. "It must be lying nearby," he replied. But although we searched everywhere, no deer was to be found. He insisted, however, that he had seen the deer's antlers fly in all directions when he shot it, yet neither he nor I could find a trace of blood or antlers.

Wenger had simply told another one of his lies, as he had become all too accustomed to do. Of course he tried to put the blame on me. Had I but loaned him my rifle the deer would now surely be ours. If I had been certain that he had actually hit it, even I would have been inclined to believe him. But since he was as unable as I to find either hair or blood, and since he had been quite close to the stag when he fired, I considered his story to be pure bluster, and I let him know it. When we returned Wenger had a deer story to tell, and Minter, who did not yet know him well, was inclined to believe him and to blame me. However, he was going to have a chance to get to know Wenger better.

37. An Evening Visit from Indians and Their Culinary Art— Minter and Wenger Intend to Trade with the Indians— The Latter's Bragging and Lying

For some time Teuss and I had noticed that Wenger and Minter were keeping some kind of secret from us. But we made no particular effort to learn what it was. However we suspected that it might involve a partnership to trade with the Indians. And one evening—it was dark already—our cabin door was literally thrown open, and a large Indian started to enter, behind whom we could see three more Indian forms. Apparently the Indians had not known that, instead of only one man, there were four of us. But, when they so unexpectedly found the attention of four white men focused upon them, they stopped in their tracks. But when they saw us smile, they came nearer, stretching out their hands toward us, saying, "How do do." They were two men and two women who had traded their various furs at present-day Prescott for knives, glass beads, whiskey (min-nesota or firewater), and some bilge water, which was supposed to be wine.

The men sat down on our wooden bench, while the women squatted on the floor close to the fireplace. One of the squaws filled the peace pipe, lit it, and then handed it to one of the Indians. He took several puffs and then offered it to his companion. That one did the same and offered it to Minter because he was sitting closest to him. After all of us had done exactly the same, the pipe was returned to the first Indian, who set it aside, and then poured a little from a brandy bottle into a tin cup, drank some of it himself, and then passed it around the circle, as he had the pipe. When it came back to him, he drank once more and let it go around the circle again. When he found, however, that the white men wished no more of it, he produced another bottle, poured some of its con-tents into a cup, drank a few gulps as before, and let it be passed around the circle. The Indians said it was wine. We took it to be a mixture of vinegar, whiskey and water. He offered us another round of this as well, for which we thanked him.

Probably satisfied from the thanks received that he had secured our friend-ship, he now asked Minter if he would be allowed to cook their evening meal on our hearth, which we gladly consented to. They had a large metal kettle with them. The women filled it half full with water. Into it they put a piece of alli-gatorfish and a duck, whose feathers had been plucked, but whose entrails had not been removed. They also added a turtle. They impaled a muskrat, which had been skinned and disemboweled, on a long pointed stick and then stuck it into the ground, close to the fire, and they slowly turned the rat, exposing its sides to the fire, until it had become as crisp as a well-baked crust of bread. In addition, they also had impaled two live turtles. They made a place for them in the hot ashes, set them in it, and covered them all over with ashes. This new environ-ment seemed to give the turtles little pleasure. At first they tried various ma-neuvers, but wherever they turned the hellish heat was the same. Apparently realizing the futility of their situation, they gave up all further attempts to free themselves.

Supper was finally ready. The broth (soup) from the kettle was eagerly slurped and drunk. The duck, entrails and all, was next, and appeared to taste wonder-ful to them, as did the alligatorfish and the turtles. The crisp muskrat and a tur-tle were taken along on the journey, after they had first invited us to share in their meal, for which we thanked them.

While the food had been cooking the Indians had shown us various articles which they had traded for animal pelts. A large portion appeared to have been muskrat, which they called zinquapins. Minter, who could speak a little Indian, asked them how many zinquapin pelts they would have given for an ordinary butcher knife, whereupon the Indian counted off at least fifteen to seventeen on his fingers. In St. Louis this kind of knife cost twenty to twenty-five cents, while each muskrat pelt would bring twenty cents, certainly a nice profit.

Minter had for the moment completely forgotten his well-kept secret with Wenger. The huge profit that traders made from zinquapins filled them with joy, and then Minter blurted out, "Wenger, by God, what a killing we are going to make with our new business venture!" "So that's your secret. We had thought so for a long time." From then on there was no need to maintain the secrecy, and we learned that they intended to build a small house on Minter's claim, there to begin their trade with the Indians.

The river level stayed high for some time, so work was out of the question, and it happened a few times that we ran short of provisions. We tried to shoot something edible: coots, ducks, and pheasants, etc., and at times these, along with catfish, were what we subsisted on. The person whose turn it was to cook—we traded off daily—stayed behind.

One fine afternoon Wenger had paddled off in the large canoe to the big slough where the water was quiet and very deep, which we thought would be a good place to catch catfish. But as often happened, Wenger, our chief hunter, which he firmly considered himself to be, came back without anything at all. Whenever Wenger had nothing to bring back he usually found some reason or other for returning empty handed. Of course today, instead of catfish, he had fished up something else, and that turned out to be a wild and fantastic story. Swearing to the truth of his tale, he told how a terrible, fearsome large fish had taken the bait on his long catfish line and had dragged him, canoe and all, around the large slough, threatening to yank him out of the canoe at any moment, and that he might have eventually been pulled from the canoe if he had not managed to catch hold of a willow tree just in time. I think Wenger found few believing ears. Mine were the least believing, for unfortunately it had been my bad luck to come to know him too well to believe, as I had previously, all his lies.

38. How Teuss and I Try to Fish in the Large Slough and the Return Canoe Trip

The following day it was Wenger's turn to cook. Teuss and I tried our luck fishing at the same place where Wenger had had his colossal fish adventure the day before. For bait we were using bird entrails, which the fish usually took quite eagerly; but although we had put out our lines and had tried various likely places, no fish would bite, not even the monstrous fish that had nearly made off with our Wenger the previous day. The sun was already low in the west when Wenger called to us to come for the evening meal. Although dissatisfied with our bad luck, we pulled in our hooks and lines and set out for home. We were looking at the water—at least twenty feet deep here—and since neither Teuss nor I knew how to swim, it seemed to me not the right place for foolishness in the canoe. Teuss, however, was full of reckless mischief, and, when he thought he could play a particularly good prank on someone, it gave him tremendous pleasure. A long slender sapling lay upon the surface of the slough. One could easily take a canoe out over it if one worked reasonably fast with the paddle. I had paddled strenuously to get over the sapling so that the canoe was nearly halfway over it, and only a few more strokes would have been required to put the sapling behind us. To the left of this spot, between the top of some tall willows, there was a place through which we could make quick turns and reach open water. As already stated, a few strong strokes of the paddle would have carried us over the slender sapling, which would have, under our weight, sunk deep into the water. At this point Teuss suddenly took it into his head to take the open but winding route, stating that we could not paddle the canoe over the trees—though there was certainly enough water to do so. The sudden turning of the canoe, and back paddling, put us in danger of capsizing. My observation that, thanks to his foolish behavior, we could easily capsize and drown, since neither of us could swim, was met with his repeated question, "What did you say?" I declared that if he intended to continue with such foolishness I would no longer paddle, to which he answered with his "What did you say?" He had almost brought the canoe to the place where we were to get out, and I was already preparing to do so, when Teuss pushed the canoe back into deep water. He had taken it into his head to make me really angry, but I ignored him. Teuss paddled back into the large slough. From this a smaller one branched off to the right, deep into the heart of the island, where its waters formed a little fall over a large tree trunk. He let the canoe glide over it, paddled to a shallow spot near the shore and then jumped out. His feet had hardly touched solid ground when I pushed off, back into deep water. He tried to stop me, but he was not quick enough. "Just look over there, you will not be able to get up there by yourself," he called to me. But I replied that, should I not make it upstream by water, I would drag the canoe by land. The trunk, however, lay deep in the water on the opposite shore, and, when I got the canoe going fast by paddling strenuously, I got it going fast enough to get across it without much difficulty.

I turned back toward Teuss, and I acted as though I were going back to take him back into the canoe, which he repeatedly asked me to do, and he was about to jump in when I backed away from the shore again. "You tried to make me angry and for no good reason. But you have been caught in your own trap, and now you will spend the night out in the open. Maybe some bears, panthers, or Indians will keep you company," I remarked. "You see how nice it is to dig a ditch for someone else only to fall in it yourself?" Although Teuss was a big strong fellow, he was not all pleased at the thought of spending an entire night alone in the open. He begged me repeatedly to let him back in, and two or three times more I tormented him. At the point of land, between the small and the large slough, he found a large, gray-headed duck with a broken leg and a broken wing. It had been shot the previous day by an Indian, who had not been able to find it. Teuss held it up high calling out to me, "Look what I have found. Now you will pick me up, won't you?" But I continued to act as though I were un-interested. Only after he had promised faithfully never again to annoy me that way, did I pick him up.

Wenger had called to us repeatedly, and was angry because we did not come to eat. I had fired my gun, and, when we got back and Wenger asked us why we had been gone so long, Teuss told him that, since my shot had not imme-diately killed the duck, it had taken some time to find it. We were now ready to eat. But there was only a little bowl of catfish, which had been picked over. Some Indians had been there in our absence, and our fine cook had presented our supper to them, and since they had picked out the choicest bits, Wenger ex-pected us to eat what was left. This time we knew how to look out for ourselves. We did not eat the leftover catfish, but instead quickly plucked our duck's feath-ers, washed it a little, and soon had it crackling in its own juices over the fire. Be-cause we had a good fire, the duck was well done after a quarter-hour's roasting. We had made coffee as well, so our duck supper tasted wonderful. Wenger would have loved to have had a bit of duck as well; it smelled so good to him. But, as punishment for having given our supper to the Indians, we gave him none of it.

At the invitation of two Germans from Austria, who lived at the mouth of the St. Croix, i.e., Prescott, and who had taken out and already worked a portion of a claim of land a short distance from the river, on the Wisconsin side, we one day set out to pay a visit. I had bolted the door of our cabin from the inside and had climbed out through the chimney. We did this so the Indians could not so easily take advantage of us during our absence. We then paddled toward a sort of bay, a deep cut or indentation, directly across from our cabin, on the high bank of the Wisconsin side of the river. This bay extended for perhaps almost a hundred feet, directly into the bank. At the upper end of the bay grayish-black rock rose perpendicularly, some twenty feet above the water. At the lower end the rock had crumbled at places, and hazel bushes and other shrubs grew in var-ious spots. At the far end the rocks were very jagged, and a perpendicular cliff rose some twenty feet in height. At the foot of this cliff was even more fallen rubble. But surrounding this cove was a border of different kinds of trees, some of which were pine. Interspersed among the trees, especially on the lower side, were bushes.

We had landed at the end of this bay and had tied our canoe to a small hazel bush. I hid our paddles among some fallen boulders at the foot of the aforementioned high cliff. I was the only one with a firearm. Wenger considered it too much trouble to carry one, and Teuss did not have one. We then walked upstream along the high bank, and soon reached the Austrians. Since there was nothing particularly noteworthy about this spot, we asked to have a look at their claim, but arriving there we found nothing that interested us very much. The soil was poor in my opinion, more bad than good, and the trees growing on it of below average quality.

It was a sunny, sultry spring day, which had an enervating effect upon us. We headed back toward the deep bay, Teuss in the lead. But as we neared it, Wenger and I noticed that Teuss must have been walking very fast, for he had already disappeared from our sight. We asked each other, "Where can Teuss be?" Knowing of his great inclination for playing pranks, I remarked that I would not be surprised to see him taking off in the canoe when we arrived at the bay. But Wenger did not want to believe it. We did begin walking a bit faster however. But as we got close to the bay Teuss came running toward us, pale and very frightened, saying, almost out of breath, "There's a big, spotted snake right where we would get into the canoe." "You good for nothing, it is probably only a branch of a tree that you mistook for a snake. Because you have been planning to annoy us for some time, you had a bad conscience. That is probably why you made the mistake," I remarked.

I had truly guessed right. Teuss did not deny it. As we had reached the place where we were to go down to the bay, I first went up to the top of the aforementioned rock, from where I could look straight down upon our canoe. But I could see no snake, only a branch. I now led the way to the bay and, on arriving at the canoe, found no snake, whereupon I called to my companions that they should come also. Wenger came, but Teuss was still apprehensive, and very carefully descended the rocky slope. I was just about to pick up our paddles from between the fallen boulders when I actually did find a snake there. The snake, not more than four to five feet long, was whitish yellowish-brown with black spots. It was in no hurry to slither away from the spot, but shot its pointed forked tongue in and out repeatedly.

I still had my gun in my hand and tried to shoot its head off; I had, however, aimed a little too low, for the bullet only blew away its lower jaw. Now it had lost all desire to remain by the paddles and tried to make a hasty retreat. But

I immediately killed it with one of the paddles. Teuss finally dared to come down. Wenger had seated himself in the rear of the canoe; Teuss had taken a seat in the middle. I laid down my unloaded weapon in the front of the canoe and was about to untie it from the hazel bush when a similar, considerably larger snake emerged from the lower crumbled bank of the bay and came swimming rapidly through the water directly at Teuss, with its head held high, its large angry eyes glaring, and its forked tongue working. At my shout, "Look at the snake!" Teuss got up like a flash, and, with a mighty leap, landed on a small rock jutting out into the water. The snake immediately turned toward Wenger. I called to him to hit it with the sharp edge of the paddle, and bang, he made a direct hit and knocked it deep into the water! The snake surfaced again but it had lost its will to fight. It turned away and swam back not half as fast as it had come to the place it had so recently left. It slowly slithered up between rocks and bushes where, at a height of some sixteen feet, it twined itself about some brush and glared down upon us from there. The snake may have been about six to seven feet long and as thick as the arm of a half-grown youth.

Teuss had climbed all the way out of the bay, to the top of the cliff, and from there asked us to paddle out of this hole and pick him up at some other place. We answered that he was in no way better than us, and was scarcely due any special consideration after his cowardly behavior. So, feeling forced, despite his great fear, to get back in the canoe, he kept looking back apprehensively at the snake, which continued to flick its tongue in our direction as we paddled near it on our way out of the bay.

Wenger and I visited the bay again some ten days later. We did so to get some resin from the few pine trees, which we put on one of Minter's index fingers, partly bitten off in a fight with another Kentuckian. It had caused him a good deal of pain, which soon eased, and then the finger quickly healed. As we approached the pine trees through the brush above the bay, we found several similar-looking snakes, though none were large. But they were not inclined to move out of the way, and they made shaking movements with their tails, producing a sound somewhat like that of a rattlesnake, only not quite so loud. I killed three of them. Wenger also killed one or two. As I was heading between some dense bushes and loose rock toward another pine, I heard a kind of growling or hissing which so alarmed me that I backed away quickly. I had seen nothing, but I was not about to linger, perhaps to be suddenly bitten by a poisonous snake.

The waters had now receded considerably, but the ground was still marshy and muddy in places. For some time chopping wood would be out of the question. Teuss, as usual, was full of mischief. He was only content when he could play some kind of trick. One time he wanted to find out which of the three of us was the strongest, and he was prepared to take on Wenger first to see who was the strongest. Teuss was about my height, but considerably heavier, had limbs he was proud of, which he liked to show off. Listening to Wenger one might fairly believe that he would be hard to overpower. But Teuss wanted to have proof, and invited Wenger to try a *Hosenlupf* with him. Wenger countered that he knew only the Berner kind of *Schwingen*,[21] which Teuss probably would not find to his liking. Teuss was willing to try the Berner variety of wrestling first, and after that they would try the Graubuenden kind.

Each now tied a handkerchief, I believe around his left thigh, after which each, with one hand, took a firm hold of the handkerchief, wrapping the other arm around the upper body. "Ready!" was the call. And now, according to Wenger, Teuss's feet should have swung into the air, just as his back was immediately thrown to the ground. Instead, as I had expected, that is not at all what happened; both fell down together, Teuss landing on top. Wenger insisted that he simply had been unable to keep from laughing, but after that he did not dare do another *Hosenlupf* with Teuss. Teuss now knew that he could beat Wenger, but he was not sure about me, and was determined to find out. So on the following day he suddenly grabbed me. He allowed me to take a similar hold on him, making several efforts to throw me. But then, thanks to my outstretched leg, he was the one who fell on his back. I pinned him there. After making several unsuccessful attempts to roll me off, he admitted defeat and declared me the stronger of the two.

Since the sun was so warm, Teuss often took off all of his clothes and wallowed in the black slime left by the flood waters, until his body was completely covered with it. Afterwards he submerged himself up to his mouth in the cold river water and began emitting certain gases from his submerged gas machine, which created large bubbles that crawled up his back and behind his head, to the surface of the water, all the while making muffled, half-strangled sounds. He repeated this experiment later.

Teuss called Wenger our *Daeti*[22] and repeatedly said to him, "*Daeti,* why do you lie so much?" One time he even wanted me to help him castrate *Daeti*. Naturally I did not help, and I had no way of knowing whether or not Teuss was serious. Unfortunately, I later learned that he actually had carried out a partial operation of this type on another lad in his homeland, and that he had persuaded another child to eat poisonous juniper berries, which caused the child's death. I have often since thought that, had I then been willing to cooperate, our Wenger probably would have found himself employed harmlessly as a eunuch in a harem somewhere.

39. Wenger's Double-Dealing of Us and Minter—
Swarms of Mosquitoes—Trip Back to Galena

Wenger had finally left our island home, had made the trip to the steamboat at Galena, intending to travel to Highland, and then later to return from St. Louis with the goods needed to carry on trade with the Indians. He told Minter, his future business partner, that he would write him from Galena.

Teuss and I stayed and tried to chop a lot of wood, for the forest offered much better opportunities than the lower island. But the more the flood waters receded on the island, the bigger the swarms of mosquitoes became, until we found it almost impossible to carry on, despite our best intentions. Our provisions were almost all used up, although we had managed to supplement our stores substantially with fish and wild fowl. There were plenty of wild doves, but the swarms of bloodsucking insects gave us no respite when we tried to shoot doves. They attacked us everywhere. They flew into our mouths, ears, noses, and eyes, slipped up our sleeves, and came up our pant legs. Their long stingers went through shirts and pants. They gave us no peace, in the cabin or outside, from the break of day in the morning, until far into the night.

To protect myself from them somewhat during the day I had to wear two shirts and a pair of black buckskin pants. Even so, they did not let up. At night I slipped into my straw sack bed, and twisted the corners together over my head, and I felt fortunate if I could thus find a little peace, all the while listening to Teuss and Minter, as they continued to be disturbed and bitten. Evenings we filled the air, inside and out, with dense smoke. But this helped only as long as the smoke lasted. Then they were back again.

Minter finally received a letter from Wenger from Galena. But since Wenger could not write English, and Minter could not read German, he was forced to ask me to read the letter. He wanted to hear something about the prospective Indian trade, for that was, I believed, the understanding between them. Teuss and I were not a little surprised when we instead received advice from Wenger to chop a lot of wood for Minter and to try to earn money. And then he intended to establish a partnership with us, rather than with Minter, and, with us, to build a house on Minter's claim (and without Minter) to trade with the Indians.

I was shocked by Wenger's false and deceitful conduct and wanted to pass the news immediately to Minter, who was waiting impatiently to hear the contents of the letter. At first Teuss did not want me to do so, but I explained that if he wanted to throw in his lot with a fellow such as Wenger, who could, with no reason, be as deceitful to us as he now was to Minter, he could do what he wished.

As for myself, I did not want anything from Wenger other than the money I had paid out for him.

Minter was almost beside himself with impatience. But when I told him about the proposal contained in the letter, he said I was a dirty liar. So I suggested he take the letter to the Austrians and have them read it. Then he would soon find out whether or not I had told him the truth. The next morning Minter followed my advice, went to the Austrians, and learned what he had not wanted to believe. When he returned I asked him about it and he admitted that I had told him the truth and that he had been mistaken about Wenger.

Minter told me that Wenger had informed him that I had money with a St. Louis merchant and that this merchant knew that Wenger and I were good friends. Wenger intended to go to him and ask him to hand over my money, and he thought the merchant would give it to him. I was indeed expecting to receive a small payment from Switzerland in care of Mr. [John] Boeschenstein in St. Louis. My presumed, upright friend Wenger knew this, and apparently in the expectation that the money might have arrived, the villainous fellow dared to try to get his hands on it without my knowledge or consent. By the way, I pointed out to Minter that he had only told me this to get even with Wenger. Had he not treated him so deceitfully he would not have told me a single word about it. Therefore he was little better than Wenger himself.

We often had opportunities to get to know the Indians, and our relations with them were mutually friendly. However, one time some Indians, to whom we had earlier given something to eat, took a fishing line we had hung out. One day, as Teuss and I were chopping wood a short distance above our cabin, an Indian and a squaw passed by very close to us in a canoe. The squaw paddled the canoe while he loaded a small carbine, probably to have it ready to fire if necessary, while he was in the vicinity of white men. He was the chief of the Sioux Indians of Red Wing, blind in one eye, about forty years old, more short than tall, but fairly stocky. His companion was his favorite wife, the most highly prized of his six or seven spouses. They had not noticed us as they passed by, and since we knew Minter was at home, we had not considered it necessary to check to see whether they would stop for a visit. When we returned to the cabin at noon, Minter told us that Mokopenoscha, the chief's name, had taken our hatchet with him, and he could not say whether we would ever get it back. We were annoyed with Minter for not having called us when the chief took our hatchet. We did not expect to see it again. One evening, when we were having our supper, a tall, good-looking, young Indian entered our cabin with our hatchet in his hand; he put it down, saying something we simply could not understand, which probably were words of thanks. We saw Mokopenoscha at our place more than once.

One day—a rather heavy rain just happened to be falling—two Sioux Indians stopped in to seek shelter from the rain. Seeing the rainwater leaking through the roof everywhere, the first one said, "Ha Mini Ahta" (Why, the water comes through). One appeared to be a great warrior. He had three eagle feathers on his head, wore various decorations, and also had a comb and a small mirror, in which he often admired his coarse, supposedly handsome face, and he no doubt considered it incomparably beautiful. Minter told us that he must have killed three Indians of another tribe, for a Sioux was only entitled to wear an eagle feather if he killed an enemy. When asked to which nation the dead warriors had belonged, he replied "Sauk and Fox."[23]

The Sioux usually kept to the area west of the Mississippi, while the Chippewa kept more to the east.[24] We had not seen any Chippewa. Because they are not on friendly terms with the Sioux, they avoid each other, and only undertake minor skirmishes as a kind of diversion.

Regarding such, Minter told us the following story. A large number of Sioux warriors undertook an expedition up the St. Croix River intending to attack the Chippewa. They stopped at the Stillwater Sawmill to get information regarding their enemies. They had hardly resumed their up-river journey when two Chippewa arrived at the same sawmill. Since the sawmill people were more in Chippewa territory than in Sioux, they were inclined to favor the former. They told the Chippewa that a large number of Sioux warriors had just left the mill to attack them, the Chippewa. Whereupon the Chippewa immediately paddled over to the left bank, and then—knowing the area well—hurried overland to a place on the St. Croix where they knew the Sioux would have to paddle close to the bank. They actually succeeded in reaching the spot unobserved, just before the Sioux got there. The latter now began to cross the spot, when two shots from the bank instantly killed two warriors. But, before the Sioux could pursue them, their enemies had disappeared. And the Sioux, realizing that pursuit was useless, went back to the right bank of the river, erected a sort of platform for each of the dead and gave each one his rifle, a kettle, fuel, and some provisions, so that they would have the things they most needed in their happy hunting grounds beyond. As soon as they had paid their brothers their last respects, they resumed their suddenly interrupted river journey, but without locating their enemies.

The sawmill people had witnessed everything from afar, and when the Sioux left their two fallen brothers behind, some of the sawmill people had gone there and had stolen the rifles and several other things, thinking the Sioux would blame the theft on the Chippewa. When the Sioux returned they stopped at the resting place and found that their brothers had been robbed. They immediately concluded that the whites, and not the Chippewa, had been the thieves. The warriors, numbering roughly two hundred, stopped at the sawmill and demanded the immediate return of the stolen items. The whites all denied having any knowledge of the items, but the Indians would not be put off. They said that, if the Chippewa had been the thieves, they would have taken the warriors' scalps and cut their hearts out of their bodies, which had not occurred. The warriors finally left, but with the express warning that they would return in a very short while. If the looted items had not been returned, they would have found ways to expose the thieves, and would have punished them harshly. After a certain time, they had returned as promised, and in great numbers. But their threats had had the desired effect, for the stolen objects had all been put back in place, and the Indians were thus satisfied. This was a just and well-deserved humiliation for the whites, and one must wonder whether or not the Christian, but hypocritical, whites would not have dealt much more harshly with the savages in similar circumstances!

The mosquitoes had been appearing lately in such huge swarms that rest was no longer possible. So we decided to leave the place as soon as the steamboat *Otter* appeared. Minter was not happy about this, for he had told us a few times about another Kentuckian at Douglas Point, who, like Minter, sold cordwood to the steamboats, and who was angry because of the competition, and had, once or twice, threatened to kill him. As long as we were with him, he considered himself comparatively safe, but he feared a return to his former perilous situation as soon as it was known that he was alone.

Teuss and I each had chopped only twenty cords of wood, and up to then I had received no payment. To Teuss, he had disposed of a rifle that cost almost ten dollars. The remainder, which he still owed Teuss, was barely enough money to pay his passage to Galena. So far Teuss had not repaid me anything, but he offered to give me a note for the amount he owed me, or if I preferred, I could keep his trunk and all of his clothes until I was paid in full. I asked him to tell me whether he was really honest or not. He claimed he was honest and promised to repay me with the very first money he earned. I told him I would take his word of honor, instead of his note or his trunk, and see whether he had deceived me or not. So that I would at least have something of his in my possession, he gave me his rifle as collateral, with the suggestion that were I able to sell it, I should then apply the proceeds against his debt.

The *Otter* had finally arrived and had tied up near our cabin. Our things were on the bank, ready to be loaded, but we still had not received our pay, and it seemed to me that Minter would have preferred that our belongings be brought on board immediately. But I told him firmly that we would not have our things brought on board until we had been paid. Minter may well have suspected that if we were prevented from leaving on the *Otter* he would not likely be able to count on our friendship from then on, and he was not mistaken. Since Minter finally seemed to realize that he could not get rid of us as easily as he seemed to have hoped, he had the ship's clerk give him the necessary money and paid us with it, after which all our things were loaded onto the *Otter,* which immediately steamed downstream. Thus ended our pinery speculation. Even though we had lost roughly two months and had suffered financially, in spite of chopping all that wood, we were both glad to say goodbye to the island and to its mosquitoes, Indians, and snakes. We had seen no large beasts of prey, but early one morning I heard an animal that sounded something like a woman with a high voice calling a child. Well after sunup I headed toward the area from which I had heard the cry of the wild animal and, sure enough, I found the footprints of some kind of panther in the soft earth.

Nothing of moment happened on our return trip. The weather was sunny and pleasant. We passed Red Wing, where the Indians were playing a game with balls, Lake Pepin, Prairie du Chien, and Prairie la Porte, which was developing into the town of Guttenberg and where several small houses had been built since we had last passed by. Then came Dubuque, and finally, hale and hearty, we arrived at the Washington Hotel in Galena.

40. Repairing Guns at Mr. Mack's—Teuss Repays Me and Declares That He Is Honest—He Later Swindles His Father—The Swabian Gardener

In Galena I became acquainted with a locksmith from Wuerttemberg by the name of Friedrich Mack. His wife was from Graubuenden and was the sister of a Mr. [Hartmann] Luetscher, a family man, who I knew had formerly lived on a farm near Highland. As a young man Mr. Mack had traveled through a good deal of Switzerland and was an enthusiastic admirer of the same. Mack repaired all kinds of firearms and, when I told him I had worked for half a year for a gunsmith in Switzerland, he offered to employ me. For the time being, he promised to provide me with room and board. I cannot say that I had much hope of earning high wages because I really did not as yet know much about making firearms. But I thought it better to at least earn my keep than to loaf about idly, using up my money. Thus, I ate at his house and slept at the Washington Hotel, for which he paid.

Mack was a thin little man with light red hair, had done a good deal of reading, and on the whole was not a bad fellow. His wife was a milliner and knew how to make beautiful artificial flowers. She seemed to be a good, industrious woman, but was somewhat delicate.

The space in Mack's house was limited. Even so, it included the workshop, which by itself took up about half of the space. There was definitely a shortage of good tools. Indeed he made the most necessary ones himself. But, since he usually used only poor material, they were generally of very inferior quality. I called this to his attention, and he agreed, but he lacked the means to acquire better. Sometimes there were days when I was able to do the work assigned me with some skill. But then there were other days when I would break the home-made tools one after another, so that I sometimes felt like giving up the work entirely. But Mr. Mack would patiently encourage me, and then I would try again.

The Fourth of July, 1845, had now drawn near. There were all kinds of used firearms to be repaired. Among others, a young man brought a little pocket pistol in for cleaning so that it could be used for shooting again. He remarked that an old bullet was stuck in it, which he had tried in vain to remove. Mr. Mack turned it over to me for cleaning, and I set to work at once. I unscrewed the stock, or breech pin, and, as well as I could, I scraped the old hardened powder from the back part of the barrel until I came to the bullet. Then I tried to remove the bullet, but it would not move backward or forward. I was of the opinion that there had to be two bullets in the barrel, because one bullet without powder could not take up so much space. This I told the master. However, he thought it was only one bullet, and told me to warm it up a bit on his outdoor forge. I thought that this would be dangerous, and that the bullet could easily discharge and wound me. But he thought otherwise, so I went to the forge, worked the bellows a few times and carefully laid the barrel down on it. I was about to remove it from the hot ashes in order to prevent it from getting so hot that it might discharge, but at that very instant, as I was cautiously reaching for it, it went off with a bang, sending the barrel quite a distance and covering me with ash and tiny sparks. Naturally I was greatly startled, but considered myself lucky not to have been injured. I was trying to brush off the ashes and sparks as quickly as I could when the master came rushing out and snapped furiously, "What stupidities are you up to there!" At first I was dumbfounded that he who had ordered me to do it, despite my stating that it might be dangerous, was reproaching me thus. My astonishment quickly gave way to a burst of anger. Without stopping to think, I asked my master whether or not he had not ordered me to lay the barrel in the hot ashes, or whether I had done so out of sheer idiocy. He did not seem to like the question very much. He was of the opinion that I could have mortally wounded his wife, who had just stepped outside before the shot went off. But that did not silence me, for I believed that I had really stood in the greatest danger of being shot, and not *I*, but *he,* was the only one to be blamed. The bullet—if no more than *one* was in the barrel—had lodged in the cabin wall opposite, and the episode had ended happily enough, except for the sheer fright. But the fact that the master had immediately wanted to blame me had infuriated me, and, when two Swiss came into the shop just after the danger had passed, I told them what had happened and asked them what they would have thought under similar circumstances. The master had not a single word to say and seemed quite glad that I also held my tongue. Probably he had spoken thoughtlessly and was now ashamed of himself.

While I was at Master Pfenniger's in Staefa, I had often had the opportunity to rebore rifle barrels that had become rough and did not shoot true, making them as good as new. I had not forgotten how to do it. A boardinghouse keeper named Keller, from the Aargau region, brought in a fine-looking double-barreled rifle, and asked Mack whether he believed he could repair it so that it would shoot straight again. He explained that it had shot accurately before, but now he would either miss entirely or it would not kill cleanly. Mr. Mack turned to me, asking me whether I could make it serviceable again; but I could not give a positive answer. However, I replied that I would work on the barrel just as I had learned to do it at Master Pfenniger's. Keller said that he would gladly sell the rifle for twelve dollars, the way it was, although it looked quite handsome. But if we could repair it so that he could shoot well with it again, he would not sell it for double the price. Mr. Keller, along with a number of other men, planned to leave shortly for the recently discovered copper mines near Lake Superior. It was therefore important to him that the gun be repaired quickly and, if possible, well. I found the bore of the gun to be quite uneven and I took pains to try to put both barrels in perfect order. After Mr. Keller had tried it, he immediately returned, declaring that he wanted to buy a round for the master and me, for the rifle hardly seemed to him to be the same gun, and the worst barrel was now the best, and if someone offered him double the price, he would not sell it. Everyone is a little vain, and I believe that I was also a little vain, and a little proud of my work.

I had been with Mr. Mack only a short time when our former employer, Minter, entered the shop unexpectedly. He was looking for Wenger, and wanted me to tell him where he would most likely find him, information I was glad to give him. I was of the opinion, however, that the money he would spend on the trip would be wasted, for if I had been in his shoes I would not have anything further to do with so deceitful a person as Wenger had proven to be. Even so, Minter undertook the journey and found him at Jacob Schuetz's farm, and then, ten to fourteen days later, returned without having achieved anything; he called on me again, telling me about his lack of success, and complained mightily about Wenger's deceitful conduct. He also pointed out to me again that Wenger would try to get his hands on my money at Mr. Boeschenstein's, if it had arrived there. Although I was fairly certain that Mr. Boeschenstein would not give up my money without written word from me, I nevertheless decided to go to St. Louis and soon after to Schuetz's farm, which I did, unfortunately at least two months too early.[25]

In the beginning, while I was working for Mack, Teuss was working for his keep at the Washington Hotel. His view was that we should never again be separated, but because of his thoughtless, mischievous pranks I could not consider him a dependable friend, though I did not dislike him. I thought that he was honest, but I took every opportunity to point out to him that we could never truly become good friends unless he gave up his heavy drinking and card playing, and I knew that was not possible for him. The money, with which he had repaid me in full, he had earned by helping float a raft of lumber from the Stillwater Sawmill to Galena. We had been able to sell his gun for ten dollars, and with that we were totally settled up. I later learned from distant relatives that he had swindled his father, who had subsequently come to America, had run off with the money that had been entrusted to him, leaving the old man penniless, a contemptible deed which I would not have believed him capable of, despite his irresponsibility.[26]

When he left the Washington Hotel a young man from Alsace was hired. He took quite a liking to me, and one day he made a well-intended proposition, which I could not accept at any price. My young friend told me of two young men he knew of who had developed a perfectly proper friendship. Eventually they had taken an oath never to undertake anything without consulting the other. They would share everything, support one another, never forsake each other, etc., and he was prepared to enter into such a union with me. I tried to explain that such a relationship was unnatural, and to talk him out of it. Hopefully he later saw the merit of my view, and, if he is still alive, has long since united with a nice young woman, instead of with a man.

During my stay at Mr. Mack's he bought his vegetables from a big, old Swabian vegetable gardener, whose name I have forgotten. The old man had his garden about six miles northeast of Galena. He had a great deal of "mother wit," which he was happy to show off. He was particularly careful not let himself be taken in by anyone, and if someone tried it, he would say, "Only a fool gladly seeks advice, and only the sick man meekly accepts it."

Haymaking time was upon us. Workers were scarce. He and his stepson were extremely busy, and, since I did not dislike the peculiar fellow, I promised to help him for a few days. His house was built down in a little valley through which a small spring-fed brook ran. In front of it was his vegetable garden, where everything seemed to be growing luxuriantly in the rich black soil. A short distance west of the house was the barn, and behind the house rose a steep hill. Freddy [his son] and I were to share a bed on the upper floor of the house, and we went to bed early to ensure that we would get up on time in the morning.

Freddy fell asleep immediately and snored so loudly that one might have thought a dozen men were taking part in the concert. Unfortunately I was not as lucky, for I had scarcely warmed up in bed when I began to be bitten here, there, and everywhere by very strong smelling little beasts. Perhaps they considered me to be especially tasty, chance prey that offered an exceptional opportunity. I was soon busy defending myself, with might and main, against the individual and concerted attacks, and whenever I felt some soft creature somewhere, I tried my best to reach it. I knew I had been successful every time, as the aromatic smell increased. Gradually I became quite feverish, scratching, cursing, and fuming, and amazed that Freddy did not awaken from his snoring concert and his peaceful slumber. I could no longer bear it. I finally shook the snorer out of his sweet slumbers, probably with words that were less than kind. Freddy, after I had expended great effort in rousing him to partial wakefulness, was more than a little surprised by my action. He wanted to know what was the matter with me. "The bed is full of bedbugs that are eating me alive. I have already killed at least ten or twelve of these bloodsucking beasts. I can't stand it any longer. Aren't they biting you?" "What are you talking about? Bedbugs here? There are no bedbugs here and none are biting me." "Then just smell and tell me if these were not bedbugs," I said, as I put the fingers I had used to kill the bloodsuckers that had driven me half-mad under his nose! To Freddy's surprise he really did smell a bedbug odor on my fingers and tried to comfort me by saying that his mother and the hired girl from Werdenberg in [Canton] St. Gallen would thoroughly clean them out the next day. Since it was my intention to stay on with these people, at least until the greater part of the haying was finished, I still wanted to get some rest in what remained of the night. I dressed and went to the hay barn and, since there were no bedbugs there, I was able to rest and slept wonderfully the rest of the night. It was almost beyond my comprehension that Freddy was not bothered by these blood-sucking creatures. Probably they had already become sick of his blood long before my arrival. And, since my arrival provided a welcome change of diet, they had seen me as a pleasant refreshment and had set out to take me by storm. Although Freddy's mother (who had a remarkably large goiter) told me the next evening that she and the hired girl had completely cleaned out the bedbug colony and that I could go to bed in peace, I nevertheless preferred to sleep on the hay in the barn, which I knew to be free of bedbugs, and where I sought and found my nightly peace for the remainder of my stay with my Swabian vegetable gardener.

Early in the morning I began mowing and, as soon as breakfast was over, started up again. The day was hot and sunny. I became thirsty and drank a good deal of water. My old Swabian appeared to have forgotten that water alone cannot keep up one's strength for long when mowing. Finally—it was about eleven o'clock—he brought me some whiskey, a drink I rarely touched. However, thirsty as I was, I quickly downed a little of it mixed with water, and it was not long before I felt its influence. Although I did not become intoxicated, the feeling was not very pleasant and, since the scythe was no longer sharp and the grass had become dry, the mowing did not go well. I explained to the old man that in the future he should bring me something to drink an hour earlier, but it should not be whiskey. This helped the following day. Instead of whiskey, there was coffee or beer.

I spent the next day as I had the first one. It was close to noon. I was mowing near a small bush growing beside the little spring-fed brook. The old man was also mowing not far from me. Suddenly I caught sight of a bluish, black, and white spotted snake, three to four feet long. When I called the old man's attention to it, he seemed very afraid of it, and wanted me to kill it. But since I considered it to be nonpoisonous, I caught it alive and, holding it behind its head, let it wind itself around my arm. The old man practically thought I was a magician. He could scarcely believe his eyes. Of course he did not want to take it when I offered it to him. He fearfully turned away from me and told me I would never touch his bread again. I even let it go without killing it. He did not at all like the fact that I was setting such a dangerous reptile free, and I feared that my behavior set back his good opinion of me considerably. However, as far as touching the bread was concerned, he continued to let me help myself to as much as I wanted, without stopping me.

As for religion, there was not much one could discuss with this man and his family. They were real died-in-the-wool Lutherans. Anyone who had a different opinion was—as the old man put it—a child of the devil. Naturally it was a great sin to assert that the earth revolved around the sun, instead of the sun around the earth, for the saying had it, "sunup to sundown," and not a single syllable of that could be changed. That I was of a different mind and called his and his family's attention to astronomical discoveries and calculations that permitted precise calculations that made possible long-range forecasts of eclipses of the sun and moon, etc., he simply could not comprehend. And of course he deemed those astronomers children of the devil. And I am afraid that in his eyes I was a downright heretic.

In the evening of the fourth day, when the grass had been mowed and a large part of the haying had been completed, I left the gardener's family, and by dusk I had arrived back at Mr. Mack's in Galena. I had stopped sleeping at the Washington Hotel some time before this, for I was no drinker and did not have much money to spend for liquor, and back then that was an affront, as it still is today, in the eyes of drinkers. Thus I could clearly tell that I was not especially popular. Also, I preferred sleeping on the floor of the workshop instead of making the trip from Mack's home to the hotel every evening. After work I often visited the auction hall diagonally across from the workshop, more to look than to buy.

One evening after supper, as I was about to go to the hotel, I went first to the auction hall instead. But, when I became bored, I left and decided to visit a neighboring shoemaker across from the hall. They were Germans and we were well acquainted. They told me that on our side of the street, quite near our door, two men had just been in conversation and that one of them had, with some instrument, struck the other's head with such heavy blows that the victim would probably die as a result. I found the fatally wounded man in a nearby pawnshop, where a good many people had gathered. His forehead appeared to be broken. It was already considerably swollen and his face was covered with blood. He was breathing deeply and seemed to be unconscious.

The doctor, who had just arrived, declared that his brain was hopelessly injured, and that the man was going to die. And the man did die that same night. No one was found who could supply reliable information about the deed. I only know that the deceased had been tried for murder earlier that day, but had had to be released for lack of evidence. Most people present seemed to be of the opinion that, even if the evidence against him was insufficient, he was nonetheless the murderer, and it was assumed that one of the murdered man's friends had taken revenge on him. And, instead of feeling sorry for the dying man, it appeared to me as though they were looking forward to the death of this man with a kind of satisfaction. The whole affair disgusted me. I had trouble understanding how anyone could judge such an act so unfeelingly and even derive satisfaction from it. The murdered man was, it appeared, an Irishman, and was said to have been a bad man. But Galena was filled with Irishmen, especially on Saturdays, and since they filled themselves with too much whiskey, many of them seemed somewhat disreputable to me.

41. My Journey by Foot to Guttenberg—I Lose My Way— A Rattlesnake—Overnight in a Barn

Prairie la Porte, as noted above, had been laid out as a town and had been named Guttenberg. Naturally there were building lots for sale. Mr. Mack told me that his brother-in-law, Mr. Luetscher, who was living in Guttenberg, also had a so-called land claim, about three miles west, on which he intended to settle. There was said to be more fine government land available in the vicinity of this claim, and Mr. Mack was also somewhat interested in settling there. Since he was not overwhelmed with work at the time, we soon agreed that I would go to Guttenberg in order to take a good look at the situation. Then it would be clear as to what the possibilities were. Of course there was no discussion about Mr. Mack paying a portion of my traveling expenses, but, since I expected to make the trip there and back on foot, a great many expenses were not anticipated. In addition to his brother-in-law, Mr. Mack also had a good friend in Guttenberg. He was a German shoemaker by the name of Huntemann,[27] whom he especially recommended that I look up and to convey to him his warm regards.

It was already toward the end of July when, on foot, I set out on my walking journey. I carried with me a kind of hunting or traveling bag, well-filled with cheese, bread, sausage, and a small flask of brandy, along with two small boxes of matches. In addition, I carried a Kentucky rifle on my shoulder and took along a traveling companion, a medium-sized brown setter, who was very fond of me and belonged to Mr. Mack. And, since it was the middle of summer, I took no blankets with me. In addition, I wore a pair of good gray woolen trousers and a short green woolen jerkin, or jacket, that was decorated with black velvet.

In good spirits, one morning I set out on my walking journey, and, according to the inquiries I had made, I should have reached Snake Hollow, some twenty to thirty miles above Galena, by the end of the first day. I had been told that about three miles above Galena the road to Dubuque would go off to my left. The road to Snake Hollow would go off to the right. I had not the slightest doubt that I would find the right road. So I strode along my route in high spirits, glancing at every road that turned off. But I believed that I had not yet come to the right road.

Suddenly it occurred to me that I certainly must have gone more than three miles. If only there had been someone able to give me information. But I met no one, and I became convinced that I had missed the right road, for this road veered more and more to the left, in the direction of the Mississippi. Unwilling to turn back, I continued along this road and around noon, a little after twelve, I arrived at the bank of the Mississippi opposite Dubuque.

I had no intention of abandoning my plan to go up the Wisconsin side and to return on the Iowa side. So I asked a boy about the road to Snake Hollow, and he advised me to follow a little footpath upstream, along the river bank, until I came to a limekiln, where I would turn right, cross a number of hills, and then follow a wagon trail that would lead me to the right road to Snake Hollow. A man working at the limekiln gave me the same directions as the boy had. I climbed the hills and passed a couple of little log cabins, where I came upon a man with bilious fever who, in response to my poor English, felt too miserable to be able to give me information.

But I had actually found the wagon tracks and I believed I was going the right way. However, they soon branched off to the right, and then to the left, and since both tracks were heavily overgrown with tall grass, one turning sharply left toward the river, while the other led to the right into an apparently deep valley, I was again at a complete loss. Since the tracks often became faint, I sometimes stooped down toward the ground. Then something moved right in front of me in the tall prairie grass, and I heard a peculiar shrill or rattling sound ahead of me. In a flash I jumped backward a few steps, for it must surely have come from a rattlesnake. I could clearly see the grasses move as the snake slithered through them. Since I did not know the nature of this most poisonous kind of snake, I did not venture to follow it through the tall grass.

The sun had already set in the west. I could see no houses along the tracks leading to the right, and, although I was halfway convinced that this probably had to be the right way, I nevertheless turned left, and followed the wagon tracks. They led me into a little valley, bisected by a small spring-fed brook that led directly to the Mississippi. The sun had already set when I came to the river bank, where I saw a frame house, but only a horse, no people in it. I went on in the expectation that people must be nearby. Sure enough there was another house similar to the first, but again no people, though it did contain some harness. People certainly cannot be far away, I thought, and again there was a house, but there was nothing at all inside.

Since it was now pitch dark, I hurried on and, sure enough, there was a large house, but no sign of life. No light was to be seen. The door was open, but my call went unanswered. I entered and found that the ground floor consisted of only one large room. In the rear, however, a broad stairway led to the upper floor, which I ascended, but again I found only one room. Here there was hay, and I quickly decided to spend the night there. My clothes, especially my shirt, were so soaking wet with sweat from walking fast in the hot July sun that the sweat streamed off me. What I had at first taken to be a house was probably just a barn, although it had window openings. Then there was a big cross beam on which I hung my wet shirt, so that it would be dry by morning. I had no appetite for food. I was very tired and longed for some rest.

Although I was at first a bit uncomfortable in my bed of hay, I nevertheless soon fell asleep. When I woke up, the day seemed scarcely to have dawned. I wanted to get under way early, but when I tried to put on my shirt it was as uncomfortably cold and wet as an eel skin. But letting it dry would have delayed me too long. The river bank was nearby, and I headed for it to drink and to wash. As soon as I had finished, I continued my journey on the road, to the extent that I could make it out in the still prevailing darkness. Behind the building in which I had spent the night the road led upstream, soon coming to a so-called lane. There were high fences on both sides, sheltering a great many cattle that apparently had spent the night there. At the far end of this lane was a fence, in the middle of which was a gate that made a loud screeching noise when opened, or closed. Not far off I now heard the deep bark of a large dog, and saw—turning my eyes in that direction—a lovely, large two-story French-style house, which I surely would have seen the evening before if I had passed that spot just ten minutes earlier. The barking became louder as I approached the house, and when I heard a sound at a window, as if someone were trying to open it, I passed by quickly, fearing that I might be mistaken for a thief and shot at.

Unfortunately, in so doing I had strayed from the path, and I now found myself at the foot of a tall, steep bluff, right on the river bank. The footpath I had initially found had ended, and the rubble of sharp-edged rocks made for most difficult walking.

Dawn was beginning to break, but I did not want to return to the house, much as I would have liked to, provided that I could have been certain that Germans lived there. I decided to climb the steep bluff, for I had often enough in Switzerland climbed hills just as steep and much higher. So why should I not try? By the time I reached the top it was nearly daylight. My clothes were once again wet with sweat, and I was already good and tired. And my dog, who often could scarcely keep up with me, seemed equally tired.

I rested a little, enjoyed the beautiful view, and saw the house I had left behind far below. The sky was overcast with gray clouds, and I feared it might rain. So I did not want to lose any time, but was anxious to push ahead. The high ground I was crossing now was what in Wisconsin were called "oak openings."[28] The oaks were slender and lovely, although not very tall. Intermittently there were patches of tall grass, with charred hazel bushes, obstructed by tangled young grape vines, which for a while, slowed my pace.

After some time I found a little path, an Indian footpath, which I followed for awhile until I feared that it would lead me too far from the river. I turned off to the left, crossed some small hills, and came, quite unexpectedly, upon two young men chopping cordwood. Expecting that these men would know the area well, I turned to them to ask if they could tell where I would find the closest route to Snake Hollow. I asked in English, but the men did not seem to understand me. I repeated the question two more times, finally receiving the answer, "Don't know," and to each other in German, "What can he want? Do you understand him?" The questions they put to each other were in a Swiss dialect. Naturally my questions were now asked in the same language, and I easily received the desired information. One of the men was from Canton Aargau and the other an Alsatian from Belfort. They had a cabin, their temporary quarters, similar to our cabin on the Mississippi island among the Indians. Of course, as a fellow countryman, I was invited to stay for breakfast, which they were about to cook right away, and I gladly accepted their invitation. Since my clothes were completely soaked from sweat and the tall grass, I took them off piece by piece and dried them by the warm fire, while my two friends cooked breakfast. I had as yet eaten but little from my own provisions, which did not appeal to me much anyway. The hot coffee, fried bacon and eggs and bread tasted far better.

42. An Exhausting Trip During Which I Lose My Jacket in the Hilly Terrain and Also Lose My Way and Spend the Night in the Open

After breakfast, my countrymen took me across the little stream that flowed past that place, and emptied into the Mississippi a few miles below. If I am not mistaken, they called the stream the Platte River.[29] It was deep there and about sixty feet wide. My countrymen told me that if I wanted to take a level route, I would have to walk between this river and the hills rising behind it down to the Mississippi, and, arriving there, heading upstream I would find fairly good roads leading to the next village. The route over the hills would be at least three miles closer, but much more difficult because it led up and down over very substantial hills. Since I had climbed up and down plenty of hills in the old country, I felt these could not compare with our Swiss mountains, and would present no particular problem to me. So I decided on the shorter, hilly route. I had just begun to climb the first hill when I shot a beautiful pheasant.

Arriving at the top, I struck out, or so I thought, in a straight westerly direction. But it took me through deep tall grass, tangled with grape vines, scattered with charred hazel bushes, among occasional oaks, then steep down to a water channel, and then, just as steep up the opposite side. I walked briskly onward and expected to arrive at a bluff overlooking the Mississippi at any moment, but there was just more of the same climbing up and down as before. It was an extremely long three miles, and I began to realize that I had lost my way again. Once more, I was at a low place between steep hills, quenching my thirst at a little spring. I had been walking very fast, and had not been looking at my feet, when I stepped into a hole left by a burnt out tree stump in grass choked with vines, resulting in my doing a fine involuntarily somersault. Although I quickly picked myself up from the wet grass, I had no wish to repeat that performance.

Only then did I notice that my dog was no longer with me, and that I had lost my beautiful green woolen jacket, which I had slung across my shoulder, and that my good trousers were missing several buttons and were torn in two places. My suspenders were beyond repair, and my white shirt was blackened by the many charred hazel bushes. Moreover, I was quite exhausted. Where I had left my dog behind me, I could not tell. I assumed that he was with my jacket, but where it had slipped from my shoulder I had no idea. Perhaps it was far behind me, perhaps not, but I was much too tired to go back and look for it. So I whistled for the dog through my fingers. He heard and returned to my side in about five minutes.

Now I continued in what I took to be a westerly direction, but instead of coming to the Mississippi, I found myself on the bluff of a little stream similar to the Platte, which I had crossed several hours earlier. Down below there was a log cabin. After pondering for some time, I realized that it was not my countrymen's cabin, but that it had to be the same bluff, although I was much farther upstream than in the morning. At first I hardly knew what to do, for I no longer trusted myself in these cursed hills and hollows.

Thinking that if I only had a compass, I finally remembered that I had one in my right vest pocket. "If one does not think, one must suffer the consequences." I applied this proverb to myself. How needlessly and thoughtlessly I had been wandering around. It served me right, and in my view, I had been a downright stupid fellow. I did not linger there very long. Carrying the compass open in my hand, I set out confidently in a westerly direction, and reached a high bluff of the Mississippi sooner than expected. In my haste I came close to falling over its edge. Just in time I saw that there was a steep precipice under my feet. I could easily have done somersaults that might have cost me my life. At the top was an open area covered with short grass. I lay down on it. I still had the pheasant with me. I wanted to give it to the dog, but he would not eat it. He only looked at me somewhat sadly, and seemed as exhausted as I was.

I had from this spot a wonderful view. At my feet was beautiful flat bottom land; about two miles further up the valley I saw several little white houses. After I had recovered a bit, I got up and walked along the crest of the gradually descending bluff, down into the valley and found, at its foot, a lovely spring, from which I again drank. This was a real "water eye," an opening about three feet wide and perhaps just as deep, so clear that I could see myself in it almost as plainly as in a mirror. This gave me an opportunity to see how dirty, or blackened, my face was. I greatly resembled a common chimney sweep and feared that as such I probably would not be very welcome anywhere. So I busily set about thoroughly washing my face and hands and combing my hair. But my jacket was gone, and my shirt was very black and dirty. I repaired my suspenders as well as I could, so that they could perform at least part of their function. In spite of all this, my outward appearance still seemed very questionable, with the result that I was afraid that if I went to any of the houses, the door would be slammed in my face.

After I had restored my appearance as well as I could, I proceeded down the good road toward the small village. On my way, I met two men driving a wagon drawn by two oxen. I asked them whether one might be able to get some milk in one of the nearby houses, whereupon they pointed to a little frame house where I could probably get what I wanted. When I arrived at the house I knocked at the door timidly, whereupon a woman's voice called, "Come in." I stepped into a modest but clean living room, in which I found a middle-aged American woman, who looked at me through her spectacles, quite surprised and perhaps frightened. I asked whether I might be able to get some cold milk and something to eat, for which I would gladly pay. In her nasal voice the woman told me to sit down, and said she would get me some milk. And indeed she returned right away with a small, full pitcher, but it was very sour buttermilk, which I could not possibly drink. The woman had also meant well for my dog; "He must surely be hungry," she thought and she brought him some ox ribs on which there was not a shred of meat. But the dog felt the same as I had with my sour buttermilk. He did not touch it. Since the woman apparently was not about to offer me anything better, I asked what I owed her. I decided I had no time to waste there to allow myself to be curiously examined through a pair of spectacles. But the woman was generous. She charged me neither for the sour buttermilk I had not been able to enjoy nor for the hard-as-rocks ribs my dog had left untouched, for which I thanked her and wished her a "Good morning." I have forgotten the name of that little village.

From here the road led away from the river through a beautiful little valley, straight back between the hills, to Snake Hollow, a scant two miles away. Along the way, near this little town, was a lone blackish frame house near which I met a Negro, of whom I asked whether he could tell me where I could get some sweet milk. He answered that if I would step into the house he would be able to give me some right away. I entered and found the house occupied only by Negroes. Because I was tired and thirsty, and the living room was not unclean, I sat down on a chair that was offered me. Shortly afterward the Negro appeared with a white, clean-looking, three-quart jug, full of cool, very good-tasting milk, of which I drank heartily, giving my dog as much as he wanted. As far as I can recall, this milk cost ten cents, and I was entirely satisfied with the price.

When I asked the Negro about the road between there and Cassville, he pointed to a two-story brick house. "You are a German, I believe, and probably would not understand me if I were to describe the route. In that brick house lives another German. You will understand him better and thus be more likely to find the right road." I did as he had advised me, and found a large, friendly German in the designated house. He invited me to sit down and asked whether I planned to go farther than Cassville. When he learned that Guttenberg was my goal, he asked if I would take a letter to Guttenberg's founder, a German by the name of Weiss,[30] a task I gladly agreed to. The man brought me a large glass of good white wine, a couple of apples, and showed me on a large county map the roads I must take. He then went away, but soon came back with a letter to Mr. Weiss. The man described the route to Cassville again. He would accept no payment for the wine and the apples he had given me.

Then I resumed my journey. At first, I found the road just as described. But soon it made a big turn to the left. It went all the way to the Mississippi bottom, so that after I had gone almost two miles I was sure I had yet again taken the wrong road. I turned back and was once more near the fork, close to Snake Hollow, when I met a man on horseback, of whom I asked directions to Cassville. The man laughed and said, "This is the right road to that town alright. You seem to be coming from there." I hardly knew what to think of myself. So I had again been wandering hither and yon, for four unnecessary miles, because I was constantly afraid I had not found the right road.

The man on horseback was, as he said, an Englishman, and he himself lived not far from the road to Cassville and about twelve miles from Snake Hollow. I was carrying my boots in my hands and walking in my Indian moccasins. The Englishman offered to carry my boots for me so I could follow along with a lighter load. I feared he might run off with my boots and hesitated at first. But since he did not look like a thief and promised to hold his horse to a walk, I allowed him to carry them for me. I found this man very talkative and entertaining and, as the sun began to sink low, he gave me back my boots, saying his route led off to the right from mine here, and so we parted. My road wound around a steep slope, down into a valley through which flowed a clear river sixty to seventy feet wide. My feet were already hurting badly. I had an opportunity to wash them in the cool water. They were swollen and had several blisters, and I was so tired that I would gladly have, there and then, given up any further travel. The Englishman had pointed out to me that I definitely should not consider going further that day, as tired as I was; that it was still eight miles to Cassville, and he advised me to spend the night down in the valley, for people lived there, and I would then be in better shape to push on the following morning.

43. Am Considered by a Squinting Miller as Probably Untrustworthy — Spending the Night in the Open — Cassville and the Turkey River

A long, wide footbridge crossed the river, and on the other bank was a grain mill. I had not only washed my feet, but also my face in the cool water, and had combed my hair. But my shirt was in even greater need of washing. My external appearance probably was therefore not especially appealing. Arriving at the mill, I found the miller standing in the door. He squinted with one eye and suspiciously looked me up and down. To my question as to whether I would be able to obtain a night's lodging and something to eat in one of those buildings, of which there were several more below the mill, if I were to ask politely and were able to pay, he answered with an emphatic "No!" It was obvious that the man did not trust me very much, and therefore he denied me shelter. The miller wanted to know whether I would sell my rifle, and asked me the price, which I set at eighteen dollars, but for which he offered me only twelve dollars. In response to my question as to whether I might be able to buy something to eat, especially sweet milk, he pointed to a neat little frame house at the lower end of this little settlement. I could ask there and say he had sent me.

Arriving there I knocked at the door of the little house, and heard a woman's voice call out, "Come in!" In a simple, but neatly kept room, I found two young females, probably single, of slender build and lovely faces, and I was always glad to see pretty young women back then, that is when I myself was properly dressed and spruced up a little, but shabbily dressed as I was, I would much rather have been greeted by older women. At the moment there was nothing I could do, and although I felt my face flushed, I tried to appear calm, saying that the miller had sent me to get a little cool sweet milk and a little food. The one girl had some sewing in front of her, and appeared to be looking at me from the corner of her eye. The other one, a slender, striking creature, had brought me a clean, white jugful of really good milk, as well as a couple of small plates with buttered bread and custard pie. I very much regretted that I was not yet in complete command of the English language so that I could have properly explained the reason for my miserable appearance and missing attire. I was soon finished with the light meal, for which I was charged only five cents, which certainly was cheap enough.

I had already left the house and had gone a short distance when I remembered that I had forgotten my cap, which I had removed at the table. Had I had another in my possession I would certainly have left the cap behind, but I was already without a jacket and simply could not go on without a covering for my head. Therefore I had to go back, regardless of how embarrassed I was. I had no alternative. When I entered the house again I certainly must not have appeared very pale, for I definitely felt more hot than cold. The girls however laughed a little as I entered. They had already discovered why I was coming back. I could not blame them, for in the end I myself had to laugh at my awkward, shy behavior.

After leaving the little valley and arriving on the prairie, which was considerably higher here, I strode on briskly, but a strong northwest wind was blowing against me, and in my sweat-soaked clothes I soon felt as if I were battling a fast current in a cold stream. On both sides of the road were huge solitary oaks, among which tall prairie grass grew. An earlier storm had blown down several of the trees, some across the road, and others beside it, their branches scattered about. If I had had a woolen blanket, I would have lain down for the night beside one of these trees. But lacking a blanket or jacket, I could not do so.

In order to keep my spirits from sinking, and perhaps to warm myself, I now walked even more briskly, singing all kinds of cheerful songs. But the faster I walked the stronger and colder the wind cut through me, until I began to regret not having stopped earlier—when I had had a good opportunity—to settle for the night. Since the sun had set it was completely dark when descending from the prairie, I found myself in a small river valley where there was no visible shelter of any kind which might have offered me protection against the night air and the dew.

Luckily I suddenly stumbled upon a dried-out, downed oak, whose branches lay strewn on the ground, broken into little pieces. I decided to wait there for the coming day, put down my bag and rifle, took out some of my matches, and tried to start a fire. But the matches had become wet from sweat coming through the bag and would not light. So I took about a quarter of the box of matches and struck it sharply against a dry spot on the fallen tree, and finally had the pleasure of being able to warm myself at a roaring fire. I had taken off all my sweat-soaked clothes and dried them at the fire, first the shirt, then the trousers and vest, putting them on again after they were thoroughly dry. Then, far enough from the fire that the flames could not reach me while I slept, I made myself a bed of fresh grass and oak leaves, laying my bag and rifle next to me, with my faithful dog as a sleeping companion, close by on the other side. While I was sleeping, the fire died down, and I woke up in the middle of the night shivering with cold; but with a new supply of dried branches, a good fire was soon going again. After I had warmed myself by the flames, I lay down upon my bed, only to wake up again, at the first sign of dawn, wet from the dew, and freezing. I jumped up quickly from my bed and, in so doing, I startled a deer standing nearby, that perhaps had been watching me while I slept, and he dashed away with mighty leaps. I again stoked the fire into a lively flame in order to warm myself and, having accomplished this, I once again set out on my journey.

With the brightening day the trees became fewer and fewer. The route led through a slightly rising prairie which stretched in a northwesterly direction. To my right was a magnificent field of shining, ripening grain, at the west end of which I could see, even from a distance, several small log farm buildings. Ahead of me were some cattle and other livestock moving in the direction of those inhabited dwellings, where they were going to be milked by the farm woman who was waiting for them. When I arrived a short time later, I asked the woman who was milking if I could get some breakfast there. She answered in the affirmative and invited me to go into her house, saying that she would bring me something as soon as she had finished milking.

In the house I found, in addition to a couple of little children, her husband, who was wearing a large pair of glasses, with green protective lenses, because his eyes were badly inflamed. The man was friendly, invited me to sit down, and asked me the usual questions, where was I coming from and where was I going, etc., all of which I tried to answer. I also tried to explain, as far as possible, my having no jacket, as well as the rest of my not especially neat appearance. They were friendly people, and I learned from them that it was only three more miles to Cassville, and I probably would not be able to lose my way again. My breakfast consisted of fresh cow's milk, small cheeses, butter, wheat bread, and cornbread, all of which tasted wonderful to me. And for all of this they asked only fifteen cents. These people had found a small place in my heart. I was grateful and departed contentedly from these simple but honest farm people. It cannot have been much after seven when the road widened, as it left the bluffs, and I arrived in Cassville.

There I asked whether someone could take me across the Mississippi. A young fellow offered to row me across for twenty-five cents. He stated he was ready to leave right away, but he let me wait two hours while he seemed to be discussing all sorts of inconsequential things with some other men. When I finally asked him again whether he intended to take me across the river, he appeared to have forgotten his promise. But he came at once and rowed me to the right bank of the river, setting me ashore however in a dense growth of willows. Since there was no road in sight, I at first hesitated to set out, but my carrier showed me some human footprints and noted that, if I followed them, they would lead me to a little path and then to a wagon trail that would lead to the Turkey River, and up it to some houses where I would find the ferry across the Turkey River, and the road to Guttenberg.

Although I feared at first that I had been misled, I did in fact find the designated path and the wagon track that brought me to an open place not far upstream where that river flowed into the Mississippi. On the bank of the smaller river were two log cabins, though no one was living in them, and I received no answer to my loud "Hello," except for the echo of my own voice from the nearby bluffs. Had my carrier told me that the ferry was somewhat farther up the river, and not near those small houses, I would of course have gone on. But, based on his directions, I had the incorrect impression that the ferry must be near these cabins. I was further strengthened in this belief when I found, down on the bank, close to the house, a canoe tied to a paddle stuck in the ground, and the fresh footprints of a man. Since my repeated calls remained unanswered, and I did not want to delay any longer, I decided to follow the American expression, "Help yourself." I jumped into the canoe, followed by my dog, and paddled to the opposite side of the Turkey River, only to find an almost impenetrable swamp, grasses and tangled thicket. I was therefore forced to paddle back, close to the right bank, and then upstream a short distance until I saw steeply rising, high bluffs, on the left bank, free of vines, weeds, and bush. While I was briskly paddling up the fast-flowing Turkey, I kept worrying that the owner of the canoe, to which I had helped myself, might be a hunter who would show up and take a shot at me. But the closer I came to the left bank the more confident I became of avoiding this danger, and when I finally reached a great protruding sandbank those fears ended. I pulled the canoe far enough up onto the sandbank to ensure that the stream could not get to it, telling myself that if this was the ferryboat the ferryman should have stayed with it and, if it was not, the man would surely know where to find it and thereby arrive back at his canoe.

At the foot of the high river bluff, from which point I now intended to proceed, there was no sign of a path, only coarse, sharp-edged rock, on which I briefly stumbled about, hurting my feet with every step. Farther on the woods were too swampy, and it was also inadvisable to go that way because of the tall, thick weeds. My dog raised a young deer, which I could have shot easily. But in my present circumstances I did not have the heart to harm the poor animal.

Thinking that I would find level land at the top, where the going would be easier, I climbed the first very steep hill. I found a steep drop, however, and then had to climb up again, just as steeply and even higher. I repeated this experiment only one time before deciding I would rather walk on the sharp rocky debris than completely use up my remaining strength by climbing up and down. But to get down I had to slide down an almost perpendicular cliff where I ran the risk of having to take some considerable somersaults over the rocky debris at its foot. My dog, who had followed me up to this point, whined and howled, and was fearful of following me down. But when he saw me go, he did try to jump, and he tumbled down without hurting himself.

Now I made but slow progress in the woods. But eventually I came to better ground in the woods. At the foot of these hills I found an old footpath and finally a small uninhabited house whose door was locked. Next to the house was a little garden in which several kinds of squash were growing. Following the narrow footpath, I arrived after awhile at another similar little house, also with a little garden and squash. But the tracks seemed fresher here, and at various places I found stacked dried barrel staves. The path now became more and more distinct, leading to a fresh wagon trail, and suddenly I came upon a fairly large inhabited house where I encountered children as well as adults. The distance from Cassville to Guttenberg was supposed to be eight miles. It seemed to me that I had covered at least twice as much. I was curious, therefore, to learn where and how far it really was to Guttenberg. In response to this question, the occupants of the house pointed out an open spot to the right between trees and bushes. There I would find the lower end of Prairie la Porte [Guttenberg].

On a nearby bridge I crossed a crystal-clear brook and found myself right at the spot on the prairie that had been pointed out to me. I found many ripe blackberries, which I ate to my heart's content. Far ahead, on the bank of the Mississippi, I saw a number of small, mostly new little houses. This was the town of Guttenberg, the goal of my, I could say crazy, journey. The road toward the houses was flat, dry and easy to follow.

44. Arrival at Mr. Huntemann's in Guttenberg — Luetscher's Claim — Return Trip and Final Arrival in Galena by Way of Dubuque

Near the houses a few people, who were gathering fresh hay, showed me where to find shoemaker Huntemann's house, where I knocked and entered. Mr. Huntemann was busy with his shoemaking. He was not yet old, and after explaining why I had come, and giving him the regards and instructions of his personal friend, Mr. Mack, I was made very welcome. Mrs. Huntemann, a slender, young and pretty woman, was asked by her husband to bring me a good clean shirt immediately and to wash mine afterwards. A hearty appetizing noon meal was also placed before me.

Although it was barely past noon, I was too exhausted for now to do much more than look around. I limited myself to a visit to the family of Mr. Luetscher, the brother of Mrs. Mack, who lived in a little house in Guttenberg. The following day we visited the prairie, a beautiful, flat bottomland, stretching a mile or more north to south, from woods to woods, between the Mississippi and some somewhat rocky bluffs, about a half a mile distant. I had not counted the little houses, but I believe there could scarcely have been more than ten, and all of them were only one story high; but this was only the beginning of what was to be. At the upper end of the prairie was a fresh water spring and several side channels of the river (sloughs), which separated the prairie from the main channel a little further downstream. Several nice perch were visible near the river bank, scarcely a foot-and-a-half beneath the surface of the water. I hit one of them in the side with a bullet, causing it to rise to the surface of the water where I was able to lift it easily out with my hand. There was no wound, but, where the bullet had hit its side, the scales were crushed and pushed apart. When I got back to the house I laid it on a block in a shed. When we went to bring it in a few minutes later the cat had already devoured a good chunk of it, so we let it have it all.

The following day Luetscher, I, and one or two of his boys, went to look at his so-called claim, about three miles to the west, passing through dense woods, brush and streams, finally reaching the higher prairie. We met several other settlers, mostly Germans, all of whom seemed to have settled in the area recently and were planning to make their home there. On the parcel of land that Luetscher called his claim there were several oak openings. The rest was beautiful rolling prairie. Judging from what Luetscher told me, however, I learned that all the land that would have made nice farms had already been claimed by others, although I found only a few settled on their claims, a requirement for a valid claim.

Since I had no intention of settling on a parcel of land I would never be content with, I realized soon enough that I had undertaken an extremely tiring journey on foot for nothing. On our way back we took a southerly route which brought us onto a road that was pointed out to me as the one to Dubuque, and was the one I was to take on my return trip the following day. I was told there were lead mines, etc., in the area, but no one could show me any minerals, and I surmised the people there had more lead in their brains than there was in the ground.

Early the next morning I set out on the road pointed out to me the day before, apparently a well-traveled one, and I briskly set out on my return journey. I had recovered from my trip, and thought I was sufficiently strong to be able to cover in one day the distance between Guttenberg and Dubuque, which I had been told was almost fifty miles. In order to reach my goal I knew that I would have to set a really good pace, and, after I had reached the right road, I did just that.

By early forenoon, I had arrived at the ferry on the Turkey River and was taken across at once. It had not taken me as long to get back there from Guttenberg as it had taken me on the trip out. The road took me through rolling countryside, among numerous fine farms and open prairies, and every so often through patches of woods. Most of the land seemed of fairly good quality. My rapid pace soon had me soaked with sweat and gave me a great thirst, which I attempted to quench at the many freshwater springs which I passed; but then I would resume my rapid march, which made me sweat more. I felt no hunger, but on the other hand I was very tired. Although the day was not unfavorable for foot travel, the sky being mostly cloudy, I nonetheless found my strength rapidly beginning to give out.

Had I had an opportunity to ask the distance to Dubuque, I felt sure the response would have been a very large number of miles. Dead tired as evening neared, I plodded along the road through a stand of oaks, over a steep hill, where another road leading from the interior crossed mine and seemed to lead down into a valley and toward the Mississippi. Several times I had thought I heard voices coming from the valley to the left. Since a man in an open horse-drawn vehicle just happened to be heading down toward the valley, I asked him whether there was a settlement down there. The man seemed or wished not to understand me. But because he looked German, I repeated my question in German. However the man put the whip to his horses, whereupon they broke into a fast trot.

From sheer exhaustion I could hardly lift my limbs. I felt that my feet must have a good many blisters, for they were hurting all over. My dog seemed even more exhausted than I. He would try to get a short distance ahead of me and then lie down to rest, letting me get about two hundred steps ahead of him. Then he would get up again and repeat the process. I would gladly have called a halt for the day, but I feared that spending the night in the open would be bad for my health, and I hoped to soon find some shelter where I would at least be protected from the night dew.

After darkness had fallen, the road led into a little valley and made a turn to the left. I could hear the sound of running water, and I soon came to the bank of a creek, and sure enough there was a roof, but it was supported on posts which rose from the stream bed. So, in spite of the roof, there was no shelter for me. So I slowly dragged myself on, looking to the right and the left to see if I could find a house or a light. Finally I actually saw to my left, close to the road, a house from which a light shone. In response to my repeated calls of "Hello," a man's voice asked, "What do you want?" My request was simply for a roof over my head for the night. The man answered that everyone in the house was sick and I should go just two hundred yards farther down the road where I would find a house in which I would surely be able to spend the night. To my reply that I was so exhausted that I could scarcely walk, he again encouraged me, coming out himself. The man was a tall, young American, who walked with me and spoke to me kindly. With great difficulty I arrived at the house, where he left me.

There I found an older man and a tall young man, the latter making it very clear to me that there was no room for me there. But the older man said I should stay there. He thought that the landlord would take me in. After awhile a large man with light, very curly hair came. In response to my questions as to whether he was the owner of the house and if I could spend the night there, he answered affirmatively to both. However, the evening meal was finished. No one thought to ask me if I would like something. I still did not have the slightest appetite, although I had not eaten since early morning but had drunk a lot. However, I did very much crave some cool milk, and, after a short pause, I asked the owner for some. The man apologized for not having asked me if I had had my evening meal and told his wife to prepare supper for me. Although I told him cool milk would be enough, he also brought me some still warm cornbread, butter, and white bread. I had drunk only two glasses of milk when I began to shiver as though from a severe chill. These good people noticed how cold I was and seemed to have genuine compassion for me. They instantly started a good fire in a fireplace, before which they had me sit. Then they made a good bed for me on the floor of the room where the first two men were sleeping, and I was told to lie down there. In addition the man of the house brought a large white jug of cool water and a glass which he set on a chair beside my bed remarking, "Young man, if at any time there is anything you wish during the night and we have it in the house, just call out, and you will have it." I can hardly say how much his kind words did for me. I felt very grateful and was touched by this entirely unexpected, kind solicitude.

At first they had wanted to chase my dog out of the house. But he would have allowed himself to be beaten and kicked before he would leave my side. Observing this, the good man gave instructions that he was not to be disturbed. I fell asleep, sooner than I had expected, with the dog at my feet. I slept soundly and did not awake until it was bright daylight and my weary muscles had recovered somewhat. But my feet were swollen and covered with blisters, which I bathed in the cool spring water nearby, and then put on my moccasins instead of my boots.

Breakfast was now ready. As soon as I had eaten and after I had paid my host forty cents—he had asked only thirty-seven—I thanked him for his kind reception, said "Goodbye," and set out on my journey to Dubuque nine miles distant. I traveled mostly across hilly prairie, but, because my aching feet hurt, it was almost eleven in the morning before I arrived. I inquired as to whether there were any steamboats expected from upriver that day. I was told that none were expected. I lay down on some dry green grass near the landing and slept, without really meaning to, for nearly two hours. When I awoke, the horse ferry was ready to go and I took it over to the left bank (to present day Dunleith),[31] a place, as I recall, with only one house. It was no easy task to cover the fifteen miles between this place and Galena in my exhausted condition. It was twilight when I reached my final destination.

45. Newly Arrived Colonists from Glarus and Their Greenhorn Behavior—Trip to St. Louis, St. Jacob and Highland—Fever Returns—Old Acquaintances

A young man by the name of Suter told me that a large group of Swiss from Canton Glarus had just arrived and were staying at a house on Liberty Street. He offered to accompany me there, but I was too exhausted from my trip and longed to get some badly needed rest. A week of rest allowed me to recuperate from the effects of my punishing journey. During this time I often had the opportunity to spend time with my fellow Glarners. On such occasions I felt it my duty to educate them regarding American customs, specifically not to walk down the middle of the street, but to keep to the side, and not to call out loudly to one another by name in public, thereby drawing the attention and contempt and disapproval of passersby. It appeared to me, however, that I earned no special thanks for my well-meant advice. It was a free country after all in which one could do as one wished, and furthermore they had always conducted themselves the same way at home. In short, I found that I was considered an arrogant young fellow for whom the customary manners of old Glarus were no longer good enough. Naturally I soon felt no further inclination to give my compatriots further advice, but comforted myself in the thought that they would eventually come to see another point of view.

I was able to see the men in their wide pants that reached to half a foot above their ankles; walking about in their great, clumsy mountain shoes; old, gray puttees wound around their legs instead of stockings; without jackets, and often without vests; with their shirt sleeves turned up to their elbows, displaying their sunburned arms, looking as if they were still haying in our old Glarus mountains. They had thin black knitted stocking caps pulled down over their uncombed heads, walked down the middle of the streets, and called out to one another in their back-country manner, things such as, "Hey, Jaegsch, where are you going?" or "I am going over there!" I noticed that the women, too, spoke unnecessarily loudly, and, wearing some kind of red handkerchief tied over their heads, also walked down the middle of the street, instead of using the sidewalks, yelling here and there into various stores, "Have you any [illegible] to sell?"

To be sure there were also some exceptions: for example, a Mr. [Balthasar] Schindler and his grown daughter, as well as an energetic, intelligent young man, also named [David?] Schindler, a draftsman, all of them from Mollis, the latter of whom seemed to be the lover of his older namesake's daughter.[32] These people were staying at Mr. Keller's inn. The way they dressed also demonstrated that they could have gone anywhere without drawing attention to themselves. I found the leader of the Glarus group, Judge [Nicholas] Duerst, to be quite a pleasant, friendly, enlightened man. I was of the opinion back then, and still feel to this day, that the group leaders made a mistake by establishing their colony seventy miles in the interior of Wisconsin, rather than seeking better land by going farther up the Mississippi where there was still plenty of top quality government land on both sides of the river to be had for $1.25 per acre. Had they settled on the upper Mississippi they would have found markets for their goods without much difficulty, for back then steamboats already provided weekly communication, while it was not all that hard to see that, when one was far removed from all communication and larger cities, selling one's products became difficult and time-consuming. I had called this to the attention of my compatriots at that time, but they seemed not to hear my words, or not to believe them.[33]

After I had recovered a bit from my recent exhausting travels, I resumed my interrupted employment with Mr. Mack and worked for him for quite a long time. But ever since Minter had told me about Wenger's intentions regarding my money, that was in the care of Mr. Boeschenstein in St. Louis, I could not rest, and decided to go to St. Louis and to Highland, although I knew I would be arriving there right at the height of the fever [malaria] season. I left most of my belongings with Mr. Mack, since I planned to return. Traveling on the steamboat *War Eagle,* one of the best boats of the time, I soon reached St. Louis. I had gone to Mr. Boeschenstein's and had learned from him that Wenger had been there and had tried to get his hands on my money. Mr. Boeschenstein said that even if he had had the money at hand he would not have given it to him without instructions from me, although he knew we had earlier been good friends. The best and simplest thing for me to do would have been to write to Mr. Boeschenstein as soon as I learned from Minter about Wenger's intentions. But I was just plain inexperienced in business affairs. As a result I undertook the trip at the most unhealthful time of the year, wasting my money on travel, although I certainly had no surplus.

In St. Louis I found Mr. Blattner from Highland, who was leaving for Highland at four in the afternoon. The heat in St. Louis was very intense, and since I did not have enough lightweight clothes, I had sweated profusely during the day in my heavy jacket, which I removed only after we were on the Illinois side. The sun set before we had reached the bluffs at Collinsville, and in the cool evening air I suddenly became chilled in my sweat-soaked clothes. Cold shivers penetrated to the marrow of my bones. I should have put my jacket back on sooner. Toward four in the morning we had reached Jacob Schuetz's farm, the present day St. Jacob, where of course I got off. I was directed to a bed where I soon warmed up again. But I believe that the fever germ definitely had got its grip on me during the trip from St. Louis.

Wenger was not at Schuetz's. The latter told me that he had gone to Highland, and Schuetz, who formerly had been fond of Wenger, now seemed to feel quite differently. Schuetz had employed another young Berner as a hired man, and he was supposed to chop firewood for him in his woods at Silver Creek. Wenger had offered to help the hired man, and, after the two had been working in the woods for several days, one day Schuetz went to see what had been accomplished. One may easily imagine how little Schuetz was pleased when he arrived and found that practically no firewood had been cut, but instead he found Wenger and the hired man paddling about Silver Creek in a hollowed-out tree trunk. To the hired man, John, as well as to Wenger, Schuetz's unexpected appearance probably was not very welcome, for it put a sudden stop to the ever-so-innocent boat trip. Wenger may have found that his presence at Schuetz's was no longer much desired, which may have led him to seek another place. As for the hired man, John, he may well have learned thereby that if one has been hired and is being paid to do useful work, the employer will not be particularly pleased if, instead of carrying out the required task, time is wasted in unproductive playing around, especially if the employer is as good a man as old Schuetz. After Schuetz had heard my story about Wenger, the latter did not rise in Schuetz's esteem.

On the following day I rode one of Schuetz's horses to Gale's farm, where my reception was as warm as I had anticipated. I was sorry to have to return with the horse the same day. In Gale's family, as almost everywhere else, they had been suffering from fever, as one could easily see in their pale, drawn faces, especially in my friend Mariet's. For my part, compared to almost all the others, I was still plump and rosy-cheeked. But Mariet told me I had returned to Highland about two months too soon and that she expected I would be just as pale as she and all the others in two weeks. She had predicted only too well.

Returning to Schuetz's by way of Highland, I met at shoemaker Schmied's tavern a cooper from Bern, whose name I have forgotten. This man was planning to accompany Wenger back up to Wisconsin. He told me that Wenger was inside the house and asked me to enter also, which I felt no inclination to do, although I wanted to see Wenger once more because he still owed me about sixteen dollars.

The next day there was an auction on a farm near Schuetz's, which Schuetz said he would have liked to attend. But because he had a piece of land, somewhat more than an acre, that badly needed plowing, which would have kept him from attending, I offered to plow it for him. Schuetz accepted my offer gladly. He estimated that it would take me little more than a half-day, but less than a full day, to plow it. Schuetz had traded his excellent horse, Bub, to his brother-in-law Joseph Mueller for a nice looking black mare, and had in my opinion made a poor trade. With this mare and with the one he had received from Karl Mueller for Claybank, both in good condition, I set to work in good spirits, determined to finish plowing the field before my midday meal. I knew that this team could get some work done, and so after Schuetz had gone, I set them to plowing at a good clip.

The day was sunny and hot. Instead of a light straw hat, I had a black cap on my head and, overheated by the fast plowing, I got a headache and became extremely dizzy, which I ignored. My thoughts were focused on finishing the plowing, perhaps before noon. By one o'clock I was finished and back home, but I felt so dizzy that everything seemed to be spinning around me. I was also unable to eat anything. I lay down on a sofa, but all kinds of visions kept whirling through my brain, so that I could scarcely recognize the faces of people I knew well. I clearly had the beginning of an attack of the bilious fever that was rampant in the community. They were the same symptoms as in the previous year. Schuetz got an emetic for me from a neighboring farmer-pharmacist named

Kohler,[34] after which I took a good dose of Epsom salts, but no quinine or other medicine to relieve the fever. Nevertheless I got better in about two weeks, so that soon, perhaps too soon, I was able to visit the Gale family.

I believe it was on the second day after I was taken ill that Wenger sought me out at Schuetz's and tried to persuade me to take part in his project to trade with the Indians, an undertaking for which I had little inclination. His conduct had done little to encourage me. I took this opportunity to reproach him for the way he deceived us, especially me, and Minter too. At first Wenger put on an injured air, saying that if we had not been such good friends, he would have taken legal action against me for what I said to him. But I had nothing to fear from his baseless claims against me, and he calmed down considerably when I told him I could prove, by both Boeschenstein and Minter, that he had tried, without consulting me, to get Mr. Boeschenstein to turn my money over to him. I only asked that he repay me the money I had loaned him, which he paid me on the spot in silver dollars, and thus my dealings with this false friend were concluded. He left and I have not seen Wenger since, and only seldom heard vague reports about him.

Naturally I had lost my red full cheeks during these two weeks; instead, like most people, I crept about with a pale, worn face. The Gales laughed when they found they had predicted correctly. Mariet and I were riding through Sugar Creek woods on horseback on some kind of errand for Mr. Gale at Squire Tompkins, who lived on the other side of the woods, on the edge of Shoal Creek Prairie. If my financial condition at that time had permitted me to support a wife and family, she and I surely would have come to an understanding. I sincerely regretted that I lacked the necessary means, for not only did I truly love this girl, but I had a high regard for her good character, her pleasant personality, and her efficiency in managing a household. Miss Gale felt that my perceived lack of means was an insufficient reason for keeping two people who loved each other apart. As an example, she told me about a young neighboring American who did not even have the money to pay for the marriage license, and had to borrow the money. Much could be accomplished through hard work and sticking together through thick and thin.

For my part, I had far less self-confidence, for I had been ill with this terrible bilious fever two years in succession. For all I knew, I might suffer a good deal more illness, and how could I then support a family? The thought that I might not only be unable to support my wife, but my wife would have to support me, was intolerable, and made my decision for me. I had only a faint hope that I might soon be able to achieve a certain level of self-sufficiency, and then revive my former love. And should she still be unmarried, I could then ask for her for her hand. As it later turned out my financial condition did improve eventually, but since I did not maintain a correspondence with the Gales, and only heard about her from others, without her knowledge, Miss Gale may have come to think that I had long since forgotten her, and so she gave her hand to another. This I learned just as it seemed that I was about to achieve my goal.[35] There is in the world no complete happiness. I also learned this, as does everyone.

Upon returning to Jacob Schuetz's farm from my visit to Gale's, I soon suffered a serious attack of intermittent fever marked by the various ups and downs and symptoms of the year before. While the terrible headaches did not recur, the shivering fevers and the sweating were just as bad as the previous year.

Bilious fever, and afterwards intermittent fever, became so widespread in 1845 that no family was spared, and in most instances not even one member escaped. There were cases where several members of a family succumbed to the terrible fever. For example, a family from Baden called Schaefer, that had immigrated that same year, lost father, mother, a son, and a daughter. At Sugar Creek, on Shoal Creek Prairie, a family of four lost three, both parents and a son; only a daughter survived. A father of seven small children died, as did a mother of nine. It was almost as if yellow fever were running rampant. Every member of the Schuetz family was ill except little Maria, although none was as ill as I. I was the only one who had bilious fever; the others suffered more or less from intermittent fever.

46. Schuetz's Only Brother Arrives Deathly Ill—His Irresponsible Son Hans—I Go to [Galena] to Bring Back My Trunk— Return Trip on the *War Eagle*

The Schuetz family had increased by two members when Schuetz's only brother, his wife, and his son emigrated from Switzerland; however his brother had already died by the second day after my arrival. As old Schuetz told me, he had been glad that his brother was coming to live with him in America because, having no children of his own, it had been his plan to make his brother's son, Johannes, who had attended good schools in Switzerland and had learned the harness-making trade, his principal heir. One day Schuetz had received a letter from St. Louis informing him that his brother had arrived there with his family, but was very ill and weak. Schuetz had intended to pick him up in his wagon the next day and had set out in plenty of time. On the American Bottom, as he neared Illinoistown, he had met a young fellow who seemed very much in love with the girl on his arm. The thought suddenly crossed his mind, "Is this perhaps my brother's son?" But the thought left his mind as quickly as it had entered, for he remembered that his brother was very weak and ill, and therefore his only son and offspring surely would have remained at his side. Soon Schuetz saw a wagon approaching, and, when they met, it turned out that the wagon carried his brother and wife, and one of his first questions was, "Where is your Johannes?" "You must have met him. He went on ahead. A girl was with him." This gave the good man his first impression of his nephew, an impression that was not favorable, and even more so when he had found his brother so weak. Having arrived at his farm, Schuetz realized that his brother would not live much longer; he tried everything to keep the dying flame of life alive, but by the next day he had died.

Johannes, or Hans as we came to call him, although the death of his father was so imminent, found it more pleasant to go up to Highland with the girl he had on his arm when he had first met Schuetz, instead of staying to be at his father's deathbed and fulfilling his duty as a son. A messenger was sent to Hans with the news that his father had died and was soon to be buried. But this report saddened Hans hardly at all. He did not show any indication of grief for his father, either at the deathbed or at the grave. On the way home from the burial Hans could not restrain himself from singing some lively songs, another indication of how little his father's death affected him. Schuetz's hopes and plans for his nephew were dashed from the very outset, for Schuetz rightly concluded that, if Hans cared so little for his own father during his final illness and on his deathbed, how could he expect to receive better treatment as an uncle under similar circumstances?

But, instead of returning to Schuetz's after the funeral, Hans went off to his girl in Highland, and finally came back only after Schuetz asked him for an explanation of his behavior. Hans attempted to put him off with all sorts of shameless lies, with the result that the good old man immediately decided that this nephew would never become his heir; indeed he thoroughly despised him. Schuetz had also learned from others that Hans had declared during the voyage that he was going to America to become the heir of a rich old childless uncle who was getting along in years.

In addition to myself, this nephew and his mother were now all somewhat ill in Schuetz's house. The relatives of Schuetz's hired man were also ill. For that reason the man had left his position to care for them. Schuetz always had some horses, cattle and many hogs. They needed to be fed, and, although Schuetz himself often felt quite ill, he never neglected to feed the stock. Although it seemed to me that Hans may often have felt unwell, I was of the opinion that, if I felt no worse than he, I would have at least been glad to help feed the livestock, for which he showed neither inclination nor interest, despite the fact that he generally managed to come up with a healthy appetite at mealtime.

One afternoon, when I learned from Mrs. Schuetz that old Schuetz was chopping corn stalks, despite having been quite ill the day before, I suggested to Hans that we might give him a little help. But Hans wanted to hear none of it. "I'm ill and don't feel like working. If uncle wants to work, let him do as he thinks best. But I'm not going to." Although I was unquestionably the sicker of the two, I dressed, took a corn knife, and joined Jacob, who at first objected to my helping him. "You're ill and will only bring about a relapse." Whereupon I replied that if he, the older man, who was also sick, could work, then the consequences could hardly be worse for me, the much younger man.

To his questions as to what Hans was up to, I could only reply that he felt too ill to help, at which Schuetz shook his head, and seemed of the opinion that the only thing ailing Hans was his lack of motivation. He then announced, "He may stay at my place until he's well again. Then he will have to see where he can earn his keep. He will not remain with me."

As often happens when one lacks good medical care, as was the case with me at that time, my illness dragged on. One day I thought I was well, my appetite improved, and I could work a bit. But then I got the chills and a violent fever followed.

I often longed for fruit, and since I knew of a wild plum tree full of fruit in nearby woods south of the farm, I was impelled, as if by force, to go there to enjoy a few plums—or so I planned. I soon found the tree, and its fruit looked ever so tempting. The branches were covered with them, and they dropped easily to the ground where they were devoured as choice morsels by a number of young hogs. The grunters were soon driven away, and I tried one of the plums, and then another, and still another. They were all so good, tasted so delicious, how could I resist? I thought of the tempting tree in Paradise and of Father Adam, and a voice in me said, "Thou shalt not eat of this fruit!" But how could I obey that? It is true, I did not stay there. Otherwise I might still be there. I finally did leave the tree, but only after filling a handkerchief I had been carrying with me. On the way I kept sampling them, now one then another, until I suddenly noticed a certain swelling and a heavy feeling in my stomach, which I immediately attributed to the many plums I had enjoyed. This was the manifestation of my punishment for not having heeded my inner voice. Beyond the woods I came across the hogs I had frightened away and, since I feared I would not stop eating those plums as long as I was carrying them, I tossed the lot to them, and they grunted happily, seeming to thank me for the unexpected plum feast. The following day I was shaking, as might have been expected, and the thought that the cursed plums were to blame would not get out of my mind. To this day I am still somewhat of that opinion.

As already indicated, old Schuetz was a kind of livestock doctor. Without doubt a full-grown cow can swallow a really large dose of medicine and take more than the strongest person can handle. Believing that any advice from the well-meaning Schuetz must be good for me, one day, when I was comparatively free of fever, I took, according to his prescription, two spoonfuls of black ground pepper in a half glass of corn whiskey. One spoonful would probably have been enough for a large horse. As far as I was concerned I felt as though I had swallowed so much liquid metal and glowing coals, and I would never have tried this radical remedy a second time. But had my fever actually gone away after that I would, for all that, have then been satisfied. Unfortunately, despite this treatment, I was not so lucky. On the following day my left side was very swollen near the spleen. I did not know what that meant, but feared something had ruptured. However, I had not done anything physically strenuous for some time. I showed this inexplicable swelling to old Schuetz, who simply laughed and said that it was really nothing to worry about. It was simply a swelling of the spleen, a "fever cake," and was caused by the fever; he had had it also, but it had long since disappeared. If old Schuetz had really had a swelling of the spleen that was as bad as mine, and if it had disappeared as readily as he claimed, he had certainly been far luckier than I, for, while the external swelling had seemingly receded, whenever I was not well or became ill in the future there was always initially a certain pain in that spot, and sometimes it tended to swell again. In short, the ailment had become chronic, and probably will never leave me entirely. I am inclined to believe that the whiskey and pepper were probably the main cause of this problem.

If I had taken my trunk with me when I left Galena, I could have saved myself the expense and trouble of returning there now. It was already October. One could not be certain as to how much longer the river would be open, so there was no time to lose. To be sure the fever had not entirely left me. It returned periodically, but that could not keep me from getting my belongings.

In St. Louis I found a second-class steamboat, on which I found an inexpensive cabin, and I left that same evening. For several days the weather was rainy and unpleasant, and I was almost constantly cold in my warm clothes and heavy overcoat, in spite of the warm stove in the cabin where I sat almost all the time. My hands and fingernails were bluish, and my fingers were a yellowish white. I often coughed up blood and feared I was getting consumption. My appetite was sometimes great, then other times would go away again almost completely. I had no real zest for living and I often looked upon myself as a burden, and felt ashamed of myself. In Galena I consulted the apothecary, who was also a physician,[36] and received from him various mixtures and medicines, for which I had to pay at least fifty cents almost every time. But unfortunately that money was wasted, for my condition failed to improve.

47. What Happened on the Boat from Galena to St. Louis—From St. Louis to Greenville

Since it was now November, I did not remain there very long, but took the opportunity to return to St. Louis again on the *War Eagle*. Since the *War Eagle* was one of the last boats to St. Louis, it was very crowded, and the fare for a cabin was expensive. I therefore chose to travel steerage and quickly assured myself of good sleeping accommodations. The weather was pleasant and mild, and, even in steerage, there were more passengers than there were places for sleeping. Most of the steerage passengers appeared to be American. But there were also some of other nationalities.

Even before the boat departed I observed an Irishman of solid, but not slender build, probably some thirty years old, who was industriously consulting a whiskey bottle and repeatedly offering it to a good-looking young American, who also drank from it several times, until finally his young fever-sick wife warned him against it. The bunks were triple-tiered along both sides. Across from the one I had taken, the young American had appropriated the two lower bunks and had installed his wife in the bottom one. The Irishman, after he had nursed his whiskey for some time and offered it in vain several times to the American, began to become somewhat bothersome to him. Finally the Irishman decided to go to bed. But he was determined to take the middle bunk that the American had chosen for himself, against which the latter naturally protested. That seemed not to bother the Irishman at all. The American, who found that rational reasoning and politeness did not deter this person, dragged him out of his bunk. And, before the American knew what was happening, he was knocked to the deck by a hefty blow from the Irishman. This unexpected attack drove the American wild. Quick as a flash he jumped up, but was knocked down again. Just as quickly the American was on his feet again, and this time he succeeded in attacking the Irishman before he could strike him again. The Irishman was immediately thrown to the deck, and suffered many blows to the head from the extraordinarily quick right hand of the American.

The sick young wife, seeing her husband battling with the Irishman, had cried out, and was close to losing consciousness, when her husband released the Irishman to take care of his wife. The Irishman immediately scrambled to his feet, and had again assumed a combative posture, just as the second mate came by to see what was going on. In response to his inquiry, the situation was soon explained to him. He then tried to make it clear to the Irishman that he was not to take the middle bunk, but rather the top bunk. He was holding a lit lantern. Suddenly he too crashed headlong to the deck, punched by the Irishman. Although the second mate was not a large man, he jumped up quick as lightning, threw the stupid fellow, and began wildly pounding him until he was bleeding profusely from his mouth and nose. He stopped only after some passengers pulled him off, fearing that he might beat the Irishman to death.

The Irishman had never asked for quarter. Indeed, he now picked himself up, but did not assume as threatening a posture as before, although he did not seem to consider himself to have been entirely defeated. At this point the first mate arrived. He had a gigantic build. He seized the Irishman and rolled him like a ball across the deck, causing him to perform several somersaults. Then he grabbed him in both hands and lifted him in the air as easily as if he were a small child and pushed him none too gently into the top bunk, where he ordered him to be very quiet if he did not wish to tangle with him again.

He remained lying almost exactly as the mate had stowed him. He did not get up until it was nearly noon the next day, when he came to me and asked how he looked. My description was even a bit worse than he really was, and he really did look bad enough. Both his eyes were black and blue and heavily swollen. His nose and lips were likewise, and almost all of his face was crusted with dried blood, which required considerable effort to wash off with water. For the rest of the trip the Irishman was one of the quietest passengers.

Some of the passengers had begun to go to bed, as I was also going to do soon. Then a large man, with a tall woolen hat, and not exactly over-clean clothes, came to me asking for permission to sleep on my bed for just a few hours in my buffalo robe, for he was suffering from a fever and had been unable to find a bunk. He promised to vacate it whenever I asked. Although I was not favorably impressed by his appearance, and although I was far from well myself, and also would have much liked to lie down, I felt sorry for him and let him use my bunk for a few hours. At about nine I awakened the man. Although he would have much preferred to lie there longer, I would have none of it. The man seemed very sluggish, which I attributed to the fever.

I was in my warm buffalo robe a short time when something bit me behind my right ear. Reaching for the spot, I felt something between my fingers, which, when I held it toward the light, looked like a gigantic head louse. Soon thereafter I was bitten again in almost the same spot, and again I found a similar small animal. I imagined that this man must have extraordinarily large head lice, for I was certain they had come from him, since I had not been plagued by lice before, and I was already sorry I had given in to his request.

I had two new attacks of chills on the steamboat, the first on the rapids on a so-called flatboat between Montrose and Keokuk,[37] the second on the day before reaching St. Louis, whereupon I, as usual, came down with a bad fever. My fellow passengers were amazed by my intense and prolonged chills, and several showed compassion for me. Gradually I began to feel a sort of biting all over my body, which I regarded as the beginning of the last stage of my fever, because I had experienced the same kind of biting when my fever ended the year before. I had absolutely no idea that this biting could be attributed to another source. But later on I will disclose the surprise that awaited me.

Before I continue, I must mention Galena one more time. During my stay there, I had come to know and became friendly with several fellow countrymen. One of them was named Heinrich Thomman, a native of Biberstein in Canton Aargau. He was barely of average height, had reddish hair, and was a bit freckle-faced. He was about eight years older than I; I found his personality rather appealing. The other, from Kienberg in Canton Solothurn was named Jacob Rippstein.[38] He was a tall, slender, good-looking man, with dark and somewhat piercing eyes, and dark, rather curly hair. He was quick moving, seemed to have a lively, excitable temperament, and was likewise about eight years older than I. With Thomman, Rippstein, and the aforementioned Suter, I had spoken several times about California and Oregon, as well as South America. I had chiefly talked with Suter, who had told me many interesting things about Alexander von Humboldt's travels, and I had become totally enthralled, filled with a great longing to see those regions. But since a trip to South America in those days presented more difficulties than it does today, we set aside thoughts of traveling there, for the time being, as a venture that could not easily be accomplished. As for Oregon or California, that was something else entirely. To get there one had no ocean to cross, no waves, and no stormy seas to fear. The ship upon which one relied was a solid, well-built wagon drawn by a team of mules, or oxen. The helm was reins or a good oxen whip.

Since Suter was a jovial and good-natured, but unfortunately dissolute fellow, I would not consider becoming close friends, or undertaking a journey, with him. Thomman and Rippstein were quite different from him in this respect, so a trip in their company to Oregon or California seemed feasible. I discussed a trip there with these two men several times, especially to California, for at the time we had already read several glowing reports about California. They had been written by a Swiss, Captain Sutter, and according to these accounts this wonderful country had to be a veritable paradise.[39] Ever since that November evening in 1843, when, on the way to Highland, I had spent the night in a stand of young oaks beyond Collinsville, with Aebli and Behler, and old Buchmann and Iberg, and Buchmann had described the trip many immigrants would undertake every spring, my plan had already taken shape, although I had not yet reached Highland, the goal of my journey. We had never made a formal commitment to travel to the shores of the Pacific, although in our hearts each of us longed to make the journey. That was as far as our plans went at that time.

Now I want to take up again the thread of my story from where I left off. After arriving in St. Louis, I looked for an opportunity to leave it as soon as possible. But the first day was Sunday, so there was no opportunity to get started. On the second day I met a former fellow traveler, Barbara Bircher of Canton Aargau, and her husband, a still older acquaintance of mine, a Glarner named Wild, who had often worked for my father as a carpenter. Wild had, I believe, landed in New Orleans about a year before with his first wife, but on the trip up the Mississippi to St. Louis she had fallen overboard and was never seen again. As a result Wild was a widower, and since he happened to meet the no longer very young Barbara, who was also not disinclined to marriage, they came to the conclusion that they suited one another, and had become husband and wife.

At the old market place,[40] near the river, which has not existed for many years now, I finally met a man from Bern, who had a farm in Bond County in Illinois, near Greenville,[41] and who had come to St. Louis to sell some of his produce. I asked him about Greenville—whether there were also German-speaking people there, or only Americans. My countryman said that Greenville was a nice little rural town and that a German-speaking family from Canton St. Gallen lived there, consisting of a husband, a wife, and a little boy. The man's name was Federer. Since my health was not good, my plan was to spend as much time as possible during the winter among Americans, and, if I could, attend the English-speaking school, so that I might thereby more quickly strengthen my command of the English language. According to my compatriot from Bern, Greenville was just the place I was looking for, and since we soon agreed on the price for my fare and belongings (I was to pay him a dollar, cheap enough for a distance of fifty miles), and since he hoped to set out on his return trip shortly, I was quite pleased, and my trunks were at once loaded on his wagon.

We had soon reached the Illinois side and were again crossing the American Bottom toward Collinsville. The weather continued to be quite mild, as fine as I could have wished for on a trip by wagon, and by nightfall we had reached the inn at which we planned to spend the night. I suggested that I sleep in the wagon, for I feared that the precarious condition of my bowels might well result in embarrassment in a closed room—though I did not tell him about my concern—but my friend refused to hear of it. And after a simple, inexpensive meal we went up some steep stairs to a large common sleeping room. There was not a single chamber pot in the entire room, nor was there a light or even a match. I cannot say that I slept well, if I slept at all, for my bowels were churning, so that I longed for the first light of day. But, since this was a long way off, I could not stay in my bed any longer. I got up, dressed, and searched for a chamber pot without finding one; likewise neither light nor matches were at hand. In the darkness I found the door, but it seemed to be locked, which drove me half-mad, and finally I began to call out for someone to open the door. My countryman had also gotten up. He may have guessed the cause of my unrest, and also called the innkeeper, who finally appeared with a light and opened the door. We were soon at the foot of the stairway, but the door below leading to the outside also was locked, trying my patience to the utmost, and it was high time that I got into the open.

After breakfast we got an early start. Instead of taking the most direct route to Greenville, by way of Troy, and then to Marine Settlement, I suggested that we cross Silver Creek and, passing by Schuetz's, take the road through Highland to Greenville. I still had a good, almost unused tree saw from our unsuccessful pinery speculation which I wanted to leave at Schuetz's, along with some other things. On the way we happened to meet Schuetz and Joseph Mueller, who were going to St. Louis, and I took the opportunity to sell Schuetz the saw at a lower price than I had paid for it. Schuetz asked me to drop the saw at his house and to tell his wife to pay me for it, which I did.

It was a pleasant trip, traveling across the still sparsely inhabited prairie northeast of Highland, in the direction of Pocahontas. We startled several deer that were grazing near the road. Pocahontas had only a few houses at that time. Nevertheless it had some of the largest orchards of its time. It lay at the edge of a forest, and from there to Greenville it was another five or six miles, mostly through oak woods. In Greenville the Berner took me to the home of Johannes Federer, where I found a place to stay for the time being. Federer's house was a fairly good, two-story, frame house. Across the street was the larger of the two Presbyterian churches, in which the Greenville schoolroom was located.

I soon came to an agreement with Federer on a price for my board and laundry. I was to pay a dollar a week, as well as help him feed his horses and cattle, chop some firewood, leaving me enough time to go to school. My bedroom was on the upper floor. In addition to a good large, clean bed, it contained a couple of chairs, and a small round table, as well as a wardrobe. The food was simple, but clean and sufficient. Federer was a small, not yet old man, quite pleasant looking, but he had a somewhat wishy-washy, restless look about him. He was a so-called peddler who took eggs, butter, etc., to St. Louis every couple of weeks, exchanging them there for other things. His wife [Frances] was of slender build, with pale, elongated facial features, and dark eyes and hair. She could be termed pretty. She seemed quite industrious and tidy. The boy may have been six years old and appeared outwardly more to resemble his father. Although an only child he was not a spoiled boy.

48. My Unpleasant Acquaintance with Invading Parasitic Creatures— Going to School—Interesting Church Music

Had my health been better I believe I would have found it not unpleasant to be with these people. However, my condition was such that, even in the supposedly fever-free season, I still experienced a lingering fever. Then, for a change, I also had severe toothaches that kept me awake. I remember sleepless nights in bed, writhing in pain, trying vainly to sleep. I had some old tooth roots that were causing the pain, and often I tried to grasp and extract them with my fingers, without achieving my objective, thereby only worsening the excruciating pain. In the darkness, half-mad with pain, I considered all kinds of remedies, until finally I reached into my pants pocket for my keys, held the largest one against the remnant of the tooth, and gave it a hefty blow with my right hand. I had actually loosened the root. Now I could easily pull it out with my fingers. But the other was still in place, and I found, after a long wait that there was no alternative but to repeat the same experiment again, and luckily it worked as well as the first time. Now at last I was able to sleep, and the next morning I only regretted that I had not thought of this solution much sooner.

Although my fever never seemed to let up, the biting and itching at various places on my body had increased. I had no idea that the cause could be attributed to another source. It was all cleared up one morning, rather unexpectedly. I had slept somewhat longer than usual, and, opening my eyes to bright daylight, I quickly jumped out of bed, threw back the covers, and was about to begin hurriedly dressing when I spied some grayish objects on the clean bed sheet. Examining them closely, I found them to be gigantic, black creatures that derived their nourishment from the human body. Since I did not remember ever having seen these creatures before, I took them for their similar but smaller relatives that, unlike them, prefer the human scalp. Their size surprised me, and I could not understand their presence, since I combed my hair thoroughly several times a day. All at once the source of this whole lousy business became clear to me. These were not the disgusting little creatures that make their homes in people's hair. They were the much larger, perhaps even more disgusting, cousins that prefer nesting under people's clothes. How could I have gotten them? That large, untidy-looking man, with the tall, woolen hat on the steamboat *War Eagle,* whom I had, out of sympathy, allowed to sleep in my buffalo robe no doubt could have told me quite easily. Probably the two I had caught behind my ear had been only a part of the first generation. Only now did it become clear to me why, in spite of all the itching, my fever never seemed to subside. After this unexpected, distasteful discovery I quickly began a thorough examination of my woolen underpants and undershirt, with a view to getting rid of the pests once and for all. If ever a creature complied completely with the command to be fruitful and multiply, it was surely these gray, unwelcome parasites on the bodies of human beings. For I had sufficient proof from personal acquaintance. I did not feel a single spark of Christian love for the meek toward my antagonists. I exercised bloody revenge, singeing and burning, and did not stop the annihilation until I believed I had eradicated them down to the last embryo. This work of destruction had taken a long time, but had finally thoroughly finished them off, and I quickly found myself freed of my apparent fever. Without giving her the reason, I asked Mrs. Federer to boil my laundry before washing it. Why? Because this way I hoped to be that much more certain of completely achieving my purpose. Whether Mrs. Federer ever discovered the reason I cannot say, for I was afraid to ask her, and she never said anything to me about it.

Because I had come to Greenville primarily to learn English, I immediately began attending the free public school there. All of the pupils were under a single teacher. The teacher was a good and upright man of about forty years of age, of slender build, and gentle manner, all good necessary characteristics of a teacher. His name was Roedies, or something like that. At first I used Kunst's German-English dictionary[42] a great deal to translate German letters into English, but Mr. Roedies explained that although the letters had admirable style, he could not tell whether the translations were accurate, because he knew no German. After a while Mr. Roedies suggested that I study spelling thoroughly. In order that, as the eldest of his pupils, I would not make myself too ridiculous, he proposed that he would listen to me recite privately until he felt I could progress with the rest of the pupils.

From then on I tried to spend some time every day on this subject, and began to think that, after a few weeks, I would be able to take the floor with the other pupils. Then Mr. Roedies unexpectedly, and in my opinion much too soon, told me I could take the floor to spell with the other pupils. I was terrified, for, although I was the oldest of the pupils, I assumed that all the others would be far ahead of me. However, Mr. Roedies usually pointed the most difficult words out to me beforehand, and I then made a special effort to spell them correctly.

In addition to myself, there were several other older boys, as well as girls, who attended the school. But I was probably the oldest. In order not to lose my place in spelldowns immediately, I went and stood at the very end with the very young boys. However, when a word came along that several of those above me missed and I spelled correctly, I felt no desire to take the place in line which I had earned thereby, although it would have been surrendered to me willingly. Several times it happened, however, that the whole class, from the top of the line down to me, missed some difficult word. Then I spelled, quite slowly, but usually correctly, since Mr. Roedies had made a point of calling my attention to such words. At such times I should have moved to the very head of the line. But, since I was afraid I would probably have to move down again the very next moment, I preferred to keep my place at the end.

Despite the fact that for some time I was the only German in Greenville who attended school, and back then the Americans considered themselves as much more intelligent than any foreign-born person, nonetheless several of the older pupils had already begun to follow my example, that is not moving up to the higher place in line which they had earned through superior spelling. As a result, in order to maintain established procedure, Mr. Roedies felt obliged to insist that everyone occupy the place he had earned, and he could not make an exception for me.

I continued translating from German into English, and I felt it was becoming ever easier for me. I still regret today that I did not continue to practice translation afterward, for it could not have done me any harm, and it could have been useful to me. If my fever had not recurred every two to three weeks I surely would have made much better progress. But the interruptions of one to two weeks certainly had adversely affected my studies. It seemed to me that it took a long time to pick up from where I had left off when the fever set in.

One time Federer took his wife and son to St. Louis, during which time I stayed at home alone and fed his cattle and pigs. Due to this circumstance, Federer arranged for me to take my board at the home of a family named Egridge,[43] a childless couple of middle age, good and upright people. The weather happened to be quite cold for Greenville. Since I always suffered more from cold than from hot weather, except during my bouts of fever, getting up in the morning and going to bed at night was a fairly difficult time for me. I could not seem to warm up at all afterward. By the time the Federers returned I had become quite fond of the Egridge couple, and I soon discovered that I liked living with them even better than living at Federers'. The board was inexpensive and even better than at the Federers'. Especially in pie baking, Mrs. Egridge could hardly be surpassed.

My bed at Egridges' was just as good and clean as at Federers', and since there was only one other boarder, a wagon maker, I soon felt very much at home. The Egridge couple had come from one of the Carolinas. Both were tall and slender, down-to-earth, good-hearted people, without a deceitful bone in their bodies. Often, when at school I felt fever creeping up on me, Mrs. Egridge was always ready to do something or other for me when I came home. After especially violent chills I would vomit considerably. It was a strange, slimy, reddish matter, which, in my ignorance back then, I thought to be pieces of lung. I would often spit blood and my breath had an unpleasant, putrid odor, so that I was ashamed to speak to anyone without holding my hand before my mouth.

One winter day, taking with me my warm winter robe, I rode as far as Highland with Johannes Federer who was going on to St. Louis. Federer asked me to let him take the robe with him, promising to leave it at Jacob Schuetz's on his way back so that I could use it again when I returned to Greenville. Expecting that he would keep his word, I let him take it with him.

I got off in Highland and went to the Gales' who still lived on the old farm. Old Mr. Gale had died in the late autumn.[44] His son John was wandering somewhere aimlessly about the world. So I found Mariet and her mother at home all alone. Of course the two women could not think of working the farm by themselves, and they could not depend on their unstable son and brother. So the farm later had to be sold. A family from Canton Glarus bought it, and the two housewives then moved over to Marine Prairie, where John had decided to rent a plot of land for the year.

When I arrived at Schuetz's farm I found that Federer had not yet returned. Nor did he come while I was there, and thus I was forced to make my return trip by post without my buffalo robe, despite the raw cold weather, thus leaving me exposed to the elements in the open wagon. Along the way I suffered greatly, and my thoughts regarding the deceitful, word-breaking Federer were far from favorable. I believe I would have been more than happy to have given him a good tanning if I had had the opportunity to do so. By the time we reached Pocahontas, where the post driver stopped for a short time on the way back to Greenville, I felt I might never again be able to warm my stiff, frozen limbs.

It had become completely dark by the time we reached Greenville, and when I got down from the wagon my limbs felt half-paralyzed, so that I could hardly walk, and for a long while I suffered ill effects from the severe exposure to the cold. Federer was unable to give me a satisfactory explanation for having broken his word. The words I said to him on this account, although not especially loud, were certainly not complimentary. But his sense of honor seemed very flexible. I scarcely think that my words bothered him very much.

Perhaps this is the place to mention some other things about Federer. I had little to do with Federer after this incident. I had observed earlier that he was somewhat avaricious and, despite his always smiling face, he was pretty good at being deceitful. Eight-and-a-half years later, when I had returned to America from Switzerland and was visiting Highland, I quite unexpectedly ran into Mrs. Federer and her son, again at Mr. Blattner's house. Naturally I had many questions about Greenville, and then I also asked about her husband. However, this seemed to upset Mrs. Federer, and I learned from her own lips that she had separated from her husband, and had divorced him, or intended to, because he had stolen something, and she did not want a thief as a husband.

In the area around Greenville at that time there was still a great deal of small game, especially rabbits, prairie hens, partridges, and such. On Saturdays there was no school, and I would use those days, when I was not sick, to go on short hunting trips, during which I usually used my gun. I generally shot the rabbits through the head, and one afternoon I shot seven or eight of them, so that I had quite a load to carry. I also often shot partridges and prairie hens. But I shot no deer, and I rarely saw any.

On Sundays I attended one or the other of the two Presbyterian churches, and I found their service quite similar to that of our Protestant churches in Switzerland. On one occasion there was a temperance meeting in one of the churches, during which much was spoken and preached in favor of it; nevertheless no one appeared to be won over. Another time some kind of church festival was being celebrated in the larger church. There were many speeches. I was told that music was also played, etc. I was curious and of course went to that church. I had always enjoyed hearing good music, and I could hardly allow such an opportunity pass by. I soon had plenty of reason to be astonished at this music, which very often commenced at a signal from the minister. I had two reasons for my astonishment: the combination of musical instruments, plus the musical selections themselves, which were familiar to me as well-known merry trillings from my old homeland. It was a kind of yodeling that took place outdoors, sung as a sort of postlude, after all the best songs had been sung and all were feeling especially merry.

The musical instruments consisted of a very out-of-tune, dissonant-sounding clarinet, a trombone, and a large drum, which were doing their best to drown out one another with an earsplitting noise that went right through me. The clarinet player happened to be a neighbor of Mr. Egridge's, so I had had the opportunity to hear that same piece of music on many occasions. Upon inquiry I found that he had learned this piece from Gallus Schneider, the son of an old neighbor. Since the clarinet player was actually the group's chief musician, and he knew how to play only this one piece, it is easy to imagine that, under such circumstances, the variety of music was not extensive. Sheet music was not used, and was not necessary, for it may have been that they knew such songs only from memory. The man who played the trombone did not seem to be concerned about which notes he produced as long as his horn was putting forth sounds that were good and loud and plentiful. After all, he had to prove to the assemblage that he was capable of doing something also, and he was not negligent with his toot, toot, tooting. And, even if the sounds from his trombone only seldom harmonized with those of the clarinet, he simply tooted all the more zealously. The virtuoso probably thought that if he produced a good many sounds, now and then one would be bound to harmonize.

As for the man playing the large drum, I must admit that he certainly was not lazy, even when he failed to keep in time, which was not infrequent. It would have been unreasonable to expect of him, that, as player of the noisiest instrument, he should not have let himself be heard. Matching the shrill marrow-penetrating sounds of the clarinet and the earsplitting toot, toot, tooting of the horn certainly did require vigorous beating of the drum, but the drummer proved himself quite capable of drowning them out whenever he wanted to, and he wanted to quite often. Then all of the squealing of the clarinet and the tooting of the horn were of no avail. They could only be heard complaining between the drumbeats. I have often heard that wooden houses are safer than stone houses during violent earthquakes, because the elasticity of wood yields more to great quakes than does stone. It was therefore quite fortunate for the church, and lucky for the many people assembled therein, that it was built of wood. Otherwise the building could not possibly have withstood the powerful, firmament-rending, explosive thundering of the large drum.

But the music seemed to meet with general approval. That was apparent from the many grateful and enthusiastic looks of those present, both the handsome and the ugly, and the many indications given by the learned ignoramuses that they wanted encores of those enchanting sounds. And I have absolutely no doubt that the entire congregation returned home highly edified by the inspired words of the preacher and enchanted by the wonderful tones of the music. Only one member of the assembly dared to be of a different opinion and that individual was a mere "Dutchman," and what do they know about music?

If I remember correctly, the free school in Greenville closed at the end of January, 1846. With that my stay there also came to an end. Mr. Roedies would have been glad to employ me as a farm hand, but I was not prepared at the moment to make such a commitment. However, if I had decided to take up farming I believe Mr. Roedies would have been a good employer. His quiet and friendly nature had won me over, and he, along with the Egridge couple, had become dear to me.

49. En route to Highland with Two Half-Drunks — Going to School in Highland — Pulling an Unfortunate Man out of the Fire

The roads were so bad that they were almost impassable. Therefore, the post was often irregular as well. On one of the warmest days in early February, I had loaded my luggage on the post wagon, with the help of the post driver, and now said goodbye to Greenville and my friends there. There was only one other passenger on the lightweight wagon, which was being used by the post driver during the time the roads were so bad, and this passenger sat next to the Irish driver, on the same seat.

A piece of the wagon's floorboard had broken out, so that smaller objects could easily fall out. My trunks were in the rear of the wagon, and I sat on a seat between the trunks and the aforementioned hole. My fellow passenger had a bottle of whiskey that was more than half full, which he consulted frequently, and then offered to the driver, who accepted it gladly. He then handed it to me, that I might have a drink also, for which I thanked him heartily, but chose not to. This passenger had a large pocketbook full of bank notes, which he carried very carelessly in his coat pocket, so that it would have fallen out many times if I had not called it to his attention. He opened the pocketbook to show us the notes, amounting to five hundred dollars, which he had inherited from a recently deceased uncle. Of course he felt lucky to have inherited so much money so unexpectedly and probably felt obliged to use a certain portion of this substantial amount for the good of his body, and the whiskey bottle provided a wonderful means of achieving that objective.

Whenever the bottle had made its rounds, he put it behind him in the wagon bed. But, due to the continual jolting, the whiskey bottle often slid quite near the hole in the wagon bed, so that I frequently had to rescue it. I called this to the owner's attention, warning him that he would lose it if he did not take better care of it. But he paid little attention to my words, and continued as before. I now began to ask myself whether it might not be better for him if the bottle were lost before its owner derived too much benefit from it, which could also result in his being separated from his many dollars. I now determined to leave the bottle to its fate, and, sure enough, it was not long before it again approached the perilous hole, and, since the wagon happened to be at another bumpy place in the road, fate permitted it to fall out, or rather to fall down. Since the ground was not hard, the bottle did not appear to break, but I forbore telling the lucky heir about his loss, and we had driven on for some time before it occurred to the heir, at about his usual interval, to take a little refreshment. "Where is the whiskey bottle?" With this question both he and the driver turned to me. "It probably fell through the hole in the wagon bed," I answered. "I warned you several times, and I have not been watching it constantly." But my two friends seemed more inclined to believe that I had tossed it out of the wagon myself, and were a bit out of sorts over this not immediately replaceable loss.

If I had felt before that the two men, especially the heir, might gradually show the effects of too much liquor, I could see now that the effect of the whiskey seemed to be giving way to normal good sense. When we reached Highland the heir had almost become himself again, and, more importantly, he was still in possession of his large number of bank notes, and would soon be able to continue his beneficence. How long this man would remain in possession of his bank notes, if he continued such behavior, was, I thought, not difficult to predict.

The free school in Highland was to continue operating for some time. A handsome young man named Johnson was the teacher. In order to be able to take advantage of the school there, I sought and found lodging with a rich farmer by the name of [James] Reynolds, who lived about four miles west of Highland, in some woods at the edge of the prairie. For my keep I had to help feed the livestock mornings and evenings, even on Sundays and holidays, which for the time was a bit much.

With Johnson I progressed more easily than I had earlier under Mr. Roedies. With him I also sometimes played the part of the teacher, and sometimes the student, for he wanted to learn German, which he was already able to read fairly well. I would often review his lessons with him and explain various points to him. I also continued translating from German into English and from English into German. Once, using a geographical history, I did a little translation into German about African termites. To my surprise he took my translation with him to be read by Squire Joseph Suppiger, who had an American wife and who, it was assumed, was well schooled in both English and German. I rather feared that my friend Johnson would report to me that Suppiger had found many mistakes in my translation. But instead Johnson told me that Suppiger had found my translation to be completely correct, and this appeared to elevate me in Johnson's esteem. Johnson revealed to me that he was going to attend a college[45] on Rock River in April in order to further his education, and he tried to persuade me to go there with him. He was of the opinion that I could work for my tuition, as well as my board and room, but I doubted this. In any event I had quite different plans.

I thought I had recovered from my lengthy sufferings from the fever, when suddenly I became quite ill again, and, instead of going to Reynold's house from school, I went to shoemaker Schmied's, Schuetz's brother-in-law, and was welcomed and well-cared for by those good elderly people, as well as by a couple from Basel named Waechli, who lived in Schmied's house. My illness was the so-called winter fever,[46] which had just broken out in many towns and had struck down several otherwise robust individuals. As for me, thanks to the doctor's appropriate and timely ministrations and the good nursing I received at the hands of Mrs. Waechli, I was soon able to leave my sickbed. Meanwhile, however, my schooling in Highland had come to an end. But I still owed Mr. Reynolds some work, so, as soon as I felt strong enough, I again spent a day sawing and splitting wood, which seemed to please Mrs. Reynolds considerably.

Sometime before I left Highland I was in Durer's Helvetia Hotel sitting at a table next to Mr. Johnson, listening to him read German. On Johnson's other side sat the aforementioned Irish mail coach driver listening to us, when through the open door of the adjoining room we heard what sounded like someone falling to the floor. Johnson and I gave it scant attention, but the Irishman slowly got up from his seat and strode toward the door. When he looked into the room, he indicated his surprise by a strange sound and rushed in. Johnson, who, had noticed it, now left my side, went to the door, also seemed surprised, and rushed in. I ran around the table, and, when I looked into the other room I was initially dumbfounded when I saw the two men lifting another man from the hearth.

At first we did not know who the unfortunate man was. But one of Durer's daughter's, who had just come in, told us the most surprising news of all: that he was from Canton Glarus. The poor young man's name was Kubli or Leutzinger. Born in Netstal, he had epilepsy, and had the misfortune of frequently suffering severe attacks of that dread malady. Since his father was well-off, and because the doctors believed that a long sea voyage and a change of air might have a positive effect, he undertook the journey, and had chosen of course to come to New Helvetia in New Switzerland where so many Swiss had come before him. The assumptions of the doctors had not proved correct in this instance. The unfortunate young man had, so to speak, leaped from the frying pan into the fire.

He had burned his face so badly in the intense fire that he lost an eye, and for a time it looked as if he might lose the other as well. His face was also badly disfigured. If he had been left in the flames just a little longer it would have been the end of him. In 1851, somewhat over five years later, as I was walking through Netstal, I met this man on the street, not far from his father's home. The unfortunate fellow had tied a little cloth over the burned part of his face. When I questioned him he clearly remembered the fall, for he had regained his senses as soon as we got him out of the fire and into a bed.

My old friend Schuetz, who had heard of my winter fever, had sent word more than once to have me brought to his place, which I was urged to regard as my home. Although not especially robust, I was nevertheless up and about, and capable of light work. One day Jacob came to get me and my few possessions. I tried to be helpful to Jacob in various ways, and did more than he asked of me. But in the spring, when I tried to plow with the two black mares for the first time, I was overtaken in the field by a major bout of chills, which put a sudden end to my plowing. The chills were, as usual, followed by fever, and so once again I was for some time indisposed. This recurring fever convinced me that I could never be really well in Highland or its environs. Even the doctors supported me in this view.

50. My Hope of Being Able to Travel to California Improves — I Leave My Position at Mr. Boeschenstein's — Schuetz's Fatherly Feelings Toward Me

Jacob Schuetz had previously suggested a number of times that, if I could acquire some knowledge of general store merchandise, he and I might open a store at his farm. A post office also would need to be opened there, and I could serve as postmaster, as well as store clerk. This idea, though not without its appeal, really did not interest me that much. My mind constantly turned toward California. But, since I was still uncertain as to whether I would ever really get there, I was prepared to try to find a job working in a store in St. Louis, where I hoped to get the appropriate merchandising experience.

Schuetz wanted to take me to St. Louis himself for this very purpose, believing that I might find a job at Mr. Boeschenstein's. But, before I went to St. Louis,

I laid out a vegetable garden for Schuetz, and planted vegetables and some peach trees I had obtained from an Englishman named Comstock, who lived on a farm which belonged to a young fellow by the name of Zwilchenbart. Since Schuetz had a few chores to do before he could get away, I first went to St. Louis alone, more to find out whether there was any possibility of finding someone with whom to make the overland journey to California than to look for a job in a store. Having arrived in St. Louis, I visited the marketplaces, which have long since disappeared, and sought wherever possible, to find out whether anyone knew of someone planning to make the overland trip across the prairies and mountains to California. I suspected that more than one of the persons I asked imagined that I must be out of my head, for many stared at me with amazement, as if I were asking about a balloon trip to the moon. "Travel to California? Where in the world is such a place?" Not one person I asked seemed to have ever heard of California or Oregon, much less about people who were considering going there. So I was forced, much as I hated to, to give up the plans for traveling there myself, which I had cherished for years.

Thus, without having accomplished what I had hoped, I returned to Schuetz's farm, only to come back a few days later when he took a load of fat hogs to St. Louis. After Schuetz had sold the hogs, we went to Mr. Boeschenstein's store at the southwest corner of the city's oldest market place. Boeschenstein was at home, and, since he was interested in hiring new help, he was more than happy, at Schuetz's recommendation, to employ me. But he did not want to pay me more than the cost of my food at the Switzerland Boarding House. Only later, after he saw what I was worth, would he be ready to pay me wages. I had to sleep in the store. Since my main purpose was to learn the business, as well as to earn money, this less than generous proposal was temporarily acceptable.

My clothes trunk was soon brought around, and I began my new job. In the morning I first had to scrub the floor clean, hang some goods outside the door, put everything in its proper place, and then prepare a half-washtub of fresh water in a back room of the building, where Mr. Boeschenstein used it daily to wash his entire body. By the time all of this had been accomplished, the customers usually began to appear. Ours was a general store, handling what would now be called dry goods and groceries, and, to my mind, the best kind of place in which a young man might learn the trade.

As far as I was concerned, I did not find the duties difficult to understand and to learn once they were explained to me, and it was not nearly so hard to learn the meaning of the letters and numbers on the wares as I first thought. The former clerk stayed on for several days after I came. He was a good-looking young German, who seemed to understand the business completely, and he was my first instructor. After two weeks I was already able to replace him adequately, although I do not claim that I had complete command of my duties. Mornings, after I had straightened things up, Mr. Boeschenstein arrived right after breakfast, and I went to my boarding house to have mine. I had already abandoned the idea of going to California that year as impossible, for I had heard nothing from Thomman and Rippstein.

I had been at Boeschenstein's nearly three weeks when, as usual, I arrived one morning at Strasser's Switzerland Boarding House to have my breakfast. Since the breakfast bell had not yet rung, I was sitting in the waiting room when there suddenly appeared in the doorway a newly arrived man, whom I immediately recognized as one of my acquaintances from Galena. It was Heinrich Thomman of Biberstein, in Canton Aargau, who had also recognized me as well, and he told me that Rippstein was there also, and that they were making preparations for a trip to California. One can scarcely imagine the feelings that suddenly awakened in me; very mixed feelings, first of regret that I had not known of it sooner, and then again concern as to whether or not I could quit my present position without thereby offending my employer. Moreover, my finances had declined considerably, so that I surely would not be able to pay my share of the cost of oxen and wagon. It was all really awkward, and I truly would have liked to have gone along, which Thomman and Rippstein tried to convince me to do. When I protested that I had only been employed at Boeschenstein's store about three weeks and that he might think badly of me if I were to leave so suddenly, they countered that Boeschenstein could easily find another sales clerk, and that he would not hesitate to fire me if he believed he might to do better with someone else, etc.

As for my money concerns, both offered to help me out, should I have the need. To be sure that they would have no misunderstandings in this regard, I told them the amount I would be able to contribute, but this seemed to make no difference to them. It seemed that I had no other choice than to go with them, but still I was uncertain, wondering also how I could honorably leave my job without offending Mr. Boeschenstein. While for the past three weeks all my thoughts had been completely focused on learning the business as quickly and as thoroughly as possible, now those thoughts were completely thrown off track. And yet I strove loyally to fulfill my obligation. I continued to consider by what means I might possibly leave Boeschenstein's decently, and I believed I finally had found the right—"I've got it"—solution.

When on the second morning Thomman and Rippstein again urged me to accompany them, I confided my plan to them whereby I was sure Mr. Boeschenstein would freely to give his consent to let me go without actually meaning to. My plan was as follows: Since a trip through the wilderness by several men, which would take up to six months, would require substantial purchases of provisions, especially coffee, sugar, tea, dried beef, lard, as well as gunpowder, lead, shot, percussion caps, matches, etc., I could guarantee that we would sell these items at cheaper prices than anywhere else in St. Louis. They were to come to the store during the day to make purchases there, at which point I would introduce them to Mr. Boeschenstein. Since I had already told my employer on the first day that friends of mine from Galena had arrived, with whom I had made a tentative agreement last summer to journey to California, and that they were demanding now that I go with them, he would be somewhat prepared. Their purchases would put him in a fairly good mood. Naturally I would be the one to wait on them, and then, within earshot of my employer, they would suddenly turn to me and say, "Lienhard, you are acting as if you were not a participant in this venture, and you well know that last summer you promised to make the trip with us. So hurry up and get ready. We were counting on your keeping your promise!" At this point I would reply that, to be sure, I had made this arrangement with them, and that I certainly would have gone along before I had entered Mr. Boeschenstein's employ. But, since I had not heard from them, I thought that they had completely given up on the trip. I was working now at Mr. Boeschenstein's, and he might not like it if I were to quit so suddenly; at which point one of them would turn to him and say, "Oh surely, Mr. Boeschenstein, you certainly can't have anything against his leaving his position in order to travel with us. There must be plenty of people you can get anytime to serve as sales clerk." Then I would expect him to reply that, if I really wanted to go, he would have nothing against it. I would then use this reply, or one of a similar nature, to promise anew, in his presence, to accompany them, since I now saw that it did not matter to Mr. Boeschenstein whether I went or stayed. I had told Mr. Boeschenstein that I had invited my friends to make their purchases in our store and that I believed we would be able to sell them what they needed as cheaply as anywhere else. With that I had done him a favor.

As we had planned, my friends arrived to make their purchases, and after I had introduced them, their purchases were packaged, a task attended to primarily by me. Mr. Boeschenstein, who ordinarily looked a bit somber, now had a friendly smile on his face, for customers such as these were really somewhat rare. It was no wonder. All that cash surely would have made anyone happy. I acted as though I was extremely busy, which in fact I was. Suddenly I heard Rippstein speaking to me, asking why I was not getting ready for the trip, etc., just as I had suggested, and I replied, just as we had planned, whereupon Thomman and Rippstein turned to Boeschenstein and spoke the above-mentioned words, that he surely would not mind, etc., at which point he used almost the very words I had predicted he would.

"There, you heard it for yourself, Lienhard?" my friends now said to me. "Your employer has nothing against your going with us. So now hurry and get ready!"

Of course I pretended to be somewhat surprised and said, "Well, if Mr. Boeschenstein does not mind, I hereby renew my promise to go with you, and will get ready for the trip in the next few days." I very much suspected that this arrangement did not exactly suit him. This was clear from the way his lips were drawn to one corner of his mouth, which was a sure sign of disapproval or displeasure.

After my friends had gone, Mr. Boeschenstein and I did not exchange a single word about the matter. I did my work as before, as if I were planning to stay a long time. The following morning I again did all my work as usual, even fetching the water for his bath in the back room. Then I turned to Mr. Boeschenstein, saying that I would now have to leave everything else to him. Mr. Boeschenstein acted very surprised. "What, you want to leave me?" I in turn did the same, and questioned why he seemed so disturbed. He had himself declared in the presence of my friends that it did not matter to him if I wanted to go with my friends, and on this basis I had given them my word again, which he certainly must have heard, and, in all decency, I could not back out again!

But Mr. Boeschenstein wanted to play the role of the injured party, and said something about being treated that way, etc., whereupon I asked him to tell me exactly how I had treated him unjustly or dishonorably. Mr. Boeschenstein was clearly in a dilemma; he was unable to say that he knew of any dishonorable act on my part, but he had expected me to stay with him, and he had after all been well satisfied with me, and had hoped that I would move to Highland with him, where he planned to transfer his business in May.[47] As for me, I was of the opinion that if he had wanted me to stay he should not have spoken in that way in front of other people, who he knew wanted me to go with them. Furthermore, no contract existed between us, and I did not really know whether or not he intended to pay me anything beyond the cost of my board. He did not really want to give me a straight answer to this, but it was clear to me that he would not pay me anything beyond board for the period I had already worked if I left him now. Then Mr. Boeschenstein attempted to describe the enormity of such a trip through the deserts, wilderness, through areas inhabited by dangerous Indian tribes, across mountains, etc., and added that he would much rather undertake a trip to Texas, which one could at least reach within fourteen days. But I remained true to my long cherished goal, and wanted to hear nothing about a journey to Texas, where cousins of mine had already gone earlier and had not liked it.

Arriving on the Illinois side of the Mississippi, I strode briskly toward the Schuetz farm, for the weather was pleasant and the road dry, and I covered the twenty-four miles in fairly good time. When I arrived at the farm, Schuetz was busy doing something or other to the west of the farm. How surprised he was to see me climbing over the fence so unexpectedly! He looked at me with a half-embarrassed smile. When I allowed him to guess why I had come, he replied that he could not imagine. When I told him I was going overland to California in the company of several other young people, he may have been somewhat regretful, for he had something else in mind for me. He explained to me that if I had stayed with him until his death he had intended to give me his farm.

"My nephew Hans," he said, "shall receive nothing from me. He is a thoughtless person who neglected his father, even on his deathbed, and has lied to me continually since he has been here. Fritz is to get nothing from me either, because I can make nothing out of him, and, whenever I have tried, I have been met with ingratitude, both from him and his mother. But Maria will receive something from me. She's become a dear child to me." I was touched by these good intentions of the good old man, but they did not cause me to change my mind. I spoke with him about it, saying that I expected, if I were not prevented by recurring illness, to make my own way in the world, since I was still a young man. Though pleased by his good intentions, I could not accept them, for if things should not always go as I hoped, which could easily happen to anyone, and I seemed some day to take something amiss, he might be inclined to think that I was impatient for him to die. But I was much too fond of him to wish him dead, and even though they were only stepchildren they still could not but resent that I might become his principal heir in their stead. Sorry as Jacob was to see me go, he told me on the last day of my stay with him that if he were still a young man he would have decided to go along also. If things went well, he asked me to write to him, and he would come too, despite his age.

51. Taking Leave of Friend Schuetz and Highland

I had had a little trunk made and, since my Swiss trunk was too large for a wagon trip, I left it with Schuetz, but he later again placed it at my disposal, since I had not sold it to him. Near Highland I bought a good, double-barreled shotgun from a man from Graubuenden named Margut, and, from a native of Glarus called Weber, I bought a hunting knife, such as Swiss sharpshooters carry, to be able, if necessary, to save my skin as well as I could during hostile Indian attacks.[48]

Afterwards I said goodbye to my friends in Highland, and on the following day did likewise to my upright friend Schuetz and his family. Schuetz had pressed a few dollars into my hand, remarking that he was sorry that he was a little short of money at the moment, otherwise he would have given me more. The mail wagon had arrived, in which I took my place, and soon it took me from my second home and from my kind-hearted, second, or American, father.

Notes
Principal Sources Consulted
Index

Notes

1. Growing Years in an Alpine Canton

1. Lienhard folio 1/1/11. A collection of small farms, jurisdictionally belonging to Bilten.

2. Lienhard folio 1/1/16. Lienhard's parents were Caspar, born October 14, 1784, died March 18, 1873, and his second wife, Dorothea Becker, born October 19, 1793, died January 30, 1842. All four children were by the second marriage. *Auszug aus der Genealogie des Landes Glarus Bilten, No. 126.* (Glarus: Landesbibliothek, 1985).

3. Lienhard folio 1/1/19. Such a hailstorm did take place, July 30, 1824, when Lienhard would have been two-and-a-half years old. Franz Winteler, *Beitraege zur Biltner Geschichte* (Niederurnen: Thomas and Co., 1973), 39.

4. Lienhard folio 3/3/35. Any translation of *Gegensaetze,* meaning contrasts, opposites, contraries, antitheses, or possibly disputations, that would be consistent with the pedagogy of the times seems speculative. However, it is quite possible that a schoolmaster as enlightened and creative as Pastor Schuler might have used the students' essays as a basis for discussion of varying viewpoints.

5. Lienhard folio 4/3/15. Glarus, Schwyz, Zurich, and St. Gallen.

6. Lienhard folio 4/3/34. Lienhard uses the word *Faehnrich,* meaning one who might be the standard-bearer of an organization or a military adjutant; but the title just as likely had a humorous connotation since names, such as Zweifel, were so common that it was often felt necessary to distinguish their bearers by a nickname.

7. Lienhard folio 4/4/39. The Aschenwald is a steep-wooded area paralleling, for a distance of perhaps two miles, the road from Bilten to the Lienhard home at the Ussbuehl.

8. Lienhard folio 5/2/32. *Santa Katerina.*

9. Lienhard folio 6/1/2. *Doppelten Golden Adler.*

10. Lienhard folio 6/1/32. *Traube Wirtshaus.*

11. Lienhard folio 6/3/2. Johann Evangelist Fuerst, *Der wohlberatene Bauer Simon Struef, eine Famliengeschichte: Allen Staenden zum Nutzen und Interesse, besonders aber jedem Bauer und Landwirthe ein Lehr- und Exempelbuch* (Augsburg: Kollmannische Buchhandlung, 1841).

12. Lienhard folio 6/3/3. *Foehn* are desiccating and generally high-velocity winds that take place on the leeward (downwind) sides of alpine mountains. They are the result

of air being forced over windward mountain slopes, whereby the cooling that occurs in the process is reduced as a result of condensation. As the air flows downward over the leeward slopes it becomes considerably warmer and drier than during its ascent. Everything in the path of the winds may become extremely dry, threatening dangerous fires. Considerable rainstorms may follow. On the positive side, a foehn can hasten the coming of spring and lengthen summers, to the benefit of agriculture. The same phenomenon is known elsewhere by other names, e.g., the Chinooks, which descend the eastern slopes of the Rocky Mountains.

13. Lienhard folio 6/3/4. Community-owned land used for grazing, etc.

14. Lienhard folio 7/2/11. So-called because the handles were bent backward, somewhat resembling the horns of a goat. The usual spelling for goat would be *Geiss* rather than *Geisse*.

15. Lienhard folio 9/1/20. *Zum Roessli.*

16. Lienhard folio 9/4/18. Fridolin and Hilary are the patron saints of Canton Glarus, and the green cheese was one of the canton's much-esteemed products.

17. Lienhard folio 9/4/28. Lienhard uses the old form of the name, Pfaeniger.

18. Lienhard folio 10/4/2. *Pistumzieher,* meaning nipple wrenches, small wrenches used for removing and reseating percussion nipples in muzzle-loading guns. Letter from Christa Landert to Spahn, October 3, 1990; George C. Nonte, *Firearms Encyclopedia* (New York: Harper and Row, 1973), 177.

19. Lienhard folio 12/4/4. Lienhard, as was common in the nineteenth century, referred to *Le Havre* as *Havre.*

20. Lienhard folio 12/4/37. A French border town, already better known as St. Louis. It was, at the time Lienhard was there, the usual point of entry into France from Basel; however, at the time Lienhard was writing, about 1874, as a result of the Franco-Prussian War it had come under German jurisdiction.

2. By Land, Sea and Upriver to St. Louis

1. Lienhard folio 13/1/35. About eleven miles northwest of Bilten, on Lake Zurich.

2. Lienhard folio 13/1/40. *Gasthof zum Baeren.*

3. Lienhard folio 13/1/43. Until 1835 these ships carried only mail, but thereafter only freight and people. Oswald Heer, *Der Kanton Glarus* (St. Gallen: Huber, 1846), 500.

4. Lienhard folio 13/2/36. A large hill overlooking Zurich.

5. Lienhard folio 13/2/44. Lienhard uses the word *Dolmetscher,* literally meaning an interpreter, but probably it was a dictionary, or perhaps a phrase book for travelers, or a combination of both.

6. Lienhard folio 13/4/11. Lienhard is referring to Salomon Koepfli's *Neu Schweizerland in den Jahren 1831 und 1841* (Lucerne: Xaver Meyer, 1842).

7. Lienhard folio 13/4/24. Probably Lienhard's memory was not clear, as a few lines later he refers to "Stein, or Steinen."

8. Lienhard folio 13/4/38. Lienhard sometimes uses the question mark to express sarcasm.

9. Lienhard folio 14/2/2. Canton Basel is divided into two demicantons, Basel-Land and the City of Basel.

10. Lienhard folio 14/2/7. *Dreikoenig.*

11. Lienhard folio 14/2/9. Lienhard spells as Chalons.

12. Lienhard folio 14/3/11. Free, candid.

13. Lienhard folio 15/1/11. Le Havre de Grâce, the old name of Le Havre.

14. Lienhard folio 15/2/20. The ship they were to take bore the Indian name—as Lienhard spells it—*Naraganset.* The usual spelling would have been *Narrangansett.* In a letter to Christa Landert from the President of the Centre Havrais de Recherche Historique Les Amis du Vieux Havre, June 15, 1985, the name is given as *Narraganset.* The passenger list for the ship, on its arrival on November 7 in New Orleans uses the spelling *Naragansett. Narragansett* will be used here. The name of the Captain was Peter [Anton?] Destebecho.

15. Lienhard folio 15/2/22. Lienhard uses the word *Hummer,* meaning lobster, a most improbable provision. According to Christa Landert, in a letter to Abbott of April, 1984, Lienhard may have meant *Hammen,* which would be Lienhard's High German version of the dialect word, *Hamme,* meaning ham.

16. Lienhard folio 16/1/5. Wuerttembergers were commonly called Swabians.

17. Lienhard folio 16/4/1. The then common name of the island that became the Dominican Republic on the east and Haiti on the west.

18. Lienhard folio 17/2/5–6. Dolphins are, of course, not "fish," but mammals, as are whales. Since Lienhard, by the time he wrote this passage, had crossed the Atlantic five times and was a keen observer of flora and fauna, it is probable that he was using the word "fish" in a general sense to designate various swimming fauna.

19. Lienhard folio 17/2/19f. The course of the *Narragansett* would have by now taken them southwestward into the Caribbean toward one of the two northern-most of the Cayman Islands, which were then known as the Tortugas, Spanish for turtles.

20. Lienhard folio 17/4/7. Apparently they had arrived on November 3 at the point where the *Black Star* met them; it took another day for them to arrive at New Orleans.

21. Lienhard folio 17/4/16. Probably bananas, a variety of plantain.

22. Lienhard folio 18/1/13. Lienhard uses the northern Andean word for buzzards.

23. Lienhard folio 18/4/35. Grand Gulf, twenty-five miles below Vicksburg, was named for the whirlpools and eddies created in the Mississippi by the Big Black River as it worked against—and eroded—the sandstone cliff that jutted into the junction of the two rivers. Well known to early travelers, Grand Gulf was, by the time Lienhard saw it, Mississippi's premier shipping place for cotton. On its way to a population of nearly 1,000, its large wharf-side shops offered fancy goods, as well as grog, and duels were fought on the bottomland sandbar below. In the spring of 1863, it took center stage in General Grant's campaign to take Vicksburg. Having failed to silence the Confederate batteries on the Bald Knob Hills below Grand Island, Grant landed on the eastern bank, thirty-five miles further south, at a place that offered dry land roads to the north; Grand Gulf was evacuated before Union troops arrived, and, barely two months later, July 4, 1863, Vicksburg fell. Today Grand Gulf is little more than a ghost

town, its main claim to glory being the Grand Gulf Military Monument, located on the heights to the south. Federal Writers' Project Mississippi, *Mississippi, A Guide to the Magnolia State* (New York: Hastings House, 1938), 326; Earl Schenck Miers, *The Web of Victory, Grant at Vicksburg* (New York: Knopf, 1955), 138–59 passim; United States Geological Survey, *Grand Gulf Quadrangle* (Washington, D.C.: U.S. Geological Survey, 1963).

24. Lienhard folio 19/2/39. Lienhard spells as Thomen. However, the correct spelling is Thomman. He was baptized in Biberstein, Canton Aargau, on April 22, 1814, and died in San Francisco on May 18, 1883. Letter from Christa Landert to Abbott dated March 13, 1994.

25. Lienhard folio 20/1/11–17. When platted in 1837 this Swiss community had been named Highland. In 1840, when word was received that a town site in northern Illinois had been given that name first, the name was changed to Helvetia. However, later the northern Illinois town was incorporated as Highland Park and the name was changed back to Highland, by which name it was again known by the time Lienhard arrived there.

26. Lienhard folio 20/1/33. St. Louis's population, more than 16,000 in 1840, rose to 34,140 in 1844, and to 35,900 in 1845. New Orleans' population was several times greater.

27. Lienhard folio 20/1/41–44. Jefferson Barracks was several miles below Carondolet. Lienhard gives Carondolet's nickname as "Weepush," a German-speaking person's hearing of the French nickname Vide Poche, empty pocket, an apparent reference either to the poverty of the inhabitants or to the financial situation of persons who had gambled away their money there.

3. Becoming More or Less American

1. Lienhard folio 20/2/1. Beginning in 1797, James Piggott began a ferry service from this site to St. Louis directly across the Mississippi. Around 1818 lots were laid out and the village began to be referred to as Illinoistown. In 1861 the town was incorporated and its name was changed to East St. Louis.

2. Lienhard folio 20/2/4. The American Bottom—or Bottoms—extends twenty-three miles along the Mississippi, from Prairie du Pont on the south to Alton, Illinois on the north. The flood plain is about nine miles wide at the portion Lienhard crossed. Collinsville, ten miles east of St. Louis, was named for the prosperous Collins brothers who settled there in 1817.

3. Lienhard folio 20/2/9–19. Lienhard is describing the Cahokia Mounds complex, the trade and cultural center of the largest population of pre-Columbian Indians (A.D. 900–1300) ever to live north of Mexico. It is now the only World Historic Site in the United States that is not also a national park. The mound that he describes as "very high and extensive" is the famous Monks Mound, actually one hundred feet in height and covering fourteen acres. Lienhard's underestimate of the mound's height was probably in part due to the circumstance that the road he took passed to the south of

the mound, which consists of several terraces, the lowest being closest to the road; his view was undoubtedly obscured by foliage. The "little" house on top was occupied by its builder, T. Ames Hill. Mikels Skele, *The Great Knob: Interpretations of Monks Mound* (Springfield: Illinois Historic Preservation Agency, 1988), 21–28.

4. Lienhard folio 20/3/1. "Wiski" is whitewash in the Glarus dialect spoken by Lienhard. Christa Landert in a letter to Spahn, July 3, 1987.

5. Lienhard folio 20/3/14 The name "Minnesota" derives from the Dakota, or Sioux, word "minne" meaning water, plus "sota" meaning somewhat clouded. Warren Upham, *Minnesota Geographic Names* (St. Paul: Minnesota Historical Society, 1969), 36; William Watts Folwell, *A History of Minnesota* (St. Paul: Minnesota Historical Society, 1921), 1: 45–57. In a letter to Abbott of June 20, 1991, Alissa Rosenberg, Reference Librarian, Minnesota Historical Society, states that Lienhard's version is "completely unsubstantiated." Lienhard was probably passing on—possibly tongue-in-cheek—an oral version.

6. Lienhard folio 20/3/36. "Looking Glass Prairie, a large, rich, beautiful, and undulating prairie lying between Silver and Sugar Creeks . . . Few prairies in the state present more eligible situations for farms than this." John Mason Peck, *A Gazetteer of Illinois*, 2nd ed., rev., corrected, and enl. (Philadelphia: Grigg and Elliot, 1837), 243. Averaging six to ten miles in width, and about twenty miles from north to south, the prairie extended from around Highland in the north to Lebanon in the south.

7. Lienhard folio 20/3/38–41. Troy was laid out as a town site in 1819. Marine Settlement, or Marine Town, as it was called during Lienhard's stay in Illinois, had been settled in 1818 by several sea captains. Silver Creek rises about eight miles northwest of Highland and runs into St. Clair County, where it enters the Kaskaskia.

8. Lienhard folio 20/4/13. A ridge named by the Koepflis after the subalpine chain stretching from southeastern France into Canton Schaffhausen.

9. Lienhard folio 20/4/15 Two Leutwiler's, Jakob and Rudolf, both from Canton Aargau, lived along the route Lienhard was taking.

10. Lienhard folio 20/4/17. Lienhard spells as Gilam. A Nic Gillom is indicated on the 1847 "Map of the Highland Area, or New Switzerland." See Raymond J. Spahn and Betty Alderton Spahn, eds. and annot. *New Switzerland in Illinois* (Edwardsville: Friends of Lovejoy Library, Southern Illinois University Edwardsville, 1977), as living exactly on the spot on the Jura indicated by Lienhard. Also, a Christian Gillomen is shown as living on the Jura, to the south, and not far up the same hill. Later Lienhard refers to a Christian Gilom, 30/4/47, also a Berner. Jacob Eggen, in his "Chronicles of Early Highland," translated as book two of *New Switzerland in Illinois,* notes on page 118 the arrival in 1835 of the large Gillomen family from the vicinity of Thun [Canton Bern]. Max Schweizer's *Neu- Schweizerland: Planung, Gruendung und Entwicklung einer schweizerischen Einwanderersiedlung in den Vereinigten Staaten von Nordamerika (Madison County, Illinois)* (Zug: Verlag Zuercher, 1980), pages 238–39, gives seven versions of the name, all with three syllables, each starting with "Gil" or "Gill," followed by an "om," and ending in "an," "ann," or "en." In recent years a fairly large number of families living in the Highland area appear solely under the name Gilomen in city

and phone directories, which form will be used here. The editor has been told by a long-time resident of Highland that all Gilomens living there today pronounce the name as though it were spelled "Gilam," thus Lienhard's phonetic spelling is vindicated.

11. Lienhard folio 21/1/1. Caspar Schneider was married to Regula Aebli. The Schneiders and the Kunderts, like Lienhard, were from Bilten in Canton Glarus.

12. Lienhard folio 21/1/14. Margaret Kundert married Balthasar Schneider in 1847.

13. Lienhard folio 21/1/49. Having arrived in the United States in 1833 at the age of twenty, and having been married in Highland in 1839 to an American woman, Rebecca Allison, Mollet was apparently well on the way toward becoming Americanized.

14. Lienhard folio 21/3/17. Lienhard, in apparent sarcasm, uses the English word.

15. Lienhard folio 21/3/37. Garrett Crownover was a storekeeper and justice of the peace at the time Lienhard saw him at the party. He later served in the Illinois legislature.

16. Lienhard folio 21/4/47. If Lienhard was referring to Michael Kaempf, a fellow Swiss, it was one of the few times, if any, that he used the diminutive form of an adult male's name.

17. Lienhard folio 22/2/9. Zimmermann and Michael Mollet were among the first members of the German Methodist Church when it was established in Highland in 1846.

18. Lienhard folio 22/3/3. At least two Swiss immigrants of this name were living in the Highland area at the time. However, one John, or Johannes, Rudolph Blattner, already a prominent citizen would have been too young—he was born in 1812—to have had a son in 1843 of Lienhard's age. It is likely that the Johannes, or Hans, Blattner whom Lienhard writes about was the son of a John, or Johannes, Blattner born in 1797 and a resident of Helvetia Township, who in 1845 had three sons between the ages of ten and twenty. *1845 Census of Madison County*, Elsie M. Wasser, comp. Madison County Naturalization Records, University Archives, Lovejoy Library, (Southern Illinois University Edwardsville, 1985), 3.

19. Lienhard folio 22/4/43. Rebecca Mollet died in 1858; Michael Mollet then married Rosina Andres from Canton Solothurn on March 15, 1860. He died May 18, 1888 and Rosina died April 13, 1890. At his death Michael Mollet left, in addition to his wife, eleven children and twenty-five grandchildren.

20. Lienhard folio 22/4/49. By law any male in Illinois could be required to work five days a year on road construction. The project on which Lienhard was required to labor was of importance to Highland, since, when completed in the fall of 1843, this portion of what was referred to as the National Road ran from Pocahontas through Highland to Troy, rather than through Marine.

21. Lienhard folio 23/2/11. Joseph Suppiger's cousin, who arrived in 1833, along with other Suppiger family members.

22. Lienhard folio 23/2/16. A well-known mountain between Lakes Lucerne and Zug.

23. Lienhard folio 23/2/18. Public land owned by the United States government was purchasable at the land office in Edwardsville, fifteen miles to the west of Highland, at $1.25 an acre.

24. Lienhard folio 23/2/30. According to Jacob Eggen, the going interest rate in Highland was twelve percent. Eggen, "Chronicles of Early Highland," 151.

25. Lienhard folio 23/3/49. Son of Francois Abeck, a blacksmith from Arth, Canton Schwyz, according to Christa Landert in a letter to Abbott of March 2, 1994.

26. Lienhard folio 24/1/19. Shoal Creek, ten miles to the east of Highland, flows south into the Kaskaskia River.

27. Lienhard folio 24/1/23. "An extensive prairie lying to the west of Shoal Creek, in Clinton, Bond, and Montgomery counties. It is slightly rolling, and contains much good land." Peck, *A Gazetteer of Illinois*, 292.

28. Lienhard folio 24/3/19. A Mr. Ruef had arrived in Highland in the spring of 1834. However, since conditions in Highland did not suit him, he moved to St. Louis in the fall and returned to Switzerland the following spring. Schuetz rented the property from the winter of 1834–35 until he moved to his permanent residence in what was to become St. Jacob in the spring of 1845. Eggen, "Chronicles of Early Highland," 111, 115.

29. Lienhard folio 25/4/40. Schuetz was born May 7, 1789, and would have been nearly fifty-five when he first employed Lienhard.

30. Lienhard folio 26/1/12. Madison County marriage records show Schuetz having been married to Mary Meyer on September 3, 1840.

31. Lienhard folio 26/1/18. The farm Schuetz had bought was on the future site of the village of St. Jacob. St. Jacob "was started as a crossroads place when Jacob Schutz built the first house, where he sold whiskey by the gallon." W. T. Norton, *Centennial History of Madison County, Illinois, and Its People, 1812–1912.* (Chicago: Lewis Publishing, 1912), 599.

32. Lienhard folio 26/2/36. *Plattdeutsch*, i.e., persons speaking North German, or Low German, dialects.

33. Lienhard folio 26/3/17. Probate records for Schuetz (Madison County Circuit Court Probate Records, Court House, Edwardsville, Ill.) give the date as May 9, 1865.

34. Lienhard folio 26/3/40.

35. Lienhard folio 27/1/1. Claybank is the name for a shade of dun that verges on sorrel. Dun ranges from buckskin to shades considerably lighter; sorrel ranges from a brownish orange to light brown. Louis Taylor, *Harper's Encyclopedia for Horsemen* (New York: Harper and Rowe, 1973), 115.

36. Lienhard folio 27/2/22. Several years before Lienhard arrived in Highland "Shoemaker Schmidt," who had come to the area in 1833, built a shop in Highland. However, because of difficulty in establishing for certain that "Shoemaker Schmidt" and Schuetz's brother-in-law, Schmied, are one and the same person, Lienhard's spelling of the name is followed here. A. P. Spencer, *Centennial History of Highland, Illinois 1837–1937.* (1937; reprint, Highland: Highland Historical Society, 1978), 36.

37. Lienhard folio 28/4/46. In his will dated May 15, 1865, Schuetz bequested $1,000 to his wife; and to his stepdaughter, Mary Meyer, he gave all of his real estate, plus all of his personal property not above disposed of, under the condition that his wife, Mary, should be maintained and provided for on the farm as long as she remained unmarried. Elsewhere it was noted that there were two stepchildren, one of whom, Mary,

was the main legatee. Fritz received nothing, but may have been allowed to live with the family. Madison County Circuit Court Probate Records.

38. Lienhard folio 29/2/37. Dr. Benjamin Brandreth's Vegetable Universal Pills, consisted of 4 oz. aloes, 2 oz. gamboge, ½ oz. extract of colocynth, 2 oz. Castile soap, ½ dram peppermint, ½ dram cayenne pepper, and an undetermined, but essential, quantity of sarsaparilla, has been described as "among the most powerful cathartic cannon in the botanical armory." In three books, many pamphlets, and thousands of newspaper ads throughout the country, Brandreth's panacea through purgation brought him and his family a large fortune, from the mid-1830s until well after his death in 1880. James Harvey Young, *The Toadstool Millionaires; A Social History of Patent Medicines in America before Federal Regulation* (Princeton: Princeton University Press, 1972), 75–89; *Consult Me, To Know How to Cook . . .* , at least three editions, London, 1871, 1884, 1902.

39. Lienhard folio 29/3/8. Lienhard appears to spell as "Richner." However, the name could only be that of Dr. Frederick Ryhiner, who was prominent in Highland, both as a physician and as a businessman for about forty years.

40. Lienhard folio 31/3/22. The Madison County Courthouse was in Edwardsville; Alton was the site of the State Penitentiary.

41. Lienhard folio 32/1/38. Since Gale died intestate all his estate passed to Mrs. Gale. Madison County Circuit Court Probate Records.

42. Lienhard folio 32/2/31. *Die Hundert Wunder der Welt & die 3 Naturreiche.*

43. Lienhard folio 32/4/23. June 27, 1844.

44. Lienhard folio 32/4/27. The "Territory of California" was never organized as such and was legally a part of Mexico until the Treaty of Guadalupe Hidalgo, February 2, 1848. The first company of Mormons arrived at the Great Salt Lake on July 24, 1847. The Territory of Utah was created by Congress in 1850. As a part of the Compromise Act of 1850, California was admitted as a state, September 9, 1850.

45. Lienhard folio 32/4/36. The name "Fever River" is usually attributed to an American hearing of *La rivière aux fevès,* meaning "Bean River." The river originates in Wisconsin, northeast of Galena. Because of the ominous implications of the name, it was changed to Galena River in 1854.

46. Lienhard folio 32/4/46. Fort Snelling was strategically located north of the mouth of the St. Peter's River, later the Minnesota, and on the west bank of the Mississippi. It remained the only military post in the territory and the northernmost fort on the upper Mississippi until 1849. It was the nucleus around which both St. Paul and Minneapolis were to form. Contrary to Lienhard's assertion, its latitude was toward the southern portions of both cities.

4. To See More of the World

1. Lienhard folio 33/1/1–8. According to H. Scott Wolfe, Historical Collections, Galena Public Library, the name "Liberty Street" does not appear on any map or directory resources. Wolfe has heard of a Liberty Street existing in an area known as "Cabbage Town," the name of the chief German community in Galena. The street de-

scribed as Liberty Street, running off Main Street and extending to the heights, could only be Hill Street, then, as now, the only street on which one can ascend from Main Street. The little valley would correspond to Spring Street. Letters to Spahn dated July 1 and 22, 1987, and to Abbott on February 5, 1995.

2. Lienhard folio 33/1/12. Bridges across the Fever River were frequently washed out by the spring floods. However, a foot bridge was built in 1844. Florence Gratiot Bale, *Historic Galena* (Galena: Harbin and Harbin, 1938), 5.

3. Lienhard folio 33/2/14. Probably a German hearing of "Hardscrabble." A few miles to the north, in Wisconsin, there was a place called Hardscrabble Diggings. At various times there were six places named Hardscrabble in Illinois. None of these places were at all close to Galena. Joseph Schaefer, *The Wisconsin Lead Region* (Madison: State Historical Society of Wisconsin, 1932), 94; James N. Adams, comp., *Illinois Place Names,* ed. William E. Keler (1968; reprint, with a new addendum by Lowell N. Volkel, Springfield: Illinois State Historical Society, 1989), 384.

4. Lienhard folio 33/3/37. The "conceited little Hessian" was William Reichardt, according to H. Scott Wolfe, in a letter to Spahn dated July 1, 1987. Wolfe enclosed a copy of a page from the "Advertisement Directory" of the *Galena City Directory* for 1848–49 listing "Washington House by Reichardt and Tufly, No. 59 Main Street," as well as a copy of an 1845 application by the two men for a city tavern license. Lienhard spells the latter's name as Duffly; however, in view of the contemporary documentation, Tufly will be used here.

5. Lienhard folio 33/4/3. The Black River, one hundred and sixty miles long, flows southwest through Wisconsin and empties into the Mississippi at La Crosse.

6. Lienhard folio 34/1/38. Dubuque, Iowa, named for Julien Dubuque, who had secured Fox Indian permission to work the mines west of the Mississippi, was the oldest city in Iowa, and was then still an important lead mining center.

7. Lienhard folio 34/1/42. Potosi was known as Snake Hollow.

8. Lienhard folio 34/1/45. The site was first known as Prairie la Porte. When the name was changed to honor the inventor of moveable type printing, a printing error on the first plat filed in the county records resulted in the town being named Guttenberg, rather than Gutenberg, the latter being Lienhard's spelling.

9. Lienhard folio 34/2/5. Named for an Indian chief, called *Le Chien*— French for dog—Prairie du Chien is located at the west end of the Fox-Wisconsin water route from the Great Lakes to the Mississippi. The four-hundred-thirty-mile long Wisconsin River flows south through central Wisconsin and turns west before entering the Mississippi.

10. Lienhard folio 34/2/14. Lienhard spells the river and the Indian tribe as Chipaway. The river flows south and southwest through central Wisconsin.

11. Lienhard folio 34/2/15. This place, now La Crosse, Wisconsin, lies at the foot of high bluffs, on the Mississippi, where the La Crosse and Black Rivers meet, forming a natural port.

12. Lienhard folio 34/2/30. Great rafts of logs and lumber from Stillwater and the upper St. Croix were pushed to Prescott, at the mouth of the St. Croix, just east of its

junction with the Mississippi, from where they drifted to Lake Pepin, through which they were pushed by other boats. Then they drifted to their destinations at various points along the Mississippi. George B. Merrick, *Old Times on the Upper Mississippi* (Cleveland: Arthur C. Clark, 1909), 29, 115.

13. Lienhard folio 34/2/32. Varying from one to three miles in width throughout the course of its twenty-two miles, Lake Pepin is an enlargement of the Mississippi, formed by sandbars heaped up by the swift-flowing Chippewa River, where it enters the sluggish Mississippi.

14. Lienhard folio 34/2/36. The Sioux (or Dakota) were one of the largest and most powerful Indian tribes in North America. By the mid-eighteenth century they inhabited the northern Great Plains and western prairies, mainly in present-day Wisconsin, Minnesota, Iowa, and the Dakotas. Equipped with horses and guns, they were later known for their battles with settlers and soldiers, which began in 1862 with the Sioux Wars, the bloodiest of all Indian wars fought in North America.

15. Lienhard folio 34/3/36. Swiss Protestant missionaries had established a post at Red Wing among the Sioux in 1836. It was abandoned in 1840, reestablished temporarily, and then abandoned in the mid-1840s. It soon became the nucleus of a substantial river town.

16. Lienhard folio 34/4/30. St. Peter's, soon to be known as Mendota, was an early settlement of traders, opposite Fort Snelling, and at the mouth of the St. Peter's or Minnesota River.

17. Lienhard folio 34/4/37. Some five hundred yards above its mouth, the St. Croix expands into Lake St. Croix, thirty-six miles long and one-and-one-half miles wide.

18. Lienhard folio 34/4/42. The first sawmill on the St. Croix commenced operations in 1842 at the St. Croix Falls, and John McKusick's sawmill at Stillwater became operational on March 30, 1844. James Taylor Dunn, *The St. Croix: Midwest Border River* (New York: Holt and Winston, 1965), 72.

19. Lienhard folio 35/1/35. Lienhard's description is undoubtedly accurate. However, a reader not well-informed about the history of logging in Wisconsin might gain the mistaken impression that the area was already well cut over. In fact the boom was just beginning and reached its peak in the late nineteenth century.

20. Lienhard folio 35/3/26. In 1827 Philander Prescott established a trading post where Prescott, Wisconsin, now stands, at the mouth of the St. Croix, just east of its junction with the Mississippi. It was not until 1851 that a village was laid out. Point Douglas lay in Minnesota, just across the St. Croix, to the north of Prescott, the site of the first post office in Minnesota, but soon to be abandoned.

21. Lienhard folio 38/4/12–13. *Schwingen* is a popular traditional Swiss sport, similar to wrestling. It commences with two men wearing short pants, around which is tied a special cotton belt (*Hosenlupf*). Before they start, each takes hold of the other's belt by his right hand. In some versions the left hand may be used to grab the opponents rolled-up pants leg. Then the combatants try to throw the opponents on their backs. As Lienhard's account makes clear, there are regional variations. Letter from Christa Landert to Abbott, April 1994.

22. Lienhard folio 38/4/38. Presumably a slang expression meaning eunuch.

23. Lienhard folio 39/2/38. The two tribes—Sac-and-Fox in government records—were Algonquian, and often associated, as at the time Lienhard mentioned them. In 1804 the Sauk were tricked into signing a treaty by which they turned over to the United States all their lands in Illinois, Wisconsin, and Missouri, but were permitted to remain on their lands until they were sold to American settlers. A minority of the Sauk, under Black Hawk, believing the treaty unfair, resisted, and were defeated in the 1832 Black Hawk War. The Fox remained neutral, but were eventually forced to cede their lands around the Rock River and Dubuque areas, after which both tribes were placed on a reservation in Kansas.

24. Lienhard folio 39/2/39. For many years prior to Lienhard's arrival in the area, the Algonquian Chippewa (or Ojibwa) and the Sioux (or Dakota), both among the largest and most far-flung of Indian tribes, had carried on sporadic warfare in the upper Mississippi Valley, including the St. Croix River area. Boundaries established by the Grand Conference in 1825 did not deter either tribe from making raids within the other's territories. In 1837, two treaties were signed, one at Fort Snelling, on August 18, with the Chippewa; the second in Washington, on September 29, when twenty-six Sioux chiefs met with the Great White Father, President Martin Van Buren. The treaty brought the Chippewa $870,000, while the Sioux were given close to $1,000,000. Although large amounts of money, even in 1837, both were authoritatively judged, in view of the immense territories given up, to be steals, monumental injustices to each tribe. At first, both treaties were little better observed by both parties than that of 1825, but by 1839 squatters felt secure enough to begin logging the St. Croix. However, the two tribes continued to roam the area, as Lienhard's observations indicate, for at least another six years. James Taylor Dunn, *The St. Croix: Midwest Border River* (New York: Holt, Rinehart and Winston, 1965), 10–49 passim.

25. Lienhard folio 40/2/30. That is to say, before the malaria season was over.

26. Lienhard folio 40/2/40. In a marginal note on 40/3 Lienhard added the final sentence of this paragraph.

27. Lienhard folio 41/2/21. An H. Hundemann or Henry Hunteman, is described as the "first shoemaker of Guttenberg," and as a "trustee" in 1851, 1854, and 1865. A "Henry Huntermann" is listed as a "trustee" in 1862 and 1867, and as "assessor" in 1868. *History of Clayton County, Iowa* (Chicago: Inter-State Publishing, 1882), 855–57.

28. Lienhard folio 41/4/35. Bur oak was

the characteristic tree of southern Wisconsin when the prairie grasses first gained possession of the region. Bur oak is the only tree that can stand up to a prairie fire and live. . . . A thick crust of corky bark covers the whole tree, even to the smallest twigs. This cork is armor. Bur oaks were the shock troops sent by the invading forest to storm the prairie; fire is what they had to fight. Each April, before the new grasses had covered the prairie with unburnable greenery, fires ran at will over the land, sparing only such old oaks as had grown bark too thick to scorch. Most of these groves of scattered veterans, known to the pioneers as 'oak openings,' consisted of bur oaks.

Aldo Leopold, *A Sand County Almanac, and Sketches Here and There* (London: Oxford University Press, 1949), 26–27.

29. Lienhard folio 42/1/18. A short river that flows southwesterly in southwest Wisconsin and enters the Mississippi above Dubuque, Iowa.

30. Lienhard folio 42/4/2. Christian Weiss is listed as Guttenberg's first mayor in 1851. *History of Clayton County, Iowa,* 855.

31. Lienhard folio 44/4/21. Renamed East Dubuque in 1879.

32. Lienhard folio 45/1/12–15. Miriam B. Theiler, *New Glarus: First 100 Years* (Madison, Wis.: Campus Publishing, 1946), 18, provides a list of "Original Colonists," giving three Schindlers, Abraham, with a wife and three children; Balthasar, with one child; and David, with neither a wife nor a child. Leo Schelbert, ed., *New Glarus, 1845–1970: The Making of a Swiss American Town,* (Glarus, Switzerland; Tschudi und Die Kommissionsverlag, 1970), 203–204, gives only one Schindler, Abraham, as being among the original "Register of Emigrants." However, Abraham, having been born in 1811 and married in 1832, could not be expected to have had a daughter old enough to be of matrimonial interest. Most likely David was the amorous suitor.

33. Lienhard folio 45/1/30. Lienhard's Glarner compatriots went on to establish the town of New Glarus in south-central Wisconsin. Surviving extreme deprivation, especially during the first year, and living in relative poverty until after the Civil War, when wheat prices plunged, the residents turned to dairying, upon which the present prosperity of the community, now grown to 1,900 residents, is largely based. Tourism now also thrives and the town proclaims itself as "America's Little Switzerland."

34. Lienhard folio 45/3/26. The name is not clearly written; it could be Stohler or Kohler.

35. Lienhard folio 45/4/32. On October 11, 1846, Marietta Gale married Andrew B. Parker.

36. Lienhard folio 46/3/43. This may well have been Augustus Wierich, who was practicing in Galena about 1837–48, according to H. Scott Wolfe in a letter to Spahn dated July 1, 1987. Wolfe enclosed a copy of a page from the *Galena City Directory* for 1847–48, describing Wierich as a "medical practitioner and wholesale druggist and chemist, No. 100 Main Street, Galena, Illinois."

37. Lienhard folio 47/1/31. Flatboats were mainly used on the Ohio and lower Mississippi where they were popular for transporting pioneer families downriver. Measuring from twenty to sixty feet in length and ten to twenty feet in width, they could not be feasibly brought back upriver, so they were usually sold for lumber, after reaching their destination. They were also sometimes used on the upper Mississippi, principally for transporting lead; however, they would have been a logical choice for conveying passengers over the Lower or Des Moines Rapids during times of low water, such as were likely to prevail in the fall, at the time Lienhard was traveling from Montrose to Keokuk, in the southernmost corner of Iowa. William J. Petersen, *Steamboating on the Upper Mississippi* (Iowa City: State Historical Society of Iowa, 1968), 50–51, 205.

38. Lienhard folio 47/1/46. Lienhard spells as Ripstein. However, according to

Christa Landert in a letter to Abbott of March 13, 1994, the correct spelling is Rippstein.

39. Lienhard folio 47/2/21. Scholarly publications cite no accounts by Captain Sutter. Doubtless they did read news stories and books on Sutter, which may have quoted him.

40. Lienhard folio 47/2/42. The following description of the "old market place," by Charles Van Ravenswaay, provides a vivid picture of the atmosphere in that location:

> At the south end of the levee, in the square bordered by Walnut, Market, Front, and Main streets, was Centre Market, which combined in happy intimacy the city market, town hall, and jail. Facing the levee was the brick Market House; its center portion housed the city offices while its wings held stores and fly-infested butcher stalls. (Visitors inquiring where the city officials could be found were often told to "keep straight ahead until you *smelled blood,*' and there you'd have 'em.") On the third floor was the mayor's office: on the second was the Recorder's Court—a dingy chamber, divided by high railings into compartments for spectators, for police, and for offenders. One day a criminal was arraigned, and the recorder inquired how often he had been there. "I don't keep count," replied the man, ". . . but you may bet high on my comin' again!" The basement of the building was divided between a jail and a groggery. "Here is the road to degradation and its consequences, side by side. Madden the brain in one chamber, and you are prepared for entry to the other," said John S. Robb in an 1848 description of Centre Market, published in the *St. Louis Reveille.*

Charles Van Ravenswaay, *Saint Louis; An Informal History of the City and Its People, 1764–1865,* ed. Candace O'Connor (St. Louis: Missouri Historical Society Press, 1991), 329.

41. Lienhard folio 47/2/44. Greenville, twenty miles northeast of Highland, was settled in 1815, and soon became the county seat of Bond County.

42. Lienhard folio 48/1/41 P. J. Kunst, *An American Dictionary of the English and German Languages* (Harrisburg, Penn.: 1838, and later editions).

43. Lienhard folio 48/2/38. In all probability the "Egridges" were John and Sarah Ackerige, described as follows:

> and who that lived within the last period named [1840s] does not remember the private boarding house of Mr. and Mrs. John Ackerige, next house east of Dr. Drake's? What nice meals at moderate prices they prepared! During court week, their table was always crowded by jurors, witnesses and those interested in court, living in the country.

William Henry Perrin, ed., *History of Bond and Montgomery Counties, Illinois* (Chicago: O. L. Baskin, 1882), 122. The 1850 U.S. Census for Bond County lists a John Akridge, then aged fifty-six, owner of eight hundred acres, born in South Carolina, and his wife, Sarah, then forty-six, born in Georgia. United States Census Office, 7th Census, *1850 United States Census of Bond County, Illinois* (Decatur: Decatur Genealogical Society, 1977), 62.

44. Lienhard folio 48/3/18. According to Gale's probate papers, Madison County Circuit Court, he probably died, intestate, around early October, 1844.

45. Lienhard folio 49/3/18. Probably any "college on the Rock River" at that time would have been no more than a short-lived secondary school.

46. Lienhard folio 49/3/26. Very likely influenza or pneumonia.

47. Lienhard folio 50/4/5. Boeschenstein had considered opening a store in Highland almost a dozen years before. Later, in 1846, he did move his store to Highland. Eggen, "Chronicles of Early Highland," 111, 153.

48. Lienhard folio 51/1/10 Two Margut's from Canton Graubuenden (Johann and Martin) lived in the Highland area, as did two Weber's from Canton Glarus (Jacob and Fridolin).

Principal Sources Consulted

Switzerland and Canton Glarus

Bonjour, E., et al. *A Short History of Switzerland.* Oxford: Clarendon Press, 1952.

Heer, Gottfried. "Geschichte des glarnischen Volksschulwesens." Vol 18 of *Jahrbuch des historischen Vereins des Kantons Glarus.* Zurich: Meyer and Zeller, 1881.

Lunn, Arnold. *The Swiss and Their Mountains; A Study of the Influence of Mountains on Man.* London: George Allen and Unwin, 1963.

Martin, William. *Switzerland from Roman Times to the Present.* New York: Praeger, 1971.

McCracken, W. D. *The Rise of the Swiss Republic.* 2d ed., rev. and enl. New York: AMS Press, 1970.

Oechsli, Wilhelm. *History of Switzerland, 1499–1914.* Translated from the German by Eden Paul and Cedar Paul. Cambridge: Cambridge University Press, 1922.

Schelbert, Leo. "On Becoming an Immigrant: A Structural View of Eighteenth- and Nineteenth-Century Swiss Data." *Perspectives in American History* 7 (1973): 441–95.

Schmidt, Fridolin. *Bericht des evangelischen Schulraths ueber den gegenwaertigen Zustand der evangelischen Volkschulen im Kanton Glarus.* Glarus: n.p., 1834. A foldout table, "Vergleichende Uebersicht des Zustandes des Elementar-Schulwesens im evangelischen Theile des Kantons Glarus in den Jahren 1801, 1811, 1824, und 1832," provides considerable information on the Protestant schools of Canton Glarus.

Siegfried, Andre. *Switzerland, A Democratic Way of Life.* Translated from the French by Edward Fitzgerald. New York: Duell, Sloan and Pearce, 1950.

Switzerland, Landscape, Art, Culture, and History. Edited by the Swiss National Tourist Office. Berne: Buechler and Co., 1955. See especially chapter, "Glarus," by Hans Thuerer, pages 160–68.

Thuerer, Georg. *Free and Swiss; The Story of Switzerland.* Adapted and translated from the German by R. P. Heller and E. Long. 1948. Reprint, London: Oswald Wolff, 1970.

Winteler, Franz. *Beitraege zur Biltner Geschichte.* Niederurnen: Thomas and Co., 1973.

New Switzerland and Nearby Areas in Illinois

The early settlers provided a remarkable body of literature on the history of New Switzerland, most of which is available in modern translations. The following is a list of the originals.

Eggen, Jacob. *Aufzeichnungen aus Highlands Gruendungszeit zum fuenfzigjaehrigen Jubilaeum* (Chronicles of Early Highland [for for Its Fiftieth Anniversary Celebration]). Highland, Ill., 1888.

———. "Aufzeichnungen von Jacob Eggen." Deutsch-Amerikanische Geschichts-blaetter 5 (1905): Heft 1, 52–55; Heft 2, 13–54; Heft 3, 1–36. Contains material expurgated from Eggen's 1888 Aufzeichnungen.

Koepfli, Kaspar. *Die Licht- & Schattenseite von New Switzerland in Nordamerika.* N.p.: Sursee, 1833. This work also was published (with slightly altered title) as part five of the Suppiger and Koepfli *Reisebericht,* 2d ed., which is described below.

———. Spiegel von Amerika: Praktische Grundsaetze, Belehrungen und Warnungen fuer Auswanderer nach Amerika: Nebst zwei Reiseberichten, einer Ansicht der Stadt Highland und Plan seiner Umgebung. Lucerne: Xaver Meyer, 1849.

Koepfli, Salomon. *Die Geschichte der Ansiedlung von Highland.* Highland, Ill., 1859. It first appeared serially as "Beitraege zur Geschichte unserer Ansiedlung" in the *Highland Bote,* ?/?/1859–27 July 1860.

———. "Highland." Gazetteer of Madison County. Compiled and published by James T. Hair. Alton, 1866. Unlike the other works listed above, this account appears only here, and in a 1973 reprint.

———. Neu-Schweizerland in den Jahren 1831 und 1841. Lucerne, 1842.

Suppiger, Joseph and Salomon Koepfli. *Reisebericht der Familie Koepfli & Suppiger nach St. Louis am Mississippi und Gruendung von New Switzerland im Staate Illinois.* Sursee, 1833. This edition contained four parts, the first three being a travel diary, with advice to prospective emigrants, written by Suppiger. Part four consists of two letters each from Salomon Koepfli and Joseph Suppiger to their respective families.

Suppiger, Joseph, Salomon Koepfli, and Kaspar Koepfli. *Reisebericht der Familie Koepfli & Suppiger nach St. Louis am Mississippi und Gruendung von New Switzerland im Staate Illinois.* 2d ed. Sursee, 1833. This edition contained a part five, Kaspar Koepfli's "Licht- & Schattenseite der Gegend, die wir zu unsern Aufenthalt auserkohren," plus a letter by Salomon Koepfli to his brother Kaspar Mauris in Sursee, who edited and supervised the publication of both editions of the *Reisebericht.*

Most of the above works are available in translation in three books:

Koepfli, Salomon. *The Story of the Settling of Highland* (Die Geschichte der Ansied-lung von Highland). Highland, Ill.: *Highland Bote,* 1859. Reprint, translated by

Jennie Latzer Kaeser, edited and annotated by Raymond J. Spahn, with an introduction by John C. Abbott, Edwardsville: Lovejoy Library, Southern Illinois University, 1970.

New Switzerland in Illinois as Described by Two Early Swiss Settlers. Edited and annotated by Raymond J. Spahn and Betty Alderton Spahn. Edwardsville: Friends of Lovejoy Library, Southern Illinois University Edwardsville, 1977. Book one is a translation by Jennie Latzer Kaeser, under the title "Mirror of America," of Dr. Koepfli's *Spiegel von Amerika;* Book two is a translation by Manfried Hartwin Driesner of Jacob Eggen's "Chronicles of Early Highland," *Aufzeichnungen aus Highlands Gruendungszeit.* "Foreword: The Pioneer Writings about Highland" is by John C. Abbott. Facsimiles of an 1847 *Plan [Map] der Umgegend von Highland, oder von Neu Schweizerland* and an 1847 *Ansicht [View] der Jungen Stadt Highland,* which appeared in Kaspar Koepfli's *Spiegel von America,* are appended to this work.

Suppiger, Joseph, Salomon Koepfli, and Kaspar Koepfli. *Journey to New Switzerland: Travel Account of the Koepfli and Suppiger Family to St. Louis on the Mississippi and the Founding of New Switzerland in the State of Illinois.* Translated by Raymond J. Spahn, with excerpts from Jennie Latzer Kaeser's translation of Salomon Koepfli's *Die Geschichte der Ansiedlung von Highland* (The Story of the Settling of Highland), edited by John C. Abbott, foreword by Joseph Blake Koepfli. Carbondale: Southern Illinois University Press, 1987.

There are no plans to republish the original or translation of Salomon Koepfli's *Neu-Schweizerland in den Jahren 1831 und 1841.* However, a typescript translation by Betty Alderton Spahn is in the University Archives, Lovejoy Library, Southern Illinois University Edwardsville.

The best history of Highland remains the following:

Spencer, A. P. *Centennial History of Highland, Illinois, 1837–1937.* Highland: Highland Centennial Association, 1937. Because it contains an index, a 1978 reprint, published by the Highland Historical Society, is especially useful.

Other useful works on Highland and nearby areas include the following:

Gazetteer of Madison County. Compiled and published by James T. Hair. Alton: 1866. See also reprint, Evansville, Ind.: Unigraphic, 1973.

History of Madison County, Illinois, Illustrated. Edwardsville: W. R. Brink, 1882.

Illustrated Encyclopedia and Atlas Map of Madison County, Illinois. St. Louis: Brink McCormick and Co. of Illinois, 1873.

Koepfli, Joseph Blake. *Koepfli (A Partial History of the Family).* Santa Barbara: J. B. Koepfli, 1981.

Meyer, Charles. *Map of Madison County, Illinois.* Highland, Ill., 1851, map.

Norton, W. T. *Centennial History of Madison County, Illinois, and Its People, 1812–1912.* 2 vols. Chicago: Lewis Publishing, 1912.

Schweizer, Max. *Neu-Schweizerland, Planung, Gruendung und Entwicklung einer schweizerischen Einwanderersiedlung in den Vereinigten Staaten von Nordamerika (Madison County, Illinois).* Zug, Switzerland: Verlag Zuercher, 1980.

The Swiss on Looking Glass Prairie: A Century and a Half, 1831–1981. Compiled by Betty Spindler Coats, with a foreword by Joseph Blake Koepfli, edited by Raymond Jurgen Spahn. Edwardsville: Friends of Lovejoy Library, Southern Illinois University Edwardsville and Highland Historical Society, 1983. This book has an extensive sources consulted section, pages 87–116, plus a genealogical supplement on the Koepflis and Suppigers, pages 118–50.

All of the above are valuable for identifying personal names. In addition, the following is specifically devoted to names of persons. It consists of a card index file of about twelve thousand name entries, compiled by Raymond and Betty Spahn, of persons of Swiss or German origin in the four-township area surrounding Highland. Records checked were cemetery records, gravestones, church records, newspapers, histories and other works. It is in the University Archives, Lovejoy Library, Southern Illinois University Edwardsville. For personal name identification, the following works were also of much value:

A Complete Surname Index to the History of Madison County, Illinois, 1882. Compiled by the Madison County Genealogical Society. Edwardsville: The Society, 1986.

1880 Federal Census of Madison County, Illinois. Compiled by Elsie M. Wasser, index by Marie T. Eberle. Miami, Okla.: Timbercreek, 1991.

1855 Census, Madison County. Compiled by Elsie M. Wasser. Madison County Naturalization Records, University Archives, Lovejoy Library, Southern Illinois University, Edwardsville, 1955.

1845 Census of Madison County, Illinois. Compiled by Elsie M. Wasser. Madison County Naturalization Records, University Archives, Lovejoy Library, Southern Illinois University, Edwardsville, 1985.

"1837 Tax List of Madison County, Illinois." Parts 1 and 2. Compiled by Jane Shelley and Elsie M. Wasser. *The Stalker* 12, no. 4 (1992): 157–62; 13, no. 1 (1993): 28–34.

Index of Biographical Sketches, Madison County, Illinois. Edwardsville: Madison County Genealogical Society, 1983. Index to ten publications on Madison County.

Madison County Circuit Court Illinois Marriage Records Index. 2 vols. Compiled and published by Jane Shelley and Elsie M. Wasser. Edwardsville: 1984–85.

Madison County, Illinois, 1850 Census. 2 vols. Transcribed by Maxine E. Wormer. Thompson, Ill.: Heritage House, 1976.

Madison County, Illinois, 1860 Census. Transcribed by Joy Upton. Utica, Ky.: McDowell Publications, 1986. *Naturalizations and Intentions of Madison County, Illinois, An Index, 1816–1900.* Compiled by Jane Shelley and Elsie M. Wasser. N.p.: Jane Shelley and Elsie M. Wasser, 1983.

Madison County Probate Index. Compiled by Barbara J. Heflin. *Illinois State Genealogical Society Quarterly* (fall 1993): 160–70; (spring 1994): 12–29; (summer 1994): 66–85. Indexes probate cases 1813–1903, transferred from the Madison County Circuit Court to the Illinois Regional Archives Depository, Carbondale.

Public Domain Sales Land Tract Record Listing. Springfield: Illinois State Archives, 1984. 432 microfiche in 3 vols. Vol. 1 is a listing in sequence by purchaser's name. Vol. 2 is a listing in sequence by geographical — county, meridian, range, township, section name. Vol. 3 is a listing in sequence by purchaser's name within county.

The Upper Mississippi Valley

Buley, R. Carlyle. *The Old Northwest, the Pioneer Period, 1815–1840.* 2 vols. Bloomington: Indiana University Press, 1950.

Dunn, James Taylor. *The St. Croix: Midwest Border River.* New York: Holt, Rinehart and Winston, 1965.

Federal Writers' Project Illinois. *Galena Guide.* Galena: City of Galena, 1937.

Federal Writers' Project Illinois. *Illinois, A Descriptive and Historical Guide.* New rev. ed. New York: Hastings House, 1974.

Federal Writers' Project Iowa. *Iowa, A Guide to the Hawkeye State.* New York: Hastings House, 1938.

Federal Writers' Project Minnesota. *Minnesota, A State Guide.* New York: Viking Press, 1938.

Folwell, William Watts. *A History of Minnesota.* Vol. 1. St. Paul: Minnesota Historical Society, 1921.

Gard, Robert E. and L. G. Sorden. *The Romance of Wisconsin Place Names.* New York: October House, 1968.

Illinois Place Names. 1968. Compiled by James N. Adams, edited by William E. Keller, with a new addendum by Lowell N. Volkel. Springfield: Illinois State Historical Society, 1989.

Lewis, Henry. *The Valley of the Mississippi, Illustrated.* Translated from the German by A. Hermina Poatgieter, edited with an introduction and notes by Bertha L. Heilbron. St. Paul: Minnesota Historical Society, 1967.

Nauvoo, An American Heritage. Prepared by Ida Blum. Carthage, Ill.: Journal Printing, 1969. The only history of Nauvoo that does justice to the post-Mormon and post-Icarian periods.

Peck, John Mason. *A Gazetteer of Illinois.* 2d ed., rev., correct., and enl. Philadelphia: Grigg and Elliott, 1837.

Petersen, William J. *Steamboating on the Upper Mississippi.* Iowa City: State Historical Society of Iowa, 1968.

Primm, James Neal. *Lion of the Valley: St. Louis, Missouri.* Boulder: Pruett Publishing, 1981.

Upham, Warren. *Minnesota Geographic Names: Their Origin and Historic Significance.* St. Paul: Minnesota Historical Society, 1920.

Writers' Program Wisconsin. *Wisconsin, A Guide to the Badger State.* New York: Duell, Sloan and Pearce, 1941.

Index

Raymond J. Spahn is a professor emeritus of German at Southern Illinois University Edwardsville. He earned his Ph.D. in German from Northwestern University. Spahn was a member of the Department of Foreign Languages from 1957 until his retirement in 1978, serving as chair of the department in 1975 and in 1977. Currently a resident of Tucson, Arizona, Spahn is the author of many articles and papers on nineteenth-century German manuscripts in America.

John C. Abbott is a professor emeritus, Lovejoy Library, at Southern Illinois University Edwardsville. Abbott, who earned a Ph.D. in librarianship at the University of Michigan, served as director of Lovejoy Library from 1960 to 1981 and as head of Research and Special Collections from 1981 until 1986. An active community volunteer, he has special interest in the history of southwestern Illinois and the Mississippi River valley.

Raymond J. Spahn and John C. Abbott have collaborated on four previous books about the Swiss in Highland, Illinois: *The Story of the Settling of Highland; New Switzerland in Illinois; The Swiss on Looking Glass Prairie;* and *Journey to New Switzerland.*